Oxford Studies in European Law

General Editors: Paul Craig and Gráinne de Búrca

RELIGION AND THE PUBLIC ORDER OF THE EUROPEAN UNION

Religion and the Public Order of the European Union

RONAN McCREA

OXFORD
UNIVERSITY PRESS

OXFORD

UNIVERSITY PRESS

Great Clarendon Street, Oxford OX2 6DP

Oxford University Press is a department of the University of Oxford.
It furthers the University's objective of excellence in research, scholarship,
and education by publishing worldwide in

Oxford New York

Auckland Cape Town Dar es Salaam Hong Kong Karachi
Kuala Lumpur Madrid Melbourne Mexico City Nairobi
New Delhi Shanghai Taipei Toronto

With offices in

Argentina Austria Brazil Chile Czech Republic France Greece
Guatemala Hungary Italy Japan Poland Portugal Singapore
South Korea Switzerland Thailand Turkey Ukraine Vietnam

Oxford is a registered trade mark of Oxford University Press
in the UK and in certain other countries

Published in the United States
by Oxford University Press Inc., New York

© Ronan McCrea, 2010

The moral rights of the author have been asserted

Crown copyright material is reproduced under Class Licence
Number C01P0000148 with the permission of OPSI
and the Queen's Printer for Scotland

Database right Oxford University Press (maker)

First published 2010

British Library Cataloguing in Publication Data

Data available

Library of Congress Cataloging in Publication Data

McCrea, Ronan.
Religion and the public order of the European Union / Ronan McCrea.
p. cm.
Includes bibliographical references (p.   ).
ISBN 978–0–19–959535–8
1. Church and state--European Union countries. 2. Freedom of religion
—European Union countries. 3. Religion and law—European Union
countries. I. Title.
KJE5530.M38 2010
342.2408'52—dc22

Typeset by Newgen Imaging Systems (P) Ltd., Chennai, India
Printed in Great Britain
on acid-free paper by
CPI Antony Rowe,
Chippenham, Wiltshire

ISBN 978–0–19–959535–8

1 3 5 7 9 10 8 6 4 2

Do mo dheartháireacha agus do Mariana Chaves

GENERAL EDITORS' PREFACE

Ronan McCrea has written a timely and welcome book on the place of religion in the public order of the European Union. From debates over the desirability of a reference to religion in the preamble to the EU constitutional treaty or the permissibility of discrimination on the basis of religion in specific employment contexts, to more recent controversies over the banning of the *burqa* and the place of the crucifix in the classroom, the relationship between religion and the public sphere in Europe is a topical and often controversial one. And while much has been written about the relationship between law and religion in the context of the European Convention on Human Rights, far less scholarly attention has so far been given to the role of religion in the public order of the European Union.

Ronan McCrea's book addresses the complex range of issues raised by this topic in an elegant and confident manner. He illustrates in a nuanced and informative way how EU law in certain ways regulates and shapes aspects of the role and treatment of religion within the law of the Member States, even while religion itself shapes and governs aspects of EU law. The core of his argument is that the particular conception of religion which informs the public order of the European Union is understood as a form of identity (individual as well as national identity) and is committed both to pluralism and to balancing religious, humanist and cultural influences. Crucially, this conception of religion accommodates certain religious traditions – namely those which are able to accept the multiple truth claims inherent in a religiously pluralist public sphere – much more easily than others, marking out certain religious identities, notably aspects of Islam, as 'unacceptable'.

In a series of chapters on the regulation of the role of religion in law-making, EU fundamental rights and religious freedom, the Single Market and the regulation of religion (as an element of national culture), and the impact of enlargement and immigration, McCrea highlights the influence of Europe's ideological and Christian inheritance in this field. The author's careful analysis demonstrates the inevitable complexity and difficulty of the relationship between religion, law and politics in the EU. Ultimately, he concludes that the EU is not strictly secular, but seeks to protect the political sphere from religious domination and to promote a degree of religious pluralism, even while constructing its own 'distinctive public order with identifiable fundamental norms'.

This is rich and intelligent work which should be of interest to EU scholars and students alike, and to all those interested in the relationship between law and religion in today's European Union.

Paul Craig
Gráinne de Búrca
July 2010

ACKNOWLEDGEMENTS

I never thought I would be able to write a book. Indeed, this book is not only the result of individual effort but is the fruit of labours that could not have been carried out if they had not been underpinned by the support of a *meitheal* made up of many people. The book grew out of a doctoral thesis completed at the European Institute of the London School of Economics and funded by an Arts and Humanities Research Council doctoral award. The largest debt of gratitude is owed to my primary supervisor, Professor Damian Chalmers, who provided truly outstanding supervision and guidance in the preparation of the thesis and afterwards.

I am also indebted to Dr Jennifer Jackson-Preece, my second supervisor, and to my examiners, Professors Conor Gearty and Neil Walker, who all provided extremely valuable insights. Professor Carolyn Evans, whose book on Article 9 of the European Convention on Human Rights was an invaluable resource, took the time to give me tremendously useful feedback at an early stage of my research, which helped me to clarify my normative approach.

I have been lucky to have been surrounded by stimulating and supportive colleagues. In the LSE, Mariana Chaves, Tine van Criekinge, Lior Herman, Emelyne Cheney, and Nadine El Enany, and all the inhabitants of the PhD room were great company on the doctoral journey. At the European Court of Justice my colleagues in cabinet Maduro, David Baez, Anne Buckinx, Francisco Costa-Cabral, Nicholas Hatzis, Advocate-General Poiares Maduro, Dominique Reitling, Maria Tavares, Daniela Kromer, and Dana Kaersveng who, along with Síofra O'Leary, Emma Jean Hinchy, Kai Ziegler, Hélène Kanellopoulos, Marina Pascual Olaguíbel, Pauline Phoa, Ignacio Signes de Mesa, Nana Sumrada, Stephanie Bodoni, and Sarah Enright, provided great company and some insights into EU law along the way. During my time at the University of Reading, my colleagues Professor Chris Hilson and Dr Anne Thies have provided valuable feedback on my work.

Books are not written in a vacuum and I have benefited enormously from the support of my friends and family over the years. My parents Carmel McCrea and Colin McCrea provided encouragement at every stage of the process. Without interest in education and in books that they gave me, I would have developed neither the desire nor the ability to write a book. There are many others who deserve thanks, especially Seána Cunningham, Romail Dhaddey, Nicola Doherty, Catherine Donnelly, Nathy Dunleavy,

Stephen Fennelly, Richard Heffernan, Sossie Kasbarian, Myles Lavan, Roddy Maguire, Barry McCrea, Killian McCrea, Claire McGrade, Paul O'Connell, Sandeep Sharma, Francis Sweeney, and my extended family, particularly Bernadette Cunningham and Katherine Garnier, who all read or discussed parts of the text or wined, dined, and listened to me during its production. Finally, I am grateful to Alex Flach, Natasha Knight, Ela Kotkowska, Sophie Softley-Pierce, and Glynis Dyson at OUP for their very valuable assistance with this project.

Chapters 3 and 6 are modified versions of articles that appeared in the 2008 *Yearbook of European Law* and Volume 16(1) of *The Columbia Journal of European Law* and have been reproduced with the kind permission of the publishers.

Ronan McCrea
London, 28 April 2010

CONTENTS

TABLE OF CASES

EUROPEAN COURT AND COMMISSION OF HUMAN RIGHTS

AUSTRALIA

FRANCE

IRELAND

UNITED KINGDOM

UNITED STATES

TABLE OF OFFICIAL DECLARATIONS, RESOLUTIONS, AND REPORTS

EUROPEAN PARLIAMENT

ORGANIZATION OF THE ISLAMIC CONFERENCE

UNITED NATIONS

Introduction

1. Introduction

Religion has not generally been seen as a central concern of the European Union (EU).[1] The EU has no specific policy on religion, nor any explicit competence in relation to religious matters. As a central and sensitive element of national identity and culture, religion would appear to be remote from core EU competences such as the regulation of the Single Market. Indeed, the few direct references to religion in the treaties stress the Union's desire to defer to Member State preferences in this area.[2] Freedom of religion, including the distinction between positive and negative religious liberty and the institutional aspect of religious freedom, is certainly an important element of the approach of any polity to matters of faith.[3] However, heavy or exclusive focus on the facilitation of religious freedom tends to underplay the complexity of the broader issues raised by the relationship between religion and the law. In particular, such an approach can fail to acknowledge sufficiently that more religious freedom for some can come at the cost of less freedom for others. In any event, while respect for the fundamental right to religious freedom is, indeed, an important part of the Union's approach, the relationship between EU law and religion is much broader.

The European Union, in exercising its functions and constructing its own identity, is inevitably required to legislate and adjudicate in relation to the claims that religion continues to make in the public and private arenas in

---

[1] C Crouch, 'The Quiet Continent: Religion and Politics in Europe' in D Marquand and RL Nettler (eds), *Religion and Democracy* (Oxford: Blackwell Publishers, 2000).

[2] See Ch 3, sections 2 and 3.

[3] For an account of some of these questions, see G Robbers (ed.), *State and Church in the European Union* (Baden-Baden: Nomos Verlagsgesellschaft, 2005).

Europe. Religion still influences law at national level through notions of public morality which provide the basis for laws restricting activities that are considered to be undesirable for religious or cultural reasons.[4] EU law in areas such as the Single Market can impact on such laws by limiting the ability of states to control or suppress certain economic activities. Religion's important institutional role in many Member States means that religious organizations are important employers. EU law in relation to employment must reach decisions that influence the degree to which religious bodies can continue to promote their ethos in these contexts, as well as the ability of Member States to reflect religious norms in market structures.[5] In areas such as broadcasting and trade marks, Community law can affect efforts to protect religious symbols and ideas as well as freedom of expression.[6] More broadly, the Union's commitments to upholding fundamental rights and liberal democracy are also relevant to religion. While it has recognized that religious freedom must be protected,[7] the EU has also identified limitations on religious influence as an important principle and has monitored national relationships between religion, the law, and the state in order to ensure that those countries that become members of the Union uphold the principles of the autonomy of the public sphere from religious domination as well as respect for individual autonomy, including freedom from religion, in the private sphere.[8] EU law can therefore potentially impact on the role of religion in contemporary Europe. However, the relationship between the Union and religion operates in both directions and Community law is itself shaped by religion. The EU recognizes the promotion of public morality as a valid basis of law thus enabling religious norms to influence the content of Community law. Religion is also recognized as part of national cultures that the Union is required to respect. Furthermore, religion has been recognized as a source of the EU's constitutional values while religious organizations have been acknowledged as making a 'particular contribution' to the Union's law-making process.[9]

The public order of the Union is therefore required to develop an approach to religion beyond merely undertaking to respect religious freedom. Indeed, the EU is a particularly interesting context in which to study the issues of competing rights, goals, and interests that characterize the increasingly controversial and complex relationship between religion, law, and polity in the

---

[4] See Ch 2, sections 3.2 and 4.2.   [5] See Ch 5, sections 2 and 3.
[6] Ibid, section 3.2.   [7] See Ch 4.   [8] See Ch 6, section 2.
[9] See Ch 3, sections 2 and 3.

contemporary world. Most states approach religion in the context of a dense cultural identity that has been heavily influenced by particular religious traditions and where certain views of religion and its role in society are the subject of, often unarticulated, shared historical and cultural assumptions.[10] The European Union, by contrast, lacks a strong cultural identity of its own and is still in the process of developing its political institutions. The weakness of its identity means that the Union lacks the authority to effect fundamental change in the relationship between religion, law, and the state in Europe. As an independent legal order encompassing 27 states with widely differing approaches to religion, the Community must, in carrying out its functions, devise its own approach to this relationship, which synthesizes a common framework within which respect for Member State autonomy is reconciled with the need for a coherent EU approach that remains true to the Union's fundamental values. Indeed, although it must be extremely careful not to interfere with Member State autonomy in this sensitive area, the very facts of the weakness of its cultural identity and the newness of its institutions mean that the EU is required to spell out in more explicit terms than most nation states, the relationship between religion, the law, and the polity. Issues of religion and identity have come to assume increasing importance in Europe in recent times. As the controversy in relation to the making of a reference to God in the preamble to the Constitutional and Lisbon Treaties showed, the nature of the EU in this regard has become the subject of major dispute and is seen as bearing on fundamental issues in relation to the future of the Union and of Europe in general.

This book gives an account of the role of religion in EU public order that addresses both issues of the relationship of religion to law and politics and the question of nature of the European Union. It analyses the relationship between religion, individual autonomy, the state, and the promotion of communal norms in the context of EU law and, in doing so, sheds light on the nature of the EU as a polity. In particular, it assesses the degree to which the Union can be seen as a secular polity or as one which regards religion, or certain versions of religion, as a legitimate basis for the exercise of legal power. This analysis touches on key issues relating to the controversial contemporary role and influence of religion in private and public life, such as the balancing of individual autonomy with the desire of communities to constitute themselves through the promotion through law of particular norms and the

---

[10] See JTS Madeley and Z Enyedi (eds), *Church and State in Contemporary Europe: The Chimera of Neutrality* (London: Frank Cass Publishing, 2003).

reconciliation of the principles of equal treatment and state neutrality with the accommodation of cultural identity and notions of community. It also involves the assessment of the degree to which the Union's approach to these issues impacts on the relationship between the law, the state, and religion at Member State level, as well as the extent to which the public order of the EU can be seen as reflecting a particular, Christian humanist, tradition.

2. An Identity-based, Balance-focused Approach

The EU integrates religion into its public order and adjudicates upon religion's claims on the basis of a commitment to balancing what it regards as the overlapping and, at times, conflicting, religious, cultural, and humanist influences underpinning its constitutional tradition and public order. The Union has seen the relationship between religion and identity as key to such balance. The notion of identity operates in two interrelated ways in this regard. The idea of balance between religious, cultural, and humanist influences is seen as a part of Europe's ethical inheritance and as a reflection of a predominant contemporary European approach to religion which arises from European history and culture. This principle of balance is regarded both as normatively desirable and as an element of European identity. At the same time, the Union's commitment to balance is seen as requiring that religion be treated primarily as a matter of identity. Balance between religious, humanist, and cultural influences within the EU legal order is therefore seen both as an element of European identity in itself and as requiring the treatment of religion largely as a form of identity. In this way the notions of identity and balance can be seen as mutually reinforcing.

3. Features of the Balance between Religious, Cultural, and Humanist Influences

The regulation of religion through the framework of identity raises certain complications. Identity has various forms whose accommodation can, at times, be mutually inconsistent. For instance, the facilitation of collective religious identity through the promotion of communal norms can be inconsistent with the freedom of individuals to develop their own identity in contravention of such norms.[11] On the other hand, protection of individual identity in contexts such as employment may impact on the collective and institutional religious identity of others. The EU's commitment to balancing cultural, religious, and humanist traditions gives scope for the assertion of collective religious identity through the Union's recognition that collective cultural identity rights may include the promotion through law of notions of public morality, of particular religio-cultural practices such as restrictions on Sunday trading, and the protection of the national institutional role and status of culturally entrenched faiths. However, although EU law permits the legal promotion of collective identities, Europe's shared identity has a self-limiting element in this regard as it is seen as also encompassing a strong tradition of respect for individual autonomy, which requires the limitation of the imposition of collective identities.[12] The humanist tradition recognized by the Union as part of its ethical inheritance is also hostile to the promotion of religious norms per se and resists the promotion of those religious norms that cannot be accommodated under the rubric of cultural identity. The Union's regulation of these conflicts shows the degree to which the Union's public order can be seen as having a particular religious identity and reveals the approach of this public order to key issues such as the balancing of individual and collective identity rights and the degree to which the Union impacts on the right of Member States to pursue their own arrangements in relation to religion.

Beyond the potential conflicts between identity's individual and collective elements, treating religion as a form of identity also affects the role it can play within the public order and the influence it can exercise over law. Identities are both attributed and chosen and, in a diverse world, are inevitably heterogeneous. Therefore, linking the legal status and role of religion within the public order to its status as an element of identity, pluralizes religion as it inevitably involves the recognition of more than one kind of religious identity. Such an approach also links and values religion's role in public and private life, not on the basis of the truth of religious claims, but as human choices, both collective and individual. Accordingly, such an approach renders it difficult for religions to achieve recognition for claims to a monopoly on truth within the political arena and would appear to regard religion as a voluntary matter—a view which is not shared by all the major religions.[13] Regarding

---

[11] See, eg K Dalacoura, *Islam, Liberalism and Human Rights: Implications for International Relations*, (London: IB Tauris, 1998).

[12] See Ch 3, section 5, Ch 5, sections 2.1 and 2.3, and Ch 6, sections 2 and 4.

[13] See Ch 4, section 2.

religion as an element of identity links it to notions of culture and of a particular communal way of life. Although culture can be a site of political conflict, it is also a state of affairs rather than an inherently normative phenomenon and is seen as in some way separate from the rationalism and ideological nature of the political sphere.[14] Accordingly, this view of religion can depoliticize religion in that it values what religions regard as normative practices and views on the basis of a normatively neutral status, namely that of element of cultural norms and practices. This emphasis on religion as an element of culture and identity also has the effect of linking the role of religion within EU law to the most powerful source of culture within the Union—the nation state. The Union's approach characterizes religion not merely as an individual or collective choice but as part of a national way of life that Member States are entitled to uphold. In taking this view, EU law connects the role of religion to ideas of inheritance and enables certain religious traditions that have achieved elevated status within national cultures to exercise a greater degree of influence and privilege than 'outsider' faiths that lack such a national cultural role. Thus, the Union's approach involves the promotion of certain collective identities to a greater degree than others. While it does not require a libertarian approach and envisages the use of the law to promote these national collective identities, such promotion must nevertheless respect the overall notion of balance and the humanist elements thereof.

Many of these features, particularly those of pluralism, the linking of religion to choice and to culture, and the restriction of truth claims within the public sphere, reinforce other elements of the balance between religious, humanist, and cultural influences which the Union sees as elements of its heritage and as necessary features of its public order. This enables the accommodation of religion to take place in a manner that does not threaten established political structures and collective identities that have grown from Europe's historical experience of conflict between different religions and between religious and secular powers. In particular, the pluralization of religion inherent in an identity-based approach helps to secure the autonomy of the public sphere from domination by any single form of religion, particularly at EU level where no single cultural identity predominates. The focus on individual identity and choice also underlines the commitment to individual choice that

---

[14] See F Inglis, *Culture* (Cambridge: USA Polity Press, 2004) 28 9. See also C Barker 'Culture' in *The SAGE Dictionary of Cultural Studies* (London: Sage, 2004) 45. In relation to the non-political and non-ideological characterization of culture, see A Gramsci, *Selections from the Prison Notebooks* (New York: International Publishers, 1971) 238 and S Žižek, *In Defense of Lost Causes* (London: Verso, 2008) 21. See also the discussion in Ch 7, section 4.

underpins the protection of individual autonomy in the private sphere. These two features have been identified by the Union as key elements of its public order whose protection can impinge on the desires of those forms of religion that wish to dominate the public sphere or to use the law to force individuals to adhere to religious teachings in the private arena.[15]

As noted above, the degree of separation between the political and religious spheres, and the individual-centred notions of personal autonomy that this can help to foster, are both results of the historical and cultural events and influences that gave rise to contemporary European culture and can in themselves be seen as elements of an identity or as the markers of the parameters of acceptable religious identity, which characterize the public order of the Union. The characterization of religion as a form of identity is an element of a broader commitment to balancing religious, humanist, and cultural influences. This commitment to balance is itself an aspect of what is thought to be a shared European inheritance and identity. This means that there will be forms of religious identity that cannot readily be accommodated within this broader balance-focused approach. Religious identities that are inconsistent with the notion of balance, characterized by the features outlined above, may be seen as threats to the Union's public order and may be restricted on this basis. In particular, approaches to religion that cannot reconcile themselves to the accommodation of humanism inherent in this idea of balance, that are unable to the make their political contributions on the basis of the implicit acceptance of multiple truth claims inherent in a religiously pluralist public sphere, or whose beliefs and practices are not rooted in, or even clash with, predominant national or European cultural norms, may struggle to achieve influence or even acceptance within such a framework.[16] Conversely, religious identities that are established elements of national identities are not seen as threats to the overall notion of balance or, therefore, to the public order, even when they retain political ambitions that may be inconsistent with principles, like respect for personal autonomy, which the Union has identified as a key element of balance and therefore of its public order.[17] Furthermore, in its attempts to protect the public order from forms of religion seen as hostile to the notion of balance, the Union has, at times, been willing to countenance the curtailment principles, such as individual autonomy in matters of belief, which are themselves regarded as key elements of such balance.[18]

---

[15] See Ch 6, sections 2 and 5.   [16] See Ch 5, section 3 and Ch 6, sections 2–5.
[17] See Ch 5, section 3.2 and Ch 6, sections 2.5 and 5.   [18] See Ch 6, sections 3 and 4.

4. Proper Balance: Cultural Religion, Political Religion, and Individual Autonomy

To summarize, the Union regards balance between the religious and humanist influences as a key element of its public order. Certain kinds of relationship between religion, the law, and the polity are not regarded by the Union as satisfying this criterion of balance. The EU's public order does therefore have its own sensibility in relation to religious matters and a particular view of what the relationship between religion should be, albeit that this view enables Member States to retain significant autonomy in religious matters. This European view of the appropriate relationship between religion, law, and polity does not preclude accommodation of religion's cultural role in Member States and even enables particular faiths to exercise a degree of indirect influence over law by virtue of their contribution to collective cultural norms and ideas of public morality. However, it does require the restriction of explicitly religious influence over law and politics and the protection of individual private autonomy from efforts to enforce collective moral norms through the law. Therefore, approaches to religion that undermine the independence of the legal and political arenas from religious domination by accommodating religious truth claims in law-making or that seek to legally enforce religious morality in private matters to too great a degree, will not be regarded as maintaining the proper balance between religious and humanist influences required by the Union's public order.

5. The Chapters

These features are sketched and analysed in five substantive chapters and a conclusion. Chapter 2 sets out the factual background to the Union's approach to religion by setting out the fundamental elements of contemporary European approaches to the relationship between religion, politics, the law, and the state. It notes how European identity originally arose out of a shared commitment to Christianity but how this identity has also been moulded by a strong humanist tradition which owed much to Christianity but which nevertheless played a significant role in the experience of secularization undergone by most Member States since the fifteenth century. Chapter 2 demonstrates that although Europe is relatively a-religious in world terms, religion remains an element of both personal and national identities. Indeed, strict separation of Church and state is rare in Europe and religion has an important institutional role in many

Member States, particularly in relation to healthcare and education. Despite its continued role in individual and collective identities, religion's political influence has waned and, although it retains some influence over law in relation to 'moral issues', such as the beginning and end of life, family structures, and sexuality, this influence is declining and has given way to liberal and humanist notions of individual autonomy to a significant degree. Religion in Europe therefore retains an important role as an element of individual and collective identities. In particular, individual denominations continue to function as parts of the national identity and institutional structures of many European states. Despite this continuing role in identity, religion in Europe is required to compete for influence over law with strong secular and humanist traditions which have resulted in significant restriction of its political role and influence.

Chapter 3 shows how the tradition outlined in Chapter 2 has been reflected in the Union's approach to the influence of religion over law-making. It reveals how religion is recognized by the Union as an element of its constitutional values but how, at the same time, this role is balanced by the recognition of potentially competing humanist and cultural influences. The limited role played by religion in the political arena, shown in Chapter 2, is reflected in the Union's approach to the role of religion in law and policy-making. Although it recognizes the 'particular contribution' of religious bodies in this area, EU law requires that this contribution be made in the context of civil society, thereby requiring religious bodies to engage in structures that implicitly recognize the legitimacy of other beliefs and the authority of secular political institutions. Accordingly, the notion of balance between the various elements of the Union's ethical inheritance is preserved by recognizing a role for religion in relation to law-making while simultaneously making such a role contingent on the limitation of claims on the part of religion to a monopoly on truth or to substantive political power in its own right.

Chapter 3 also shows how religion's role in national identity and culture and as a source of communal moral norms has been accommodated by EU law through the pluralist nature of the Union's public order, which enables Member States to reflect particular national and religiously specific visions of public morality in EU law, provided that such states respect the notion of balance between religious, humanist, and cultural influences inherent in EU fundamental rights commitments (most notably respect for individual autonomy), as well as the moral pluralism involved in principles such as freedom of movement. This approach has been justified on grounds of cultural autonomy. The EU level of this pluralist public order lacks a strong cultural identity and is therefore marked by a strict adherence to formal neutrality in religious matters and by notions of public morality that are derived from the Union's fundamental rights commitments. Although formally neutral, such commitments have been heavily influenced by the historical and cultural role of particular religious traditions in Europe, most notably that of Christian humanism, and can be experienced as more restrictive by adherents to religions that struggle to accept the limitations on religious influence inherent in a balance between religious and humanist values and in respect for Europe's strong cultural tradition of individual autonomy and popular (as opposed to divine) sovereignty.

Chapter 4 demonstrates how this same framework fits in with the Union's fundamental rights obligations, which also envisage religion exercising influence over law on the basis of its status as an element of individual and collective identities. It analyses the various justifications for religious freedom and notes how respect for individual and collective religious rights can often come into conflict. In line with both the pluralist and humanist elements of its public order, and with its fundamental rights obligations, seen primarily in the requirements of the European Convention on Human Rights ('ECHR'), EU law has recognized individual and collective religious freedom as largely private rights linked to notions of personal autonomy in matters of identity. However, both sets of rights have also been seen as being required to give way to certain public interests in non-private contexts. In particular, the right to develop and adhere to a religious identity has been seen as being legitimately required to yield to the general public interest in the maintenance of a non-theocratic, democratic system, a requirement that can be seen as reflecting the limitations on assertion of religious claims to truth in the public sphere in Chapter 3. Furthermore, although some recent decisions have shown an increasing concern on the part of the Strasbourg Court to police, in the context of public schools, the boundary between state recognition of a particular faith as an element of national culture and state recognition of the truth claims of a particular religion, in general, the case law of the European Court of Human Rights ('ECtHR') indicates that respect for religious freedom does not require the accommodation of individual or collective religious choices in non-private contexts such as the labour market when such choices clash with prevailing cultural norms. Chapter 4 therefore suggests that the basic framework provided by the Union's fundamental rights obligations in relation to religious freedom is one that requires that individual and collective religious identities receive a significant degree of protection in private but that enables Member States to curtail such identity rights in non-private contexts in order to promote either their communal cultural identity or the democratic nature of the public order.

Chapter 5 addresses the application of the identity-based framework set out in Chapter 4 within the context of EU Single Market law and the reconciliation of the potentially clashing collective and individual identity rights in this area. The idea that religion is an element of personal identity entitled to protection on the basis of respect for individual autonomy can be seen in the characterization of religion as an economic choice within Single Market law. Chapter 5 shows how EU law has taken a broader view of the need to protect individual religious identity in non-private contexts than that contained in the minimum standard prescribed by the ECtHR and has legislated in order to require accommodation of individual religious identity in the workplace. By embracing the principle of indirect discrimination, EU law not only protects individual religious identity outside purely private contexts, but also ensures the formal neutrality of the marketplace, thereby pluralizing the workplace in religious terms. On the other hand, such facilitation of religious and individual identity is still required to give way to certain public interests such as the commercial nature of the market economy, the need to protect the non-theocratic nature of the public order, and pre-existing religious privileges in the market. The Union has, in fact, shown considerable deference towards existing structures and privileges held by particular denominations in the market place and has exempted such structures from the duty to comply with anti-discrimination measures in order to enable the preservation of the institutional role played by particular religions in individual Member States. Such deference facilitates collective religious identity by enabling religious employers to promote their 'ethos' in the workplace. It also, however, restricts individual religious identity rights by permitting discrimination against employees on religious grounds.

This facilitation of the collective role of religion is also seen in the Union's recognition of religion as an element of culture. Respect for cultural influences is explicitly recognized as an element of the respect for inheritance and the balance between the religious, humanist, and cultural elements that underpin the Union's public order. Chapter 5 shows how the Union has, in line with its approach in relation to pre-existing religious privilege in the marketplace, recognized particular approaches to individual denominations and institutional arrangements linking such denominations to particular Member States, as parts of national culture. This cultural approach reinforces some of the features of the 'balance' pursued by the Union outlined in previous chapters. For instance, given that culture relates to a state of affairs which is not necessarily normative, characterizing religion as an element of culture reinforces its status as a human choice or element of identity rather than a claim to truth or ideological matter. Such a view of religion reinforces the limits on the role of explicitly religious claims in the political arena set out in Chapter 3. However, Chapter 5 also demonstrates how recognition of particular religions as elements of national culture enables such faiths to access a degree of influence over law that is denied to other faiths. Such status also enables these insider faiths to promote their worldview, or protect their elevated status, through EU law, by means of exemptions from free market rules and public morality clauses that Member States see as necessary to preserve religiously influenced elements of their culture.

Furthermore, Chapter 5 shows how the EU has not fully appreciated the complexity of the relationship between culturally entrenched 'insider' faiths and the limitations on religious influence over law and politics required by the humanist elements of the Union's identity. Its culturally centred view of religion's relationship to law causes the Union to view as 'cultural', and therefore acceptable, demands which, coming from 'outsider' religions, would be seen as unduly political and threatening to notions such as the pluralism of the public sphere or respect for individual autonomy, which underpin the balance between religious and humanist influences to which the public order of the Union is committed. Finally, Chapter 5 demonstrates how religions that are regarded as contrary to European culture have received scant recognition of their rights under EU law and have, in some cases, been characterized as contrary to the public order and liable to restriction on that basis.

The Union's regulation of religion in the Single Market therefore demonstrates that, while it is committed to facilitating religion as an element of individual, collective, and national cultural identity, there are also kinds of identity which, within a framework dedicated to maintenance of the balance between the religious, humanist, and cultural influences that forms Europe's ideological inheritance, are considered unacceptable. Chapter 5 notes how religions that fall outside of the protection of national cultural identity and fail to respect the limitations on religion's political role seen as inherent in this inheritance, are considered to be identities which will receive more limited protection and facilitation under the EU law.

Chapter 6 further investigates this notion of unacceptable religious identities. It analyses how the limitations on the political influence of religion inherent in the vision of balance pursued by the Union have been highlighted in its dealings with outsiders whose religions cannot as readily be accommodated under the rubric of national cultural identity. Chapter 6 assesses the EU's approach to enlargement and the integration of immigrants to demonstrate how religions that attempt to dominate the public sphere have been seen as violating the duty to respect the principle of pluralism, while attempts to interfere with private autonomy in order to impose religious morality similarly breach the requirement that the role accorded to religion respect the notion of balance between religious and humanist influences. Failures on the part of religion to respect public and private autonomy are therefore viewed as inconsistent with a European identity that the Union regards as encompassing not only a strong (predominantly Christian) religious tradition but also the equally strong traditions of questioning religion, of imposing a degree of separation between the religious and political realms, and of respecting individual autonomy. Chapter 6 goes on to show that in defending this identity, the Union has been willing to interfere with individual autonomy itself by seeking to regulate private religious identity and that, in doing so, the Union has at times appeared, at least implicitly, to regard some forms of religion, most notably Islam, as inherently less compatible with Europe's religious inheritance and identity than others. Furthermore, it demonstrates that while the Union has accommodated the reflection in law of norms of religions that are recognized as part of national cultures and identities, as elements of 'public morality' or national cultural norms, attempts on the part of outsider religions to mould the law to reflect their religious beliefs are seen as political rather than cultural and as representing, on that basis, a threat to the limitations on religious political influence inherent in the Union's interpretation of the requirements of balance between religious, humanist, and cultural influences.

Chapter 7 ties these themes together and argues that the Union's approach to religion is characterized by a commitment to reconciling the two dominant and partially conflicting approaches to religion that have emerged from European history, namely the tradition of Christian religiosity and the humanist tradition, which partly grew out of Christianity but which also fostered a strong tradition of secularism and of questioning and challenging religion. These traditions are reconciled by the Union through a commitment to balancing the religious, humanist, and cultural influences that it sees as marking its religious inheritance. This commitment to balancing a strong religious tradition, which has included promotion of religious goals and norms through law, with a strong humanist tradition stressing individual autonomy, equality, and separation between the religious and political realms, is effected by the recognition of religion as an element of identity, both individual and collective. The framework of identity enables religions to pursue their goals in relation to the promotion of communal moral norms through recognition of religion's status as an element of collective identity and as a contributor to the definition of shared norms. At the same time, viewing religion as a form of identity defines it as an element of human choice, thus pluralizing it and limiting its ability to assert a monopoly on truth in the public sphere while also strengthening claims for autonomy in relation to individual identity formation, all of which place limits on religion's ability to dominate the legal and political arenas. Therefore, while an identity-based framework does allow the Union's approach to display considerable pluralism and thereby to accommodate divergent Member State approaches to religion to a significant degree, there are limits to such pluralism and the Union regards a *proper* balance between religion as being a fundamental element of its public order and a prerequisite of membership. Approaches that base law-making on recognition of religious truth claims and permit religious domination of the legal and political arenas or that enable the enforcement of religious morality to a degree that fails to respect individual private autonomy, will not be seen as maintaining such proper balance and will be contrary to the Union's public order. These features give the Union a public order that is unambiguously linked to a Christian humanist tradition and facilitates the, predominantly Christian, cultural role of religion in influencing the law. On the other hand, while not strictly secular, such a public order is avowedly non-theocratic and, while recognizing religion and privileging certain culturally entrenched forms thereof, the Union also recognizes the importance of non-religious perspectives.

Difficult issues are raised by the fact that the restrictions on religious influence in the political arena that are required by the EU's public order may be less restrictive of the influence of 'insider' faiths than that of 'outsider' faiths. By treating the influence exercised by culturally entrenched insider religions over law as a result of their role in the identities of particular Member States as cultural rather than political or ideological, the Union does exempt, to a limited degree, the claims made by such religions on this basis from requirements of rational justification and reciprocal respect for other identity claims, despite the political and ideological elements of these cultural demands. The recognition of such claims as cultural is therefore undoubtedly an important source of privilege and influence over law. Indeed, relationships between religion, law, and state are in flux across Europe as greater religious diversity places strains on established, often implicit, arrangements between the state and culturally entrenched faiths. The Union's approach is problematic, not because it seeks to safeguard limitations on religious influence over law and politics but because, in common with some of its Member States, it attributes an uncomplicated and wholehearted acceptance of such limitations to culturally entrenched faiths and has often failed to impose them on such insider religions with the same rigour as it does in the case of outsider religions. However, in the light of the continuing importance of particular religions in the cultural identity of Member States, the Union's limited powers, its legal pluralism, and its commitment to respecting Member State cultural autonomy, it is inevitable that those faiths that play a major role in national identities will exercise greater indirect influence over laws than those faiths that do not play a similar role.

Nevertheless, although it is not capable of radically reshaping the relationship between religion and law within Member States, the Union does not merely reflect Member State preferences, but places limits, albeit limited ones, on such relationships. Indeed, by exempting 'cultural' claims from requirements of rational justification and reciprocal recognition on the grounds of their ostensibly non-political nature, the Union can impose these very requirements on insider religions when they make demands that are explicitly political in nature or that cannot be cannot be characterized as a claim for protection of national cultural identity. The EU's public order therefore establishes its political sphere as a formally neutral environment in religious terms to which all religious viewpoints may contribute and within which claims to exclusive possession of the truth and a refusal to recognize the validity of other religious identities are not possible. Furthermore, the combination of this protection of the autonomy of the political sphere from religious domination with the Union's requirement that Member States respect the fundamental elements of its own public morality, such as respect for the principle of proportionality and fundamental rights including individual private autonomy, non-discrimination, and free movement rights, provides an impediment to attempts to expand the influence of particular faiths over law and political life and the subjugation of individual autonomy to the promotion of collective religious and cultural goals at Member State level,[19] thereby promoting the degree of pluralism necessary for cultural evolution to remain sufficiently open and reflexive to enable groups that are currently outsiders to contribute to the process of cultural evolution.

While the EU is not strictly secular, if predictions of the return of religion to the political arena[20] prove correct, the Union may well provide limitations on the impact of such a return in the coming decades and may play an important role in the evolution of the relationship between the law, politics, the state, and religion in Europe. Although there are serious issues in relation to the selective application of limitations on religious influence to outsider faiths, not all of which can be accounted for by the linking of religion's public role to its cultural status (which an identity-focused approach involves), the Union's attempts to distinguish between religion's cultural role and explicitly religious claims within the political arena represent a justifiable balance between ensuring respect for the its cultural and legal pluralism while constructing a distinctive public order with identifiable fundamental norms.

---

[19] See Ch 5.
[20] P Berger and G Weigel (eds), *The Desecularization of the Modern World: Resurgent Religion and Modern Politics* (Grand Rapids, Mich: Erdemans Publishing Company and Public Policy Center, 1999).

2

Europe's Religious Inheritance: Religion, Law, and Identity in Contemporary Europe

1. Introduction

Under the public order of the European Union (EU), religion is dealt with largely as a matter of identity and on the basis of what the Union sees as Europe's ethical tradition of a balance between religious, humanist, and cultural influences. The Union's regulation of religion takes place in a context in which the majority of political power and religious practice remains within national contexts[1] and through a public order that is committed to respecting pluralism and national cultural autonomy. The approaches of Member States to religion are characterized by Europe's common heritage of Christianity and by humanist and secular influences that have emerged from European history and have limited religious influence over law and politics in Europe to a greater degree than elsewhere.

However, the balance between these influences is struck differently in differing Member States and arrangements in relation to the official status of religion or religions, the political and legal influence of religion, and the cultural and institutional role of religious bodies, vary significantly from state to state. Despite such diversity, certain common themes and patterns can be identified. All current EU Member States share a largely Christian past but have also been exposed to humanist and secular influences which have reduced religious influence over law and politics.

[1] Although international religions such as the Catholic Church are by definition not national bodies, their hierarchies and clergy are nevertheless organized along national lines to a significant extent.

Nevertheless, religion has retained a significant role in both personal and collective identities. Religious institutions retain important roles in areas such as healthcare and education in almost all Member States, while many states retain official links to particular Christian denominations which remain an important element of national identities. No EU Member State is a fully fledged theocracy and limitations on religious influence are a key element of the shared European ethical and political traditions. On the other hand, religious groups have retained some influence over law and policy in certain areas, albeit to a declining degree. The approach of EU Member States to religion is therefore characterized by a significant degree of diversity but also by a common view of religion as an important aspect of national, collective, and individual identities, which has both a particular institutional position and a degree of influence (albeit one which must be limited and which is declining) over law and politics.

An appreciation of contemporary European approaches to religion requires an awareness of the role played by Christianity in European history and identity and some knowledge of the secularization process that has led to the establishment of significant limitations on religious influence over law, politics, and society in Europe. These developments have given rise to competing versions of European identity centred on Christianity and secularism. Indeed, the degree of secularization undergone by European societies is rather exceptional in international terms. Nevertheless, even in secularized societies, religion has not disappeared and continues to exercise influence in certain areas, most notably issues relating to sexual morality and the beginning and end of life ('lifeworld' issues), as well as questions of communal identity. Religion's continuing role in individual identity is shown by the high levels of nominal adherence to religion, as well as by the widely divergent levels of religious practice shown by the populations of European states. Religious influence over law and politics has declined, even in relation to 'lifeworld' issues, but religious bodies nevertheless retain a degree of influence in these matters. Finally, a key element of the Union's relationship to religion centres on the role played by religion in national identity and the constitutional and institutional position of religion in the Member States. There is a wide degree of divergence between states, with options from official embrace of a single religion to official secularism being found among EU members. Nevertheless, almost all states provide some degree of recognition or support of religion and religious bodies retain significant roles in the provision of healthcare and education.

While religion exercises a comparatively low level of influence over Euro-pean societies, attachment to a particular form of religion, or way of deal-ing with religion, is a key element of both personal and national identities in many Member States. Furthermore, while religious influence over law and politics has declined, it is not entirely a thing of the past. However, the role played by religion in these areas is counterbalanced by strong humanist and secular influences that have marked European history, and the overall picture is therefore one of balance between religious and secular influences, which is struck in differing ways in the various Member States. This chapter outlines the broader context that underpins the Union's regulation of reli-gion and its development of a distinctive constitutional approach to religious issues.

2. A Legacy of Christianity and Secularization

Religion, and Western Christianity in particular, have played a foundational role in the establishment of the very ideas of Europe and European iden-tity. Le Goff suggests that 'it was Christianization above all that brought uniformity to the West in the Early Middle Ages'.[2] He notes that the first time medieval chroniclers described an event as 'European' was the victory of Christian Frankish forces over a Muslim army at Poitiers in 732[3] and how, with the crusades of the eleventh century, Western Christianity became syn-onymous with a European identity which defined itself against the Islamic and Byzantine Orthodox Christian civilizations to its south and east, a proc-ess that was reinforced with the fall of the Byzantine Empire to the Turks and the military threat posed by Ottoman Empire until the seventeenth century.[4] Le Goff also describes how certain features of Western Christianity gave rise to key ideas and distinctions which were to have a profound effect on the political development of Europe. In particular he suggests that the separa-tion of the laity and the clergy by Pope Gregory VII helped to bring about a degree of separation between Caesar and God that distinguished European civilisation from the Caesaro-Papism of the Eastern Orthodox Church and Islamic approaches which did not differentiate between the religious and

---

[2] J Le Goff, *The Birth of Europe* (Malden, MA: Blackwell, 2005) 22.   [3] Ibid 26.
[4] Ibid 10.

political domains.[5] Furthermore, he notes how the emergence, during the eleventh and twelfth centuries, of a strong emphasis on the belief that man was made in the image of God gave rise to a strain of humanism which was to have important consequences in terms of the importance accorded to the individual in European society in future centuries.

Although Le Goff suggests that these features 'involved the rejection of theocracy [....] and a balance between faith and reason',[6] both he and other authors such as Taylor and Casanova agree that up to the fifteenth century all areas of European life were dominated by religion and by Western Christianity in particular.[7] However, beginning in the late fifteenth century, Europe embarked on a long process of secularization or what Taylor calls 'disenchantment', which led to a decline in religious influence over political and, ultimately, personal, life that has few parallels elsewhere in the world. Various explanations have been provided for this development. Casanova argues that this reduction in religious influence was caused by four main factors. The Protestant Reformation undermined the universalist claims of the Catholic Church, the rise of the modern state with its monopolization of force undermined the compulsory nature of religion, the rise of capitalism and markets removed economic life from the control of religious bodies and ideas, and, finally, early modern science brought about new and autonomous methods of verifying truth.[8] This combination of factors eventually brought about a situation in modern Europe where 'the quest for subjective meaning is a strictly personal affair [and] the primary "public" institutions (state, economy) no longer need or are interested in maintaining a sacred cosmos or public religious worldview'.[9]

Similarly, Bruce[10] argues that it was the increase in both individualism and rationality engendered by the Reformation that began the process which was to result in the secularization of modern Europe. He submitted that 'individualism threatened the communal basis of religious belief and behaviour, while rationality removed many of the purposes of religion and made many of its beliefs implausible'.[11] The decline of religious influence was strengthened by the rise of the nation state in the post-Reformation period. In particular, Bruce suggests that the adoption of a policy based on a degree of mutual tolerance following the Treaty of Westphalia enabled a

---

[5] Ibid 60.   [6] Ibid 196.

[7] Ibid 200. See also J Casanova, *Public Religions in the Modern World* (Chicago: University of Chicago Press, 1994) 20.   [8] Ibid 21–4.   [9] Ibid 37.

[10] S Bruce, *From Cathedrals to Cults: Religion in the Modern World* (Oxford: Oxford University Press, 1996).   [11] Ibid 230.

'live and let live' attitude towards religion that came to predominate over the unbending convictions of previous generations. This acceptance of a degree of pluralism eventually brought about a situation where religion (and, eventually, even the idea of God) became part of a world of choices and preferences. Previously dominant churches therefore lost the central role they once had in society as an increasingly rational citizenry exercised their choice in religious matters to follow individualistic and subjective forms of religion, with a consequent decline in the role and influence of traditional religious denominations.

Weber and Durkheim both attributed major importance to the emergence of capitalism and saw religious decline as an inevitable by-product of modernity. Weber saw the Industrial Revolution as having encouraged a process of 'capitalist secularization' where 'irrational compulsion' was replaced by 'sober economic virtue' and utilitarianism.[12] Durkheim, on the other hand, stressed the role of modern industrial society in promoting 'functional differentiation' under which specialized autonomous professions rather than ecclesiastical institutions became the providers of goods such as healthcare, education, and welfare.[13]

Other theorists have focused on internal developments within religion. Stark and Iannaccone put forward what has been called a 'supply side' theory, arguing that the dominance of single denominations and state subsidy brought about a complacent clergy and unadaptive ecclesiastical environment that depressed levels of belief and practice.[14] Taylor, on the other hand, emphasizes political and moral changes which, he suggests, arose from within Christianity. He suggests that religious reformers such as Luther and Calvin built on the humanistic elements of Christianity and gave new importance and dignity to ordinary human flourishing by abolishing the distinction between sacred and profane activities. Christian humanism also facilitated the growth of Deism, which centred religious belief around personal experience and reason rather than revelation. Such an approach, Taylor suggests, empowered individuals to determine their own relationship to

---

[12] M Weber, *The Protestant Ethic and the Spirit of Capitalism* (New York: Scribner's, 1930 [1904]) 176.

[13] É Durkheim, *The Elementary Forms of the Religious Life* (Oxford: Oxford World's Classics, Oxford University Press, 2001).

[14] R Stark and LR Iannaccone, 'A supply-side reinterpretation of the "secularization" of Europe' (1994) 33(3) *Journal for the Scientific Study of Religion* 230, 231.

the divine and led to the modern 'age of authenticity' where individuals are encouraged to develop their own identities and approaches to life.[15]

Whatever its origins, the process of secularization was vigorously resisted by many religious bodies, particularly the Catholic Church, but has nevertheless led to a situation where the levels of religious practice, belief, and influence over the legal and political domains are weaker in Europe than in any other continent.[16] However, both Taylor and Casanova agree that this process has not resulted in the removal of religious influence from European life. As is shown below, religion continues to seek to influence law and public policy, particularly in relation to 'lifeworld' issues such as family, sexuality, and the beginning and end of life.[17] Furthermore, Taylor argues that, even in secularized societies such as Europe, there is an 'irrepressible desire for the transcendent'.[18] This has been seen in recent centuries in the romantic and nationalist movements as well as in the success of evangelical religious movements and the anti-humanist movements such as fascism, which saw a purely rationally based worldview and the cooperative demands made by such an approach as suffocating the human spirit.[19] Moreover, as Davie points out,[20] levels of nominal adherence to religion remain high in Europe, while Christian religious institutions and symbols remain important elements of the national life and identity of most EU Member States. This dualism has been highlighted by Olivier Roy who, while agreeing that 'Western secularism actually has a Christian origin',[21] nevertheless notes that secularism and Christianity provide two potentially competing poles around which Western identity can be defined. In this vein he suggests that the West (and therefore also Europe) is defined either:

in Christian terms or [...] in reference to the philosophy of the Enlightenment, human rights, and democracy that developed against the Catholic Church through first the Protestant Reformation, then the Enlightenment, and finally the secular and democratic ideal.[22]

---

[15]   C Taylor, *A Secular Age* (Cambridge MA: Harvard University Press, 2007).

[16]   P Norris and R Inglehart, *Sacred and Secular: Religion and Politics Worldwide* (Cambridge: Cambridge University Press, 2004).   [17]   See sections 3.2 and 4.2 below.

[18]   Taylor (n 15 above) 473.   [19]   Ibid.

[20]   G Davie, *Europe: The Exceptional Case: Parameters of Faith in the Modern World* (London: Longman Todd, 2002).

[21]   O Roy, *Secularism Confronts Islam* (translated by George Holoch) (New York: Columbia University Press, 2007) ix.

[22]   Ibid vii.

3. The Post-secularization Role of Religion in Contemporary Europe

3.1 Europe as a Secular Exception

Despite the near-universal acceptance of secularization theory in academic circles up until the 1960s, religion in the outside world stubbornly refused to wither away as predicted. Furthermore, the persistence of religion was limited to pre-industrial countries in the less-developed world. Berger, previously a committed advocate of secularization theory, recanted and conceded that the non-Western world was 'as furiously religious as ever' and that evidence of religious decline in the United States was largely absent. The continuing religious vitality of the United States (with its highly developed religious pluralism) called into question the link between pluralism, relativism, and secularity.[23]

However, although religion remained strong in many areas of the world, in Europe it was undeniable that a significant degree of secularization had taken place. In this context, Europe, as a progressively secularizing continent, eventually came to be seen as the exception to the rule of a persistently religious world rather than the trail blazer to a secular future. Although, as is discussed below, most Europeans retained at least a nominal affiliation to Christianity, as Cox pointed out: 'an unwillingness by most Europeans to declare themselves entirely atheistic, or to abandon irrevocably all hope of life after death, is not persuasive evidence that Berlin and Amsterdam are throbbing with a hidden Durkheimian numinosity'.[24] Furthermore, he notes that the fact that 'in large areas of modern Europe, religious men and women who attempt to create new religious institutions run into a brick wall of resistance and indifference'.[25] Attempts to introduce televangelism to Europe, for example, have found that that kind of religion simply does not find an appreciative audience among Europeans in the way it clearly does elsewhere.[26]

Whatever the merits of their arguments in relation to secularization theory as it applies to the world in general, attempts to deny Europe's progressive

---

[23] P Berger, *A Far Glory: The Quest for Faith in an Age of Credulity* (New York: Free Press, 1992) 32.
[24] J Cox, 'Master Narratives of Long-Term Religious Change' in H McLeod and W Ustof (eds), *The Decline of Christendom in Western Europe, 175–2000* (Cambridge: Cambridge University Press, 2003) 203–4.   [25] Ibid.   [26] Davie (n 20 above) 32.

secularization, like those who used confidently to predict the eventual dis-appearance of religion altogether, run into what Cox describes as the 'tri-umphant empirical rebuttal'[27] of a welter of statistics showing a continuing decline in levels of religious practice and belief among Europeans in general.

3.2 The Post-secularization Political and Legal Role of Religion

Nevertheless, it was also clear that, although secularization had occurred, it had not meant that religion had disappeared altogether from European life. Casanova[28] has adapted secularization theory to take account of the continu-ing influence exercised by religious organizations and worldviews over certain areas of law and politics. He agrees that this process has brought about a funda-mental change in the role of religion in society but departs more radically from traditional secularization theories in rejecting the idea that the emancipation of the secular spheres meant that religion would inevitably decline and dis-appear. He rejects the idea that religion in the modern world has been relegated to the private sphere, arguing that religion and politics have a symbiotic rela-tionship and that 'the walls separating church and state continually develop cracks through which they penetrate each other'.[29] Religions, he asserts, have refused to accept the marginal role allocated to them under the liberal state model of separation. The Catholic Church in particular has refused to accept that separation of Church and state means the privatization of morality.[30] While he agrees that churches neither can nor should seek to control the state, Casanova rejects the secularist idea of a neutral public square as damaging to both religion and politics[31] and as biased against those who have religious faith.[32] Accordingly, he sees three circumstances under which modern reli-gions should and in fact do intervene in the public square. These are:

1. to protect modern freedoms and rights against an absolutist authoritarian state (such as the ecclesiastical opposition to dictatorship in Brazil and Spain);
2. to contest the absolute lawful autonomy of secular spheres and their claim to be organized according to principles of functional differentiation without regard to extraneous moral/ethical considerations (Casanova gives the example of the opposition to arms race in the United States by the Catholic Church in the 1980s, but, in the EU context, a more relevant

---

[27] Cox (n 24 above) 205.   [28] Casanova (n 7 above).   [29] Ibid 41.   [30] Ibid 57.
[31] Ibid 61.   [32] Ibid 64.

example may be the consistent warnings of the Catholic hierarchy and clerics of other religions against the absolute primacy of the market in modern society);

3. to protect what he terms the 'traditional life-world' (ie questions relating to the beginning and end of life, such as euthanasia, bio-ethics and abortion, family policy, and sexuality) from administrative or juridical state penetration and in the process to open up issues of norm and will formation to the public and collective self-reflection of modern discursive ethics.

Casanova gives the example of the public mobilization of the so-called Moral Majority and the Catholic public stand on abortion in support of 'the right to life' in the United States as examples of this third instance.[33] In the European context, the Catholic Church has been equally active in relation to EU policies related to these 'lifeworld' issues.

In summary, Casanova accepts that modernization has played a key role in bringing about a significant decline in religious influence in modern society. The emancipation of the secular spheres from ecclesiastical control is, he believes, 'incontestable and a modern structural trend'.[34] However, he rejects the idea that this process of secularization will inevitably bring about the disappearance and privatization of religion, asserting that where churches have avoided excessive entanglement with the state, religion can retain vitality, and that in the modern democratic state, religions continue to play a public role in certain areas.

Casanova's adaptation of secularization theory would appear to account successfully for many (though not all) of the features of the role of religion in contemporary Europe. It is clear that, in European terms at least, processes such as the rise of the nation state and the capitalist economy, coupled with scientific and educational advances, have brought about a decline in the influence of religion on society. Indeed, even the Catholic Church, having fought the emergence of the secular state for centuries, began in the mid-1960s 'a tortuous process of official aggiornamento to secular modernity [in which it] accepted the legitimacy of the modern age'.[35] However, this has not meant that religion has disappeared from European life in either its private or public forms.

---

[33] Ibid 228. He does not explain how such a role for religion is not biased against forms of religion that are hostile to 'modern freedoms and rights'.   [34] Ibid 212.
[35] Ibid 9.

More importantly, the churches themselves have not abandoned their public, political role. As Casanova pointed out, the Catholic Church in particular, despite its acceptance of the legitimacy of the secular state, has explicitly rejected the notion of religion as a purely private matter and continues to challenge the absolute autonomy of the key secular spheres of the market and the state and to intervene in public affairs on a wide range of issues, particularly those connected to the 'lifeworld'. In its 'Doctrinal Note on Some Questions Regarding the Participation of Catholics in Political Life',[36] the Vatican authorities stated bluntly that legislators had 'a grave and clear obligation to oppose' any law that attacks human life, and that it was 'impossible' for any Catholic to vote for such laws.[37] More broadly, the same document states that 'a well-formed Christian conscience does not permit one to vote for a political program or an individual law which contradicts the fundamental contents of faith and morals'.[38]

Support for the argument that the churches do retain an influential public role is provided by Halman and Riis, who argue that what they term 'modern people' are 'less prone to accept the churches as moral authorities though they may still accept them as advisors on a limited range of moral issues'.[39] Thus, while religious bodies express views on a wide range of matters, their influence is concentrated on certain issues. This hypothesis is further supported by Procter and Hornsby-Smith's work, which showed that while political values on socio-economic issues could not be predicted on the basis of levels of religious practice and identification, a significant relationship could be shown between the latter and attitudes to questions of 'family values'.[40] Thus, even in highly secularized societies such as Europe, churches

---

[36] 'Doctrinal Note on Some Questions Regarding the Participation of Catholics in Political Life', 16 January 2003, issued by the Congregation for the Doctrine of the Faith (quoted in D Yamane, *The Catholic Church in State Politics: Negotiating Prophetic Demands and Political Realities* (Lanham: Rowman and Littlefield Publishers, 2005) 151).   [37] Ibid para 4.

[38] Ibid para 4.

[39] L Halman and O Riis (eds), *Religion in Secularizing Society: The Europeans' Religion at the End of the 20th Century* (Leiden: Brill, 2003) 5.

[40] M Procter and M Hornsby-Smith, 'Individual Context Religiosity, Religious [sic.] and Values in Europe and North America' in Halman and Riis (n 39 above) 110–111. Norris and Inglehart (n 16 above) 228 also note a weakening in the relationship between a general right political orientation and religiosity over the last 20 years in most industrial and post-industrial societies apart from the United States and Austria. While several commentators note that there continues to be a link between religiosity and support of right-wing political parties, the significance of Procter and Hornsby-Smith's work is that this orientation is influenced to a greater degree by the attitudes of right wing parties to lifeworld issues rather than their stances on socio-economic matters.

act most strongly and have most influence in relation to state attempts to regulate the private sphere (namely those areas of policy impinging on the 'lifeworld' of family policy, the beginning and ending of life, sexuality, and bio-ethics). Indeed, in a 2006 address to the European People's Party, Pope Benedict XVI stated that: '[a]s far as the Catholic Church is concerned, the principal focus of her interventions in the public arena is the protection and promotion of the dignity of the person, and she is thereby consciously drawing particular attention to principles which are not negotiable'.[41]

As to the specific areas of policy related to the dignity of the person, the Pope mentioned three areas upon which the Church had focused:

—protection of life in all its stages, from the first moment of conception until natural death;
—recognition and promotion of the natural structure of the family—as a union between a man and a woman based on marriage—and its defence from attempts to make it juridically equivalent to radically different forms of union which in reality harm it and contribute to its destabilization, obscuring its particular character and its irreplaceable social role;
—the protection of the right of parents to educate their children.[42]

These issues are both at the forefront of contemporary political debate within Europe[43] and at the crux of the value differences separating values of the West from those of less-economically developed regions.[44] Large-scale immigration into Europe, particularly from Muslim countries, has given these issues a new lease of life[45] and has reopened conflicts which the proponents of traditional Christian morality had thought lost for many years. In late 2004 an expert group appointed by the EU issued a report entitled *Islam and Fundamental Rights in Europe*, which concluded that:

the major area of conflict between Islam and Human Rights is not politics but on Civil Law and culture as demonstrated in the debate over secularism and Islam. The highest divergence between Muslims and non-Muslims seems to concern the

---

[41] Address of Pope Benedict XVI to the European People's Party of 30 March 2006, full text available at <http://www.vatican.va/holy_father/benedict_xvi/speeches/2006/march/documents/hf_ben-xvi_spe_20060330_eu-parliamentarians_en.html> (last visited 11 May 2010).
[42] Ibid.
[43] See, eg B Bawer, *While Europe Slept: How Radical Islam Is Destroying the West from Within* (New York: Doubleday, 2006).   [44] Norris and Inglehart (n 16 above).
[45] J Klausen, *The Islamic Challenge: Politics and Religion in Western Europe* (Oxford: Oxford University Press, 2005) 15, 16, 92.

questions of morality and sexuality as shown in the debate over the headscarf but also on the question of sexual orientation.[46]

This conclusion was underlined by leading figures from a range of Islamic organizations in a joint statement condemning homosexuality in early 2006, which was published in the London *Times* newspaper.[47]

Thus, although significant secularization has taken place, and although most mainstream European religions have come to accept the legitimacy of secular political authority, this has not meant that religion has been removed from law or political life. Instead, in certain areas, religion continues to seek to play a role in relation to, and to varying degrees, succeeds in influencing, law and politics in the Member States of the European Union.

3.3 Religion and Identity

In addition to its continuing role in the legal and political arenas, theorists have noted the continuing importance of religion in matters of identity in Europe. Davie acknowledges that there has been a striking decline in religious belief and practice in Europe. She argues, however, that large numbers of Europeans who do not themselves practice their religion actively, nevertheless retain a religious sensitivity, approve of religion in a general way, and are pleased that the smaller number of active religious participants do practice their faith.[48] This Davie terms 'vicarious religion' and sees it as representing a uniquely European frame of mind in which the actively religious are seen as carrying out religious activities 'on behalf of' the non-actively religious. In an approach reminiscent of supply-side theories, she regards such an attitude as springing partly from European attitudes to public utilities which they may never use themselves but whose existence they nevertheless approve of. Churches, Davie argues, have become *de facto* influential voluntary organizations capable of operating in a variety of ways. As members of civil society, churches are 'central to the structures of a modern democracy and attract more members than almost all of their organisational

---

[46] See J Césari, A Caeiro, and D Hussain, *Islam and Fundamental Rights in Europe*, Final Report, October 2004, European Commission, DG Justice and Home Affairs Centre National de la Recherche Scientifique, Ecole Pratique des Hautes Etudes, Groupe de Sociologie des Religions et de la Laïcité, Executive Summary, para 3.

[47] Available at <http://www.timesonline.co.uk/article/0,,59-1984362,00.html> (last visited 11 May 2010).

[48] G Davie, *Religion in Europe: A Memory Mutates* (Oxford: Oxford University Press, 2000).

equivalents'.[49] She therefore concludes that Europeans have not become less religious but differently so. They are content for a minority of the population to enact their 'religious memory'[50] on their behalf with a level of awareness that they may need to draw on such religious facilities at certain times in their lives. In this regard, Davie notes the almost universal take-up of religious ceremonies at the time of death, the prominent role accorded to churches in times of national crisis such as the sinking of the ferry *Estonia* in the Baltic Sea in 1994 or after the death of Princess Diana in 1997, and the growth in 'new age' spirituality among Europeans in recent times.[51]

Hervieu-Léger also focuses on religion's role in terms of collective identity. She views religion as an aspect of a shared memory, awareness of which is an essential feature of both individual and social identity.[52] It is also an important element of the chain that links past, current, and future members of a community. The tradition of collective memory of the community becomes the basis of that community's existence. Modern societies, by their nature, are less capable of maintaining the communal memory that is central to their religious existence, and it is the resultant amnesia rather than increased rationalism that causes the decline in religion. Although she believes that modern societies are corrosive of traditional religion,[53] Hervieu-Léger believes that such societies, through their emphasis on progress, which can only ever be partially attained, also produce 'utopian' spaces that can only be filled by religion. This analysis supports Davie's view of a Europe that has become differently religious rather than secular.

4. Religious Practice, Belief, and Influence in Europe: The Current Situation

4.1 Practice and Belief

This theoretical picture of a decline in religious belief, practice, and influence over society, but the persistence of a religious element to collective and individual identity, is borne out by the statistics on religious identity and practice in Europe. According to the *World Values Survey*, some 49 per cent of those in agrarian societies reported attending a religious service at

---

[49] Ibid 18.   [50] Davie (n 20 above) 46.
[51] Ibid 19.   [52] D Hervieu-Léger, *La Religion pour mémoire* (Paris: Le Cerf, 1993).
[53] D Hervieu-Léger, *Vers un nouveau christianisme* (Paris: Le Cerf, 1993).

least once a week.[54] In the developed United States, the figure is almost as high at 46 per cent.[55] The *European Values Survey*, by contrast, found that in 1999/2000 only 20.5 per cent of Western Europeans reported similar levels of church attendance.[56] Similarly, in relation to core religious beliefs, only 53.3 per cent of Western Europeans said they believed in life after death,[57] a figure some 23 per cent lower than that given by respondents in the United States.[58] Europeans also demonstrate significantly lower levels of belief in notions such as heaven, hell, sin, and the existence of a deity than either less-developed societies or developed countries such as Canada and the United States.[59] Furthermore, according to the 2006 Eurobarometer survey, religion is an important source of values for a mere seven per cent of Europeans. Values such as peace (52 per cent), respect for human life (43 per cent), human rights (41 per cent), democracy (24 per cent), and individual freedom (22 per cent) were viewed as significantly more important in this regard.[60]

The picture across Europe is, however, far from uniform. In Scandinavia, for example, levels of weekly church attendance are extremely low, with both Denmark and Sweden coming in at under four per cent and Finland barely exceeding five per cent. In Ireland, by contrast, some 56.9 per cent of respondents are weekly churchgoers.[61] Several commentators[62] argue that, in terms of religion, Europe can be divided into a traditionally Protestant North characterized by low levels of practice and belief, a traditionally Catholic South, with higher (though declining) levels, and a denominationally mixed zone, which is between the two.[63] These groups show considerable diversity (traditionally Catholic France, for example, manifests patterns of belief and practice which are closer to those of the Protestant North) and include countries that simply fail to fit the pattern (Ireland, which is geographically part

---

[54] Norris and Inglehart (n 16 above) 70.

[55] Ibid 74. The figure in relation to the United States is the figure from the 2001 survey, while the figure for agrarian societies represents a composite of the figures for all surveys between 1981 and 2001.

[56] Davie (n 20 above) 6.   [57] Ibid 7.   [58] Ibid.

[59] Ibid 6, 7. See also data from the Gallup Opinion Index and World Values Survey quoted in Norris and Inglehart (n 16 above) 90.

[60] Eurobarometer 66 (2006) *Standard Eurobarometer: Public Opinion in the European Union*, available at <http://ec.europa.eu/public_opinion/archives/eb/eb66/eb66_highlights_en.pdf> (last visited 30 May 2007).

[61] Davie (n 20 above) 6–7.

[62] Ibid 11; and L Halman and T Pettersson, 'Differential Patterns of Secularization in Europe: Exploring the Impact of Religion on Social Values' in Halman and Riis (n 39 above) 54.

[63] Davie (n 20 above) 11.

of the North, shows a greater resemblance to its fellow Catholic countries in the South in relation to levels of belief and practice).

The situation is further complicated by the growth of immigrant populations which not only adhere to religions not traditionally present in Europe, but which come from societies where religion and religiously influenced values continue to play a dominant role.[64] Both France and Germany, for instance, now have Muslim populations several million strong, while Britain plays host to large numbers of evangelical Christians from its African and Caribbean ex-colonies as well as significant populations of Muslims, Sikhs, and Hindus with origins in the Indian sub-continent. In several countries, most notably the Netherlands, Germany, and France, the persistence and strength of traditional religious values among immigrant communities has come to be seen as a problem by a significant section of society and has increased tensions between migrant groups and host populations. Indeed, some of those opposed to further immigration and others who favour immigration but oppose multiculturalism have stressed secularity rather than Christianity as a non-negotiable feature of European identity to which incomers must conform.[65]

Furthermore, despite the sustained secularization, religion in general and Christianity in particular does continue to exercise an influence over European society. A large (though declining) number of Europeans (77.4 per cent) continue to profess a belief in God,[66] while a significant number continue to use religious services to mark key life events such as marriage or death. Indeed, even in highly secularized Scandinavian countries such as Denmark and Sweden, where levels of belief in key elements of Christian theology such as the existence of a life after death are under 50 per cent, the vast majority of the population continue to belong to the Lutheran state churches (a step which requires them to pay a proportion of their income to those churches). Questions may well be asked as to whether the use of familiar ceremonies

---

[64] Ibid 38–9.

[65] See Chs 4 and 5. The rise of the List Pim Fortuyn in the Netherlands was closely connected to a desire to require Muslim immigrants to adopt 'European Values', particularly the separation of religious norms from questions of gender equality and sexuality. These arguments have since been incorporated into immigration policy in several countries including the Netherlands. Davie has argued that the difference in attitude to religion of native Europeans and immigrant communities 'has led to persistent and damaging misunderstandings, not least amongst groups whose religious commitments form the very core of their existence and for whom a pick-and-mix, live-and-let-live attitude simply will not do': G Davie, 'Religion in Britain: Changing sociological assumptions' (2000) 34 *Sociology* 113; quoted in Davey (n 20 above) 40.

[66] Davie (n 20 above) 7.

to mark life events represents any meaningful level of religious engage-ment or belief, or whether high church membership in Scandinavia is in fact merely an instance of cultural nationalism rather than cultural religiosity. However, the fact remains that, despite unprecedented declines in religious belief and practice, European life continues to be marked by certain features which are, at the very least, arguably religious. Furthermore, 'alternative' or 'new age' spirituality has been growing steadily as mainstream religion has declined, enabling some to argue that it is merely the form and not the level of religiosity that has changed.[67]

The overall picture, however, particularly in international terms, remains one of a Europe whose people are more secular than either their contempor-aries in other continents or their ancestors at any time during the past two millennia. The inhabitants of Europe are, as a whole, less likely than any other people in the world to believe in God, sin, heaven, hell, or life after death than those of any other continent and are even less likely to attend any kind of religious ceremony on a frequent basis. Having dominated the social, political, legal, and economic life of Europe for centuries, mainstream Christian denominations now find themselves in a position of weakness that has no parallel either in history or in the rest of the modern world and at the time when the nation states of Europe have been attempting to create a new and common political community based on common values of which Christianity would once have been the primary source. Indeed, Martin once argued that 'Europe is a unity by virtue of having one God and one Caesar'.[68] This argument is given credence by the fact that, historically, Catholic and Protestant countries of the former Soviet bloc have found it significantly easier to achieve membership of the Union than their Orthodox equiva-lents. However, although the emergence of a European identity grew out of a shared Christian identity, as the debates on the Preamble to the proposed Constitutional Treaty showed,[69] the applicability of Martin's assertion to contemporary Europe is highly controversial.

4.2 Declining Influence over Law and Politics

Furthermore, while Casanova is correct that religious bodies retain a degree of influence in relation to 'lifeworld' issues, this influence is comparatively weak and declining. The increasing de-ideologization of politics since the

---

[67] Ibid 19.
[68] D Martin, *A General Theory of Secularisation*, (Oxford: Blackwell, 1978) 100.
[69] See Ch 2.

end of the Cold War, with its emphasis on economics as a technocratic sphere subject more to its internal laws than those of any overarching ideology, has made it increasingly difficult for organizations such as churches, which retain comprehensive worldviews, to remain relevant in relation to issues of socio-economic policy. Even in relation to 'lifeworld' issues, European religious groups have had far less success than their American counterparts in opposing the liberalization of policy in relation to family structures and sexuality.

The post-war period in Europe has been characterized by a steady decline in religious influence in this area. For instance, in 1940, homosexuality was illegal in 17 of the 25 states that were members of the EU in 2004.[70] Only two states had decriminalized homosexuality since 1822, with Portugal reintroducing its ban in 1912. However, beginning with Sweden in 1944, states began to remove the criminal law from this area. The process was gradual at first, with Portugal (1945) and Greece (1951) being the only countries to change their policy between the end of the Second World War and the beginning of the 1960s. The next two decades saw this trend increase, with nine states wholly or partially decriminalizing homosexual conduct by 1980.[71] In 1993, Ireland was the only member of the Union to maintain a policy of complete criminalization, reforming its laws later that year. The countries of central and Eastern Europe, which sought to join the Union following the fall of the Iron Curtain, all decriminalized before accession (although, in the case of Romania and Cyprus, only as a result of pressure from European institutions).[72] The Catholic and Orthodox Churches in particular were opposed to this process.[73]

The law in relation to abortion was subject to a similar process.[74] By the end of the Second World War only Sweden had legalized the practice. During the

---

[70] See The International Lesbian and Gay Association, World Legal Survey, available at <http://ilga.org/ilga/en/organisations/ILGA%20EUROPE> (last visited 25 May 2010).

[71] Decriminalization occurred in the following order: Hungary (1961); Czechoslovakia (1961); England and Wales (1967) (though the law was not changed in Scotland until 1980 and Northern Ireland until 1982); Germany (1968) (in the East) and 1969 (in the West); Austria (1971); Finland (1971); Malta (1973); and Slovenia (1977).

[72] The Baltic states decriminalized in 1992 (Latvia and Estonia), 1993 (Lithuania), and 2000 (Romania and Cyprus).

[73] K Rose, *Diverse Communities: The Evolution of Gay and Lesbian Politics in Ireland* (Cork: Cork University Press, 1993). For an account of the opposition of the Cypriot and Romanian Orthodox Churches and the attitude of the EU to this process, see Ch 6.

[74] International Planned Parenthood Federation, 'Abortion Legislation in Europe' European Network, Brussels, January 2007, available at <http://www.ippfen.org/NR/rdonlyres/

1950s, Hungary (1956), Poland (1956), the USSR (which contained the Baltic Republics at the time) (1955), and Denmark (1956) all decriminalized abortion in certain circumstances. During this time, the Netherlands also introduced a policy of *de facto* toleration, although the relevant legislation was not passed until 1981. The United Kingdom (apart from Northern Ireland, where religious feelings ran much more strongly) passed legislation providing for a liberal abortion regime in 1967. During the 1970s, and despite the fervent opposition of religious figures in general (and the Catholic Church in particular), bans on abortion were relaxed or abolished in Finland (1970), East Germany (1972), France (1975), and West Germany (1976). This trend continued throughout the 1980s with Portugal (1984), Spain (1985), and Greece (1986) liberalizing their legislation in this area. A notable exception to this trend was Ireland, where, following a campaign in which the Catholic Church was heavily involved, the constitution was amended in 1983 to grant the unborn an equal right to life to that of the mother. Similarly, following the removal of restrictions on religious influence on public life which resulted from the overthrow of communism in Poland, the previously liberal abortion law was significantly tightened in 1993.

The law in relation to other 'lifeworld' issues such as adultery and divorce has also been subject to a decreasing degree of religious influence. Adultery, for instance, was considered a crime in several European countries until the 1970s, all of which subsequently decriminalized the practice, while divorce was finally legalized in Ireland in 1997.[75] On the other hand, traditional attitudes towards 'lifeworld' issues persist in many Member States, particularly those that have joined since 2004.[76] Furthermore, laws in relation to issues such as euthanasia and same-sex marriage continue to be influenced, at least partially, by religious teachings, and in all Member States religious figures are prominent participants in debate on such matters. Therefore, although the ability of religious organizations to influence law in this area has steeply declined since the end of the Second World War, there is considerable diversity between Member States, and a degree of religious influence remains.

2EB28750-BA71-43F8-AE2A-8B55A275F86C/0/Abortion_legislation_Europe_Jan2007.pdf> (last visited 25 May 2010).

[75] Irish law criminalized adultery until 1981, French law until 1975, and Austrian law until 1997. See K Gajendra Singh, 'EU-Turkish Engagement: A Must for Stability of the Region', South Asia Analysis Group Papers, available at <http://www.southasiaanalysis.org/papers12/paper1127.html> (last visited 25 May 2010).

[76] Eurobarometer 66 (2006), *Standard Eurobarometer: Public Opinion in the European Union*, available at <http://ec.europa.eu/public_opinion/archives/eb/eb66/eb66_highlights_en.pdf> (last visited 11 May 2010).

Nevertheless, in world terms, the balance struck in Europe between the promotion of traditional religious morality and humanist notions of individual autonomy favours the latter to a notable degree.

4.3 *Continuing Role in National Identity*

The religious history and background of Member States continues to exercise an influence, even following intensive secularization. As Norris and Inglehart put it: 'the distinctive world views that were originally linked with religious traditions have shaped the cultures of each nation in an enduring fashion; today, these distinctive values are transmitted to the citizens even if they never set foot in a church, temple or mosque'.[77] They argue that Sweden, for example, continues to manifest a distinctive Protestant value system, although less than five per cent of the population attends church on a weekly basis.[78] To a degree, therefore, religions continue to influence the values of very secularized societies, with Norris and Inglehart noting the particular relevance of orientations towards work ethic, sexual liberalization, and democracy in Catholic and Protestant societies. There are, it is therefore argued, 'Lutheran atheists' and 'Catholic atheists' with religious influence on values continuing after actual belief and practice have fallen away.[79] Of course, the secularization of European society has had a significant impact on the potency of these religious values. This is something which is recognized by Norris and Inglehart, who argue that:

[t]oday, these values are not transmitted primarily by the church, but by the educational system and the mass media, with the result that although the value systems of historically Protestant countries differ markedly and consistently from those of historically Catholic countries—the values of Dutch Catholics are much more similar to those of Dutch Protestants than to those of French, Italian or Spanish Catholics.[80]

Even among the secular, therefore, religion continues to play a values-forming role. However, as the level of contact with purely religious institutions falls, this role is increasingly mediated through state institutions and national cultures.

Furthermore, state identity and state institutions continue to maintain links to particular religious traditions in many Member States. Davie has pointed out that the 'vicarious' European approach to religion means that the

---

[77] Norris and Inglehart (n 16 above) 17.   [78] Ibid 17–18.   [79] Ibid.   [80] Ibid.

attitude of Europeans towards traditional churches is akin to their attitude to public services in general in that they have a benign attitude towards their existence and activities but are not actively involved with them, other than at times of particular personal or communal significance or crisis (such as birth, death, state occasions).[81] In fact, this idea of publicized religion (or even the 'socialized religion' of the supply side theorists) does fit with the legal and institutional reality of European church-state relations. Absolute separation of church and state is, in fact, extremely rare in Europe. National symbols in many European states retain religious connotations. The flags of Scandinavian countries, the United Kingdom, Greece, and Slovakia all contain symbols linked to the crucifix, while the symbol of the Irish police force is cruciform in shape and is linked to the tradition of Celtic monastic art, which is seen as an important element of national identity. European religions retain a prominent role in both Member State constitutions and as key elements of national education and (to a lesser extent) healthcare provision.[82] Indeed, Norris and Inglehart's attribution of a key role to national educational systems in the propagation of religious values in secular society is mirrored by the strenuous efforts made by traditional churches to retain and enhance their role in educational systems and to defend this role from any interference from EU institutions. The same churches have been equally keen to ensure that the prominent role of religion as a source of underlying constitutional values in several Member States has been similarly insulated from challenges at European level.[83]

4.4 Constitutional and Institutional Position

Given that the idea of state neutrality in relation to religion has been 'a central plank of liberal thinking about the state and its ethical dimensions',[84] the

---

[81] Davie (n 48 above) 44.

[82] JTS Madeley, 'European Liberal Democracy and the Principle of State Religious Neutrality' in JTS Madeley and Z Enyedi (eds), *Church and State in Contemporary Europe: The Chimera of Neutrality* (London: Frank Cass Publishing, 2003) 1. The European Court of Human Rights has recently ruled in *Lautsi v Italy* (Application No 30814/06) 3 November 2009, that the presence of crucifixes in Italian state schools violates the European Convention on Human Rights. This may indicate a greater strictness in relation to state endorsement of religious symbols, at least in the context of the state education system. This ruling which is under appeal is analysed in greater depth in Ch 4.

[83] See, eg Protocol 11 of the Amsterdam Treaty guaranteeing the status of national churches in national law and the watering-down of the Employment Discrimination Directive to allow discrimination in order to maintain the ethos of religious institutions, discussed in Ch 5.

[84] Madeley (n 82 above) 4.

most striking feature of church-state relations in Europe is the almost total absence of such neutrality. While many commentators, such as Jones, have seen substantive religious neutrality as a defining characteristic of the liberal state, arguing that 'a liberal state is a state which imposes no conception of the good upon its citizens but which allows individuals to pursue their own good in their own way',[85] other commentators have suggested that 'arrangements based on Enlightenment liberal assumptions actually offend against the principle of governmental religious neutrality because they privilege secular liberal beliefs over religious ones and consign religion to the margins of social life'.[86] The latter argue that true freedom of religion requires active facilitation by the state of religion and religious practice.

Ironically, in the highly religious United States, the constitutional prohibition on the establishment of any religion has led to the imposition of far more strictly secular standards of state neutrality than in less religious Europe, with state funding and endorsement of religion strictly prohibited under the jurisprudence of the US Supreme Court.[87] In Europe, by contrast, although the legislative imposition of religious views of the good life on individuals has been significantly curtailed by secularization, church and state are, in general, both financially and legally intertwined. In his 1982 survey of church–state relations in the world, Barrett found that of the 35 sovereign territories in Europe, only five could be termed secular in the sense that the state promoted neither religion nor irreligion. Nine communist countries were atheistic, 14 were associated with a single confessional tradition, while Finland supported two (state Russian orthodox and Lutheran). Six states were committed to the support of a plurality of religious organizations, with Belgium, for example, paying salaries to the clergy of six different denominations.[88] Furthermore, as Madeley points out, even the five states classified as secular had arrangements which would fall foul of the version of non-establishment developed by the US Supreme Court (with even famously secular France falling short of the ideal of strict neutrality

---

[85] P Jones, 'The Ideal of the Neutral State' in R Goodin and A Reeve (eds), *Liberal Neutrality* (London: Routledge, 1989), quoted in Madeley (n 82 above) 5.

[86] S Monsma and C Soper, *The Challenges of Pluralism; Church and State in Five Democracies* (Oxford: Rowman and Littlefield, 1997), quoted in Madeley (n 82 above) 5.

[87] See, eg *Zobrest v Catalina Foothills School District* 509 US 1 (1997) where the Supreme Court held that governmental action which supported religion must have a secular purpose and avoid 'an excessive governmental entanglement with religion' to pass constitutional muster.

[88] D Barrett (ed.), *World Christian Encyclopedia: A Comparative Study of Churches and Religions in the Modern World AD 1900–2000* (New York: Oxford University Press, 1982), quoted in Madeley (n 82 above) 13.

in several respects). Indeed, when *de facto* circumstances were taken into account, no European state could be said to have a fully neutral approach towards religion, with most states offering large-scale subsidies to certain denominations.[89] A review of the situation in 2000 showed that there had been no large-scale shift towards state neutrality. Despite the large increase in the number of cases (there were 47 independent states, some 12 more than in 1980), only Sweden and newly reunified Germany had moved towards a greater degree of neutrality (though both still provided large subsidies to religious organizations). By far the largest trend was towards the removal of previous restrictions on religious life (a relic of the communist era) and their replacement with state support for recognized denominations (either through the taxation system or through direct state funding of church buildings and facilities).[90]

A second striking feature of European church–state relations is the sheer diversity of arrangements among Member States. Indeed, Massignon argues that within Europe, 'attachment to a specific model of church–state relations is one of the elements of identity and national political culture',[91] while Meny and Knapp suggest that there is a European tradition of a dominant church or religion which continues to mark the political systems of Italy and the United Kingdom.[92] Both this specificity and the close relationship between the church and state are reinforced by the fact very few countries are divided anywhere close to equally along religious lines. In fact most countries are overwhelmingly of one denomination.[93] Furthermore, adherence to particular religions has been a central feature of the identity of states such as Ireland, Belgium, and the United Kingdom, while relationships to particular religions were key elements in the foundation of the modern French, Spanish, Italian, and German states. Thus, particularly where a single denomination has traditionally made up a large majority of the population (a situation which applies to 23 of 27 EU Member States), it was natural that the welfare of the relevant church (which would have been an important part of the

---

[89] Madeley (n 82 above) 15.

[90] Ibid 17.

[91] See B Massignon, 'Les relations des organismes Européens religieux et humanistes avec les institutions de l'Union Européene: Logiques nationales et confessionnelles et dynamiques d'européanisation' in Commissariat Général du Plan, *Croyances religieuses, morales et ethiques dans le processus de construction européenne* (Institut Universitaire de Florence: Chaire Jean Monnet d'études Européennes, 2002). Translation mine.

[92] Y Meny and A Knapp, *Government and Politics in Western Europe* (Oxford: Oxford University Press, 1998) 26.   [93] Madeley (n 82 above) 15.

communal identity of the dominant ethnic group in that nation state) came to be seen as a proper task for organs of that state. Therefore, despite the great diversity and national particularity of church–state arrangements in Europe, an amount of state aid for recognized denominations, either direct or indirect, is a common thread in almost all countries.

Almost all Member States of the EU have a constitutional guarantee of freedom of religion and all are, in any event, required to uphold the freedom to practice one's religion by the provisions of the European Convention on Human Rights.[94] Beyond this minimum, diversity reigns. However, despite this diversity of constitutional arrangements, relatively similar approaches are adopted by several groups of Member States. The Nordic countries were, until very recently, characterized by officially established Lutheran state churches. Part I, §4 of the Danish Constitution states: 'The Evangelical Lutheran Church shall be the Established Church of Denmark, and as such shall be supported by the State'.[95] Part II, §6 of the Constitution also lays down a requirement that the monarch 'be a member of the Evangelical Lutheran Church'.[96] In Finland, the Evangelical Lutheran Church is also established by law (the Finnish Orthodox Church is also established).[97] In both countries the vast majority of citizens are members of the established (Lutheran) churches, with 83.1 per cent of Finns and 84.3 per cent of Danes being members despite low and falling rates of belief and practice.[98] In 2000, Sweden formally disestablished the Church of Sweden, motivated by a feeling that the existence of a state church was no longer appropriate in a pluralist society. However, in all three countries, the state continues to collect a religious tax from those who are members of the established (and formerly established) churches. The funds from these taxes are passed on to

[94] This has not prevented the suppression of several new religions such as Scientology in many Member States. Greece has made efforts to restrict the ability of religions other than Greek Orthodoxy to recruit new members and has found itself before the Strasbourg Court on this basis. These questions will be dealt with in greater detail in Ch 4.

[95] See Danish Constitution. Full text available at <http://www.southasiaanalysis.org/papers12/paper1127.html> (last visited 25 May 2010).   [96] Ibid.

[97] Section 76 of the Finnish Constitution provides that 'Provisions on the organisation and administration of the Evangelical Lutheran Church are laid down in the Church Act': see The Constitution of Finland, 11 June 1999 (731/1999), available at <http://evl.fi/EVLUutiset.nsf/Documents/F322C5D68B64DB62C225728700454792?OpenDocument&lang=FI> (last visited 11 May 2010).

[98] Source: Danish Ministry for Church Affairs, available at <http://www.kirkeministeriet.dk/kirkestatistik.html> and the Evangelical Lutheran Church of Finland, available at <http://evl.fi/EVLUutiset.nsf/Documents/F322C5D68B64DB62C225728700454792?OpenDocument&lang=FI> (last visited 11 May 2010).

the denominations in question, which are therefore among the richest and best-funded churches in Europe, despite the tiny and shrinking nature of their active congregations.

The Greek model represents a very different version of establishment. Article 3 of the Greek Constitution recognizes the Greek Orthodox Church as 'the prevailing religion in Greece'. The same article states that '[t]he text of the Holy Scripture shall be maintained unaltered' and prohibits '[o]fficial translation of the text into any other form of language, without prior sanction by the Autocephalous Church of Greece and the Great Church of Christ in Constantinople'.[99] Article 14(3) also permits an exception to the prohibition on the seizure of newspapers and other publications in cases of 'an offence against the Christian or any other known religion'. Indeed, membership in the Orthodox Church is seen as being inseparable from Greek identity (97 per cent of Greeks are members of the Orthodox Church) and, during the most recent revision of the Constitution completed in April 2001, the main parties of left and right agreed that the issue of amending the status of the Orthodox Church would not even be raised.[100] The constitutional primacy of the Orthodox Church in Greece is an entirely different phenomenon from that of established Scandinavian churches, having a much more concrete impact on religious life. The Constitution lays down that church administration is to be regulated by state law. Orthodox clergy are paid by the state and the Archbishop of Athens receives the same honours as a head of state. More importantly, the construction of any religious buildings requires the permission of the local Orthodox bishop, a rule which has severely restricted the provision of mosques outside of Thrace (home to an indigenous Muslim minority). Both proselytism and blasphemy are criminal offences (though rarely invoked), and in 1998 the Council of State ruled unconstitutional a reduction in the hours of religious instruction (which relates exclusively to Greek Orthodoxy) in schools. An earlier decision of the same court required parents who wished their children to withdraw from such classes to make a formal request, citing specifically different religious beliefs for them to do so.[101] The Greek State does recognize other religions, namely the Muslims of Thrace and the Jews, whose clergy are employed by the state and who are regulated by state law. However, as Mavrogordatos points out, 'to speak of

---

[99] The Constitution of Greece, Arts 3.1 and 3.3.

[100] See G Th Mavrogordatos, 'Orthodoxy and Nationalism in the Greek Case' in Madeley and Enyedi (n 82 above) 120.

[101] Ibid 121.

"plural establishment"... would be misleading, since no equal treatment is implied'.[102] Other faiths are generally treated as private associations (though the status of the Catholic Church as a legal person was subject to dispute until relatively recently).[103] The Greek model of church–state relations is, therefore, somewhat removed from the European mainstream and aspects of these arrangements have been challenged several times before the European Court of Human Rights.[104]

Although it is the major Christian denomination in Europe, full establishment of the Catholic Church is rare. In fact, tiny Malta is the sole example among all 27 Member States of full establishment of the Roman Catholic Church. Article 2(1) of the Maltese Constitution declares that '[t]he religion of Malta is the Roman Catholic Apostolic Religion'.[105] The Constitution explicitly envisages a prominent role for the Catholic Church in the public life of the country in Article 2(2), which states: 'The authorities of the Roman Catholic Apostolic Church have the duty and the right to teach which principles are right and which principles are wrong'.[106] Article 2(3) provides constitutional status for compulsory religious education, stating: 'Religious teaching of the Roman Catholic Apostolic Faith shall be provided in all State schools as part of compulsory education'.[107] This rather uncompromising approach does not, however, typify the approach of most largely Catholic Member States. The Slovenian and Lithuanian Constitutions both declare that there is to be no state church,[108] while Article 41(4) of the Portuguese Constitution states that '[t]he churches and religious communities are separate from the State'.[109] The Slovenian Constitution also includes a guarantee of equal treatment of religious denominations. Other countries, such as Luxembourg, Austria, and Slovakia, make no reference to any specific denomination (in contrast to his Danish counterpart, the Grand Duke of Luxembourg appears to be free to belong to the religion of his choice). Several traditionally Catholic states do make limited special provision for the Catholic religion in their constitutions. Article 16(3) of the 1978 Spanish Constitution, for example, states that '[t]he public authorities shall take the religious beliefs of Spanish society into account and shall in consequence

---

[102] Ibid 123.   [103] Ibid.

[104] See, eg Case 14707/88 *Kokkinakis v Greece* (unreported) 25 May 1993.

[105] Constitution of Malta, Ministry of Justice of the Republic of Malta, available at <http://docs.justice.gov.mt/lom/legislation/english/leg/vol_1/chapt0.pdf> (last visited 12 May 2010).

[106] Constitution of Malta, Art 2.   [107] Ibid.

[108] Constitution of Slovenia, Art 7(1) and Constitution of Lithuania, Art 43(7).

[109] Constitution of the Portuguese Republic, Art 41.

maintain appropriate co-operation with the Catholic Church and the other confessions'.[110] However, the same article also states in unequivocal terms that '[t]here shall be no State religion'. The Irish Constitution accords religion in general a more prominent role. Although it guarantees not to endow any religion, and despite the removal of an article referring to the 'special position' of the Catholic Church by referendum in 1972, the Constitution as a whole retains a strikingly religious air. The Preamble to the Constitution begins: 'In the Name of the Most Holy Trinity, from Whom is all authority and to Whom, as our final end, all actions both of men and States must be referred, We, the people of Éire, Humbly acknowledging our obligations to our Divine Lord, Jesus Christ'.[111] The religious influence is not restricted to mere declarations. The oaths of office for the president and judiciary are couched in religious terms with no secular alternatives provided.[112] More importantly, such religious rhetoric has had concrete effects on the interpretation of the Constitution, with the Supreme Court invoking the terms of the Preamble as a ground for its refusal to strike down as unconstitutional a ban on homosexual intercourse.[113] Blasphemy is declared by Article 40.6(1)(i) to be a criminal offence, and Catholic teaching in relation to abortion, divorce, and the authority of the family in matters of education were all given constitutional status.[114] While this constitutional model may appear to be closer to that contained in the Greek Constitution (with the enshrining of privilege for a single denomination), the Irish Constitution does contain provisions that moderate the heavily Catholic influence on much of the document.

[110] Constitution of Spain, Art 16(3).
[111] Bunreacht na h-Éireann, Preamble.
[112] Ibid, Arts 12.8 and 34.5(1).
[113] *Norris v AG* [1984] IR 36, where O'Higgins CJ for a majority of the court stated:

The preamble to the Constitution proudly asserts the existence of God in the Most Holy Trinity and recites that the people of Ireland humbly acknowledge their obligation to 'our Divine Lord, Jesus Christ'. It cannot be doubted that the people, so asserting and acknowledging their obligations to our Divine Lord Jesus Christ, were proclaiming a deep religious conviction and faith and an intention to adopt a Constitution consistent with that conviction and faith and with Christian beliefs. Yet it is suggested that, in the very act of so doing, the people rendered inoperative laws which had existed for hundreds of years prohibiting unnatural sexual conduct which Christian teaching held to be gravely sinful. It would require very clear and express provisions in the Constitution itself to convince me that such took place. When one considers that the conduct in question had been condemned consistently in the name of Christ for almost two thousand...the suggestion becomes more incomprehensible and difficult of acceptance.

[114] See Arts 40.3(3) (abortion), 41.3(2) (which previously prohibited divorce, but was repealed by a wafer-thin majority in a referendum in 1995), and 41.1(1), 41.1(2), 42(1), 42.3(1) (family authority in education).

For instance, discrimination on religious grounds is forbidden by Article 44.2(3), while Article 44.2(2) contains a prohibition on state endowment of any religion. In a similar vein, the Italian Constitution states that '[s]tate and Catholic Church are, each within their own reign, independent and sovereign' (Article 7(1)).[115] Article 8(1) provides that '[r]eligious denominations are equally free before the law'.[116] In practice, however, Italy recognizes only certain denominations, such as the Jews and the Waldensians, with many other religious groups, including Muslims, being excluded from significant privileges.[117] Like the Irish Constitution, the Preamble to the Polish Constitution speaks of a 'culture rooted in the Christian heritage of the nation' but also contains some concessions towards secularists in that it is enacted in the name of 'those who believe in God as the source of truth, justice, good and beauty, as well as those not sharing such a faith but respecting those universal values as arising from other sources'[118] and of 'recognizing our responsibility before God or our own consciences'.[119] It also states in Article 25(2) that the public authorities 'shall be impartial in matters of public conviction, whether religious or philosophical'.[120] Significantly, both the Italian and Polish Constitutions make provision for relations with the Catholic Church to be regulated by means of a concordat.[121] These concordats have been a source of fierce controversy in many countries, including Poland, Hungary, and Slovakia, where critics arguing that they have institutionalized preferential treatment for the Catholic Church in key areas such as healthcare and education, with negative consequences for non-Catholics using such services.

Catholic countries have adopted equally diverse approaches to state financing. Spain and Italy operate a church tax system through which taxpayers can opt to contribute a proportion of their income to religious bodies. In both cases existing arrangements favour the Catholic Church,[122] although the Socialist Government elected in Spain in 2004 has curtailed such privileges. It is notable that, although levels of belief and practice are much higher than in Scandinavian countries, levels of payment of the voluntary church tax are much lower in both Spain and Italy. In Portugal no direct subsidies are provided but indirect aid is generous. The concordat arrangements

---

[115] Constitution of the Italian Republic, Art 7(1).   [116] Ibid, Art 8.

[117] See Davie (n 48 above) 17–21.

[118] Constitution of the Republic of Poland, Preamble.   [119] Ibid.

[120] Ibid, Art 25(2).

[121] Constitution of the Italian Republic, Art 7(2) and Constitution of the Republic of Poland, Art 25(4).   [122] See Davie (n 48 above) 39–41.

agreed between the Vatican and several Eastern European countries have also tended to provide a degree of state funding of religious institutions, either directly or indirectly. In Ireland, by contrast, religious bodies, particularly the Catholic Church, have played, and continue to play, a major role in the provision of social services such as health and education. Nowadays, such services are largely state-funded but churches have retained control of healthcare and educational institutions, meaning that, although religions receive no direct financial help from the state, a major degree of indirect financial support is provided. Catholic Belgium, on the other hand, while eschewing the idea of a state church, pays the salaries of Catholic priests along with the ministers of other religions.

Religiously mixed countries such as Germany and the Netherlands do not have state churches. In the Netherlands the Constitution is largely silent on the question of religion other than brief provisions providing freedom from discrimination and for respect for religious preferences in education. Direct subvention of religion is not a feature of the Dutch system, although some indirect aid is provided. In Germany the Constitution embodies the model of 'positive neutrality' towards religion where the state does not establish or privilege any denomination but nevertheless actively facilitates institutional religion. The German Basic Law carries over the provisions relating to religion from the Weimar Constitution and provides for 'a constitutionally structured form of cooperation between the state and churches structured around the principles of neutrality, tolerance and parity'.[123] Article 137(1) provides that there is to be no state church, but Articles 137(6) and 138(1) establish the right of churches to levy religious taxes on their members and the right to public subsidies from the Länder. In Germany, the major religious denominations are considered to be public corporations. Taxes are levied on their behalf by the state and the churches are heavily involved in the provision of state-funded social services. Other religiously mixed countries, such as Hungary, have also established a degree of state funding for religious denominations (with funding of the Catholic Church regulated by a concordat). The level of financial support has, however, fluctuated with changes in government (the left being more parsimonious in relation to religious funding). A voluntary church tax system has also failed to attract more than 20 per cent of taxpayers.[124]

---

[123] Ibid 17–21.
[124] Z Enyedi, 'The Contested Politics of Positive Neutrality in Hungary' in Madeley and Enyedi (n 82 above) 157.

Finally, France is unique in that its Constitution does not merely fail to establish a state church, but instead establishes the secular ('laïque') nature of the Republic under which the state is meant to have a strictly neutral public sphere from which religion is excluded altogether. However, even famously secular France does not achieve total separation. The province of Alsace was not part of France at the time of the separation of church and state in 1905 and, to this day, church–state relations in the region are governed by the concordat in force prior to that date under which Catholicism was officially recognized. This proved controversial when, in 1997, gay rights protesters were fined for protesting against the Archbishop of Strasbourg outside Strasbourg Cathedral because, under the relevant legislation (Article 167 of the Prussian Penal Code of 1871), any offence against the church under canon law was punishable as a breach of the criminal law.[125] Furthermore, even beyond Alsace, the French state remains responsible for the upkeep of all pre-1905 church buildings. It also pays the salaries of chaplains in military and penal institutions, as well as providing limited financial support for religious schools. The requirement of secularity is, however, rigorously enforced in other arenas, most notably and controversially in relation to the wearing of religious clothing such as headscarves or turbans in public schools.[126] This robust secularity is by no means typical of the educational systems of Member States in general. However, education is a key arena within which the battle for the hearts and minds of the next generation is being fought and which, insofar as religious educational institutions act as employers and providers of services, may fall within EU law. It is for these reasons that it deserves separate consideration.

4.5 Service Provision: Religion and Education

As both Davie and Casanova point out, education, like healthcare and welfare, was part of the domain of the churches for centuries. However, as Davie also says, 'the emergence of a discrete and autonomous educational sector is an almost universal characteristic of modernization; it is part of the

---

[125] See 'La Charia à la française: Affaire Elchinger dernière minute', *La France Gaie et Lesbienne*, March 1998, available at <http://www.france.qrd.org/assocs/gage/gageure67/charia.html> (last visited 25 May 2010).

[126] French immigration law also permits the refusal of citizenship to those who do not accept the values of the Republic, including secularism (see the decision of the Conseil d'État, Section du contentieux, 2ème et 7ème sous-sections réunies. Séance du 26 mai 2008. Lecture du 27 juin 2008, Mme Faiza M No 286798, available at <http://www.conseil-etat.fr/ce/jurispd/index_ac_ld0820.shtml> (last visited 12 May 2010)). This is further discussed in Ch 6.

undisputed structural differentiation of modern societies',[127] which Casanova sees as the still valid core of secularization theory.[128] In modern-day Europe, the state has assumed a responsibility for ensuring that citizens have access to adequate educational facilities. However, in the context of falling levels of belief and practice, church involvement in education represents perhaps the best opportunity for religions to pass on the 'religious memory' identified as vital by Davie and Hérvieu-Léger. Indeed, Davie argues that in France the exclusion of religion from the state school system, along with the decline in religious practice, means that the younger generation are experiencing 'religious illiteracy', with negative consequences for their ability to understand European culture and history.[129] Accordingly, religious denominations have fought particularly hard to maintain their role within education systems. Almost all Member State constitutions, as well as the European Convention on Human Rights, protect the right to some form of denominational education or, at least, to a degree of respect for parental preferences in the carrying-out of education by the state.[130] This respect for parental rights can also have the effect of restricting religious influence, at least in the state system. In *Lautsi v Italy*[131] the European Court of Human Rights ruled that the obligatory display of crucifixes in Italian state schools amounted to a violation of the rights of non-religious parents. This ruling, currently under appeal to the Court's Grand Chamber, indicated that the Strasbourg institutions may police the boundaries of state endorsement and facilitation of religion more strictly in order to ensure the rights of religious minorities and the non-religious. Nevertheless, in all EU Member States, religion continues to play a role in education, either where religious denominations own and manage schools or through the provision of religious education in state schools. The precise nature of the role varies greatly between states. In Greece and Italy religious instruction in state schools is almost entirely specific to Greek Orthodoxy and Roman Catholicism respectively, with a prominent role being given to the clerical authorities in

[127] Davie (n 48 above) 84.   [128] Casanova (n 7 above) 84.

[129] Davie (n 48 above) 93. The phrase 'religious illiteracy' is a translation of the phrase 'analphabétisme religieux' popularized by Henri Tincq, the religious correspondent of *Le Monde* newspaper.

[130] ECHR, First Protocol, Art 2 states that '[i]n the exercise of any functions which it assumes in relation to education and teaching, the State shall respect the right of parents to ensure such education and teaching in conformity with their own religious and philosophical convictions'. See also, eg Dutch Constitution, Art 23(3), Belgian Constitution, Art 24(1), Irish Constitution, Art 42, and Spanish Constitution, Art 27(3).

[131] *Lautsi v Italy* (Application No 30814/06) 3 November 2009.

the selection of textbooks and design of curricula.[132] In France, by contrast, religion is entirely excluded from the public school system. Somewhere in the middle are pluralist countries, such as the Netherlands, where the state system provides a form of religious instruction which consists of what Davie calls the 'conscious preparation of children for a world where a variety of religious ideas forms a significant part of cultural exchange'.[133] While the overall trend across Europe appears to be one of growing pluralism, Davie is concerned that '[a] so-called multi-faith education can end up respecting the faith of no-one and devaluing the concept of religion altogether'.[134] Individual denominations have therefore been keen to retain control of their own schools, in which their individual ethos can be imparted to pupils. The extent to which they have been able to do so while retaining state funding varies across Europe.

The role of religious education in schools can be seen as a reflection of its wider constitutional status. In Finland, for example, where the Lutheran religion is the established faith, religious instruction remains central to primary and secondary curricula. There is some provision for minorities (notably the Orthodox community, which also has official status), but in 1992 (despite very low levels of practice and belief in the main tenets of the Lutheran faith) 97 per cent of pupils followed the courses related to the Lutheran Church.[135] This underlines not only the dominance of the state church but also the significant social aspect of its nature as well as its formative influence in national identity. Although alternative courses can be provided at parental request, the Lutheran Church course is seen as such a non-threatening, national identity-related phenomenon that parents who are not church members are happy for their children to take part. In religiously plural countries like Germany and the Netherlands, separate types of education are provided for the respective denominations. In Germany, although the individual Länder have a great deal of power over education, the system reflects the historically bi-confessional nature of the country and the Basic Law lays down that religious education must be a regular subject in the public school system.[136] In general, two types of religious education are provided, one Lutheran and one Catholic. The curriculum and textbooks used are formally scrutinized by the state and churches and include a mixture of confessional teaching, alongside more general philosophical themes, such as social issues, church

---

[132] Davie (n 48 above) 91.   [133] Ibid 95.   [134] Ibid.   [135] Ibid 90–1.

[136] M Minkenberg, 'The Policy Impact of Church–State Relations: Family Policy and Abortion in Britain, France and Germany' in Madeley and Enyedi (n 82 above) 202.

history, and world religions. The state of Brandenburg, which is particularly secular given its history as part of the formerly Communist East, considered the introduction of a non-confessional ethics course to replace religious instruction.[137] This was strongly resisted by the historic churches. Overall, the German system reflects the tension (inherent in the approach of the Basic Law to the question of religion in general) between religious tolerance and pluralism and a wish to inculcate Christian moral values, which were seen by the founders of the Federal Republic as a bulwark against fascism and communism. The system does permit pupils to withdraw from religious education with the written permission of their parents. Regional differences have also placed this system under strain with the more secular East manifesting discontent with the overtly religious nature of the system, and Catholic Bavaria resenting prohibitions on the placing of crucifixes in the classroom imposed by the Constitutional Court.[138] Furthermore, the essentially bi-confessional nature of the system means that overall there is less provision for the largely Muslim Turkish minority than for the majority who come from Christian backgrounds.[139]

Similarly, in France, a relatively large network of private Catholic schools continues to exist alongside the state system, while private Muslim schools are relatively rare. Although the status of these private schools has been a source of friction, the Loi Debré of 1959, which regulates their status, provides them with a degree of state funding. The low number of private Muslim schools became more controversial when the French Government banned the wearing of conspicuous religious symbols, including the *hijab*, in state schools in 2004. The British system has grappled with similar issues. It contains a network of denominational but state-funded schools that make up approximately 25 per cent of the state system. These schools have traditionally been exclusively Christian but other denominations are now seeking to open their own schools. In recent years, Muslims and Seventh Day Adventists have received permission to open state-funded schools. This has proved controversial as inspections of some such schools have called into question values being promoted and the teaching and curriculum offered in such institutions.[140]

Education remains a key issue for the churches. The Vatican has made education a key priority in its negotiations of concordats with Eastern European

---

[137] Davie (n 48 above) 90–91.   [138] BverfGE 93, 1 (1995).

[139] Davie (n 48 above) 90–91.

[140] Ibid 87. See, eg 'Muslim Schools Citizenship Warning', *BBC News*, 17 January 2005, available at <http://news.bbc.co.uk/1/hi/education/4180845.stm> (last visited 25 February 2010).

countries such as Poland, Hungary, and Slovakia (where the issue of the concordat brought down the government in early 2006).[141] Indeed, Crouch notes that education has been one of the few issues in relation to which European churches have retained a capacity to act as rallying points for political and moral claims, with attempts to undermine the place of church schools in France and Spain having generated mass protests in recent times.[142] At Member State level, the churches have been extremely successful in acquiring and protecting a state-funded role for religion in national educational systems, even in supposedly robustly secular France. The churches have been keen to protect this role from challenge at European level, lobbying to have their status under national law recognized under the Amsterdam Treaty as well as to protect their right to discriminate in order to maintain the ethos of their educational and healthcare institutions.[143] This has not been restricted to the Catholic Church, with the Council of the Evangelical Church in Germany describing the 'public mandate' of religion as 'indispensable' in 1997.[144] This role is often very specific to the individual Member State and can be closely linked to an individual denomination's role as part of the national identity of the state in question. It is therefore an area which is particularly sensitive for a supranational organism such as the EU.

5. Conclusion

The relationship between religion, politics, the law, and the state in EU Member States is characterized by a significant degree of diversity. Europe as a whole is marked by a common heritage of Christianity, which formed the basis for the emergence of a common European identity. However, full-scale theocracy is entirely absent from Europe and its Christian-influenced

---

[141] See 'Slovak Government Falls over Concordat with Vatican', *Conscience*, June 2006, available at <http://findarticles.com/p/articles/mi_hb064> (last visited 12 May 2010).

[142] C Crouch, 'The Quiet Continent: Religion and Politics in Europe' in D Marquand and RL Nettler (eds), *Religion and Democracy* (Oxford: Blackwell Publishers, 2000).

[143] The churches are also involved in healthcare provision in many Member States. Their profile in this area is, however, much lower than in education. It is also of less significance in sociological and constitutional terms than education and will not therefore be addressed in detail. The right of the Catholic Church to fire employees in its medical facilities who publicly dissent from its core teachings was upheld by the European Commission on Human Rights in *Rommelfanger v Federal Republic of Germany* (unreported) 6 September 1989.

[144] See Minkenberg (n 136 above) 202.

common identity has been moulded by other shared experiences such as the Reformation and the Enlightenment, which reduced the influence of religion over the law and the state. These experiences, and the secularization they brought about, owe much to Christianity and, in particular, to its strong humanist tradition. Nevertheless, they have served to limit the public ambitions of Christian religions as well as those of other faiths whose presence in Europe has increased in recent years. This is particularly notable in relation to 'lifeworld' issues, where the large-scale enforcement of traditional Christian morality in relation to matters of sexuality and family has been replaced by an approach that places much greater emphasis on individual autonomy and equality. Nevertheless, the approach of Member States in this area is by no means uniform. Religious ideas continue to influence the law in relation to issues such as marriage, abortion, and euthanasia in many Member States. Furthermore, religion is an important element of communal identity and culture and maintains a strong institutional presence in many Member States, particularly in the area of healthcare and education. Thus, despite its continuing role, religion must compete for influence with secular and humanist traditions. The relationship between religion, the state, and the law in contemporary Europe is therefore characterized by a balance between largely, but not exclusively, Christian religious influences and secular influences. This balance has shifted notably in a secularist direction in the period since the Second World War and varies from state to state.

These features of the European approach to religion are all potentially relevant to EU law. Given that the balance between religious and secular/ humanist influences is different in each Member State, the balance stuck by the Union in its own public order may conflict with the approaches of individual states. In developing a common European identity, it must take account both of the formative influence of Christianity on European identity, and of the difficult relationship that has existed between Christianity and the humanist notions which have lessened Christian influence over law and politics.

While freedom of religion is recognized by all Member States, the contours of such a right, particularly in its collective and institutional forms, are the subject of dispute especially when claims to freedom of religion clash with claims to personal autonomy and to freedom from religion. The Union's embrace of the principles of equal treatment and gender equality can impinge on the role played by religious bodies in the provision of healthcare and educational services. In particular, EU legal norms in relation to anti-discrimination in employment may impede the ability of religious bodies to promote their religious beliefs and identity through their employment practices. The Union must also decide whether, in exercising its regulatory functions (most notably in relation to the Single Market), its duties to respect religious freedom require it merely to adopt a neutral approach, or whether active facilitation of religious practice is needed. Overhanging all of these issues is the question of the relative powers of the Union and its Member States. As the EU's competences expand, the potential for EU law and policy to interfere with the ability of individual Member States to uphold the religiously specific element of their communal identities increases. Thus, the approach adopted by EU law to these issues may also have to take account of the need to avoid interfering with sensitive issues of identity, particularly in the light of the weak democratic legitimacy of the Union itself. On the other hand, the status of EU law as the autonomous constitutional order of a 'Community of Values' may also impel it towards interfering with the religious particularities of Member States in so far as such particularities are inconsistent with the values to which the Union has declared itself to be committed.

3

Balance, Inheritance, and Religion as a Basis of Law in the Public Order of the European Union

1. Introduction

A key element of the role of religion in any polity is the degree to which religion, or religious arguments, can be used as the basis of law and policy. In several countries in the world religion plays a major role in this regard. In Saudi Arabia, Iraq, and Iran, for example, the issue of whether a particular policy is compatible with Islam is a major factor in law-making.[1] As shown in Chapter 2, religious arguments are significantly less prominent in most European states, although they do play a limited role in some areas. This chapter shows how the public order of the European Union (EU) permits religion to play a role in law- and policy-making by virtue of its recognition of religion as part of the Union's ethical inheritance, as a phenomenon which has a particular contribution to make to law-making, and as part of a wider public morality that the Union and its Member States are entitled to legislate to uphold. However, although religion is recognized as part of the Union's constitutional order, the EU also imposes limitations on religious influence in this regard. The Union's public order is characterized by a balance between religious, humanist, and cultural elements, all of which can reinforce or restrict each other's influence. Its commitment to balance between conflicting influences and to respect for the ethical 'inheritance'

---

[1] The constitutions of all three countries make it clear that all legislation must be compatible with the *Sharia* (see Constitution of Iraq, Art (1st)(a), Constitution of the Islamic Republic of Iran, Arts 2–5, and Saudi Arabian Constitution, Chs 1, 2, 6.

of Europe means that religion cannot be accorded a degree of political and legal influence inconsistent with this heritage. The Union regards a proper balance between the religious and humanist elements of its inheritance as enabling religion to influence law through its role in national cultural identity and through recognition of religious bodies as important contributors to moral debates. On the other hand, it requires that such facilitation be balanced by relativization of religious arguments in the law-making and policy-making arena and by the protection of key liberal principles, such as individual autonomy, from violation on religiously influenced grounds.

This approach restricts the political ambitions of all religions but has permitted those religions with significant cultural roots in Europe and which are capable of reconciling themselves to humanist influences, to exercise greater influence over EU law than those faiths which lack such characteristics.

Religion's role as a basis of law in the EU legal order operates at three levels. The first section of the chapter analyses how the notion of an ethical inheritance characterized by a balance between religious, cultural, and humanist influences has been recognized as a source of the Union's constitutional values. The second section examines how religious institutions have been recognized as playing a particularly important and privileged role in the law-making process. However, it also discusses the way this role has conformed to the notions of balance and inheritance by showing how the recognition of religions as part of civil society has been linked to their role at national level and has required them to relativize, and therefore partly secularize, their perspectives.

Finally, the third section of this chapter addresses the role played by religion in the substantive law of the Union. It demonstrates how religious perspectives have been recognized as a valid basis for EU legislation and for derogation by Member States from EU law duties, on the basis of the status of such perspectives as part of a broader public morality which Member States and the Union may use to promote particular communal norms and visions of the nature of a community. Under the EU's public order, this public morality is pluralist and accommodates religion's role in national cultural identities in that it encompasses divergent Member State moralities as well as a common European element. The common European element both restricts and reflects the pluralism of EU public morality in that, in addition to facilitating Member State moral decisions, it requires that such decisions respect certain values such as pluralism, the rule of law, and the fundamental rights commitments of the Union. These fundamental rights principles provide a broad ethical framework that is marked by Europe's ethical inheritance and accommodates only those moral goals that are compatible with the notion of a proper balance between religion and humanism and with certain common European cultural norms that have emerged from the balance between Christian and humanist influences, which has characterized European history. Perspectives that are contrary to these norms are not recognized as valid elements of EU public morality. Thus, EU law protects, through its promotion of a particular public morality, the broad outlines of the settlement between religious and secular influences in Europe and the 'way of life' it represents.

This settlement gives Member States a degree of leeway within which they can develop their approach to the relationship of religion and law. Nevertheless, although the Union's approach facilitates religious influence as a matter of culture, it rejects the assertion of religious claims to truth in the legal and political arenas it does lay down boundaries that Member States may not cross. Although internally the Union has adhered to strict formal neutrality in religious matters, faiths that lack cultural roots in Europe or are incapable of reconciling themselves to the limitations on religious influence inherent in the notion of balance between religion and humanism will have a more limited influence over EU law and are implicitly characterized as contrary to the public morality of the Union.

2. Religion as a Source of the Union's Constitutional Values

As noted in Chapter 2, European identity has been notably marked by both Christianity and humanism, and there is no consensus in relation to the relationship between religion and the state at Member State level.[2] Indeed, as Roy has stated, secularism and Christianity each provide a competing pole around which European identity can be defined.[3] The tensions in this dual approach to religion and European identity became a major feature of the negotiations relating to the drafting of the Constitutional Treaty in 2003 and focused on the issue of whether the Preamble to the Treaty would contain a specific reference to either God or Christianity as a source of the Union's constitutional values. The Catholic

---

[2] See Ch 2.
[3] O Roy, *Secularism Confronts Islam* (translated by George Holoch) (New York: Columbia University Press, 2007).

Church was particularly vocal on this issue. Pope John Paul II repeatedly called for the inclusion of 'a reference to the religious and in particular the Christian heritage of Europe'.[4] These requests were forcefully pursued by COMECE,[5] the organization representing the Catholic Bishops to the European Union. The Bishops argued that the Union's values and its Charter of Fundamental Rights in particular were 'inspired by the Judaeo-Christian image of mankind' and that:

in order therefore to facilitate citizens' identification with the values of the European Union, and to acknowledge that public power is not absolute, the COMECE secretariat recommends that a future Constitutional Treaty of the European Union should recognise the openness and ultimate otherness associated with the name of God. An inclusive reference to the transcendent provides a guarantee for the freedom of the human person.[6]

The making of such a reference was actively opposed by secularist groups and states such as France with its strong separation of church and state.[7] The initial draft proposed by the Constitutional Convention President Valéry Giscard-d'Estaing suggested the following formulation:

Conscious that Europe is a continent that has brought forth civilisation; that its inhabitants, arriving in successive waves since the first ages of mankind, have gradually developed the values underlying humanism: equality of persons, freedom, respect for reason,

Drawing inspiration from the cultural, religious and humanist inheritance of Europe, which, nourished first by the civilisations of Greece and Rome, characterised by spiritual impulse always present in its heritage and later by the philosophical currents of the Enlightenment...[8]

This reference to a 'spiritual impulse' and the failure to refer explicitly to religion in general or to Christianity in particular was heavily criticized by

---

[4] 'Post-Synodal Apostolic Exhortation Ecclesia in Europa of His Holiness Pope John Paul II to the Bishops, Men and Women in the Consecrated Life and All the Lay Faithful on Jesus Christ Alive in His Church the Source of Hope for Europe', 28 June 2003, para 114; quoted in COMECE, *The Treaty Establishing a Constitution for Europe: Elements for an Evaluation*, 11 March 2005, available at <http://www.comece.org/content/site/en/publications/pubsec/article/k3163.html> (last visited 26 May 2010).

[5] Commission des Episcopats de la Communauté Européenne.

[6] COMECE, *The Future of Europe, Political Commitment, Values and Religion: Contribution of the COMECE Secretariat to the Debate on the Future of the European Union in the European Convention*, Brussels, 21 May 2002.

[7] See 'God Missing from EU Constitution', *BBC News*, 6 February 2003, available at <http://news.bbc.co.uk/2/hi/europe/2734345.stm> (last visited 12 May 2010).

[8] Draft Treaty Establishing a Constitution for Europe [2003] OJ C169/1.

religious groups and significant sections of the Convention that was tasked with drawing up the Treaty. The Catholic Church and several Member States argued that it was historically inaccurate to refer to the Enlightenment but not Christianity as a source of European values, while a slew of amendments referring to either the Christian or Judaeo-Christian roots of such values were put down by Convention members.[9] The representative of the Polish Government to the Convention argued that 'Religions and Christianity among them have been part and parcel of our continent's history',[10] while a Hungarian representative argued that '[w]e, Europeans know it very well that the Judeo-Christian culture is at the very foundation of our idea of a common Europe'.[11] On the other hand, those such as Socialist MEP Josep Borrell, whose views fell on the opposite side of Roy's dual characterization of the role of religion in European identity, argued that:

a lot of our values have been forged against the Church or the churches. If we are to celebrate historical heritages we should remember the whole story: with its religious wars, the massacres of the Crusades; the nights of Saint Bartholomew and the Inquisition's autos-da-fe; Galileo and the forced evangelisations; the pogroms and the turning of a blind eye to fascism. . . . when it comes to democracy, human rights and equality, God is a recent convert.[12]

The final version of the Constitutional Treaty agreed by the Member States amended the relevant section of the Preamble so that it read as follows:

Drawing inspiration from the cultural, religious and humanist inheritance of Europe, from which have developed the universal values of the inviolable and inalienable rights of the human person, freedom, democracy, equality and the rule of law.[13]

---

[9] See, eg 'Suggestion for amendment of title by Mr Brok on behalf of the EPP Convention Group co signed by Antonio Tajani, member, and Mr Martikonis, member', available at <http://european-convention.eu.int/Docs/Treaty/pdf/1000/1000_Pre%20Brok%20EN.pdf>   (last visited 12 May 2010). Other similar amendments are available at <http://european-convention.eu.int/amendments.asp?content=1000&lang=EN> (last visited 12 May 2010).

[10] See 'Personal Remarks by Professor Danuta Hubner, Representative of the Government of Poland to the European Convention Plenary Session, 27–28 February 2003', available at <http://european-convention.eu.int/docs/speeches/7171.pdf> (last visited 12 May 2010).

[11] See 'Speech Delivered by Jozsef Szajer, Hungary, at the European Convention, 27 February 2007, available at <http://european-convention.eu.int/docs/speeches/9468.pdf> (last visited 12 May 2010).

[12] See 'Contribution submitted by Mr Josep Borrell Fontelles, member of the Convention: "Let's Leave God Out of This"', Brussels, 22 January 2003, CONV 501/03, available at <http://register.consilium.europa.eu/pdf/en/03/cv00/cv00501.en03.pdf> (last visited 26 May 2010).

[13] See Treaty of Lisbon amending the Treaty on European Union and the Treaty establishing the European Community, signed at Lisbon, 13 December 2007 [2007] OJ C306/01.

This formula was retained in the Lisbon Treaty.[14] The Preamble charac-terizes the constitutional values of the Union as deriving from a balance of religious, humanist, and cultural influences.[15] These three influences both reinforce, and are inconsistent with, each other. For instance, humanist influences can compliment religious influences due to the strong humanist tradition within Christianity which has also been reflected in European cul-ture. On the other hand, the secularist elements of the humanist tradition, with its emphasis on human self-government, can also restrict the influence that religious organizations, including Christian ones, may seek to assert over law and politics.

This approach involves, in contrast to strictly secular public orders, the recognition of a religious element to the Union's constitutional values and public morality. On the other hand, the reference to religion is balanced by references to cultural and humanist influences, the latter of which have, as Taylor has argued,[16] functioned so as to reduce the influence of religion over public life in Europe. Furthermore, these religious and humanist influ-ences are recognized in their instrumental capacity as contributors to the emergence of values such as respect for individual rights, democracy, equal-ity, etc. Thus, the balance struck by the Union in this area grants humanist ideas significant influence by defining the various influences on the Union's public morality as valuable by virtue of their contribution to certain forms of human government. In contrast to religiously based constitutions such as the Irish Constitution, which defines its ultimate notion of the good in explicitly religious terms,[17] the Preamble to the Lisbon Treaty portrays democracy and respect for individual rights as the ultimate goods to which Europe's cultural, religious, and humanist influences have contributed. Thus, the role accorded to Europe's religious inheritance is substantially counterbalanced by ideas that owe much to humanist notions of human self-government.

As the text of the Preamble makes clear, this balance between religious and humanist influences is also affected by cultural factors. The predominant

[14] Ibid, Preamble.

[15] Of course European culture and therefore its inheritance have contained many highly negative elements such as patriarchy and racism (particularly in the form of anti-semitism and colonialism). Therefore, in deciding on its fundamental values, the Union does not draw on Europe's entire heritage but rather draws selectively on a common heritage while distancing itself from elements of that heritage. Indeed, in many ways it is the presence of these undesirable elements in Europe's past that allows it to see more clearly what the desirable elements of a public order should be.

[16] C Taylor, *A Secular Age* (Cambridge, MA: Harvard University Press, 2007).

[17] See Bunreacht na h-Éireann, Preamble.

contemporary view of culture is of a broad ethnographic or anthropological state of affairs which represents a broad 'way of life' encompassing established patterns in relation to values and beliefs and matters such as food, clothing, or leisure activities.[18] The invocation of cultural influences themselves and the notion of the importance of Europe's 'cultural, religious and humanist *inheritance*' (emphasis added) imply that the fundamental constitutional norms of the Union are influenced by, and therefore reinforce, a shared European way of life. Such an approach entails greater recognition of those forms of religion that have been historically predominant in Europe, that have left a greater mark on national cultures, and that are therefore compatible with established European cultural norms. Indeed, the Union has been at pains to ensure that EU law does not undermine the cultural or institutional role of particular religions at Member State level, including, for instance, the arrangement of leisure periods around particular religious patterns or the role of particular religions as sources of national identity.[19] The Lisbon Treaty gave explicit recognition to this approach in Article 17(1), which states that 'The Union respects and does not prejudice the status under national law of churches and religious associations or communities in the Member States'.[20]

The importance attached to culture and to the notion of inheritance therefore has the potential to grant certain forms of religion greater influence over the Union's public morality than others. In particular, as Europe's 'religious inheritance' is overwhelmingly Christian, Christianity is likely to exercise a greater influence than other faiths over a public morality which draws on a mixture of Europe's 'cultural, humanist and religious inheritance'. This was the view of the Catholic Bishops who regarded the Preamble to the Treaty as 'implicitly referring to the centre of this [religious] tradition, which is Christianity'.[21] Indeed, the importance of balancing religious influences with those of the humanist tradition and cultural norms can be seen as implicitly categorizing forms of religion which are anti-humanist or

---

[18] See F Inglis, *Culture* (Cambridge: Polity Press, 2004) 28–29; and C Barker, 'Culture' in *The SAGE Dictionary of Cultural Studies* (London: Sage, 2004) 45.

[19] See Chs 4 and 5.

[20] Consolidated Version of the Treaty on the Functioning of the European Union [2008] OJ C115/47, Art 17(1), available at <http://eur-lex.europa.eu/LexUriServ/LexUriServ.do?uri=OJ:C :2008:115:0047:0199:EN:PDF> (last visited 12 May 2010).

[21] COMECE, 'The Treaty Establishing a Constitution for Europe: Elements for an Evaluation', 11 March 2005, available at <http://www.comece.org/content/site/en/publications/ pubsec/article/k3163.html> (last visited 26 May 2010).

which contravene other European cultural values as contrary to European public morality.

This balancing of religious, humanist, and cultural elements was criticized from both religious and secular perspectives. Although, as noted above, the Catholic Bishops welcomed what they regarded as an implicit reference to Christianity, they nevertheless stated that:

An explicit mentioning of God or Christianity would have been a strong signal supporting the identity of Europe. It is therefore regrettable that neither the European Convention nor the Intergovernmental Conference agreed to the inclusion of such a reference. As a matter of historical fact, it is Christianity and the Christian message that have built the 'inheritance of Europe' from which have developed the universal values of the inviolable and inalienable rights of the human person, democracy, equality and the rule of law.[22]

On the other hand, a group of secularist Convention members argued that 'the wording of the Preamble was already stretching the tolerance of non-Christians to the limit [and that] religion has not always been an unqualified blessing for Europe'.[23]

The balance struck by the Preamble is, indeed, neither entirely secularist nor fully endorses the theory of the religious basis of European public morality. The academic debate has reflected this lack of clarity. On the one hand, some have argued that the Preamble's failure to grant specific recognition to Christianity as the source of Europe's common moral and political norms is unduly secularist and misleading. Weigel, for instance, argues that the Preamble presents a 'false and distorting' view on the basis that 'Christianity is the story that has arguably had more to do with constituting Europe than anything else'.[24] The Treaty, he suggests, embodies a secular view of Europe which 'cannot identify with precision and accuracy, the sources of Europe's commitments to human rights, democracy and the rule of law'.[25] Weigel draws heavily on Weiler's *Un'Europa Cristiana*,[26] which is equally critical. Weiler argues that the failure to mention God or Christianity in the Preamble represented, according to Weiler, an 'EU-enforced

[22] Ibid.
[23] Convention Meeting of 5–6 June 2003, Reform of Institutions and Revisions of Parts I and IV of the Draft: Comments of members Borrell, Duhamel, and Abitol, available at < http:// www.europarl.europa.eu/sides/getDoc.do?pubRef=-//EP//TEXT+PRESS+BI-20030606 -1+0+DOC+XML+V0//EN> (last visited 26 May 2010).
[24] G Weigel, *The Cube and the Cathedral: Europe, America and Politics without God* (New York: Basic Books, 2005) 70.   [25] Ibid 85.
[26] JHH Weiler, *Un'Europa Cristiana: Un saggio esplorativo* (Milan: BUR Saggi, 2003).

laïcité on European public life'.[27] The approach embodied in the Constitutional and Lisbon Treaties, he suggests, endorses the right to freedom from religion which he sees as partisan and less desirable than freedom of religion.

This approach has rightly been criticized for failing to take account of the full picture of the relationship between Christianity and liberalism, which has often been characterized by conflict. As Cvijic and Zucca note, Weiler's 'claim that the liberal ideal derives directly from Christian philosophy and that it is accordingly illogical that the Preamble of the European Constitution invokes humanist values but refuses to make a direct allusion to Christian values, fails to give due recognition to the full picture of the relationship between humanism and Christianity'.[28]

Indeed, although Christian thought, and Christian humanism in particular, played an influential and perhaps indispensable role in the development of principles such as individual autonomy and equality, such principles have also on occasion come into conflict with Christian teachings and, in particular, with the desire of many Christian churches to have religious teachings in areas such as the family and sexuality reflected in the law of the land. The Catholic Church has, in the past, explicitly rejected notions such as freedom of religion[29] and even today has endorsed the use of the criminal law to promote and enforce adherence to biblical standards of sexual behaviour.[30] Although it has come to accept the legitimacy of the secular state and to actively embrace liberal democracy, such acceptance has, as Roy points

---

[27] See discussion in AJ Menendez, 'Review of A Christian Europe' (2005) 30(1) ELR 133.

[28] S Cvijic and L Zucca, 'Does the European Constitution need Christian Values?' (2004) 24(4) OJLS 744.

[29] See the condemnation of liberty of conscience, freedom of expression and opposition to monarchical rule in *Mirari Vos: On Liberalism and Religious Indifferentism*, Encyclical of Pope Gregory XVI, 15 August 1832 (in particular paras 13–24, full text available at <http://www.papalencyclicals.net/Pius09/p9quanta.htm> (last visited 26 May 2010). See also Propositions 15 and 78 of the *Syllabus of Errors Condemned by Pope Pius IX*, full text available at <http://www.papalencyclicals.net/Pius09/p9syll.htm> (last visited 26 May 2010).

[30] See K Rose, *Diverse Communities: The Evolution of Lesbian and Gay Politics in Ireland* (Cork: Cork University Press, 1994). More generally, see E O'Reilly, *Masterminds of the Right* (Dublin: Attic Press, 1992). See also the Vatican's opposition to a United Nations resolution calling for an end to the criminalization and punishment of individuals on the grounds of their sexual orientation: 'The Pope's Christmas Gift: A Hard Line on Church Doctrine', *Time Magazine*, 3 December 2008. The Vatican later clarified that it was not necessarily in favour of criminalization of homosexuality. However, it did not object to the principle of criminalization of homosexuality in Uganda in 2009–2010 and, as Rose notes (above) 27, 44, opposed moves to decriminalize homosexual conduct in Ireland as late as 1993.

out,[31] on occasion, been prompted by considerations of *realpolitik* rather than theological reform. Furthermore, Weigel's complaint that the Preamble does not identify the source of Europe's commitments to democracy and human rights not only appears to assume a congruent relationship between these principles and Christianity but also fails to take into account that such commitments can arise from multiple sources, or, as Dershowitz suggests, from historical experience of injustice and oppression rather than from religious worldviews.[32]

On the other hand, some secularist authors have failed to note the degree to which religion (and, implicitly, Christianity) is a major part of European national identities, is in fact recognized as part of European public morality, and is accorded special treatment by EU law in other areas.[33] Thus, Menendez's defence of the Preamble, on the basis that 'defining constitutional ethics in Christian terms may obstruct the integration of those with other or no religious beliefs who face other barriers to full membership of our society',[34] assumes that the failure to make an explicit reference means that a purely non-religious approach has been adopted. This approach fails to give adequate recognition to the fact that by recognizing Europe's religious and cultural 'inheritance' as part of European public morality, the Treaty does, in fact, recognize that Christian perspectives partly constitute the Union's constitutional ethics, albeit that such recognition is implicit and balanced by the simultaneous recognition of humanist influences.

The fact that neither those who see European identity as secular nor those who see it as Christian were satisfied by the approach adopted in the Lisbon Treaty underlines the fact that the Union has identified a balance between these two influences as characteristic of its public morality. The Preamble recognizes religion and religious values as part of the mix of influences that constitute the values underpinning the Union's constitutional order. In this way the EU's constitutional values could be seen as reflecting what MacCormick calls 'value pluralism', under which conflicts between differing rights or approaches are seen as the norm and are resolved through balancing conflicting elements rather than according priority to one over another in a

---

[31] Roy (n 3 above) 21–2.

[32] A Dershowitz, *Rights from Wrongs: A Secular Theory of the Origins of Rights* (New York: Basic Books, 2004).

[33] See the discussion of the overlap between recognition of Member State cultural autonomy and the promotion of the values of particular religions in sections 4 and 5 below and Ch 5 in particular the discussion of the Framework Directive on discrimination in employment.

[34] See Menendez (n 27 above).

hierarchical fashion.[35] Thus, religion is not entirely excluded from a public role and the Union does not follow a strictly secular approach under which religious norms and ideas are by definition excluded from influence over public life. However, it is significant that the recognition of religion in the Preamble is not only limited but is also, at least formally, denomination-neutral. Although the notion of inheritance and the influence of cultural matters mean that forms of religion that were historically dominant in Europe are likely to exercise greater influence over the EU's public morality, the Union has pointedly refused to associate explicitly itself with a particular religion. Indeed, the EU has repeatedly indicated its rhetorical commitment to the equality of religious and other forms of belief or philosophy, for example in relation to the privileges of religious bodies in the Framework Directive[36] or in the Declaration on the Status of Churches,[37] both of which conferred equal recognition on other forms of belief or philosophy. It is this formal neutrality which religious groups, most notably the Catholic Church, have found objectionable.

Beyond the formal neutrality of its provisions, what is notable about the approach reflected in the Preamble to the Constitutional and Lisbon Treaties is that while religion is recognized and may therefore play some role in the determination of public policy, recognition is also granted to other influences, such as humanism, which may limit the realization of the ambitions of religions in the political and legal arenas. Furthermore, both religious and humanist values are seen in the Preamble as instruments leading to the recognition of values, such as equality and respect for individual rights, which have, as some contributors to the debate surrounding the Preamble pointed out, had complex and sometimes antagonistic relationships to certain forms of religion, including Christianity. Thus, while recognition is granted to religion, such recognition is counterbalanced by humanist values

[35] J Bengoetxea, N MacCormick, and L Moral Soriano, 'Integration and Integrity in the Legal Reasoning of the European Court of Justice' in G de Búrca and JHH Weiler (eds), *The European Court of Justice* (Oxford: Oxford University Press, 2001) 64.

[36] Article 4(2) of the Directive states: 'churches and *other public or private organisations* the ethos of which is based on religion *or belief*' (Council Directive (EC) 2000/78 establishing a general framework for equal treatment in employment and occupation Article 2(5) [2000] OJ L303/16).

[37] Declaration on the status of churches and non-confessional organisations, Declaration No 11 to the last act of the Treaty of Amsterdam [1997] OJ C340/133 provides that: 'The European Union respects and does not prejudice the status under national law of churches and religious associations or communities in the Member States. The European Union equally respects the status of philosophical and non-confessional organisations.'

that emphasize notions of human autonomy and self-government independent of any appeal to the divine. Therefore, a commitment to 'balance' does not mean that any kind of balance will do and that absolute 'value pluralism' prevails. It is more accurate to say that the EU's public order is committed to upholding a *proper* balance between religious and humanist influences that allows Member States a significant degree of leeway but nevertheless imposes limitations that prevent either the Union or the Member States from according particular types of legal and political influence to religion. The kind of balance chosen by a Member State must, for example, be compatible with the respect for individual rights and democracy that are characterized by the Preamble as the ultimate goods to which the Union's public order is committed.

This notion of a public order characterized by a partly contested balance between religious, humanist, and cultural influences is repeated in other areas of EU law. Religions that lack deep cultural roots in Europe or are incapable of reconciling themselves to the accommodation of humanist influences will struggle to achieve influence under such a public order and may even be seen as contrary to it.[38] Thus, the EU has a preference for those forms of religion that are compatible with the accommodation of the humanist and secular elements of European culture. Such compatibility is not an easy matter for all religions because the accommodation of humanist influences can require significant limitation of the influence of religion over law and political life. Such approaches have been criticized as a violation of the duty of neutrality towards religion. Modood argues that it is 'a contradiction to require both that the state be neutral about religion and that the state should require religions with public ambitions to give them up'.[39] However, it is unclear how a polity that is committed to values such as individual autonomy and gender equality could possibly uphold those values while simultaneously refusing to limit the realization of the desires of forms of religion which, for instance, desire to mould law and policy in line with patriarchal religious teachings in relation to sexuality and gender. Certain limitations on the political and legal ambitions of religion are an indispensable element of liberal democracy and failing to restrict the realization of the ambitions of faiths that desire to establish theocracy would mean the end of liberal democracy. Indeed, the greater inequality would be to vary the limitations on religious influence in

[38] See Chs 5 and 6.
[39] T Modood, 'Anti-Essentialism, Multiculturalism and the "Recognition" of Religious Groups' (1998) 6 *Journal of Political Philosophy* 378, 393.

accordance with the demands of individual faiths. As long as limitations on religious influence over law and politics are applied to all faiths, the fact that they may impinge to a greater degree on forms of religion that reject aspects of key liberal and democratic values does not mean that such limitations violate the religious neutrality of the polity in question.

It is true that, had the EU chosen merely to affirm its commitment to democracy and individual rights and remained silent on the sources of its commitments to such principles, the issue of religious neutrality need not have arisen. However, it is a matter of historical reality that certain religious traditions have been more influential than others in the formation of shared European culture and norms. This means that by choosing to open up the contentious issue of the source of its ethical commitments and recognizing an instrumental role for religion in the determination of their content, the Union implicitly associates itself with certain religious traditions. This approach underlines the importance attached to the notion of balance between religious and humanist influences within the public morality of the Union. Preserving a balance between these influences means that approaches involving a negation of any of the elements of such balance will be seen as contrary to the Union's public order. This principle, which will be discussed in more detail below, can cut both ways. Just as an attempt to introduce *Sharia* as the basis of a legal system has been identified as unacceptable on grounds of its failure to respect the autonomy of the public sphere and individual autonomy in the private sphere,[40] approaches that are particularly restrictive of religion have also been seen as potentially problematic in the light of the Union's commitments to religious freedom.[41]

3. Recognition of the Role of Religion in Law-making

Religious influence over EU law is not restricted to acting as a source of constitutional values. Religious perspectives have also been recognized as having a special and privileged role to play in law-making. This section analyses the approach adopted by the Union in this field and suggests that, in common with the role of religion in the constitutional values of the Union outlined above, the role granted to religious bodies in law-making is characterized by the requirement of proper balance between religious,

---

[40] See the discussion of *Refah Partisi v Turkey* in Ch 6.   [41] See section 5.2 below.

humanist, and cultural influences. It begins with an analysis of the informal links between religious bodies and EU institutions, before considering the status granted to such bodies by the Treaty. It notes how religious perspectives have been recognized as a necessary and uniquely important element of law-making but concludes by showing how, on the other hand, the Union's recognition of the religious contribution to law-making in the context of civil society has the effect of relativizing and, thereby, partly secularizing, religious perspectives.

Recognition that churches and religious organizations are, by virtue of their religious nature and perspective, valid contributors to policy formation and law-making implies, at least in theory, that religious perspectives may form part of law and public policy. This is an approach which deviates from secular notions of the state. For instance, theorists such as Rawls and Habermas have argued that the justification of law or policy on religious grounds is inconsistent with a liberal constitutional order. Rawls suggests that:

the self-understanding of the constitutional state has developed within the framework of a contractualist tradition that relies on 'natural' reason, in other words solely public arguments to which supposedly all persons have equal access. The assumption of a common human reason forms the basis of justification for a secular state that no longer depends on religious legitimation.[42]

Similarly, Habermas advocates that state officials (including politicians) must 'justify their political statements independently of their religious convictions or world views'[43] and that '[m]ajority rule turns into oppression if the majority deploys religious arguments in the process of political opinion and will formation and refuses to offer those publicly accessible justifications which the losing minority be it secular or of a different faith, is able to follow'.[44]

However, in line with its rejection of purely secular notions of Europe's constitutional ethics, the EU does recognize the validity, importance, and particular nature of the contribution of religious bodies to law-making and would therefore seem, to some degree, to accept the notion that the law may, at least in part, be based on religious arguments. Religious bodies have had informal links to European Institutions for many years.[45] The Catholic

---

[42] J Habermas, 'Religion in the Public Sphere' (2006) 14(1) *European Journal of Philosophy* 1, 4, referring to J Rawls, *Political Liberalism* (New York: Columbia University Press, 1993).

[43] Habermas (n 42 above) 9.   [44] Ibid 12.

[45] See T Jansen, 'Europe and Religions: the Dialogue between the European Commission and Churches or Religious Communities' (2000) 47(1) *Social Compass* 103.

Church (COMECE), the Protestant Churches (KEK-CEC), and Jewish, Muslim, Orthodox, and Humanist groups all have full-time representation in Brussels.[46] These informal links to European institutions were largely developed at the behest of religious groups themselves.[47] However, the European Commission in particular has come to see such links as potential contributors to the attainment of its broader political goals. Links between religious bodies and the Union were placed on a more formal basis in 1992 when Commission President Jacques Delors established a programme called 'A Soul for Europe' whose aim was described by the Commission as 'giving a spiritual and ethical dimension to the European Union'.[48] The facilitation of religious contributions to policy-making was not merely a result of a desire to accommodate religious perspectives within EU law and policy but was also seen as an opportunity to use religious organizations to develop civil society at the European level, something which was regarded as necessary to sustain European integration. Commission President Delors made this point explicitly in an address to the 'Soul for Europe' initiative, in which he stated that '[w]e won't succeed with Europe solely on the basis of legal expertise or economic know how... If in the next ten years we have not managed to give a soul to Europe, to give it spirituality and meaning, the game will be up',[49] thus explicitly linking the participation of religious bodies in European public life and the accommodation of religious perspectives in the EU's activities, to the sustainability of the Union as a political project. Subsequently, the Bureau of European Policy Advisors (BEPA),[50] which reported to the Commission President, became responsible for what was described as a 'Dialogue with Religions, Churches, Humanisms'.[51] This process of dialogue consisted mainly of a series of seminars and discussion groups on

---

[46] M Rynkowski, 'Remarks on Art. I-52 of the Constitutional Treaty: new Aspects of the European Ecclesiastical Law?' (2005) 6(11) *German Law Journal* 343.

[47] See Jansen (n 45 above).

[48] See European Commission, 'Archives of GOPA, Dialogue with Religions, Churches and Humanisms—Issues: A Soul for Europe', available at <http://www.ec.europa.eu/dgs/policy _advisers/archives/activities/dialogue_religions_humanisms/index_en.htm> (last visited 12 May 2010).

[49] Quoted in H Alfeyev, 'Christian Witness to Uniting Europe: A View from a Representative of the Russian Orthodox Church', *The Ecumenical Review*, January 2003. See also European Commission (n 48 above).

[50] This organization was previously known as the Forward Studies Unit and the Group of Policy Advisors.

[51] Rynkowski (n 46 above).

the role of religious bodies in the Union.[52] The fact the EU institutions reached out to religious bodies in this way underlines the degree to which the Union has recognized religious bodies as playing a particularly important role in policy-making. The contributions of other elements of civil society have not been sought out or recognized in this way.

The specific recognition of 'churches' in the context of this 'Dialogue with Religions, Churches, Humanisms' also provides some indication of the influence of cultural and historical factors. Although the term has been applied to certain newer religious movements such as Scientology, 'churches' are a Christian concept which is generally still taken to refer to the organizational structure or branches of the Christian religion. Christian religious structures also fall within the term 'religions', so the singling-out of churches can be seen as indicative of the prominent role European institutions expected the religious institutions of traditionally dominant Christian churches to play in this dialogue. Indeed, the importance of cultural matters to the Union's approach to religion, and in particular its desire to respect the public role of traditionally dominant Christian denominations at Member State level, is seen elsewhere in EU law. The 1998 Declaration on the status of churches[53] appended to the Amsterdam Treaty also signified a formalization of the Union's relationship to religious bodies in that it stated that the Union 'respects and does not prejudice the status under national law of churches and religious associations or communities in the Member States', thus recognizing the status of such bodies at national level in a formal way. Indeed, this deference towards the cultural role of religion in Member States has also been reflected in the Union's substantive legislation, most notably in relation to employment law and religiously managed healthcare and educational institutions.[54]

The Commission White Paper on Governance of 2001 also indicated the openness of the Union to the recognition of the role of religious perspectives in policy-making by recognizing the 'particular contribution' of 'churches and religious communities' to policy-making.[55] Thus, not only did the Commission recognize religious bodies as particularly important elements of civil society, it also recognized the particular nature of their contribution. Such recognition indicates that religious bodies are seen as

[52] See Bureau of European Policy Advisers, available at <http://ec.europa.eu/dgs/policy_advisers/index_en.htm> (last visited 12 May 2010).
[53] Declaration on the status of churches and non-confessional organisations (n 37 above).
[54] See Ch 5.
[55] European Governance: A White Paper, COM (2001) 428 final, Brussels, 25 July 2001.

having particular qualifications or that they bring perspectives to law-making which other institutions are not capable of providing to the same degree. The combination of the recognition of both the importance and the particular nature of religious contributions by the Commission underlines the notion of religious bodies as particularly important and privileged players in the articulation of a European public morality by civil society. Thus, the Union appears to recognize to some degree the historic role of churches and religions as moral guardians with a special authority on moral matters. Of course, morality is not the sole preserve of religious bodies; however, the Union's explicit references to churches along with its identification of the 'particular contribution' of religious bodies in this regard would appear to defer to the historic role played by religions in relation to notions of morality, a role which is consistent with the continuing public role of religion in Western society identified by theorists such as Casanova.[56]

This identification of religious perspectives as necessary and particularly important elements of law-making was reflected in the Constitutional and Lisbon Treaties, which explicitly recognized this 'particular contribution' by according (following a strenuous campaign on the part of the Catholic Church)[57] a privileged consultative status to religious groups. While Article 11(2) of the Lisbon Treaty commits the Union to maintaining an 'an open, transparent and regular dialogue with representative associations and Civil Society',[58] Article 17 singles out religious bodies and specifically undertakes to maintain a dialogue with them. Article 17, which also incorporates the 1998 Declaration on the Status of Churches, reads:

(1) The Union respects and does not prejudice the status under national law of churches and religious associations or communities in the Member States.

(2) The Union equally respects the status under national law of philosophical and non-confessional organisations.

(3) Recognising their identity and their specific contribution, the Union shall maintain an open, transparent and regular dialogue with these churches and organisations.[59]

---

[56] J Casanova, *Public Religions in the Modern World* (Chicago: University of Chicago Press, 1994), discussed in Ch 2.

[57] See COMECE, 'The Future of Europe: Political Commitment, Values and Religion: Contribution of the COMECE Secretariat to the Debate on the Future of the European Union in the European Convention', Brussels, 21 May 2002.

[58] Consolidated Version of the Treaty on the Functioning of the European Union, Art 11(2).

[59] Ibid, Art 17.

The granting of this special status was strenuously opposed by secularist organizations which characterized Article 17 as 'incompatible with secularism',[60] challenging 'the principle of separation of church and state',[61] and granting religion 'a privileged status in European public policy making'.[62] Although the dialogue is open to all religions, the combination in Article 17 of the recognition of the national status of churches with the recognition of the special importance of religious contributions to policy-making, links the recognition accorded to and role played by, religious bodies at EU level with the national status of such bodies, because the identity and contribution of such bodies will be influenced by their role in the lives of particular Member States.

The Union does therefore seem to accord religious perspectives a particular degree of recognition and facilitation in policy-making. Religious bodies are recognized as elements of civil society with which the Union will maintain a dialogue. However, such bodies are seen as making a 'specific contribution' and as representing a particularly important part of civil society which is accorded specific and explicit recognition. By recognizing the specificity of the contribution of religious bodies to law-making, the Union implicitly identifies religious perspectives as a legitimate and necessary element of policy formation. Furthermore, the recognition of the right of religious bodies to be consulted by law-making institutions in a separate article from that dedicated to civil society in general, characterizes this religious contribution to law-making as distinctive and particularly important.

Nevertheless, in line with the Union's approach in other areas, the notion of proper balance requires that this facilitation of religious influence be limited by other influences which draw on the humanist and secular influences within the EU public order. First, Article 17 itself also recognizes the equal status of 'philosophical and non-confessional organisations'. One of the most prominent of these is the International Humanist and Ethical Union, which has been part of the dialogue with European institutions and which has a vigorously secular outlook. Furthermore, the fact that, even in an article dedicated to the facilitation of religions, the Union felt constrained to provide equal recognition to non-confessional groups, indicates that, although religion is recognized within the legal and political arenas, such perspectives

---

[60] See 'Catholics Join European NGOs in Coalition in Appeal to Convention Not to Give Religion Unfair Influence in Constitutional Treaty', *US Newswire*, 22 May 2003, available at <http://www.forf.org/news/2003/cje.html> (last visited 12 May 20108).   [61] Ibid.   [62] Ibid.

will not necessarily be predominant. Indeed, the importance of religious bodies is seen in line with humanist approaches, as deriving, to a significant degree, from their human dimensions and the attachment of individuals to religious organizations. This approach is echoed in the Commission's documents in relation to the dialogue with 'Religions, Churches and Humanisms', which stresses the status of religious bodies as part of civil society and which justifies dialogue with such bodies on the grounds that '[t]hey are representatives of European citizens. In this respect, Community law protects the churches and religious communities, as they would any other partner in Civil Society.'[63]

Thus, while the historical and cultural role of religions in Europe as moral guardians means that the 'specific contribution' of churches and religious communities is recognized by the Union, and while this contribution is seen as representing a particularly important perspective, the right of such bodies to play a part in the law-making process is seen as deriving from their historic role as moral guardians and their status as representative organizations, rather than from the inherent truth of their message or the importance of ensuring compliance with divine mandates. Indeed, it is simply inconceivable that EU legislation would explicitly base itself on revelation or seek to justify itself on the basis of its compatibility with a religious text. EU legislation is not justified in theological terms and one does not, for example, find biblical justifications in the preambles of directives and regulations, which instead rely on what might be termed generally accessible justifications. Even legislation such as the Preamble to the Framework Directive, a piece of legislation that touches on religious issues to a significant degree, justifies the measures contained therein on the basis of non-religious goals, such as their contribution to the 'attainment of a high level of employment and social protection, raising the standard of living and quality of life, economic and social cohesion and solidarity'.[64] Indeed, the statements of the Commission, the rulings of the European Court of Human Rights, and EU enlargement policy have all indicated that a failure to maintain limits on religious influence over the political and legal domains is incompatible with membership

[63] See Group of Policy Advisers, 'Commission Document on Dialogue with Religions, Churches and Humanisms: Introduction to the legal aspects of the relations between the European Union and the communities of faith and conviction', available at <http://ec.europe.dgs/policy_advisers/archives/activities/dialogue_religions_humanisms/legal_en.htm> (last visited 5 April 2008).

[64] Council Directive (EC) 2000/78 establishing a general framework for equal treatment in employment and occupation [2000] OJ L303/16, para 11.

of the Union.[65] In fact, despite its facilitation of religious participation in law-making, the Union's conception of a proper balance in this area can be seen as reflecting, to a significant degree, humanist perspectives, which stress human autonomy and reject the idea of law as something subordinate to, or merely a means to promote, divine authority on earth.

Furthermore, the Union also balances its recognition and facilitation of religious influence by providing such recognition within the framework of civil society, a context that requires relativization of religious arguments. The manner in which the dialogue with religious bodies has operated demonstrates that the Union has refused to associate itself explicitly with particular religious viewpoints and has instead operated a process in which differing religious, and even non-religious, perspectives have been accorded equal recognition. As noted above, Article 17 specifically recognizes the equal status of 'philosophical and non-confessional organisations', and thus the legitimacy of non-religious worldviews. Not only have avowedly secularist and atheist groups taken part in the dialogue, new religious movements, which have received little protection in other areas of EU law, have also been permitted to participate. Rynkowski notes that members of what he calls 'sects' 'are present during meetings, even those concerning combating the illegal activities of sects'.[66] He argues that their presence is 'inappropriate' and that the Commission 'is a hostage of political correctness'.[67] Whatever the merits of these arguments (Rynkowski provides neither reasons supporting the inappropriateness of their presence nor indeed a method of distinguishing 'sects' from bona fide religions), the denomination-neutral approach adopted by the Commission highlights both the conspicuous reluctance of the Union to grant recognition to, or associate itself officially with, any individual religious denomination, and the commitment to restricting the accommodation of religious truth claims in the legal and political arenas, as elements of the maintenance of proper balance between religious and humanist perspectives.

Thus, the Union does recognize and privilege religious bodies as particularly important articulators of, and contributors to, European public morality and, on this basis, acknowledges them as important contributors to law- and policy-making. However, the fact that such recognition is provided within the context of civil society (albeit with the privileged status conferred by the Treaty article dedicated to religious bodies), requires that religious bodies exercise the rights attached to such recognition in the context of a

---

[65] See Ch 6.   [66] Rynkowski (n 46 above).   [67] Ibid.

process which relativizes their claims. Furthermore, by participating in a process in which religious bodies are required to persuade law-makers and to articulate their religious contribution in a forum which equally recognizes different religious, or anti-religious, perspectives, religious bodies implicitly accept the legitimacy of secular political institutions, along with the reality that the ultimate decision in relation to matters of law lies with such institutions. Indeed, as the justifications provided by Commission President Delors for the original dialogue with religious groups made clear, the Union's engagement with religious groups has been partly related to efforts to create a European public sphere and to enhance the legitimacy and sustainability of the political institutions of the Union.[68] Thus, the Union's approach to the facilitation of religious contributions to law-making can be seen as balancing religious and humanist influences by recognizing religion as one influence among many in the process of law-making. Engagement in such a process requires religious groups to acknowledge the legitimacy of other religious and non-religious worldviews. Such acceptance is not an easy matter for all religions. As Habermas points out:

missionary doctrines such as Christianity or Islam are intrinsically intolerant of other beliefs. Love of your neighbour includes active care for his or her salvation. And because,—as Thomas Aquinas, among others, argue—eternal salvation has absolute priority over all goods, care for the salvation of others does not per se exclude the application of force to convert someone to the right faith or to protect them against heresy.[69]

The recognition of such groups within the context of civil society is therefore based on certain prerequisites. Thus, '[t]he liberal state expects that the religious consciousness of the faithful will become modernised by way of cognitive adaptation to the individualistic and egalitarian nature of the laws of the secular community'.[70]

The recognition of religious communities in this way can be seen as encouraging a process where each religious body 'locks the moral and legal principles of secular society onto its own ethos'[71] and where religious bodies

---

[68] See 'The New Crusade; Fighting for God in a secular Europe, conservative Christians, the Vatican and Islamic militants', *Newsweek*, 1 November 2004, available at <http://www .religiousconsultation.org/News_Tracker/the_new_crusade_fighting_for_God_in_a_secular_ Europe.htm> (last visited 12 May 2010).

[69] J Habermas, 'Intolerance and Discrimination' (2003) (1)(1) *International Journal of Constitutional Law* 2, 7.   [70] Ibid 6.

[71] Ibid 8.

in general 'have to make the civic principle of equal inclusion their own'.[72] As Habermas acknowledges, such a process means 'accepting mutually exclusive validity claims'[73] which requires a neutralization of the 'practical impact of the cognitive dissonance'[74] this produces.

Indeed, it is notable how recognition of religion in the context of a pluralist civil society, linked to secular political institutions, has pushed religious bodies to phrase their contributions in precisely the kind of generally accessible reasons required by theorists such as Rawls and which appeal to views of 'the good life' that are not necessarily religious. For instance, COMECE justified its calls for the recognition of the specific contribution of churches and religious organizations on the basis that churches 'are committed to serve society—inter alia, in the fields of education, culture, media and social work—and they play an important role in promoting mutual respect, participation, citizenship, dialogue and reconciliation between the peoples of Europe, East and West'.[75] Its campaign in favour of the making of a reference to Christianity in the Preamble to the Constitutional Treaty was justified on similarly generally accessible grounds, with the Bishops stressing Christianity's role in developing human rights and democracy and suggesting that such a reference 'would have been a strong signal supporting the identity of Europe'.[76] Similarly, Pope John II also declared that the Catholic Church was committed to 'fully respecting the secular nature of the institutions'[77] of the Union, thus acknowledging the legitimacy and contribution of secular political institutions.

The Catholic Church's invocation of European identity not only underlines the instrumental polity-building aspects of the process, it also demonstrates, along with the reliance on the facilitative role of religion in relation to religiously neutral civic activities and values, how, in engaging in the law-making process at EU level, religious bodies have internalized what Habermas termed 'civic principles' and 'the moral and legal principles of secular society'. Thus, while religion is recognized by the Union, this recognition of religious influence is balanced by the nature of the forum

---

[72] Ibid 10.   [73] Ibid 12.   [74] Ibid.

[75] COMECE, *The Future of Europe, Political Commitment, Values and Religion: Contribution of the COMECE Secretariat to the Debate on the Future of the European Union in the European Convention*, Brussels, 21 May 2002, available at <http://www.comece.org/content/site/en/publications/pubsec/article/k3130.html> (last visited 26 May 2010).

[76] COMECE, *The Treaty Establishing a Constitution for Europe: Elements for an Evaluation*, 11 March 2005, available at <http://www.comece.org/content/site/en/publications/pubsec/article/k3163.html> (last visited 26 May 2010).   [77] See n 4 above.

in which such recognition is granted, which requires religions to relativize their claims and accept the legitimacy of other worldviews.

The Union's Treaty commitment to engagement with civil society recognizes that its law- and policy-making must be informed by diverse perspectives and views of the good life from across Europe. Thus, civil society plays a role in forming a European public morality that informs the Union's law-making. Religion, as noted above, has been recognized by the Union as a particularly important contributor to this public morality, which enables certain religious traditions to exercise greater influence than others. The explicit recognition of the status and role of national churches in Article 17 of the Lisbon Treaty encourages the according of greater weight to the contributions of religions that are culturally and institutionally entrenched at national level. Furthermore, as was the case in relation to the influence of religion on the constitutional values of the Union set out in the Preamble to the Lisbon Treaty, the recognition of religion's role in law-making in the context of civil society renders those forms of religion that can reconcile themselves to the notion of balance between humanist and religious influences and to the European cultural norms, more capable of exercising influence than religions that lack such characteristics and are, for instance, anti-humanist in nature or do not acknowledge the legitimacy of secular political institutions. While these limitations are challenging for all European religions, including those that are culturally entrenched, the cultural influence and long (though still contested) tradition of humanism within the historically dominant Christian churches may render them more capable of exerting influence within the structures established by the Union to engage with religious perspectives than outsider religions, such as Islam, which have had less cultural impact on Europe or may have more antagonistic attitudes to humanist principles.[78]

---

[78] Christian religions have often had antagonistic relationships towards elements of humanism and democracy, liberalism, and secularism. However, strong humanist traditions within Christianity have made it easier for such faiths to accept, even if only as a matter of *realpolitik*, the limitations on religious influence that emerged from European history. Roy notes that secular and humanist traditions have not had the same impact on Islam as on Christianity and that 'Western secularism actually has a Christian origin': Roy (n 3 above) ix. Le Goff notes that, as early as the eleventh and twelfth centuries, a strong emphasis on the belief that God was made in man's image gave rise to a strong strain of humanism within Western Christianity: J Le Goff, *The Birth of Europe* (Malden MA: Blackwell, 2005. Similarly, Taylor notes how the humanist elements of Western Christianity were responsible to a significant degree for the secularization of Western societies: C Taylor, *A Secular Age* (Cambridge, MA: Harvard University Press, 2007). As Esposito notes, the notion of religion as primarily a system of personal beliefs rather than a

4. The Pluralist Public Morality of EU Law

The recognition of religious perspectives within EU law is not restricted to institutional and symbolic roles. In contrast to libertarian views of the relationship between law and morality, which stress the idea of morality as a largely private matter and see the promotion of communal moral standards by the law as legitimate only when necessary to prevent harm to others,[79] EU law does permit the promotion of certain communal, moral, or cultural norms through law, provided that such promotion can be reconciled with the balance between religious, humanist, and cultural elements underpinning the Union's public order and, in particular, its commitments to individual autonomy and equality reflected in the Charter of Fundamental Rights. Thus, the right of Member States to promote a particular way of life or view of the good life through law is, within certain boundaries, recognized by EU law. Indeed, as is shown below, the Union has repeatedly and explicitly recognized notions of 'morality', 'ordre public', and 'public policy' as valid grounds for legislation.[80] Given its explicit recognition as part of the Union's constitutional values in the Lisbon Treaty and in light of its heavy influence over national cultures and views of morality, religion plays an important part in these notions of public policy and morality. Thus, while the public morality is not explicitly or exclusively religious, as Davies notes, in relation to issues such as sexual morality, bioethics, gambling, or alcohol consumption, people's views 'do derive directly or indirectly—via modern secular philosophies that have been influenced by religion—from religious values that pervade societies'.[81] Thus, he argues that morality clauses in trade law both 'have a clear and traditional link with conventional interpretations of major religions'[82] and facilitate the recognition of such religious perspectives in trade agreements. The same is true of the morality clauses in EU law, which enable Member States, notwithstanding their EU law duties, to promote particular communal cultural or religious norms. For instance, in assessing the compatibility with EU law of Member State restrictions on gambling in the *Schindler* case, the European Court of Justice stated

---

comprehensive phenomenon 'integral to politics and society' is both 'modern and Western in origins': J Esposito, *The Islamic Threat: Myth or Reality* (Oxford: Oxford University Press, 2002) 199.

[79] EP Foley, *Liberty for All: Reclaiming Individual Privacy in a New Era of Public Morality* (New Haven, CT: Yale University Press, 2006).   [80] See below.

[81] G Davie, 'Morality Clauses and Decision Making in Situations of Scientific Uncertainty: the Case of GMOs' (2007) 6(2) *World Trade Review* 249, 262.   [82] Ibid.

that it was 'not possible to disregard the moral, religious or cultural aspects of lotteries, like other types of gambling in Member States',[83] which were held to grant the Member State in question a 'degree of latitude' entitling it to restrict gambling notwithstanding the EU law duty to respect the freedom to provide services.[84] The Treaty also makes room for Member States to derogate from EU legal duties in order to promote certain communal cultural, religious, or moral norms. Articles 30 and 55 recognize 'public morality'[85] and 'public policy'[86] as legitimate grounds for the derogation from the duty of Member States to permit the free movement of goods and services.

Not only is religion recognized as a basis for derogation from EU law duties, it is also a valid element of EU legislation itself. Community legislation repeatedly refers to notions of ordre public or morality. In *Netherlands v Council*[87] Advocate-General Jacobs cited several examples of the recognition of notions of morality in EU legislation, noting that:

The Community Trade Mark Regulation[88] and the Trade Marks Directive[89] both provide for the refusal of registration or invalidity of a mark which is contrary to public policy or to accepted principles of morality (contraire à l'ordre public ou aux bonnes mœurs).[90] The Community Plant Variety Rights Regulation[91] provides that there is an impediment to the designation of a variety denomination where it is liable to give offence in one of the Member States or is contrary to public policy (est susceptible de contrevenir aux bonnes mœurs dans un des États membres ou est contraire à l'ordre public).[92] Directive 98/71 on the legal protection of designs[93]

---

[83]   Case C-275/92 *Her Majesty's Customs and Excise v Schindler* [1994] ECR I-1039 para 60.

[84]   Ibid para 61.

[85]   Article 30 provides that: 'The provisions of Articles 28 and 29 shall not preclude prohibitions or restrictions on imports, exports or goods in transit justified on grounds of public morality, public policy or public security; the protection of health and life of humans, animals or plants; the protection of national treasures possessing artistic, historic or archaeological value; or the protection of industrial and commercial property. Such prohibitions or restrictions shall not, however, constitute a means of arbitrary discrimination or a disguised restriction on trade between Member States.'   [86]   Lisbon Treaty, Art 55.

[87]   Case C-377/98 *Netherlands v Council* [2001] ECR I-7079 para 96.

[88]   Council Regulation (EC) No 40/94 of 20 December 1993 on the Community trade mark [1994] OJ L11/1.

[89]   Council Directive (EC) 89/104 to approximate the laws of the Member States relating to trade marks [1989] OJ L40/1.

[90]   Article 7(1)(f) of the Regulation and Art 3(1)(f) of the Directive. It may be noted that in his opinion delivered on 23 January 2001 in Case C-299/99 *Philips Electronics* [2002] ECR I-5475 para 18, Advocate-General Ruiz-Jarabo Colomer gave as an example of a trade mark registration which would be barred because it was contrary to public policy the mark 'Babykiller' for a pharmaceutical abortifacient.   [91]   [1994] OJ L227/1

[92]   Article 63(3)(e).   [93]   Council Directive (EC) 98/71 [1998] OJ L289/28.

provides that a design right shall not subsist in a design which is contrary to public policy or to accepted principles of morality (contraire à l'ordre public ou à la moralité publique).[94] The amended proposal for a European Parliament and Council Directive approximating the legal arrangements for the protection of inventions by utility model[95] provides that utility models shall not be granted in respect of inventions the exploitation of which would be contrary to public policy or morality (contraire à l'ordre public ou aux bonnes mœurs).[96]

Thus, 'public morality' and, therefore, religion, is well-recognized as a permissible basis for legal and policy choices in Community law and as a permissible basis for Member States to derogate from the EU law duties. Individual autonomy is an important principle in the EU legal order and the Union requires that the accommodation of religious influence over law, and the promotion of communal moral standards that this may involve, not be such as to unduly curtail such autonomy.[97] Nevertheless, as the acceptance of restrictions on gambling in *Schindler* on the basis of its particular 'moral, religious or cultural aspects' shows, the Court of Justice accepts that EU law does, in certain circumstances, permit such moral notions to be invoked to restrict the autonomy of individuals to engage in activities regarded as damaging or sinful for cultural or religious reasons in order to allow Member States to promote their own collective vision of the good life and morality. Thus, although the Union has consistently required that the autonomy of public sphere institutions to legislate for that which contravenes religious morality be respected,[98] it does permit some restriction of individual autonomy in the private sphere on religious grounds.

EU public morality is also inherently pluralist in that it encompasses a shared European, and differing national, ethical frameworks. This pluralism is further reflected in the Union's acceptance that most ethical choices are to be taken at national level and upheld as part of EU law, provided they are compatible within the broad parameters of an independent European public morality.[99] These aspects of EU public morality were seen in the *Schindler* case, where the Court of Justice recognized that particular national religious

---

[94] Article 8.   [95] [2000] OJ C248E/56.   [96] Article 4(a).   [97] See Ch 6.
[98] Ibid.

[99] For a discussion of constitutional pluralism and the development of heterarchic rather than hierarchical interaction of legal orders, see N Walker, 'The Idea of Constitutional Pluralism', EUI Working Papers, Law 2002/1, available at <http://cadmus.iue.it/dspace/bitstream/1814/179/1/law02-1.pdf> (last visited 12 May 2010).

and cultural notions of morality in relation to gambling were a valid basis for the restriction of the freedom to provide gambling services.[100]

This focus on the recognition within EU law of the individual public moralities of the Member States and the consequent prioritization of Member State ethical choices is shown even more markedly in cases such as *Grogan*[101] and *Jany*.[102] In these cases the Court of Justice was faced with differing Member State regulation of the morally and religiously sensitive issues of abortion and prostitution. In *Grogan* the combination of differing moral judgments of Ireland and other Member States in relation to abortion and the EU law principle of free movement of services threatened to undermine the ability of the Irish authorities to give effect to that moral judgment in a domestic context. In this case, student groups facing prosecution for distributing, in violation of the Irish Constitution's protection of the life of the unborn, information in relation to abortion services in other Member States, argued that such restrictions violated the freedom to provide services under EU law. The Court found that the lack of commercial links between the student organizations and the abortion providers in question precluded the invocation of Community law. Nevertheless, its judgment threw significant light on the pluralistic nature of public morality within EU law. The Society for the Protection of Unborn Children (SPUC) had argued that abortion should not be recognized as a service under EU law on grounds of what they saw as its grossly immoral nature. The Court's decision on this point was as follows:

Whatever the merits of those arguments on the moral plane, they cannot influence the answer to the national court's first question. It is not for the Court to substitute its assessment for that of the legislature in those Member States where the activities in question are practised legally.[103]

The Court therefore explicitly refused to come to a 'one size fits all' conclusion in relation to the morality of abortion in EU law and stated that it would not second guess the decision of the legislatures of Member States in which abortion was legally acceptable. On the other hand, although its decision in relation to the lack of commercial links meant that the Court did not address the issue of the curtailment of the freedom to provide services on the basis of the differing moral choice of the Irish authorities, this issue

---

[100] Case C-275/92 *Her Majesty's Customs and Excise v Schindler* [1994] ECR I-01039.
[101] Case C-159/90 *SPUC v Grogan* [1991] ECR I-4685.
[102] Case C-268/99 *Jany and others v Staatssecretaris van Justitie* [2001] ECR I-8615.
[103] Case C-159/90 *SPUC v Grogan* [1991] ECR I-4685 paras 19, 20.

was dealt with by Advocate-General Van Gerven in his opinion. Having concluded that the provision of information in relation to abortion services in other Member States was covered by the principle of free movement of services, he held that restriction of such information was permissible on the basis that Ireland's anti-abortion laws represented 'a policy choice of a moral and philosophical nature the assessment of which is a matter for the Member States and in respect of which they are entitled to invoke the ground of public policy'.[104] As this moral choice in relation to abortion was, in the view of the Member State, 'a genuinely and sufficiently serious threat to public policy affecting one of the fundamental interests of society'[105] and in the light of 'the area of discretion within the limits imposed by the Treaty'[106] which Community law provided to national authorities, Advocate-General Van Gerven was prepared to uphold the restriction in question as a proportionate derogation from the free movement of services on grounds of public policy.[107]

Thus, in deciding what would qualify as a service for the purposes of EU law, the Court indicated that it would respect the moral pluralism of the Union by refusing to second guess the decision of those Member States in which abortion was acceptable. On the other hand, in relation to the impact that the decision of certain Member States to tolerate abortion and its consequent recognition as a service under Community law could have on the enforcement within Ireland of anti-abortion laws, EU law, according to Advocate-General Van Gerven, was equally willing to recognize a public morality derogation by the Irish authorities from freedom of movement of services in order to uphold Ireland's different moral conclusions in relation to this issue.

A similar commitment to the value of pluralism and a consequent desire to enable the notion of public morality within Community law to accommodate differing moral perspectives of Member States, was seen in *Jany*, where the Court assessed whether prostitution could be categorized as a service under Community law and again based its affirmative decision on the basis that:

[s]o far as concerns [sic] the question of the immorality of that activity, raised by the referring court, it must be borne in mind that, as the Court has already held, it is not for the Court to substitute its own assessment for that of the legislatures of the Member States where an allegedly immoral activity is practised legally.[108]

---

[104] Ibid para 26 (AGO).   [105] Ibid.   [106] Ibid.   [107] Ibid para 29.
[108]   Case C-268/99 *Jany and others v Staatssecretaris van Justitie* [2001] ECR I-8615 para 56.

The approach of the Court in *Grogan* and *Jany* underlines the importance of pluralism in the public morality of the EU. In both cases the Court stressed that the primary forum within which the ethical choices that influence the content of the public morality recognized and operationalized within EU law, is the individual Member States, which are permitted to come to differing moral conclusions in relation to issues and to have these differing conclusions reflected in EU law. The deference to Member State ethical and cultural choices inherent in this endorsement of pluralism was further noted by the French Conseil constitutionnel in its 2004 decision in relation to the constitutionality of the Constitutional Treaty where, in discussing the compatibility of the French approach to secularism with EU human rights norms, it noted the 'considerable leeway' granted to Member States 'to define the most appropriate measures, taking into account their national traditions'.[109]

However, the Union's commitment to proper balance between religious an humanist influences requires limitations on 'value pluralism' within its public order. The commitment to pluralism can, in fact, cut both ways. Just as EU law is required to respect the principle of pluralism by accommodating divergent Member State moral choices, the moral choices of Member States themselves must respect the moral pluralism inherent in the notion of free movement guaranteed by Community law. Free movement rights enable individuals to place themselves under differing ethical regimes and therefore permit them to carry out activities that may be prohibited for reasons of public morality in their home country. EU law requires that Member State laws that reflect particular moral choices must be compatible with the right of individuals to choose, by means of free movement rights, to be bound by the moral choices of other Member States. Such a right can contribute significantly to individual autonomy by enabling, for example, those who wish to provide or use the services of prostitutes, to do so in another Member State despite the prohibition on doing so in their own country. The right to move across European borders is a fundamental right under EU law, whose violation is particularly likely to be characterized as disproportionate. The requirement of respect for the moral pluralism engendered by free movement rights can therefore be said to be a feature of the European element

---

[109] Decision No 2004-505 DC of 19 November 2004, Treaty establishing a Constitution for Europe, para 18, available at <http://www.conseil-constitutionnel.fr/conseil-constitutionnel/francais/les-decisions/acces-par-date/decisions-depuis-1959/2004/2004-505-dc/decision-n-2004-505-dc-du-19-novembre-2004.888.html> (last visited 26 May 2010).

of the EU's public morality. Thus, the plural nature of EU public morality, which finds its expression in the reflection of Member State moral choices in EU law, is itself restricted by the requirement of respect for the moral pluralism inherent in the free movement rights guaranteed by the Union.

This requirement that Member State public morality take account of the right of individuals to access different ethical regimes in other Member States was seen in Advocate-General Van Gerven's opinion in *Grogan* where, as noted above, he suggested that, while measures restricting abortion information were acceptable within EU law 'a ban on pregnant women going abroad or a rule under which they would be subjected to unsolicited examinations upon their return from abroad... would be disproportionate [and] would excessively impede the freedom to provide services'.[110]

Similarly, in *R v Human Fertilisation and Embryology Authority, ex p Blood*,[111] the UK Court of Appeal found, in a judgment that explicitly referred to the opinion in *Grogan*, that, in principle, EU law gives the right to receive medical treatment in another Member State and that moral choices in national law must take account of this right. In this case, a widow who was prevented from using her husband's sperm for the purposes of artificial insemination due to a requirement in British legislation that he must have given his written consent for its use, sought the right to bring the sperm to Belgium, which had no such requirement. The Court of Appeal held that the medical treatment in question was insemination with her husband's sperm rather than insemination in general, and consequently a refusal to permit the export of his sperm amounted to an interference with her EU law rights.[112] The judgment noted that, as the Court of Justice had held in *Schindler*, Member States had 'a sufficient degree of latitude to determine the moral or religious or ethical values which it regards as appropriate in its territory'.[113] Thus, provided that the interference in question was proportionate and justified by 'some imperative requirement in the public interest' EU law could 'not be relied upon as preventing [the British authorities] from imposing any restriction on the export of sperm'.[114] However, the UK's Human Fertilisation and Embryology Authority, which had taken the decision to refuse permission to remove the sperm to Belgium, had a degree of discretion under the relevant legislation and, in coming to its decision, was obliged to 'balance Mrs Blood's cross border rights as a Community citizen' against the UK's ethical

---

[110] Case C-159/90 *SPUC v Grogan* [1991] ECR I-4685 para 29.
[111] *R v Human Fertilisation and Embryology Authority, ex p Blood* [1997] 2 All ER 687.
[112] Ibid 698–700.   [113] Ibid 700.   [114] Ibid 701.

decision to 'attach great importance to consent, the quality of that consent and the certainty of it'.[115] Although the Court of Appeal was clear that it was 'not possible to say, even taking into account E.C. law that the authority are bound to come to a decision in Mrs Blood's favour', the failure to take her Community law rights into account and to 'provide reasons which meet the standards set by European law'[116] led to the quashing of the decision to prevent export.[117] Accordingly, the Court of Appeal recognized that the right of EU citizens to travel between Member States in order to be bound by the differing ethical choices of another Member State must be taken into account in relation to the implementation of British public morality-based policies. The UK authorities were therefore required to respect the pluralism inherent in the Single Market in deciding whether to countenance the removal of sperm from the United Kingdom in order that it be used according to Belgian norms for purposes the British authorities had held to be illegal on moral grounds.

This respect for the moral pluralism inherent in the notion of free movement and access for individuals to the differing ethical regimes of the Member States is also seen in cases such as *Jany* where, as noted above, the Court held that the status of prostitution as legal under Dutch law prevented the invocation of public morality as a reason to refuse the registration of Polish prostitutes as 'self-employed' for the purposes of the Pre-Accession Agreement. Issues of discrimination on grounds of nationality were clearly also an important factor in the decision; nevertheless, by ensuring that non-nationals could not be subjected to more rigorous standards than those imposed on nationals, the ruling also underlines the right of individuals under EU law to access, by means of free movement, the opportunity to be bound by the ethical decisions of another Member State.

The judgment in *Blood*, where the issue of moving between ethical frameworks was complicated by the impact on domestic moral choices over the issue of the export of sperm, made it clear that the right to access services in another Member State may not always override the right of individual Member States to enforce collective moral preferences. Nevertheless, Advocate-General Van Gerven's statement in *Grogan*, that attempts to prevent pregnant women from travelling to other Member States to have abortions would be unacceptable under EU law despite what he recognized as the grave importance of the moral principle that such a ban would be seeking to

---

[115] Ibid 702.   [116] Ibid 703.   [117] Ibid.

uphold,[118] indicates that the right to move between Member States is taken extremely seriously by EU law and represents a real limitation on the ability of Member States to legislate to enforce particular moral, religious, or cultural norms. Thus, the reflection by a particular Member State of communal religious norms in its legislation is required by EU law to take account of the overall pluralism inherent in the European project, which has opened up ethical horizons beyond the nation state to individual Europeans, thereby limiting the degree to which such communal moral norms can be imposed on individuals who have, under Community law, what Hirschman terms[119] the right of exit in addition to the voice with which domestic democratic structures provide them.

5. Limitations on Public Morality within EU Law

EU law does not merely require that Member State public morality choices respect the principle of pluralism. EU public morality is both national *and* European, and the requirements of this independent, European element of EU public morality can be such as to provide limitations on the reflection of Member State moral choices. Becoming and remaining a Member State of the European Union involves moral commitments to certain notions of the good that go beyond respect for pluralism and influence both the Union's public order and what that public order considers to constitute a proper balance between religious and humanist influences. These notions of the good have been linked by the Union to respect for fundamental rights and democracy. At least as a matter of politics, the duty to respect them applies to Member States even when they act outside the Union's areas of competence. The 1993 Copenhagen Criteria explicitly established respect for fundamental rights as an explicit criterion for membership of the Union.[120] The Nice and Lisbon Treaties also reiterated the Member States' 'attachment to the principles of liberty, democracy and respect for human rights and fundamental

---

[118] Case C-159/90 *SPUC v Grogan* [1991] ECR I-4685 (AGO).

[119] AO Hirschman, *Exit, Voice, and Loyalty: Responses to Decline in Firms, Organizations, and States* (Cambridge, MA: Harvard University Press, 1970).

[120] European Council in Copenhagen, 21–22 June 1993, 'Conclusions of the Presidency', SN 180/1/93 REV 1, available at <http://ue.eu.int/ueDocs/cms_Data/docs/pressdata/en/ec/72921 .pdf> (last visited 12 May 2010). The requirement that applicant states respect fundamental rights achieved recognition in the Amsterdam Treaty (TEU) in Art 6.

freedoms and of the rule of law'[121] and laid down in Article 7 respect for such principles as an ongoing duty of membership. This article envisaged the removal of voting rights from Member States which it stated was in 'serious and persistent breach' of this obligation.[122] Furthermore, the adoption of the Charter of Fundamental Rights has committed both the Union and the Member States to upholding, within the sphere of operation of EU law, a certain view of the good, albeit one that preserves a significant degree of latitude for Member States. This view does, however, encompass certain principles, such as privacy and equality, which embody notions of the good that preclude attempts to enshrine in law certain moral or religious notions inconsistent with such principles.

These duties have been used as a basis to restrict the ability of applicant states and Member States to use their legal systems to reflect religious and moral perspectives in a way that is inconsistent with notions of equality and individual autonomy, even in areas that lie outside of the scope of the Treaties. Romania and Turkey were required by the Union not to criminalize homosexuality and adultery respectively as conditions of membership,[123] while in 2005 Poland's newly elected Conservative Government was warned by the Commission that it risked losing voting rights in EU institutions if it failed to respect gay rights.[124]

These obligations are not merely political, and the European element of EU public morality can act as a legal limitation on the accommodation of Member State moral choices in EU law. Contrary to some readings of the judgments in *Grogan* and *Jany*,[125] the Court's conclusion that 'arguments on the moral plane cannot influence the answer' in relation to the status of abortion or prostitution as a service does not mean that EU law is merely a passive reflector of Member State public moralities. In addition to the political and legal commitments to fundamental rights, EU legislation includes numerous morality clauses such as those noted by Advocate-General Jacobs in *Netherlands v Council* (above). Not all of these clauses deal with the issue of Member State derogations on morality grounds, but refer to the notion of public morality within EU law, independent of the status of such notions at Member State level. Advocate-General Ruiz-Jarabo Colomer gave an example of the operation of the notion of morality within Community law in the *Phillips*

---

[121] Preamble to the TEU. See also the Preamble to the TFEU.

[122] Article 7 TEU as amended.   [123] See Ch 6, section 2.

[124] 'Polish President Warned over Ultra-Right Shift' The Independent, 25 October 2005, available at: http://www.independent.co.uk/news/world/europe/polish-president-warned-over-ultraright-shift-512413.html (last visited 26 May 2010).

[125] See DR Phelan, 'The Right to Life of the Unborn v the Promotion of Trade in Services' (1992) 55 MLR 670.

Electronics[126] case where he suggested by way of example that the registration of an abortifacient under the trade mark 'Babykiller' would be barred under Community law on the grounds that it would be contrary to public policy.[127]

In relation to derogations from EU law on the basis of Member State moral choices, the Court has repeatedly made it clear that the 'concept of public policy cannot be unilaterally decided by each Member State without being subject to control by the institutions of the Community'.[128] Thus, rather than demonstrating that EU law merely reflects and does not independently assess the moral nature of such derogations, cases like *Grogan* merely show that such assessments take very seriously the need to respect the inherent pluralism of the EU's public morality and also, therefore, the autonomy of Member States in moral matters. This reading of *Grogan* is supported by the fact that the jurisprudence of the Court has made it clear that it *will* assess Member State moral choices for compliance with the Community moral norms which make up a European element of the Union's public morality and may intervene when such moral choices are divergent to too great a degree from these Community moral norms. Such an approach has much in common with what Weiler has argued is the 'constitutional tolerance' of EU law, which recognizes that European integration does not involve a replacement of Member State national identity by the EU but does involve a degree of commitment to shared values which is necessary in order that Europeans are willing to be bound by the decisions of common European institutions in certain areas.[129] The Community morality that is an element of shared values, as will be shown below, is rather thin but does, in addition to the principle of pluralism discussed above, encompass the notion of proper balance between religious, cultural, and humanist elements reflected in requirements of respect for the idea of the individual as an autonomous and equal actor and for certain communal European norms, all of which are assessed in relation to the broad notion of the good reflected in the Union's commitments to fundamental rights.

5.1 Consistency with a Common Ethical Template

The case law of the European Court of Justice has suggested that Member State derogations from EU norms on grounds of public morality will

---

[126] Case C-299/99 *Koninklijke Philips Electronics NV v Remington Consumer Products Ltd* [2002] ECR I-5475 (AGO).   [127] Ibid para 18.
[128] See Case 30/77 *Bouchereau* [1977] ECR 1999 paras 33, 34.
[129] JHH Weiler, *The Constitution of Europe* (Cambridge: Cambridge University Press, 1999).

be accepted only where they in some way echo, or are congruent with, an independent set of EU moral norms. The limitation on Member State moral choices imposed in this regard requires that the moral choice in question fall within the broad definition of the good seen in the fundamental principles of EU law (most notably in relation to fundamental rights).

In *Omega Spielhallen*,[130] the Court explicitly looked to find echoes in the Union's legal order for the moral value relied upon by the German authorities in order to prohibit a game that was alleged to contravene public morality. Here, the provider of a game, which was alleged to allow players to simulate killing by shooting lasers at one another, challenged the action of the German authorities, which had prohibited the game on the grounds that it 'was contrary to fundamental values prevailing in public opinion',[131] in particular the respect for human dignity required by the German Constitution. The applicant alleged that the prohibition violated the freedom to provide services guaranteed by the EC Treaty. The German authorities argued that their actions were protected by the public policy and public morality exceptions recognized by EU law.

In assessing the German derogation, the Court recognized that Member States had a margin of discretion in relation to the concept of public policy and that the restrictive measures in question did not need 'to correspond to a conception shared by all Member States as regards the precise way in which the fundamental right or legitimate interest in question is to be protected'.[132] Nevertheless, the Court explicitly assessed whether the fundamental value invoked by the Member State was also reflected in the autonomous values of the Community legal order. In paragraphs 34 and 35 it held that:

the Community legal order undeniably strives to ensure respect for human dignity as a general principle of law. There can therefore be no doubt that the objective of protecting human dignity is compatible with Community law, it being immaterial in that respect that, in Germany, the principle of respect for human dignity has a particular status as an independent fundamental right.

Since both the Community and its Member-States are required to respect fundamental rights, the protection of those rights is a legitimate interest which, in principle, justifies a restriction of the obligations imposed by Community law.[133]

The conclusion that human dignity was a general principle of EU law was based on the analysis of Advocate-General Stix-Hackl, who noted in her

---

[130] Case C-36/02 *Omega Spielhallen* [2004] ECR I-9609. [131] Ibid para 7.
[132] Ibid para 37. [133] Ibid paras 34 and 35.

opinion that 'a variety of religious, philosophical and ideological reasoning could be given as the basis of this analysis',[134] before noting the recognition of the right in various international human rights treaties,[135] Member State constitutions,[136] directives and regulations,[137] and decisions of the Court of Justice.[138] In other words, the accommodation within EU law of the German public morality exception in respect of the dignity of the human being was dependent on the recognition of a similar moral value by the Community legal order, which, as the Court noted in paragraph 33 and in cases such as *Hauer*,[139] draws on, but is independent of, the common constitutional traditions of the Member States. This is in line with Advocate-General Stix-Hackl's conclusion that the assessment of Member State derogations on grounds of public morality includes review of 'appropriateness' in addition to proportionality.[140]

The notion of assessing the 'appropriateness' of such derogations would seem to imply that national moral judgments are to be assessed for their compatibility with an independent set of standards within EU law. Indeed, in the case of *Netherlands v Council*,[141] which involved a challenge, *inter alia*, on public morality grounds, to the 1998 Biotechnology Directive, Advocate-General Jacobs implied that the scope of common EU morality may evolve and come to cover an increasingly broad range of areas, arguing, in relation to Member State morality derogations in the area of biotechnology, that:

the discretion of a Member State to determine the scope of the concept of public morality in accordance with its own scale of values, so defined by the Court more that 20 years ago, should perhaps now be read with some caution. In this area, as in many others, common standards evolve over the years. It may be that the ethical dimension of some of the basic issues within the scope of the Directive is now more appropriately regarded as governed by common standards.[142]

The progressive embrace by the Union of shared fundamental values as an element of its identity and legal order may therefore be increasing the degree to which that legal order reflects and upholds an independent framework of moral values. This potentially limits the pluralism of the EU's public morality in that the emergence of common standards, on Advocate-General

---

[134] Ibid para 78 (AGO).   [135] Ibid para 82.   [136] Ibid para 83.   [137] Ibid para 87.
[138] Ibid paras 88, 89, 90.
[139] Case 44/79 *Hauer v Land Rheinland-Pfalz* (unreported) 13 December 1979.
[140] Case C-36/02 *Omega Spielhallen* [2004] ECR I-9609 para 103 (AGO).
[141] Case C-377/98 *Netherlands v Council* [2001] ECR I-7079.   [142] Ibid para 102 (AGO).

Jacobs' analysis, results in the restriction of the discretion of Member States to pursue approaches that differ from such standards.

The development of the fundamental rights obligations of the Union has had a notable impact in this regard. In the *ERT*[143] case it was held that all Member State derogations from EU law duties (including those based on public morality) are subject to compliance with the common commitment of all Members States Union to comply with fundamental rights obligations. Furthermore, given their fundamental status in the ethical and legal order of the Union, the fundamental rights recognized by EU law must have a major impact on the content of EU public morality as well as on the limitations imposed on the reflection of the public moralities of individual states within the Union's legal order. This analysis is further underlined by the fact that in *Omega*, the inquiry into the legitimacy of a derogation from the freedom to provide services on the basis of the need to protect human dignity was regarded by both the Court and Advocate-General as conclusively resolved (although issues of proportionality remained outstanding) by the identification of this principle as one of the general principles of law protected by the Community legal order.[144] In other words, once the protection of human dignity had been categorized as part of the general principles of law through which fundamental rights are protected within EU law, a derogation based thereon was in principle acceptable and no further identification of the source or broader significance of the relevant principle was required.

The reflection of Member State moral choices in the public morality of the EU is therefore dependent on the compatibility of such moral choices with the Union's fundamental rights obligations and general principles of law, which are now given expression in the Union's Charter of Fundamental Rights, which itself acts to 'reaffirm' the fundamental rights resulting from the common constitutional traditions of the Member States. As Foley has suggested, all constitutions depend on a failure to definitively resolve certain fraught issues and contain unwritten, tacit 'abeyances' that enable such constitutions to survive by fulfilling the need for 'protective obscurity' around certain issues.[145] In line with this approach and in common with the Lisbon Treaty, the Charter of Fundamental Rights does not explicitly identify itself with any particular religious worldview. Neither does it claim that the rights it contains derive from any particular religious tradition or

[143] Case C-260/89 *ERT* [1991] ECR I-2925.
[144] Case C-36/02 *Omega Spielhallen* [2004] ECR I-9609.
[145] M Foley, *The Silence of Constitutions* (London: Routledge, 1989) 81.

divine authority. This, as Weiler notes,[146] is in contrast to the constitutions of several EU Member States, which specifically invoke either God or the Christian Trinity or which recognize a particular religion as underpinning their constitutional order.[147] However, the Charter does invoke Europe's 'spiritual and moral heritage'[148] and undertakes to respect 'the diversity of the cultures and traditions of the peoples of Europe as well as the national identities of the Member States'.[149]

Thus, the rights contained in the Charter are seen as emerging from a particular religious and moral heritage which, as noted above, has been markedly affected by Christian and humanist influences. The interpretation of these rights is, therefore, likely to reflect and accommodate established European ways of life and to prove less challenging to the ambitions and public role of culturally entrenched religions or religions that can reconcile themselves to humanist influences than to religions that lack such characteristics. Indeed, the influence of humanist principles is clearly seen in the Preamble to the Charter, which speaks of 'universal values of human dignity, freedom, equality and solidarity' and of the Union's commitment to place 'the individual at the heart of its activities'. The importance of the individual human as an equal and autonomous agent is also recognized in Articles 3, 5, 6, 7, 11, and 21, which protect the rights to bodily integrity, liberty of the person, freedom from slavery, privacy, freedom of expression, and equality.[150] On the other hand, the Charter also recognizes religion and religious freedom as another 'good', while the Preamble to, and Article 17 of, the Lisbon Treaty specifically endorse the notion of at least some religious influence over law. Furthermore, the national cultures and identities which the Charter undertakes to respect may themselves involve the promotion of religiously influenced communal moral standards. Thus, the notion of the good with which Member State moral choices must be compatible is broad and offers significant scope for the maintenance of the pluralism of EU public morality. The Court of Justice has not identified any overarching worldview within which its general principles and defence of human rights are based and thus has not required Member State public moralities to fall in line with any such worldview. Indeed, as Habermas notes, '[t]he acknowledgement of differences—the reciprocal acknowledgment of the Other in his otherness—can also be a feature of a common

---

[146] Weiler (n 26 above).   [147] See Ch 2.
[148] Charter of Fundamental Rights of the European Union [2007] OJ C303/01, Preamble.
[149] Ibid.   [150] These values are, of course, shared by many religious traditions.

identity'.[151] Nevertheless, although the Union does grant a significant degree of leeway to Member States in relation to questions of public morality, and although doubts have been expressed about the ability of Europeans to agree on common values,[152] within the European Union, as in any sustainable political community, there must be forms of 'otherness' that are not acceptable. The vast majority of Europeans would, for instance, surely reject the accession to the Union of a state committed to the annihilation of the Jewish race or to theocracy and the subjugation of women. There are therefore some common basic values to which all Member States of the Union must be committed. These values operate so as to place limits on the accommodation of Member State choices in matters of public morality within EU law.

5.2 *The Importance of Balance*

Despite the relatively broad and flexible nature of the ethical template set out in the EU's Charter of Fundamental Rights, there are aspects of the Union's approach that can potentially restrict Member State autonomy in moral and religious matters. Indeed, the very pluralism that is the source of Member State autonomy in moral matters itself operates so as to restrict this autonomy. EU public morality is characterized by a commitment to balancing what are seen as the potentially conflicting 'goods' of Europe's religious, humanist, and cultural inheritance. EU law requires that Member States respect this element of European public morality and that, in seeking to promote their own versions of public morality, they respect this notion of balance and do not accord absolute priority to any single element. The notion of balance between conflicting goods has been a central concern of the jurisprudence of the Court of Justice. In contrast to the more absolutist approach adopted by US constitutional law, in relation to matters such as freedom of speech, EU law has tended to seek to balance conflicting rights. MacCormick and others have noted how, when faced with clashes of two 'goods',[153] the Court has not sought to establish a 'hierarchical structure among these values' but instead its decisions 'are a matter of weighing and balancing'.[154]

---

[151] J Habermas and J Derrida, 'February 15, or What Binds Europeans Together: A Plea for a Common Foreign Policy, Beginning in the Core of Europe' (2003) 10(3) *Constellations* 291, 294.

[152] R Bellamy and D Castiglione, 'Lacroix's European Constitutional Patriotism: Response' (2004) 52 *Political Studies* 187.

[153] Bengoetxea, MacCormick, and Moral Soriano (n 35 above). In this instance the authors were discussing the clash between the goals of market freedoms and environmental protection.

[154] Ibid 65.

The Court has followed the same approach in relation to fundamental rights. In *Promusciae* the Court assessed the implementation of EU copyright legislation by Spain in the light of a request by an organization representing the owners of intellectual property rights to an internet provider to disclose the identities of internet users who had violated such rights using file-sharing software. It held that:

> the Member States must, *when transposing the directives mentioned above, take care to rely on an interpretation of the directives which allows fair balance to be struck between the various fundamental rights protected by the Community legal order.* Further, when implementing the measures transposing those directives, the authorities and courts of the Member States must not only interpret their national law in a manner consistent with those directives *but also make sure that they do not rely on an interpretation of them which would be in conflict with those fundamental rights or with other general principles of Community* law such as the principle of proportionality.[155] (emphasis added)

Thus, faced with a clash between the 'goods' of privacy and property rights, the Court did not assign priority to one over the other but required that the Member State in question strike a 'fair balance' between them.

MacCormick *et al.* note that an approach centred on balancing reflects a 'value pluralism' where 'values and principles cannot be reduced to a single value or coherent set of values, nor should conflicts between reasons be interpreted as a sign of imperfection, but rather as the normal state for human beings'.[156] The Court's focus on notions of balance can be seen as reflecting the value pluralism of EU public morality in that it does not require uniform moral outcomes in each Member State but permits differing national conclusions in relation to moral issues provided that such conclusions respect the concept of 'fair balance'. This concept grants Member States a considerable degree of latitude and thereby may grant a degree of what Foley would term 'protective obscurity' to the EU legal order. On this view, EU law does not seek perfection or pursue a single outcome of the reconciliation of conflicting rights, but embraces the notion of pragmatic reconciliation of rights rather than according of priority to one set of rights over another. On the other hand, it is not correct to regard the Union's role as simply one of ensuring that balancing has taken place. Member States do not have the right to strike the balance between rights in any way they choose. Approaches that, for example, fail to give any or adequate weight to principles identified as

---

[155] Case C-275/06 *Promusicae v Telefónica de España SAU* (not yet reported) 29 January 2008 para 68.   [156] Bengoetxea, MacCormick, and Moral Soriano (n 35 above) 64.

'goods' by the Community legal order will fall foul of EU law. In fact, the Union's approach is one that is committed to the protection of particular rights and principles that cannot be set aside in certain circumstances, even when a degree of balancing has occurred. Indeed, if fundamental rights are to have meaningful content there must be circumstances in which a particular right cannot be set aside, even when balancing is said to be taking place. The right to be free from torture, for example, cannot simply be balanced against other rights but must, in almost all circumstances, take absolute priority over other rights. Similarly, rulings of the European Court of Human Rights make it clear that idea of a *fair* balance means that in some balancing exercises, for example in relation to the clash between private sexual autonomy and the promotion of public morality, one of the rights must be accorded priority.[157] Certainly, the extensiveness of such rights and the range of circumstances in which these rights will be accorded priority over other goals under EU law may be circumscribed by the Union's commitments to pluralism and to respect for Member State autonomy, but that will not prevent the Union from requiring that priority be accorded to a particular right in particular circumstances.

The fact that, as is shown below, the Union is committed to protecting certain rights to a degree that goes beyond mere verification that balancing has taken place, has the potential to significantly impact upon what is thought to be a proper balance between religious and humanist influences within EU law. Given that religion, the protection of national culture and identity, and the rights to individual autonomy and equality (which can be threatened by the imposition of communal religious or cultural standards) have been identified as 'goods' by Community law, Member States must ensure that the moral choices they make which impinge on these goods do not fail to respect the duty of maintaining a proper balance between these goods that respects the Union's fundamental rights norms. This commitment to a balance between religious, cultural, and humanist influences is seen in EU anti-discrimination legislation, which attempts to balance the institutional rights of religious bodies and the cultural role of religious institutions in many Member States with the right of individuals to privacy and equal treatment.[158] A concern that a failure to maintain such a balance between these elements could invite the intervention of EU law was seen in relation to the concerns in France that the incorporation of the Charter of Fundamental Rights into the

[157] See *Norris v Ireland* (1991) 13 EHRR 186.
[158] See Ch 5, in particular sections 2 and 3.

Constitutional Treaty might, due to its commitments to religious freedom, compromise France's strictly secular approach to the wearing of religious clothing in schools. This was referred to by the Conseil constitutionnel in its decision on the Constitutional Treaty[159] in which it held that the French approach to this issue was not imperilled by the Treaty. It concluded that the French approach was characterized by a degree of balance between the competing goods of religion, the secular identity of the French state, and the protection of individual rights inherent in this secularist approach. The Conseil held that the relevant French laws had 'reconcile[d] the principle of freedom of religion and that of secularism'[160] and that, since the Court of Human Rights had given individual states 'considerable leeway to define the most appropriate measures, taking into account their national traditions',[161] the French approach was not endangered by the Constitutional Treaty's recognition of the Charter of Fundamental Rights. Thus, the Conseil did not simply conclude that Member States had sufficient cultural autonomy to define an approach to these issues without European interference, but that the French approach, in the light of both the considerable autonomy retained by Member States in this area *and* the fact that it balanced the relevant rights in a way that gave adequate protection to freedom of religion, would not violate any European right.

5.3 'Fair Balance' and the Autonomy and Equality of the Individual

Although an approach that leaves it to Member States to strike a fair or proper balance between rights grants significant leeway to national authorities, the notion of what is 'fair' or 'proper' is influenced by certain fundamental, shared European norms that restrict Member State autonomy in this area. Legislation, on the part of either the Union or it Member States, which seeks to promote notions of public morality, is required to respect certain key principles such as coherence, proportionality, and non-discrimination, which are centred on the strong tradition of individual liberty within Western liberal thought. Thus, while a margin of discretion in relation to public policy is provided by the willingness of the Court to permit public policy derogations to be assessed 'in accordance with [a Member State's] own scale of values and in the form selected by it',[162] the Court has repeatedly affirmed that, as Advocate-General Van Gerven stated in *Grogan*, this

---

[159] Decision No 2004-505 (n 109 above).   [160] Ibid para h 18.   [161] Ibid.
[162] Case 121/85 *Conegate Limited v HM Customs and Excise* [1986] ECR 1007.

margin of discretion is subject to 'the limits set by Community law,' which includes a proportionality test requiring that the derogation 'be justified by some imperative requirement in the general interest, ... be suitable for securing the attainment of the objects which it pursues and...must not go beyond what is necessary to attain that objective'.[163]

Member State morality-based derogations that are held by the Court to interfere in a disproportionate way with Community law rights will, therefore, not be accepted in EU law. Advocate-General Van Gerven, for example, suggested in *Grogan* that a ban on pregnant women travelling, or mandatory pregnancy tests on women on departure from or return to Ireland, would fail this test.[164]

The Court has also been clear that derogations based on the need to promote public morality must also respect the principle of non-discrimination between nationals and citizens of other Member States. In both *Jany*[165] and *Adoui and Cornouaille*[166] the Court refused to accept attempts to curtail, on grounds of public morality, the Community law rights of non-national prostitutes to work in Member States on the basis that:

Although Community law does not impose on Member States a uniform scale of values as regards the assessment of conduct which may be considered to be contrary to public policy, conduct may not be considered to be of a sufficiently serious nature to justify restrictions on entry to, or residence within, the territory of a Member State of a national of another Member State where the former Member State does not adopt, with respect to the same conduct on the part of its own nationals, repressive measures or other genuine and effective measures intended to combat such conduct.[167]

As discussed above, this principle is also linked to the moral pluralism inherent in the European project which confers on those individuals with the abilities, resources and skills to do so, the right to choose, by exercising freedom of movement, to be bound by the ethical choices of different Member States. In addition, it is connected to the broader requirement that Member State derogations be coherent and internally consistent in order to achieve acceptance within EU law. This was seen most notably in the *Conegate*[168] case,

---

[163] As summarised in *R v Human Fertilisation and Embryology Authority, ex p Blood* [1997] 2 All ER 687, 700. [164] Case C-159/90 *SPUC v Grogan* [1991] ECR I-4685 para 29.

[165] Case C-268/99 *Jany and others v Staatssecretaris van Justitie* [2001] ECR I-8615.

[166] Joined Cases 115 and 116/81 *Adoui and Cornouaille v Belgian State* [1982] ECR 1665.

[167] Ibid para 60.

[168] Case 121/85 *Conegate Limited v HM Customs and Excise* [1986] ECR 1007.

where a challenge was brought to the refusal of the British authorities to permit the import of certain pornographic items on the basis that domestic law
permitted their domestic manufacture and sale (subject to a ban on sending
them through the post). The Court upheld the challenge on the basis that '[a]
Member State may not rely on grounds of public morality in order to prohibit
the importation of goods from other Member States when its legislation contains no prohibition on the manufacture or marketing of the same goods on
its territory'.[169] It further stated that '[i]t must at least be possible to conclude
from the applicable rules, taken as a whole that their purpose is, in substance,
to prohibit the manufacture and marketing of those products'.[170]

The decision in *Conegate* clearly has much in common with the approach
adopted in *Jany* and *Adoui and Cornouaille*, which precluded the imposition of
stricter moral standards on outsiders than on a Member State's own nationals. However, as the above paragraph shows, it also underlines a second aspect
of the approach of EU law to public morality in that the Court made it clear
that Member State derogations on grounds of public morality would also
be assessed for their internal coherence and that measures which failed to
indicate the requisite degree of coherence would not be accepted in EU law.
The importance attached by the Court to the coherence of Member State
morality derogations reflects Fuller's notion of the 'internal morality' of law,
which requires that laws be sufficiently general, intelligible, and free of contradictions.[171] As MacCormick and others have pointed out, the notion of
coherence has been an important element in the jurisprudence of the Court
of Justice and derives from 'the idea crucial to the rule of law that the different parts of the whole legal order should hang together and make sense
as a whole',[172] or, at the very least, should not actively contradict each other.
Such ideas are central to the principle of the rule of law, which the Union
has explicitly embraced as part of the Copenhagen Criteria setting out the
prerequisites of membership,[173] and as one of the EU's fundamental constitutional values, which finds expression in general terms in the Preamble to

---

[169]   Ibid para 16.   [170]   Ibid para 17.

[171]   L Fuller, *The Morality of Law* (New Haven: Yale University Press, 1969).

[172]   Bengoetxea, MacCormick, and Moral Soriano (n 35 above) 47.

[173]   The Copenhagen Criteria provide that: 'Membership requires that candidate country has
achieved stability of institutions guaranteeing democracy, the rule of law, human rights and
respect for and, protection of minorities, the existence of a functioning market economy as
well as the capacity to cope with competitive pressure and market forces within the Union'.
See European Council in Copenhagen, 21–22 June 1993, Conclusions of the Presidency, SN
180/1/93 REV 1, available at <http://ue.eu.int/ueDocs/cms_Data/docs/pressdata/en/ec/72921
.pdf> (last visited 13 May 2010).

the Charter of Fundamental Rights, as well as more concrete expression in the prohibition of retroactive or extra legal punishment in Article 49(1).

These requirements establish a broad framework that is centred on individual liberty. The Union's approach implicitly distinguishes between law and morality, regards individual freedom to act as the default position, and requires that all curtailments of such freedom be coherent and as narrowly tailored as possible. These notions of the centrality of individual autonomy and the view of morality as a largely private matter whose enforcement by law must be limited and specifically justified have a long history in Western liberal thought but have been less influential in other contexts, most notably in largely Muslim societies.[174] Combined with the emphasis placed on non-discrimination in *Jany*, *Conegate*, and *Adoui*, the requirements of coherence and proportionality underline the importance placed by the EU legal order on respect for the idea of the individual as an equal and autonomous actor whose ability to take decisions and plan his or her own life must be respected. Thus, the promotion of public morality by law places significant emphasis on the principle of individual liberty against which the promotion of communal moral standards must be balanced. Member State approaches that fail to give adequate weight to this principle will not satisfy the requirement of proper balance imposed by the Union.

5.4 Public Morality and Perspectives Contrary to Common European Norms

Such an approach is likely to prove less challenging for religions that have reconciled themselves to the emphasis placed on human autonomy within Western societies. Indeed, the importance attached to individual autonomy by EU law can be seen as merely indicative of a wider point, namely that certain norms, which for cultural and historical reasons have come to be widely shared in Europe, influence the kind of moral goals that can validly be pursued by legislative means under EU law. As Advocate-General Jacobs' point in relation to the restriction of Member State autonomy in moral matters through the emergence of common European standards,[175] and the notion of assessing the 'appropriateness' of the moral goal pursued by the Member

---

[174] See T Gabriel, 'Is Islam against the West?' in R Geaves *et al.* (eds), *Islam and the West Post 9/11* (Aldershot: Ashgate, 2004) 15. See also P Norris and R Inglehart, *Sacred and Secular: Religion and Politics Worldwide* (Cambridge: Cambridge University Press, 2004).

[175] Case C-377/98 *Netherlands v Council* [2001] ECR I-7079.

State in question in *Omega*,[176] suggest, moral goals that run counter to the notion of the good reflected in the Charter which, as noted above, is broad but nevertheless affected by a common European inheritance of Christian, humanist, and cultural influences, are seen as illegitimate and unacceptable within EU law, even if balanced against other countervailing influences.

To take an example, the emergence of a common European norm of gender equality may operate so as to reduce the ability of Member States to make differing moral choices in this area. For instance, Article 41.2 of the Irish Constitution provides that:

1. In particular, the State recognises that by her life within the home, woman gives to the State a support without which the common good cannot be achieved.

2. The State shall, therefore, endeavour to ensure that mothers shall not be obliged by economic necessity to engage in labour to the neglect of their duties in the home.[177]

Article 41.2 could be seen as representing a deeply held, religiously influenced moral notion in relation to the upholding of differences between the sexes and the role of women and mothers in family life.[178] If the Irish authorities were to introduce legislation that discouraged mothers of young children from taking paid employment, such measures would fall foul of the principle of gender equality in the workplace enshrined in EU law. Even if the Irish Government could demonstrate that the measure in question was very limited and attempted to balance the rights of individuals to equal treatment against the religious and moral imperative to maintain traditional gender roles, it is difficult to imagine that such a choice could be categorized as, to use the language of Advocate-General Stix-Hackl in *Omega*, 'appropriate' by the Court in the light of the emphasis placed by Community law on gender equality in the workplace and the principle of equal treatment in general. Indeed, in *Kreil* the Court was willing to interfere with an explicit constitutional mandate in the extremely sensitive area of military policy when the policy in question violated the norm of gender equality.[179] On the other hand, where common standards have not yet emerged to the same degree, as, for example, is the case in relation to sexual orientation discrimination, compromises on the principle of equal treatment on the basis of respect for religious and cultural norms

---

[176] Case C-36/02 *Omega Spielhallen* [2004] ECR I-9609.

[177] Bunreacht na h-Éireann, Arts 41.2.1, 41.2.2.

[178] It should be noted that this article may not represent the majority view of the appropriate role of women in contemporary Ireland.

[179] Case C-285/98 *Kreil v Germany* [2000] ECR I-69.

have been accepted by EU law, most notably in relation to the Framework Directive, which has explicitly permitted discrimination in employment on grounds of sexual orientation in organizations that have a religious ethos, on the ground that the limited exemptions achieve a balance between the rights of religious bodies and those of individuals.[180]

Notions of religious morality that deviate from established European cultural norms are, of course, more likely to come into conflict with 'common standards'. Thus, notions of European public morality are, to a degree, linked to the promotion of a common European way or ways of life which are respectful of the balance between largely Christian religious influences and humanist influences that characterize much of European history, in addition to cultural norms such as gender equality that have emerged from this history. Therefore, common European norms around the mixing of the genders may prevent the recognition on public morality grounds of a Member State law that seeks to enforce in the workplace the separation of the genders, which is required by some forms of Islam. Similarly, it is interesting to consider how the Court of Justice would react to notions of morality deriving from religions such as Scientology, which have little cultural purchase in Europe. A law passed by a Member State at the instigation of Scientologists which, for instance, banned the practice of psychiatry (towards which the Church of Scientology is very hostile) and placed the kind of restrictions on the advertising of psychiatric services that Ireland had placed on abortion services in *Grogan*, would present the Court of Justice with the prospect of recognizing as part of European public morality a moral stance rejected by the overwhelming majority of Europeans.

Were such laws passed by the Union's own legislature there is, it is submitted, little likelihood that they would survive review by the Court. However, the pluralism of the EU's public morality means that when Member States seek to make such choices, difficulties arise. The Union's commitment to certain values means that it must place some limits on what can be accepted as part of the public morality recognized by EU law. Therefore, Member States are required to respect what the Union sees as a proper balance between rights and religious and humanist influences, not merely to balance them as they see fit. This places restrictions, albeit limited ones, on the Union's value pluralism. Notions of proportionality, coherence, and a duty to respect rights to move between countries do provide some limits.

[180] *R (Amicus and others) v Secretary of State for Trade and Industry* [2004] EWHC 860 (Admin).

However, the judgment in *Omega* and the importance placed by the Union on compliance with fundamental rights, particularly in the *ERT* judgment, means that certain religious and moral viewpoints that contradict the balance between religion and humanism inherent in the Union's public morality (seen particularly in its fundamental rights instruments) may simply not be capable of being accommodated by European public morality or, therefore, EU law. Indeed, such an approach is arguably implicit in Articles 6 and 7 TEU, which require Member States to uphold human rights and democracy on pain of loss of voting rights in the Council, and thereby stress the notion of EU membership as involving a commitment to a certain shared European notion of the good.

Therefore, if the Union is to be a 'Community of Values' and its commitments to fundamental rights and shared norms are to have any meaning, certain moral or religious goals that deviate from established European cultural norms or common standards will be held to be contrary to European public morality even before issues of balance or coherence arise. On this view, particular historical and cultural experiences, such as Europe's collective guilt in relation to the holocaust or its long experience of Christianity and humanism, will influence the Union's view of what can 'count' as valid religious or cultural aims in striking a balance between religious cultural and humanist influences.[181] From such a viewpoint, when the Court of Justice, as it did in *Omega*, investigates the appropriateness of a moral choice that a Member State is seeking to have recognized within EU law, or when the special contribution of religious bodies to policy formation is being sought by EU institutions, all forms of religious morality may, for cultural, historic, moral, or other reasons, not 'count' to the same degree in striking a fair balance between religious influences and humanist-influenced notions of individual autonomy. Rather, as in *Promusicae*, the Court will assess the balance only in relation to forms of religion whose influence *can* be balanced against humanist influences or established European cultural norms. Approaches which, like radical Islam, are radically opposed to key influences such as humanism or which, by promoting racist ideas, clash with the legacy of key cultural and historical experiences such as the holocaust simply will not be recognized as a valid contributor for the purposes of such balancing exercises.

---

[181] This is in line with Kumm's argument that European constitutional patriotism should be 'embedded in a historical narrative about how the European polity evolved to become what it is today': see M Kumm, 'The Idea of Thick Constitutional Patriotism and Its Implications for the Role and Structure of European Legal History' (2005) 6(2) *German Law Journal, Special Issue– Confronting Memories* 319.

Therefore, perhaps unsurprisingly, the reflection of religion in EU law by means of the recognition of public morality is likely to favour those forms of religion that can reconcile themselves to the balance between religious and humanist influences that has emerged from European history and characterizes much of European culture. As Taylor and Le Goff have pointed out, humanism's success in Europe occurred partly because of the humanistic elements of Europe's historically dominant religion—Christianity. As noted in section 2 above, it has been suggested that many of the fundamental values of the Union, such as democracy, equality, and individual autonomy, have roots in Christianity. Thus, it is not unreasonable to conclude that, given its enormous cultural influence and its links to humanism, mainstream Christianity may exercise a greater influence over European public morality (and thereby EU law) than other faiths. Nevertheless, the humanist influences over European culture, which gave rise to the secularization of Europe, have, despite their religious roots, served to limit religious influence over law and politics. This is particularly true in relation to what Casanova termed 'lifeworld' issues of family, sexuality, and the beginning and end of life in relation to which mainstream Christian denominations have continued to attempt to influence law so that it conforms to their moral teachings. Thus, even if liberal notions such as autonomy and equality can be seen as the offspring of Christianity, they represent rebellious 'offspring' which, as adults, have come to clash with their 'parents' in the legal and political arenas. The Union's commitment to balancing religious and humanist influences therefore restricts all religions, including those with deep roots in national and European culture.

6. Conclusion

The notions of pluralism, balance, and inheritance are key features of the recognition of religion as a basis of law in the EU public order. The legitimacy of religious input into law is recognized at a symbolic level through the recognition of religion as an element of the Union's constitutional values, at an institutional level in the recognition of religious bodies in the law-making process, and in substantive law through the recognition of religion as part of a public morality the Union and Member States may legislate to protect.

However, in all these three areas religion must share its role as an element of public morality with cultural and humanist influences. Although these elements can reinforce each other (as in the case of the Christian influence on Member State cultures) they can also be in conflict (as when humanism's stress on individual autonomy clashes with religious desires to promote communal morality). Thus, the overall public morality through which religion influences EU law is characterized by a balance between these religious, cultural, and humanist elements. These features are seen in relation to religion's institutional position, where the recognition of the special importance and contribution of religious institutions to law-making is balanced by the secularizing effect of providing recognition in the context of a pluralist civil society.

In relation to substantive EU law, religion exercises influence by means of morality clauses that allow both the Union and its Member States to promote communal moral standards by means of law. This EU public morality is pluralist in that it recognizes that the primary forum within which ethical choices are made is still the individual Member State, and therefore permits the recognition of differing national religious, cultural, and moral viewpoints within EU law. However, membership of the Union also involves certain moral commitments and a degree of common agreement around fundamental political and legal values. Thus, an autonomous EU public morality also restricts the degree to which particular moral choices of individual Member States can be reflected in EU law. These restrictions require that the ethical choices of Member States do not deviate from a common European element of EU public morality containing commitments to proportionality, coherence, free movement rights, and the notion of fair balance between competing values, all of which reflect, *inter alia*, a degree of respect for individual autonomy inherent in the commitment to balance religious, cultural, and humanist influences, which underpins the Union's public order.

Such an approach to public morality has, on one view, much in common with MacCormick's notion of the Union characterized by a legal pluralism, itself characterized by the interaction of legal systems.[182] Indeed, the analogy can extend to other areas of EU law such as freedom of movement, where it could be argued that, just as EU law requires national regulatory decisions to take into account the principle of free movement of goods, similarly it requires that national ethical choices take into account the moral commitments of EU membership embodied by the Union's public morality and

---

[182] N MacCormick, 'The Maastricht Urteil: Sovereignty Now' (1995) 1 *European Law Journal* 259, 264–265.

fundamental rights commitments. This is seen in the judgments in *Promusicae* and *Omega*, which indicate that Member States must take account of the various 'goods' and elements of public morality recognized by EU law in coming to their ethical decisions.

On the other hand, there are clear limits to value pluralism, as the commitment to balance is in reality a commitment to a 'fair' or 'proper' balance, which is assessed in the light of the fundamental values to which the Union is committed. Thus, institutional recognition of religion in the context of law-making and policy-making does not extend to the accommodation of religious truth claims in the legal and political arenas. Although the Union has adhered to a relatively strict formal neutrality in its dealings with religions, ideas of what constitute 'goods', the fundamental rights and values protected by the Union, and the notion of what constitutes a fair balance between competing rights, are all influenced by European culture and history. Indeed, the importance of Europe's ethical and religious 'inheritance' in the determination of the content of the public morality of the EU has been explicitly acknowledged in the Treaties. Combined with deference towards Member State cultural and moral autonomy and the promotion of the notion of balance between religious and humanist influences, the notion of respect for an ethical inheritance permits culturally entrenched Christian religions and those faiths that can reconcile themselves to the limitation on religious influence that respect for Europe's humanist tradition entails, to exercise greater influence over EU law. Nevertheless, the Union recognizes the complexity of the relationship between liberal democracy and religion in general, and provides limits to the public ambitions of all faiths, even those with strong humanist traditions and deep cultural roots in Europe. Thus, the notion of balance can be seen as attempting to reconcile religion's important role in communal identity with the protection of the religious neutrality of the political arena and of individual identity rights, including the right not to be forced to adhere to particular religiously inspired communal moral norms, both of which derive, in part, from the humanist elements of the Union's public order.

The Union's public order therefore upholds the broad outlines of the balance between religion and secular/humanist influences in Europe, and the cultural values and way of life to which this balance gives rise. Its approach is not absolutely religiously neutral. Indeed, given the disproportionate contribution of particular faiths to European culture it is hard to see how it could realistically be so. It more readily accommodates culturally entrenched faiths that play a strong role in communal cultural identities in Europe and that can reconcile themselves to the principle of balance between humanist and religious influences. Religions that do not exercise significant cultural influence in a Member State have significantly less influence within EU law. Furthermore, faiths that are opposed to certain shared European cultural norms or are anti-humanist are, at least implicitly, identified as in some ways contrary to the Union's public morality and notion of the good. On the other hand, religions such as mainstream Christian churches, which have deep cultural roots and a strong humanist tradition, exercise a greater influence over European public morality than other faiths. Nevertheless, although the strong humanist elements of European public morality, and the secular influences to which they gave rise, may owe something to Christian humanism, even mainstream Christian faiths have a complicated relationship with humanism, liberalism, and the secular state. The limitations imposed by the Union therefore also restrict the influence which all religions, including Christianity, can exercise over the law. Thus, the Union's approach is characterized by a complex and shifting balance between religious, cultural, and humanist influences. This balance is struck in a context of very significant, but nevertheless limited, value pluralism, which attempts to reconcile the differing balances between such influences in individual Member States with the need to maintain the open and sufficiently religiously neutral common European ethical framework necessary for the functioning of the Union as a polity.

4

Religion as Identity and the Fundamental Rights Obligations of the EU

1. Introduction

We have already seen how the European Union (EU), although limiting the role of religions in the political and law-making arena in important respects, also permits religion to exercise influence over law as an element of civil society and, perhaps more importantly, as an element of a public morality which, provided that individual autonomy is respected, is promoted out of respect for national cultural autonomy. This chapter discusses the importance of religion's status as an element of identity within this framework and how such an approach fits in with the Union's fundamental rights obligations in respect of religious freedom. The constraints imposed on the Union in this regard are determined largely, but not entirely, by the European Convention on Human Rights ('ECHR'), which provides much of the basis for the protection of religious freedom in EU law. The European Court of Human Rights ('ECtHR') has had to reconcile principles such as equality and individual autonomy in religious matters that underpin liberal rationales for religious freedom, with more communal rationales that recognize religion's communal nature and the right of Member States to promote a communal identity, which may be religiously specific, through their public institutions.

The ECtHR views individual religious freedom as a right that is principally private in nature and focuses on an individual right to develop and adhere to a religious identity. The Court has generally refused to require states to provide special accommodation for religion in non-private contexts such as the labour market. At times, the Court has seen the relationship between religion in the public arena and the liberal democratic state in essentially competitive terms and has empowered states to limit religious expression in the public contexts in order to defend principles and interests such as state neutrality, equal treatment, or public order. Such an approach appears to be consistent with notions of the neutral state and the defence of religious freedom, albeit to a degree that is limited by the needs of the state in the public sphere and by the principle of respect for individual autonomy, both of which are linked to Europe's (and the Union's) humanist heritage. Of course, the collective culture within which individual religious freedom is asserted is inevitably influenced by cultural norms to which particular faiths have disproportionately contributed. Therefore, the protection of private religious freedom may allow adherents to culturally entrenched religions a greater degree of freedom to adhere to their faith in public situations, not because the Court accords them a more extensive right to religious freedom, but because there is no clash between the collective norms and structures of the society in which they live and the requirements of their faith. As such norms evolve and change, culturally entrenched religions may find, as Christian groups in the United Kingdom have found in recent years, that the scope of the right to religious freedom is somewhat less than they had imagined.[1]

The ECtHR has had to deal with the institutional, in addition to the individual, elements of the right to religious freedom. While it has endorsed the right of states to confine religion to the private sphere in order to ensure the neutrality of the public contexts, it has not always seen the relationship between non-private religion and the state in competitive terms. In an approach that is reflective of communal notions of religion and the protection of religion's broader role in communal identity, ECtHR judgments have shown a willingness to uphold the conferral of significant public sector privileges by Member States on certain denominations, even when such privileges interfere with individual rights such as the right to equal treatment and personal autonomy (although there have recently been some indications of changes in this regard).

Confining individual religious freedom to the private sphere, coupled with the right of the state to protect the institutional role and social status of certain religions, reveals an approach to the relationship between the state

---

[1] This is seen most clearly in relation to conflicts over the application of laws prohibiting discrimination on grounds of sexual orientation to organizations run by Christian churches in the United Kingdom, such as adoption agencies and schools.

and religion that, by and large, respects the right of states to define their own relationship to religion, including relationships that involve the close identification of certain states with individual denominations. It shows how the ECHR has been interpreted so as to permit the use of coercive state power to promote the interests of certain religions and how liberal principles such as equal treatment and freedom of expression have, at times, been required to give way to the right of states to promote a religiously specific communal identity.

There are therefore two sets of rights relevant to the Union's duties in respect of religious freedom. The first is a duty to respect the right of individuals to develop and adhere to a religious identity of their choosing in the private sphere, while the second is more permissive than mandatory in nature and focuses on the right of the state to define religion's role in collective identity. Therefore, the constraints imposed by the ECHR on the choices of both the EU and its Member States in this area have been, until now, relatively limited and have consisted mainly of a duty to respect religion in the private sphere and to ensure that the identification of the state with a particular religion is not such as to imperil the level of pluralism inherent in the liberal democratic nature of the Convention system.

The fundamental rights obligations of the Union in relation to religious freedom have therefore left it free to grant priority to the right of Member States to define their own relationship to religion, to defend their public spheres and state institutions from religion, or, conversely, to promote certain denominations through state institutions, and do not require it to ensure adherence on the part of Member States to principles such as state neutrality and equal treatment of religions. That said, this analysis must also take on board the recent ruling of the Strasbourg Court in the *Lautsi*[2] case, where a requirement that Italian state schools display the crucifix in classrooms was held to violate the Convention. This ruling relates to the very specific context of state schools, in which issues of compulsion are particularly sensitive. However, the judgment also explicitly distinguished between state recognition of particular religious symbols as part of national cultural heritage (which is acceptable) and state endorsement of the truth of a particular faith (which is not). The *Lautsi* decision could therefore indicate that, as later chapters suggest, greater religious diversity in Europe and greater awareness of threats to the secular elements of European public orders may be leading

---

[2] *Lautsi v Italy* (Application No 30814/06) 3 November 2009.

to greater strictness in relation to according symbolic privilege by states to particular faiths, including greater vigilance on the part of the ECtHR in ensuring that acknowledgment of the cultural role of a particular religion by the state does not shade into acknowledgement of the truth claims of that faith. The distinction between religion as an element of national culture and religion as a truth claim is one which, as Chapters 3, 5, and 6 show, underpins the approach of the Union's public order to religion. However, it is possible that the emphasis placed by the *Lautsi* ruling on the need for states to maintain a neutral attitude to religions *qua* religions may mean that in the future, the ECHR will require stricter limitations on state endorsement of particular religions. This may well have the effect of encouraging the Union to police the boundary between cultural and political recognition with greater strictness. The *Lautsi* decision is, however, currently on appeal to the Grand Chamber, so whether these developments will come to pass remains to be seen.

This chapter analyses the major rationales for the protection of religious freedom in contemporary Europe and how such rationales accommodate the diverse nature of religion. After tracing the emergence of the Union's fundamental rights obligations in EU law, and the role of religion and the ECHR in those obligations, this chapter considers the protection of religious freedom in its individual and collective forms by the ECtHR, before concluding with an assessment of the implications of the Court's evolving approach for the relationship of religion to both the EU and its Member States.

2. Rationales for Protecting Religious Freedom in Contemporary Europe

The complex, and at times contradictory, nature of religion makes the issues arising out of its legal protection particularly complex. Religion is both a matter of individual choice and a type of communal action that may impinge on individual choice. It is also an ideological matter of beliefs and opinions that nevertheless also involves significant elements of cultural identity, which set it apart from purely political beliefs. This section analyses the major rationales advanced for the protection of religious freedom in contemporary Europe and the degree to which each can accommodate religion's complex nature, as well as the further complications relating to the balance of power between the Union and Member States that arise in the context of the EU.

Four rationales for the protection of religious freedom are generally advanced in the modern European context.[3] The first two focus on religious conflict as a source of suffering and disorder, the third relies on religious justifications for religious tolerance, and the fourth emphasises the role of religious freedom as part of a wider commitment to liberalism and personal autonomy.[4] The first two rationales are closely related and emphasize the historical strife caused by religious conflict. The first approach sees religious freedom as an instrument to avoid the suffering brought about by religious intolerance. It recognizes religious diversity as inevitable and protects religious freedom as a means to avoid the conflict that a failure to tolerate such diversity would inevitably bring. This argument has found favour in some international human rights instruments such as the United Nations Declaration on the Elimination of All Forms of Intolerance and Discrimination Based on Religion or Belief.[5] The Preamble to the Declaration specifically refers to the suffering caused by a failure to respect religious freedom, arguing for religious tolerance on the basis that 'the disregard and infringement of human rights and fundamental freedoms, in particular of the right to freedom of thought conscience, religion or whatever belief, have brought, directly or indirectly, wars and great suffering to mankind'.[6]

The second and related approach focuses on the fact that, historically, religion has often been the ground for persecution. Respect for religious freedom is therefore seen as a means of avoiding the recurrence of such persecution. The highlighting of the fact that, as in the case of race and ethnicity, persecution has often been focused on religion provides a rationale for the inclusion of specific guarantees of religious freedom in addition to more general commitments to freedom of opinion and expression.[7] This historical and pragmatic approach has certainly had some influence on the emergence of the principle of freedom of religion in Europe. Indeed, it was the destruction and suffering occasioned by the religiously fuelled conflicts that convulsed

---

[3] C Evans, *Freedom of Religion under the European Convention on Human Rights* (Oxford: Oxford University Press, 2001) 22–33.   [4] Ibid.
[5] United Nations Declaration on the Elimination of All Forms of Intolerance and Discrimination Based on Religion or Belief, Proclaimed by General Assembly Resolution 36/55 of 25 November 1981, available at <http://www.conseil-constitutionnel.fr/conseil-constitutionnel/francais/les-decisions/acces-par-date/decisions-depuis-1959/2004/2004-505-dc/decision-n-2004-505-dc-du-19-novembre-2004.888.html> (last visited 26 May 2010).
[6] Ibid, Preamble.   [7] Evans (n 3 above) 24–5.

post-Reformation Europe that prompted the recognition of the degree (albeit a rather limited one) of religious diversity embodied in the *cuius regio eius religio* principle enshrined in the Peace of Augsburg of 1555 and the Treaty of Westphalia of 1648. Such principles retain relevance today; the European Union, as will be shown below,[8] has been markedly reluctant to interfere with the relationships developed between some of its Member States and certain religions. On the other hand, the wording of the relevant articles of both the ECHR and EU Charter of Fundamental Rights focuses on a concrete personal right to choose and practice one's religion,[9] not on the need to avoid persecution or discrimination on religious grounds. Discrimination on religious grounds is addressed by the EU Charter[10] in a general anti-discrimination article covering grounds such as racial, gender, and sexual orientation discrimination, which, unlike religious freedom, are not therefore addressed by separate and specific articles. Indeed, when the issue of the avoidance of conflict has arisen in the ECHR case law the Strasbourg Court has invoked the possibility of conflict as a reason to *restrict* religious freedom.[11]

The third justification relies on religious grounds. A policy of toleration of religious difference can serve as a means by which adherents of the majority faith can ensure that their faith will be tolerated in places where other faiths predominate. John Stuart Mill, for instance, argued from a Christian perspective that religious truth is most easily established in an environment free of religious coercion,[12] while Locke considered that religious coercion merely bred hypocrisy and deceit and that forcing Christianity was futile as insincere Christians would not, in any event, be 'saved'.[13] However, Evans notes that while 'religious tolerance may be part of the teachings of some religions, . . . it is not common to all religions and even religious groups that contain some commitment to the notion of freedom of religion may disagree fundamentally as to the meaning of and limits to that freedom'.[14]

The Catholic Church, for instance, vigorously opposed the idea of religious freedom for many years (and only finally reconciled itself to the principle after the Second Vatican Council in the 1960s). For example, in 1864 the 'Syllabus of Errors' issued by Pope Pius IX explicitly condemned the idea that '[e]very

---

[8]   See sections 4.3 and 4.4 and n 39 below.   [9]   See sections 3 and 4.1 below.

[10]   See Charter of Fundamental Rights of the European Union, [2007] OJ C303/01, Art 21(1).

[11]   See, eg *Sahin v Turkey* (Application No 44774/98) [2004] ECHR 299 paras 97, 98.

[12]   JS Mill, *On Liberty* (London: Wordsworth Classic edition, 1996); cited in Evans (n 3 above) 25.

[13]   J Locke, 'Letters on Toleration' in the *Works of John Locke* (1823), Vol VI, 28, quoted in Evans (n 3 above) 25.   [14]   Evans (n 3 above) 26.

man is free to embrace and profess that religion which, guided by the light of reason, he shall consider true',[15] or that people in Catholic countries should be free to 'enjoy the public exercise of their own peculiar form of worship'.[16]

While the modern Catholic Church has embraced the notion of religious freedom,[17] this is not true of all major religions. Although the *Koran* does state 'let there be no coercion in religion',[18] it also mandates the death penalty for apostasy, which remains a crime in several Muslim states. Saudi Arabia argued strongly against the inclusion of a right to change one's religion in the Universal Declaration of Human Rights[19] and, more recently, the Cairo Declaration on Human Rights in Islam,[20] agreed by the Islamic Conference of Foreign Ministers in 1990, demonstrates a notably ambivalent attitude towards religious freedom. Article 10 of the Declaration states that 'Islam is the religion of unspoiled nature. It is prohibited to exercise any form of compulsion on man or to exploit his poverty or ignorance in order to convert him to another religion or to atheism.'

The Declaration makes no mention of a corresponding right not to be compelled to remain within Islam. Therefore, while some faiths do provide reasons to protect freedom of religion, others have not done so in the past or do not do so in the present. In contrast to approaches that see religious freedom as part of respect for individual or communal cultural rights, this religiously based view considers religious freedom as something that comes from the divine and transcends the state. How such a right would be operationalized within a legal system such as the European Union, in which nation states are extremely powerful, which is not a theocracy, and which has never sought to justify its laws in explicitly theological terms, remains problematic.

[15] See the condemnation of liberty of conscience, freedom of expression and opposition to monarchical rule in *Mirari Vos: On Liberalism and Religious Indifferentism*, Encyclical of Pope Gregory XVI, 15 August 1832 (in particular paras 13–24), full text available at <http://www.papalencyclicals.net/Pius09/p9quanta.htm> (last visited 26 May 2010). See also Propositions 15 and 78 of the *Syllabus of Errors Condemned by Pope Pius IX*, full text available at <http://www.papalencyclicals.net/Pius09/p9syll.htm> (last visited 26 May 2010).

[16] *Syllabus of Errors*, ibid, Proposition 78.

[17] Vatican II, 'Declaration on Religious Freedom' in WM Abbott (ed.), *The Documents of Vatican II* (Piscataway: American Press, 1966) 677.   [18] *Koran, Sûrah al-Baqarah*: 256.

[19] M Evans, *Religious Liberty and International Law in Europe* (Cambridge: Cambridge University Press, 1997) 187.

[20] The Cairo Declaration on Human Rights in Islam, adopted and issued at the Nineteenth Islamic Conference of Foreign Ministers in Cairo, 5 August 1990, available at <http://www.religlaw.org/interdocs/docs/cairohrislam1990.htm> (last visited 13 May 2010).

The final rationale sees freedom of religion as an important part of a liberal society. Raz argues that 'freedom of religion or belief is an essential and independent component of treating human beings as autonomous persons deserving of dignity and respect' and that 'if society does so treat people it will allow for choice between a variety of religious beliefs'.[21] Similarly, Rawls views religions as 'a fundamental aspect of human life and self-definition',[22] while Dworkin argues that states must treat citizens 'as human beings who are capable of forming and acting on intelligent conceptions of how their lives should be lived'.[23] These views are echoed in the UN Declaration on Religious Intolerance, which states that '[r]eligion or belief, for anyone who professes either, is one of the fundamental elements in his conception of life and that freedom of religion should be fully respected and guaranteed'.[24]

According to Evans, these arguments are based on the ideas that 'individuals are in the best position to determine their own concept of the good life and should, within certain constraints, be free to pursue their ideal without governmental interference'.[25] This justification of religious freedom on the basis of liberal respect for individual autonomy and the right to form one's own identity, fits in with the overall thrust of European human rights protection in the post-war period which, in common with many modern human rights instruments, protects freedom of thought and conscience as well as providing specific protection for religious freedom. Such instruments also generally guarantee other rights such as the right to privacy and freedom of expression as part of a wider, more general commitment to the protection of individual autonomy. The protection of freedom of religion at international level has, as Malcolm Evans suggests, 'been bound up with the development of the concept of individual human rights'.[26] As shown in Chapter 3, the European Union has identified the humanist tradition with its strong streak of individual autonomy as a major influence on its constitutional values, which have also been declared to include the 'rights of the human person, freedom, equality and the rule of law',[27] all of which would seem to be consistent with this view of religious freedom.

---

[21] J Raz, *The Morality of Freedom* (Oxford: Clarendon Press, 1988) 396.

[22] J Rawls, *A Theory of Justice*, (Cambridge, MA: Harvard University Press, 1971) 17–22; quoted in Evans (n 3 above) 31.

[23] R Dworkin *Taking Rights Seriously* (Cambridge MA: Harvard University Press, 1977) 272–273.

[24] See n 5 above.

[25] Evans (n 3 above) 30.

[26] Evans (n 19 above) 172–173.

[27] See Treaty of Lisbon amending the Treaty on European Union and the Treaty establishing the European Community, signed at Lisbon, 13 December 2007 [2007] OJ C306/01, Preamble.

However, such an approach raises certain difficulties for religions themselves. It embodies a very secular view of religion, seeing it as a phenomenon worthy of protection only in so far as our commitment to human choice and autonomy compels us to ensure that all items are on the 'menu' in the cultural and philosophical 'restaurant'. This raises the question of why specific protection for religious freedom should be provided rather than a more general commitment to respect for personal autonomy. Furthermore, this approach fails to take account of religion's broader social role and ideological nature. Religion is not a phenomenon that can be neatly contained within the private and individual realm, in which liberal states are content to grant the decisions of individuals the maximum of respect, but has communal aspects and wider social and political ramifications. Thus, an approach to religious freedom based solely on a respect for individual choice is, to some extent, inconsistent with the communal and social nature of many aspects of mainstream European religions, many of which play important public roles both institutionally and as sources of identity in several Member States. As Dalacoura points out, a purely individualistic approach to religion undermines its ability to retain social relevance. Religion, she argues,

is a social affair, as well as a matter of personal belief. Its strength rests on socialisation, worship and the existence of taboos. Religion confined to the private sphere eventually loses its hold on the individual conscience, as the history of the Western world after the nineteenth century clearly demonstrates. If religion is not to guide us in our relationships with one another, it loses its relevance to our existence and therefore withers away.[28]

For many religions, therefore, to protect only religion's individual aspects is to undermine its ability to maintain the taboos and social presence necessary to avoid its decline as a relevant force in society. The maintenance of such taboos requires interference with individual choice and autonomy and is somewhat inconsistent with the liberal rationale for religious liberty. Most major European religions reject the notion of religion as a purely individual and private matter.[29] Although it is true that, in the period since the

---

[28] K Dalacoura, *Islam, Liberalism and Human Rights: Implications for International Relations* (London: IB Tauris, 1998) 11. It should however be said that this fact in itself is hardly a satisfactory rationale for involving the state in the forcible promotion of particular religions or the enforcement of religious teachings through coercive means.

[29] See, eg the statements of the leader of the Anglican Communion, Archbishop of Canterbury, in 'Down with godless government', *The Sunday Times*, 22 April 2007, available at <http://www.timesonline.co.uk/tol/comment/columnists/guest_contributors/article1687465.ece> (last

Enlightenment and Reformation, the influence of religions over the public sphere in Europe has declined significantly, the major Christian denominations all continue to engage in the public sphere and to attempt to influence law and public policy in certain areas.[30] For many religions, whose presence on the European scene is more recent and whose relationship to the public arena and to post-Enlightenment values has not been as influenced by the key experiences of European history, the notion of religion as a private individual matter is even more problematic. Cantwell-Smith argues that most religions, apart from the traditional European faiths, view religion more as a way of life and behaviour than as a series of beliefs and opinions,[31] while Esposito suggests that the idea of religion as a primarily personal and private matter of individual belief is largely a Western one.[32] For such religions, an approach to religious freedom based solely on protection of individual autonomy would appear gravely deficient.

The fact that religion remains involved in public and political life reveals a further limitation in an approach based purely on respect for individual autonomy. Liberal theorists speak of religious freedom as an element of individual choice, to be asserted by individuals against the state.[33] However, given its communal, social, and political roles, religion itself can be a threat to individual autonomy. Religiously motivated actions can, for instance, have political consequences, including the undermining of liberal democratic systems and the principle of individual choice and autonomy. The difficulties posed by the need to respect religious choices while defending liberal democratic values from theocratic forces can be seen in the discussion on the Union's pursuit of 'balance' in Chapter 3 and in the limitations on the political role of religion which such balance requires. It is also seen in the approach of certain European bodies to the impact of religious freedom on the public sphere. Some bodies have sought to place limits on the degree to which such freedom can be used to protect actions inconsistent with

visited 13 May 2010), and the Address of Pope Benedict XVI to the European People's Party of 30 March 2006, full text available at <http://www.vatican.va/holy_father/benedict_xvi/speeches/2006/march/documents/hf_ben-xvi_spe_20060330_eu-parliamentarians_en.html> (last visited 13 May 2010), both of which call for active religious involvement in the political process.   [30] Ibid.

[31] W Cantwell Smith, *The Meaning and the End of Religion* (New York: The Macmillan Company, 1963) Chs 2, 3, which state that the notion of religion, let alone the primacy of particular beliefs as opposed to a religious way of life, is alien outside traditional European religions (quoted in Evans (n 3 above) 75).

[32] J Esposito, *The Islamic Threat: Myth or Reality* (Oxford: Oxford University Press, 2002) 199.

[33] See nn 21–23 above.

liberal democratic principles. The Parliamentary Assembly of the Council of Europe, for example, has stated that: '[t]he recourse to religion [as a source of values] has, however, to be reconciled with the principles of democracy and human rights',[34] while decisions of the ECtHR, such as *Refah Partisi v Turkey*,[35] indicate clearly that freedom of religion is subject to a requirement that religious ideas or practices must not, particularly in the public sphere, threaten the wider liberal democratic values that underpin the European public order.

Indeed, the broader role of the state and national identity is an element that is not adequately addressed by an exclusive focus on personal autonomy as the rationale for the protection of religious freedom. This autonomy-centred approach is very much part of the broader liberal vision of the generally neutral state, which does not embody any particular vision of 'the good life'.[36] However, several human rights instruments place strong emphasis on the rights of parents to pass on their religion to their offspring[37] (for example by ensuring that the right to religious education is protected), which would seem to stress religion's role as an element of communal culture rather than solely a matter of individual choice. Furthermore, religion has been repeatedly defined by EU institutions as a partly cultural matter.[38] In more general terms, the emphasis on religion's cultural role would seem to contradict an entirely individualistic and autonomy-based view of religion given that one's cultural identity is, for many people, influenced by involuntary factors such as nationality, race, and upbringing. Most European states are not religiously neutral and have strong cultural, historical, and institutional links to certain religions which are a key element of the collective national identity that such states embody. To give a few examples, questions of religious identity were fundamental elements of the nationalist revolts which saw Belgium secede from the Netherlands and Ireland secede from the United Kingdom. Orthodox Christian identity was also fundamental to the Greek struggle for independence, while Protestantism was a key element in the formation of the British state. Relations between religious communities were hugely important internally in Germany and the Netherlands, while conflict over the role of the Catholic Church represented the major cleavage in France, Spain, and Italy for much of the nineteenth century. Indeed, these struggles were

[34] Parliamentary Assembly of the Church of England, Recommendation 1202 of 2 February 1993 on religious tolerance in a democratic society, para 9.
[35] *Refah Partisi v Turkey* (Applications Nos 41340/98, 41342/98, 41343/88, and 41344/98) (2003) 37 EHRR 1.   [36] See, eg Rawls (n 22 above).
[37] See, eg European Convention on Human Rights, First Protocol, Art 2.   [38] See Ch 5.

fundamental elements in the creation of the modern French, Spanish, and Italian states. Even today, a primary element of the identity of many Member States is provided by their relationship to religion or a particular denomination. France's status as a secular republic is fundamental to its identity, the Catholic and Greek Orthodox Churches remain key elements of Greek and Polish identity, while the changed relationship of countries like Ireland and Spain to the Catholic Church is seen by their citizens as representing a major change in their national identities.

This national and cultural role is at the centre of a further complication in the analysis of the protection of religious freedom under EU law. While EU fundamental rights law is very much part of the worldwide and regional post-war developments in human rights, the Union itself is an organization of multi-level governance in which issues of subsidiarity and the relative powers of its constituent parts are particularly important. The Union's status as a functional organization of restricted competence and limited democratic legitimacy means that the extent to which it is capable of articulating and imposing a distinctive approach to the issue of religious freedom is restricted by its duty to respect the autonomy and identity of its Member States. Indeed, its founders deliberately sought to avoid entangling the Community with sensitive questions such as religion and identity on the grounds that it was only through functional integration that European unification could advance. Accordingly, the Union has had to be particularly sensitive not to appear to interfere with Member State choices in this area. Indeed, in a contemporary variation on the *cuius regio eius religio* theme, a Declaration appended to the Amsterdam Treaty, and more recently a substantive article of the Reform Treaty, state that '[t]he Union respects and does not prejudice the status under national law of churches and religious associations or communities in the Member States',[39] thus deliberately attempting to limit the degree to which EU law will interfere with the *religius* established by modern day *reges* (Member State governments).

Apart from purely religious rationales, which struggle to achieve recognition within the European context, the protection of freedom of religion in the contemporary European context is underpinned by a mix of potentially mutually inconsistent rationales that focus on religion as an element

---

[39] See Declaration 11, annexed to the Treaty of Amsterdam [1997] OJ C340/308. See also Art 16C of the Treaty of Lisbon, which states: 'The Union respects and does not prejudice the status under national law of churches and religious associations or communities in the Member States'.

of identity but emphasize different elements of religion and view its relationship to the state in very different ways. These differing approaches see religion as an element of individual identity to be protected from state power and as part of the culture that constitutes the state. The EU's attempts to define a distinctive relationship to religion and religious freedom in its public order is likely to be influenced by liberal ideas of individual autonomy, which are at the heart of its identity as a 'Community of Values'. However, such ideas potentially clash with several other factors, notably religion's claim to transcendence, the problematic relationship between some religions and individual autonomy, and the immense historical and cultural role of certain denominations in many Member States with which, as an institution of limited democratic legitimacy, the Union is ill-equipped to interfere.

3. The Scope of Freedom of Religion in EU Law as Part of the EU's Fundamental Rights Commitments

It has been seen how the competing rationales for the protection of religious freedom offer very different visions of the role of religion within the modern state. The Union's balancing of these competing visions takes place within certain constraints, most notably its commitment to uphold certain fundamental rights. Over the course of its history the Union's fundamental rights obligations have broadened and deepened steadily. Undertakings by the Union and its Member States to respect certain fundamental principles have become increasingly explicit and have been turned into key elements of the EU's legal and political orders.[40] This commitment to upholding certain fundamental rights informs the assessment of what can be considered to be a proper balance between religious, humanist, and cultural influences over the law and can therefore potentially influence the EU's approach to the relationship between religion and state and the ability of Member States to pursue relationships to religion that violate such undertakings. Thus, the Union's commitment to upholding freedom of religion can affect not merely the role of religion in the its own public order, but can also call into question the established structures and relationships that constitute part of the role of religion in the public orders of individual Member States.

---

[40] A Williams, *EU Human Rights Policies: A Study in Irony* (Oxford: Oxford University Press, 2004).

The evolution of the EU's legal obligations in relation to human rights began in the late 1960s, when the European Court of Justice began to develop the idea of 'general principles' of Community law, which included fundamental rights obligations and whose observance the Court declared it would ensure. In 1969, in *Stauder v City of Ulm*[41] the Court examined the implementation by the German authorities of a Commission decision enabling the sale of surplus butter. It found that the arrangements in question were compatible with Community law but at the same time held that fundamental rights were 'enshrined in the general principles of law and protected by the Court'.[42] A year later, in *Internationale Handelsgesellschaft*,[43] it established that acts by the Community that violated such fundamental rights would be held to be illegal.

The decisions in *Stauder* and *Internationale Handelsgesellschaft* effectively created what was to become an unenumerated bill of rights in Community law. In *Internationale Handelsgesellschaft* the Court attempted to give some indication as to the content of these rights by invoking the 'constitutional traditions' of the Member States as their source. In *Nold v Commission*[44] the Court recognized that international treaties to which Member States were party could also act as a source of fundamental rights. Such an approach created great scope for the ECHR, as a treaty that all Member States had ratified, to play a role in the determination of the content of rights resulting from the 'common constitutional traditions' of the Member States. The Court of Justice's judgment in *Rutlili v Ministre de l'Intérieur*[45] explicitly recognized the ECHR as such a source.[46] By the time of its 1989 decision in *Wachauf v Bundesamt für Ernährung und Fortwirtschaft*[47] the Court could summarize the situation as follows:

The Court has consistently held...that fundamental rights form an integral part of the law, the observance of which is ensured by the Court. In safeguarding those rights, the Court has to look to the constitutional traditions common to the Member States, so that measures which are incompatible with the fundamental rights recognised by the Community may not find acceptance in the Community. International treaties concerning the protection of human rights on which the Member

[41] Case 29/69 *Stauder v City of Ulm* [1969] ECR 419.
[42] Ibid para 7.   [43] Case 11/70 *Internationale Handelsgesellschaft* [1970] ECR 1125.
[44] Case 4/73 *Nold v Commission* [1974] ECR 491.
[45] Case 36/75 *Rutlili v Ministre de l'Intérieur* [1975] ECR 1219.
[46] The Court has also mentioned other treaties as sources of fundamental rights in Community law. The International Covenant on Civil and Political Rights (ICCPR), for example, was mentioned in Case 374/87 *Orkem v Commission* [1989] ECR 3283, while the European Social Charter was mentioned in Case 24/86 *Blaziot v Beligum* [1988] ECR 379.
[47] Case 5/88 *Wachauf v Bundesamt für Ernährung und Fortwirtschaft* [1989] ECR 2609.

States have collaborated or to which they have acceded can also supply guidelines to which regard should be had in the context of Community law.[48]

This obligation to respect human rights principles has been held to apply not merely to EU legislation itself but to all measures implementing or derogating from EU law. In the *ERT* case[49] the Court was faced with a challenge to the award of a monopoly to a Greek broadcasting service by the Greek Government. The award amounted to a derogation from the market freedoms protected by EU law. While such derogations are not in themselves necessarily incompatible with Community law,[50] the derogation in this case was challenged on the basis that, *inter alia*, it interfered with the right to freedom of expression protected by Article 10 of the ECHR. The Court therefore had to decide whether a national law measure, *derogating* from EU law, was itself subject to compliance with Community fundamental rights norms. It held that 'the national rules in question can fall under the exceptions provided ... only if they are compatible with the fundamental rights the observance of which is ensured by the Court'.[51]

This extensive view of the reach of EU fundamental rights norms means that the duty to respect the principle of religious freedom applies not only to EU law itself but also to measures implementing or derogating from EU law. In *Segi v Council*[52] the Court addressed the issue of the status of anti-terrorism measures adopted under the Third Pillar and held that all acts of the Union which created legal effects in relation to third parties, including those taken under the Third Pillar, could be the subject of a reference to the Court of Justice for the purposes of obtaining a preliminary ruling on, *inter alia*, the compatibility of such measures with fundamental rights norms. In the light of these judgments, it is clear that the Union's duty to respect fundamental rights applies across a wide range of areas of EU activity, including all areas of the Single Market, such as employment, regulation of advertising, and commercial activities, as well as politically sensitive areas, such as justice and home affairs and anti-terrorism policy.[53]

[48] Ibid para 17.   [49] Case C-260/89 *ERT* [1991] ECR I-2925.   [50] Ibid para 1.
[51] Ibid para 43.
[52] Case C-355/04P *Segi v Council* (not yet reported) 27 February 2007 paras 53–56.
[53] For an example of the relevance of religious freedom to EU law in this area, see the Council Decision implementing the UN Convention Against Transnational Organised Crime, which provides that Member States will not be required by the Convention to extradite an individual if there are 'substantial grounds' for believing that the request for extradition was made for the purpose of prosecuting or punishing the person in question on grounds, *inter alia*, of religion or if extradition would 'cause prejudice' to that person on that basis (Art 16(14) of Council Decision

The Court of Justice's development of a fundamental rights jurisprudence has been part of a broader deepening of the Union's political commitment to fundamental rights. In 1977, the Parliament, Council, and Commission adopted a Joint Declaration on Fundamental Rights in which they undertook to respect the provisions of the ECHR.[54] In 1992, Article 6 of the Maastricht Treaty made a similar commitment to 'respect fundamental rights as guaranteed by the European Convention for the Protection of Human Rights and Fundamental Freedoms signed in Rome on 4 November 1950 and as they result from the constitutional traditions common to the Member States, as general principles of law'.[55]

The Constitutional Treaty and its successor, the Lisbon Treaty, both viewed the Union as a 'Community of Values' and defined the upholding of fundamental rights as a key element of EU membership. This reflected the approach adopted by the Union in the enlargement process with the Copenhagen Criteria of 1993, which governs the accession of new members to the Union specifically requiring applicant states to ensure respect for human rights as part of the accession process.[56] In 2000 the Union went further and adopted its own Charter of Fundamental Rights, which became part of EU law, with a status equal to the treaties, under the Lisbon Treaty.

A commitment to the protection of fundamental rights is therefore a key element of the EU's legal and political orders. It is also clear that protection of religious freedom is one such fundamental right. As far back as 1976 the Court of Justice recognized in *Prais v Council*[57] that freedom of religion was part of the 'general principles' of law it was committed to upholding. In doing so the Court invoked Article 9 of the ECHR, thereby indicating the Convention's special status in EU law fundamental rights jurisprudence.

2004/579/EC of 29 April 2005 on the conclusion on behalf of the European Community, of the United Nations Convention Against Transnational Organised Crime [2004] OJ L261/69). Similarly, the Council Decision on the mutual recognition of financial penalties allows Member States not to execute the relevant penalty if there are 'reasons to believe, based on objective elements that the financial penalty has the purpose of punishing a person on the grounds of his or her...religion' (Preamble, para 5 to Council Framework Decision 2005/214/JHA of 24 February 2005 on the application of the principle of mutual recognition to financial penalties [2005] OJ L76/16). Respect for freedom of religion is also regularly required by the EU in its external relations (see, eg Art 3(a) of the Council Common Position on Nigeria of 27 May 2002, 2002/401/CFSP).

[54]   [1977] OJ C103/1.
[55]   Treaty on European Union, [1992] OJ C191/1 , Art F.
[56]   These fundamental rights have included the right to religious freedom: see, eg the Commission's Turkey 2005 Progress Report SEC (2005) 1426 (ECOM (2005) 561 final) 29, which highlighted respect for religious freedom as one of the requirements of accession.
[57]   Case 130/75 *Prais v Council* (unreported) 27 October 1976.

The influence of the ECHR can be seen in Article 10 of the Charter, which states:

Freedom of thought, conscience and religion

1. Everyone has the right to freedom of thought, conscience and religion. This right includes freedom to change religion or belief and freedom, either alone or in community with others and in public and private, to manifest religion or belief, in worship, teaching, practice and observance.
2. The right to conscientious objection is recognised in accordance with the national laws governing the exercise of this right.

Apart from the specific reference to conscientious objection in the second section, the text of Article 10 is almost identical to that of Article 9 of the ECHR.[58] The fact that its text very largely reproduces the wording of Article 9 of the ECHR indicates that the Union envisages that, although initially the Charter was not in itself legally binding, the level and scope of the protection of religious freedom in EU law were intended to overlap significantly with the protection provided under the ECHR. This approach has been further strengthened by the rulings of the Court of Justice in the cases of *Akrich v Secretary of State for the Home Department*[59] and *Parliament v Council*[60] both of which accorded a dominant role to the jurisprudence of the ECtHR in the determination of the requirements of the Union's commitment to fundamental rights. In *Parliament v Council*, for example, the Parliament requested that the Court of Justice annul certain provisions of a directive on the basis that they constituted a violation of the right to family life. In reaching its decision to uphold the directive, the Court of Justice based its analysis of the requirements of the EU's fundamental rights norms (including the EU's Charter of Fundamental Rights)[61] on the interpretation of Article 8 of the ECHR by the ECtHR, noting the 'special significance' of its jurisprudence in this regard.[62] It cited several judgments of the Strasbourg Court[63] before upholding the impugned provisions on the basis that they '[did] not run counter to the right to respect for family rights set out in

---

[58] See section 4.1 below.

[59] Case C-109/01 *Akrich v Secretary of State for the Home Department* [2003] ECR I-9607.

[60] Case C-540/03 *Parliament v Council* (unreported) 27 June 2006.

[61] Ibid para 38, where the Court acknowledged the Charter's importance in the determination of the content of the EU's fundamental rights norms. This was reaffirmed in Case C-303/05 *Advocaten voor de Wereld VZW v Leden van de Ministerraad* [2006] ECR I-10597 para 78 (AGO).

[62] Case C-540/03 *Parliament v Council* (unreported) 27 June 2006 para 35.

[63] Ibid para 54.

particular in Article 8 of the ECHR as interpreted by the European Court of Human Rights'.[64]

Apart from noting that the relevant provisions appeared to be consistent with the Strasbourg Court's view of the requirements of Article 8, the Court of Justice offered no other reasons for its conclusion that the directive was consistent with EU fundamental rights norms. This would seem to indicate that the Court of Justice regards the Charter as merely confirming the rights that were already protected by EU law as a result of national constitutional traditions, of which the ECHR is a primary element. The Lisbon Treaty permits the EU to accede to the ECHR, meaning that the need for EU measures to comply with the Convention is likely to be further strengthened.

The jurisprudence of the ECtHR will therefore have a significant impact on the relationship between religion and the public order of the EU. The ECHR provides the framework within which the Union can construct its relationship to religion. Politically, the Union has repeatedly committed itself to respecting the requirements of the ECHR, while legally, the Court of Justice has made it clear that not only is the Convention a key source of fundamental rights obligations within EU law itself, but that measures in violation of such rights will be struck down. Therefore, whatever balance the Union strikes between the rights of individuals, religious organizations, and Member States, must respect the fundamental norms laid down by the Strasbourg Court in its interpretation of the Convention.

4. Jurisprudence of the European Court of Human Rights Relating to Religious Freedom

The jurisprudence of the ECtHR is of major importance not merely to the regulation of religious freedom but also to the relationship between religion and the state in contemporary Europe. The ECtHR has had to reconcile principles such as equality and individual autonomy in religious matters which underpin liberal rationales for religious freedom and reinforce notions of state neutrality vis-à-vis religion, with more communal rationales that recognize religion's communal nature and the right of Member States to promote a communal identity, which may be religiously specific, through its

---

[64] Ibid para 98.

public institutions. The constraints imposed by the ECHR on state choice in this area are, with a few exceptions, limited to a duty to respect religion in the private sphere. The ECtHR, through an approach that has granted priority to the right of states to define their own relationship to religion, to defend the public sphere and state institutions from religion, or, conversely, to promote certain denominations through state institutions, over approaches that stress ideas such as state neutrality and equal treatment, has reflected the continuing intertwining of the state, national identity, and certain forms of religion in Europe.

4.1 *Article 9*

The ECHR specifically identifies religious freedom as one of the key rights protected by the Convention system. Article 9 provides that:

1. Everyone has the right to freedom of thought, conscience and religion; this right includes freedom to change his religion or belief, and freedom, either alone or in community with others and in public or private, to manifest his religion or belief, in worship, teaching, practice and observance.
2. Freedom to manifest one's religion or beliefs shall be subject only to such limitations as are prescribed by law and are necessary in a democratic society in the interests of public safety, for the protection of public order, health or morals, or the protection of the rights and freedoms of others.

The wording of the article highlights the major issues arising in its interpretation by showing the tension between the potentially competing communal and individual elements of religious freedom. The first phrase defines religion as an individual right and as a matter of thought rather than culture or identity ('everyone has the right to freedom of thought, conscience or religion'). However, it goes on to acknowledge its public and communal aspects (the right 'either alone or in community with others and in public or private, to manifest his religion or belief in worship, teaching, practice and observance'). The second section deals with limitations on religious freedom. Although the use of the phrase 'necessary in a democratic society' would seem to indicate that only weighty considerations would justify interference with Article 9 rights, the relatively extensive grounds mentioned ('the protection of public order', 'health or morals', and 'the protection of the rights and freedoms of others') indicate that broader interference may be permitted. Thus, the text of the article itself provides no simple answers to the complex issues of individual, communal, and state rights and duties brought up by religious freedom and, as will be shown below, the balance struck by the Strasbourg institutions between these rights and interests has appeared to differ in different circumstances.

4.2 Individual Religious Freedom as a Private Right

The ECtHR has, despite Article 9's protection of the right to 'manifest' one's religion, seen protection of individual religious freedom as being largely confined to the private sphere. In particular it has not required signatory states to provide religious individuals with special accommodations to allow them to adhere to their religious identities in public contexts. In *Arrowsmith v United Kingdom*[65] the European Commission of Human Rights[66] (ECommHR) stated that Article 9 did 'not give individuals the right to behave in the public sphere in compliance with all the demands of their religion or belief',[67] a statement which it has repeated on several occasions.[68] The Court has shown a concern to protect the state's ability to regulate public space and public matters from demands to actively accommodate religious belief and practice. It has therefore adopted a relatively restrictive interpretation of the notion of 'manifestation' of religion, refusing, for example, to acknowledge 'commercial activities' on the part of a church (the selling of 'e-meters' by Scientologists)[69] or the contracting of a religious marriage[70] as falling within the meaning of this term. Furthermore, it has refused to acknowledge indirect discrimination on religious grounds as a violation of Article 9. The Court has repeatedly upheld laws challenged under Article 9

---

[65] *Arrowsmith v United Kingdom* (Application No 7050/75) (1978) 19 DR 5.

[66] Until 1998 the admissibility of applications under the Convention was decided by a separate European Commission of Human Rights, which referred on successful applications to the Court for a final decision.

[67] *Arrowsmith v United Kingdom* (Application No 7050/75) (1978) 19 DR 5. Here the term 'public sphere' seems to be used in a broader sense meaning non-private contexts as opposed to what Asen calls the 'realm of social life in which public opinion can be formed': R Asen, 'Toward a Normative Conception of Difference in Public Deliberation' (1999) 25 *Argumentation and Advocacy* (Winter) 115.

[68] See, eg cases relating to cattle vaccination: *X v Netherlands* (Application No 1068/61) (1962) Yearbook V 278 (in relation to cattle vaccination); *C v United Kingdom* (Application No 10358/83) (1983) 37 DR 142 (taxation); and *X v Austria* (Application No 1718/62) (1965) Yearbook VIII 168 (mandatory voting) (all quoted in Evans (n 3 above) 180).

[69] *Church of Scientology v Sweden* (Application No 7895/77) (1979) 16 DR 00 (quoted in Evans (n 3 above) 108–9).

[70] *Khan v United Kingdom* (Application No 11579/85) (1986) 48 DR 253.

on the basis that they were 'generally applicable and neutral'.[71] In *C v United Kingdom*,[72] for example, the applicant, who was a Quaker, objected to being required to pay income tax which might be used for purposes incompatible with his pacifist beliefs. The Commission, in rejecting his claim, noted that 'Article 9 primarily protects the sphere of personal beliefs and creeds'[73] and that it 'does not always guarantee the right to behave in the public sphere in a way which is dictated by such a belief,'[74] before concluding that there was no violation of the Convention on the basis, *inter alia*, that the legislation in question 'applies neutrally and generally in the public sphere'.[75] Challenges to taxation arrangements, the compulsory vaccination of farm animals,[76] and mandatory voting[77] have been upheld on a similar basis. These cases all involved consideration of a clash between the needs of the state in public matters, such as regulation of the market, taxation, and the political sphere, and the religious beliefs and practices of individuals who enter into such areas, for example consumers, producers, or citizens. In each case the ECtHR upheld the right of the state to interfere with individual religious identities in order to ensure that the attainment of government goals in these areas would not be compromised and refused to require states to provide to religious beliefs, protections not given to other beliefs or opinions.

The subjugation of religious freedom in public contexts to the needs of the state is seen equally clearly in cases where the presence of religion in public spaces such as educational institutions or the military is seen as a potential threat to the identity of the state or even to the state itself. Turkish authorities were permitted to maintain strict limitations on the wearing of Islamic dress in educational institutions in *Karaduman v Turkey*,[78] and in *Kalaç v Turkey*[79] they were permitted to purge the army of those with connections to Islamic fundamentalist movements as part of their attempts to defend the secular nature of the Turkish state.[80] In both cases the ECtHR and ECommHR argued that the state's need to defend its secular nature rendered legitimate restrictions on the individual religious identity of those who chose to study in or work for public bodies such as universities and the military. Similarly,

---

[71] *Chappell v United Kingdom* (Application No 12587/86) 53 DR 146.
[72] *C v United Kingdom* (Application No 10358/83) (1983) 37 DR 142.   [73] Ibid 147.
[74] Ibid. See n 65 above.   [75] Ibid.
[76] *X v Netherlands* (Application No 1068/61) (1962) Yearbook V 278.
[77] *X v Austria* (Application No 1718/62) (1965) Yearbook VIII 168.
[78] *Karaduman v Turkey* (Application No 16278/90) (1993) DR 74.
[79] *Kalaç v Turkey* (1997-IV) 41 ECtHR (Series A) 1199, 1203.
[80] In 1998 the Commission (which had decided on the admissibility of cases) was merged with the Court under a series of reforms of the operation of the Court.

in *Dahlab v Switzerland*[81] the Court upheld the right of the Swiss authorities to prevent state primary school teachers from wearing the Islamic headscarf on the basis that it was legitimate for the state to attempt to ensure the neutrality of the educational system. The Court's decision in *Sahin v Turkey*,[82] in which restrictions on wearing the Islamic headscarf in universities were again upheld, also invoked notions of public order and the possible impact on the rights of the less religious, of an assertive religious presence in public institutions. On the other hand, the Court's sensitivity to the impact on the rights of religious minorities of the presence of religious symbols in state institutions led it to restrict the right of states to promote particular religions in the context of the state school system in *Lautsi v Italy*.[83] In this case the Court held that in the context of public schools 'where people are dependent on the state and vulnerable',[84] individuals have the right not to be subject to state-sponsored proselytism and that the state's duty of 'confessional neutrality'[85] prevents it from aligning itself symbolically with a particular religion by placing the symbols of that particular faith (in this case the crucifix) in the classroom. Similarly, in *Buscarini v San Marino*, it held that San Marino could not maintain its traditional oath for legislators, which required those elected to Parliament to swear an oath which included the phrase 'I swear on the Holy Gospels'.[86]

It should also be pointed out that not all 'generally applicable and neutral' laws have been upheld by the Court. In *Thlimmenos v Greece*[87] it held that Greek laws which did not provide for exemptions for those who objected to national service on religious grounds violated Article 9. This, however, was very much an exception with the Court, as Evans states, viewing 'the fact that a law is general and neutral [as] at least a powerful indicator that it cannot interfere with freedom of religion or belief'.[88]

---

[81]   *Dahlab v Switzerland* (Application No 42393/98) 15 February 2001.

[82]   *Sahin v Turkey* (2005) 41 EHRR 8.

[83]   *Lautsi v Italy* (Application No 30814/06) 3 November 2009. This ruling built on the 2007 decisions in *Folgerø v Norway* (2007) 46 EHRR 1147 and *Hasan and Eylem Zengin v Turkey* (2007) 46 EHRR 1060 where the Court held that the failure to allow parents to exempt their children from lessons in religion or religious culture in state schools violated ECHR, First Protocol, Art 2. In *Zengin* it also stated that requiring parents to reveal their religious beliefs to the authorities in order to obtain such an exemption would violate the Convention.

[84]   *Lautsi v Italy* (Application No 30814/06) 3 November 2009 para 48.

[85]   Ibid para 53.

[86]   *Buscarini v San Marino* (1999) 30 EHRR 208.

[87]   *Thlimmenos v Greece* (2001) 31 EHRR 15.

[88]   *Ahmad v United Kingdom* (1982) 4 EHRR 126.

The Court's view that, apart from circumstances where the state in some way imposes a particular religion on individuals in public contexts such as state schools or the legislature, individual religious freedom is a right that is largely restricted to the private sphere and does not generally provide an entitlement to special accommodation beyond this sphere, is also seen in its characterization of religion as a purely voluntary matter whose adherents can be taken to have waived their right to adhere fully to their religion when they leave the private and personal arena. In *Ahmad v United Kingdom*,[89] for example, the case of a Muslim teacher who was refused time off by his employer to attend the Mosque on Fridays, failed partly on the basis that he had agreed to such limitations on his freedom of religion when he had accepted a contract of employment which did not provide for time off on Fridays. In *Stedman v United Kingdom*[90] no violation of Article 9 was found in the case of an applicant who refused to work on Sundays on the basis that she was free to leave her employment; while in the case of *Karaduman v Turkey*, as noted above, the applicant's decision to attend a university whose regulations forbade the wearing of headscarves was seen by the court as having constituted agreement to waive her right to wear the garment while being photographed for her university ID card.

The Court's failure to require Member States to provide protection for the right to have one's religious practices accommodated in areas such as employment gives rise to the risk that the religious practices of adherents of majority religions will receive greater protection given that social and economic life is, for historical reasons, likely to be arranged around their practices (with, for example, holidays covering the Christmas period and the weekly rest period including Sundays in mainly Christian countries). However, in such circumstances, the greater ability of adherents to particular faiths to adhere to their religion in public is not a result of the Court granting them more extensive protection of their religious freedom, but reflects the fact that, due to the cultural influence of their faith on the cultural norms and structures of individual states, there is no clash between the needs of their faith and collective norms and structures. In such circumstances the issue of protection of religious freedom and Article 9 rights simply does not arise. Were collective norms and structures to evolve in ways which clashed with the needs of adherents to a historically dominant faith, such adherents

---

[89] Ibid 130.
[90] *Stedman v United Kingdom* (Application No 29107/95) (1997) 23 EHRR CD 168.

would not be able to rely on Article 9 for more extensive protection than is currently provided to religious minorities by the Court.[91]

Perhaps more worrying in terms of the protection of the religious freedom of minority groups, is the Court's approach to the notion of 'manifestation' of one religious belief. It has held that only acts 'required' by a particular religion will be covered by the right to manifest one's religion and, in contrast to the approach of the US Supreme Court,[92] the Strasbourg Court has taken upon itself to determine 'objectively' what constitutes manifestation for these purposes, rather than relying on the subjective views of applicants. Thus, in *Ahmad v United Kingdom* the Court held that Mosque attendance was not a requirement of the religion of a Muslim teacher who was refused permission to take time off school to attend Friday Prayers,[93] while in *Karaduman v Turkey* it was held that the right of a female applicant to wear an Islamic headscarf was not 'manifestation' for the purposes of Article 9. Similarly, in *Valsamis v Greece*[94] the Court simply substituted its view for that of the Jehovah's Witness applicants who felt that being required to take part in a Greek national day parade violated their pacifist beliefs, deciding that the parade was not military in character. Although the Court has been relatively liberal in its definition of religion,[95] its insistence that its views, rather than those of the applicants, should decide what is required by the relevant religion has meant that, as Evans notes, there is a risk that the Court 'will single out for protection religious rites and practices with which the members of the Court are familiar and feel comfortable'.[96] Cumper notes that 'the Commission and Court have, at times, been accused of being unsympathetic

---

[91]   Confirmation that Art 9 does not provide adherents to culturally entrenched religions with the right to follow the dictates of their faith in the workplace when social change causes previously dominant teachings of that faith to lose influence over the law can be seen in *Ladele v London Borough of Islington* [2009] EWCA Civ 1357 where acceptance of the right of gays and lesbians to equal treatment meant that a registrar could not refuse to conduct civil partnership ceremonies to which she, as a Christian, took exception

[92]   *Thomas v Review Board of Indiana Social Security Division* 450 US 707, 714 (1981).

[93]   *Ahmad v UK* (1982) 4 EHRR 126.

[94]   *Valsamis v Greece* (1996-VI) 2 ECtHR (Series A) 2312 (discussed in Evans (n 3 above) 121).

[95]   The Strasbourg institutions have not engaged in detailed analysis of the issue of what qualifies as a 'religion or belief' for Art 9 purposes and have instead tended not to dispute that the belief systems at the centre of claims fall within the definition of 'religion or belief'. Thus, the claims of movements such as Scientology (see *X and Church of Scientology v Sweden* (Application No 7805/77) (1979) 16 DR 68) and the 'Divine Light Zentrum' (see *Omkaranda and the Divine Light Zentrum v Switzerland* (Application No 8118/77) (1981) 25 DR 105, both cases discussed in Evans (n 3 above) 55) have been analysed on the basis that they fall within Art 9, as have the claims of certain non-religious movements such as pacifism (*Arrowsmith v UK* (Application No 7050/75) (1978) 19 DR 5).   [96]   Evans (n 3 above) 125.

to the claims of those from non-Christian traditions or religions without a long history in Europe'.[97] By taking it upon itself to decide what is and is not required by an applicant's religion, the Court has set itself upon a path that may require it to act as an arbiter of scriptural interpretation, a task to which it is manifestly unsuited and which risks compromising the respect for the internal autonomy of religious bodies required by its own case law.[98] As importantly, it has deviated from an understanding of religious liberty based on recognition of the importance of protecting the right of individuals to decide for themselves on matters of conscience and religion in favour of an approach that stresses the protection of doctrinally orthodox religious practice. Such an approach may also make it difficult for the Court to deal with claims to freedom of conscience on the part of those whose fundamental beliefs are not religious and which may lack the theological underpinnings or supernatural orientation of religious beliefs. Some national courts have followed the ECtHR's lead in this regard, with the British Court of Appeal holding in *Eweida v British Airways* that the desire of a Christian worker to wear a cross over her uniform was not a requirement of her faith, on the grounds that other Christian employees at her workplace did not have a similar desire.[99]

There are, however, limits to the degree to which individuals can be required to modify their behaviour in order to maintain their religious freedom. As already noted, in *Buscarini* and *Lautsi*, the Court held that a state could not require legislators to take a Christian oath in order to take up their seats or to symbolically endorse the truth of a particular faith within the public education system. It has also ruled that parents must be able to exempt their children from lessons in religion or religious culture.[100] The Court has upheld claims beyond these very particular contexts of state schools (where

[97] P Cumper, 'The Rights of Religious Minorities: The Legal Regulation of New Religious Movements' in P Cumper and S Wheatley (eds), *Minority Rights in the 'New' Europe* (The Hague: Martinus Nijhoff Publishers, 1999) 174 and TJ Gunn, 'Adjudicating Rights of Conscience under the European Convention on Human Rights' in JD Van Der Vyver and J Witte J (eds), *Religious Human Rights in Global Perspective: Legal Perspectives* (Hague: Martinus Nijhoff Publishers, 1996) 305, 322. Evans (n 3 above) 125 notes that the Court has never found in favour of an applicant seeking the right to wear an item of religious apparel. He states that '[the judges of the Court] have never held in favour of an applicant in cases dealing with the wearing of religious apparel or having particular appearance, for example, which can be important to people from some religious traditions despite having little relevance in Christianity. On the other hand they have been quick to hold that there is a right to proselytize or "bear Christian witness".'
[98] *Hasan and Chaush v Bulgaria* (Application No 30985/96) 24 EHRR 55.
[99] *Eweida v British Airways* [2010] EWCA Civ 80.   [100] See n 83 above.

the additional protections of Article 2 of the First Protocol apply) and the legislature. In *Darby v Sweden*[101] the ECommHR rejected the argument that an applicant's decision to reside chiefly in another state meant that he had voluntarily waived his right to avoid the compulsory church taxes imposed by the Swedish Government on temporary residents. Notably, however, the law to which the Commission took exception in *Darby* imposed the duty on the applicant to pay the relevant church tax merely as a result of his living in Sweden, rather than as a result of his having engaged in public activities. Accordingly, this decision can be seen more as a vindication of a private right to individual religious freedom than a right to have one's faith accommodated by public authorities. This is similar to the situation in *Lautsi* where it was held that the state, by requiring school attendance, interfered with private religious liberty by promoting a particular faith in its schools.

The case law shows, however, that other than when the state seeks to actively promote a particular faith within state institutions, the ECtHR's general approach has been to characterize individual religious freedom as a right that does not necessarily include an entitlement to have one's religious identity accommodated in contexts, such as the employment relationship, that are not purely private. Clashes between the state's interest in preserving the religious neutrality of the public sphere and claims to religious freedom have generally been resolved in favour of the state. This approach is largely consistent with the secular idea of the public sphere as a religiously neutral place in which religious concerns deserve no special consideration and with the idea of religious freedom as primarily a matter of individual freedom of thought rather than a way of life. The ECtHR's emphasis on the neutrality and general applicability of laws as a reason for their compatibility with the Convention seems to draw heavily on liberal and secular conceptions of the neutral state, while its emphasis on voluntarism and choice seem to place it firmly in line with the notion of religious freedom as an element of a wider respect for individual autonomy, rather than approaches that stress the need to protect religion's communal and social role.[102] Indeed, the Court has referred approvingly to secularism as a notion that is in harmony with the values of the Convention on more than one occasion.[103] In *Lautsi* and *Buscarini* it distinguished between state recognition of the cultural role of

---

[101] *Darby v Sweden* (1990) 13 EHRR 774 (discussed in Evans (n 3 above) 127).

[102] As noted above, the Court's willingness to decide for itself what an individual's faith requires is inconsistent with such an approach.

[103] See *Refah Partisi and others v Turkey* (2003) 37 EHRR 1 para 93; and *Sahin v Turkey* (Application No 44774/98) [2004] ECHR 299 para 99.

a particular faith (which is acceptable) and state recognition of the truth claims of a religion (which would violate what it termed the state's duty of 'confessional neutrality').[104] Furthermore, by regarding religion, in cases such as *Refah Partisi* and *Dahlab v Swizerland* (above), as a potential rival to the liberal democratic state and by focusing on the need to restrict religious freedom in the public arena in order to protect 'the rights and freedoms of others', the Court's approach appears to recognize that despite its status as an important part of individual identity, religion can itself pose a threat to individual autonomy.

However, while the Court's reluctance to require accommodation of religion in public contexts may be consistent with notions of neutrality and individual autonomy, it does not necessarily imply that the Court has embraced the absolute religious neutrality of the state as the foundation of its approach to the regulation of the relationship between religion, the individual, and the state. First, as noted above, the Court has faced allegations that its approach to the issue of the right to manifest one's religion has been tainted with bias towards traditionally European forms of religion. In addition, the Court's decisions have facilitated the right of states to develop a particular relationship to religion or individual religions to a significant degree. As the *Lautsi* decision made clear, states are entitled to recognize the cultural role of particular faiths in national identities, provided that such recognition does not spill over into state recognition of the truth claims of a particular faith. Indeed, the Court has repeatedly upheld the public role of individual denominations in states that maintain particular ties to certain religions. Seen in this way, the restriction of the requirement to respect religious freedom to the private sphere helps to enable the state to define its own relationship to religion (which may include recognition of the cultural role of a particular faith that brings significant public and communal privileges to certain religions). Liberal ideas of the religious neutrality of the state have achieved prominence only relatively recently and have been enforced only in relation to state recognition of the truth claims of particular faiths. The Court's greater vigilance in policing the boundaries of European secularism may, as Chapter 6 discusses, be linked to rising concerns in relation to the influence of Islam in Europe. Nevertheless, despite such concerns the Court has, in general, been very accommodating of the institutional and symbolic links between states and certain religions that are common in Europe, and to which discussion now turns.

---

[104] See *Lautsi v Italy* (Application No 30814/06) 3 November 2009 para 56.

4.3 Institutional Religious Freedom

The Strasbourg Court's approach to the regulation of the institutional aspect of religious freedom and the relationship of religious institutions to the state also, in general, reflects the prioritization of the right of the state to choose to define a particular communal religious identity, at least in relation to the definition of national cultural identity. While the Court has been unsympathetic to attempts to require states to accord special accommodation for individual religiosity in the public arena, it has upheld the granting by Member States of significant public privileges to state-favoured religious institutions. The Court has placed boundaries on the rights of states in this area. As noted above, the *Lautsi* and *Buscarini* decisions limit the degree to which the state can endorse the truth claims of a particular religion. The flipside of holding religion at a certain distance from the state is the internal autonomy of religious institutions. In *Hasan and Chaush v Bulgaria*,[105] the Court was faced with a situation where, in reaction to internal disputes, the Bulgarian Government had dismissed the leadership of the Bulgarian Muslim community in order to ensure that each religious community would have a unified leadership. In ruling on a complaint by those dismissed, the Court recognized the importance of the institutional element of religious freedom, stating that '[w]ere the organisational life of the community not protected by Article 9 of the Convention, all other aspects of the individual's freedom of religion would become vulnerable'.[106] It went on to find that attempts by the state to interfere in the internal affairs of religious communities constituted a violation of Article 9[107] and could not, in a democratic society, be justified by the need to ensure unified religious leadership.[108]

Indeed, the Court has gone further and has recognized that the internal autonomy of religious institutions can also legitimately be recognized as extending to cover situations where religious organizations engage in otherwise regulated activities, such as employment, in order to carry out religious activities. In *Knudsen v Norway*[109] the Norwegian State Church had dismissed one of its ministers, who disagreed with recent abortion legislation and who refused to perform certain tasks which he felt required him to act in violation of his conscience. The minister's application under Article

---

[105] *Hasan and Chaush v Bulgaria* (2002) 34 EHRR 1339.   [106] Ibid para 62.
[107] Ibid para 82.
[108] Ibid para 78. See also *Church of Scientology Moscow v Russia* (Application No 18147/02) 5 April 2007 where the deregistration of the Church of Scientology was held to violate Art 11 in conjunction with Art 9.   [109] *Knudsen v Norway* (1986) 8 EHRR 45.

9 was dismissed on the grounds that the Church was entitled to require its ministers to behave in a certain way or to resign. Although the church in question was a state church, the central holding in the case applies equally to religions that are not similarly connected to an individual state. It would seem therefore that religious freedom under the ECHR involves a degree of internal autonomy for religious institutions that may not be provided to other institutions. Religions, by virtue of their religious nature, are seen as being exempt from certain otherwise generally applicable norms. The Catholic Church, for example, is not required to obey gender equality laws in its recruitment of priests. To hold otherwise would have serious implications for the ability of religious institutions to organize themselves in accordance with their beliefs. This willingness to uphold the autonomy of religious institutions does, in effect, permit states to enable religious organizations to claim exemptions from generally applicable laws on grounds of religious freedom.

In relation to tasks such as acting as a member of the clergy or a political campaigner, where the job in question has a clear ideological element, it can be appreciated why respect for freedom of conscience can be invoked to justify some discrimination. However, in relation to religion, the Court (and, prior to its abolition, the Commission of Human Rights) has gone further and has upheld such privileges even when institutions were engaging in regulated activities, such as employment in jobs not directly related to religious activities but instead related to a religion's broader public role. In *Rommelfanger v Federal Republic of Germany*[110] the Strasbourg institutions upheld the dismissal of a doctor in a Catholic hospital who was fired after he criticized in a letter to a newspaper the Catholic Church's attitude to abortion. The German Constitutional Court upheld the decision to dismiss the applicant on the basis that his letter had constituted a breach of his contractual duty of loyalty to his employer. The Commission of Human Rights dismissed his application under the Convention on the basis that the enforcement of the employer's contractual rights did not violate an interference with his ECHR

---

[110] *Rommelfanger v Federal Republic of Germany* (1989) 62 DR 151, ECommHR; German Constitutional Court Decision: BNr 12242/86. EU discrimination law may take a different view of this issue. In late 2009 the European Commission sent the British Government a 'reasoned opinion' arguing that the failure of British legislation to restrict the exemptions from the duty not to discriminate on grounds of sexual orientation granted to religious employers to situations where adherence to religious teaching is proportionate and a genuine and determining occupational requirement amounted to a breach of Directive (EC) 2000/78 establishing a general framework for equal treatment in employment and occupation Article 2(5) [2000] OJ L303/16.

rights. In doing so, the Commission was supporting the right of a religious institution to terminate the employment of an employee of a partly state-funded body (the Catholic hospital), whose functions were largely secular, on the basis of his disagreement with the religious teachings of the owner of that institution. Robbers sees this decision as representing acknowledgment 'to a great degree' of the 'right of self-determination of the religious communities in its substance'[111] by the Convention institutions. In this case the relevant 'right to self-determination' involves the exemption of such religious institutions from norms generally applied to bodies engaged in the public sphere activity of employment in institutions that are not exclusively religious in nature. Moreover, these privileges were held to comply with Article 9 despite their impact on the rights of individual employees of such organizations. As has been noted above, the Court has repeatedly held that individuals cannot rely on claims of religious freedom to demand exemptions from generally applicable government regulations in areas such as employment. However, the rulings in *Knudsen* and *Rommelfanger* seem to indicate that the Strasbourg institutions are sympathetic to the granting by Member States of precisely such exemptions to certain religious institutions.

Such an approach could be interpreted as the Court embracing a version of collective religious freedom that recognizes religion's cultural and communal aspects and enables religious institutions to make demands of the state in public contexts. However, it would be a mistake to view this conferral of public privilege on religious institutions as an instance of the Convention institutions requiring the state to subjugate its interests to those of religious freedom. First, in both cases the Court was upholding the choice made by the state to grant such privilege, rather than laying down rights enforceable against the state. Secondly, the wider Convention case law shows very little support for the prioritization of religious freedom to such an extent. Not only would this be inconsistent, as noted above, with the Court's approach to individual religious freedom; the Strasbourg institutions have repeatedly accorded priority to the rights of states to ensure the religious neutrality of public contexts over those of individuals' religious freedom. This has occurred not only in relation to its upholding of 'neutral and generally applicable' laws but in cases such as *Sahin*, *Kalaç*, and *Dahlab*, where the efforts of the Turkish and Swiss states to control the wearing of religious apparel in educational and military establishments in order to uphold the secularity of

---

[111] G Robbers, 'State and Church in the European Union' in G Robbers (ed.), *State and Church in the European Union* (Baden Baden: Nomos Verlagsgesellschaft, 1996).

public institutions were upheld by the Court. The primacy of the needs of the secular state and the particular public orders of individual states is also seen in the analysis of the Article 9 jurisprudence of the Court of Human Rights by the French Conseil Constitutionnel as part of its 2004 decision in relation to the proposed EU Constitutional Treaty.[112] The Conseil analysed the Treaty's protection of religious freedom in order to assess its compatibility with France's constitutional principle of secularism. It noted that the protection afforded to freedom of religion under the proposed Treaty was substantially similar to that provided by Article 9 of the ECHR. Having reviewed the relevant case law, the Conseil noted that Convention rights were to be interpreted in harmony with the constitutional traditions common to the Member States and concluded that Article 9 had been interpreted by the Strasbourg institutions in such a way as to confer on Member States a wide margin of appreciation. This margin of appreciation was considered by the Conseil as being sufficiently broad to prevent the protection provided to religious freedom by the EU's Charter of Fundamental Rights (which it viewed as having the same substance as that provided by Article 9) from undermining the constitutional principle of strict secularism laid down in the French Constitution, notwithstanding any impact the application of this principle might have on religious freedom.[113] In other words, the religious freedom protected by Article 9 was, under the jurisprudence of the Strasbourg Court, not so extensive as to preclude measures aimed at defending the public order of the state or at structuring and regulating the public sphere in accordance with that state's particular communal cultural identity (so long as the facilitation of religion in this regard did not, as in *Lautsi*, reach the level of state endorsement of the truth claims of a particular faith). The Conseil's assessment of the limited impact of Article 9 on the ability of individual states to define their own relationship to religion would appear to be largely correct. In circumstances such as those in *Kalaç*, *Karaduman*, and *Sahin*[114] where states have seen public expressions of religiosity as a threat to the identity of the state, or even in cases like *Dahlab*, where the objection was

---

[112] See Decision No 2004-505 DC of 19 November 2004, Treaty establishing a Constitution for Europe, available at <http://www.conseil-constitutionnel.fr/decision/2004/2004505/eng.htm> (last visited 12 May 2010). See also G Carcassonne, 'France: Conseil Constitutionnel on the European Constitutional Treaty' (2005) 1 *European Constitutional Law Review* 293.

[113] See Decision No 2004-505 DC of 19 November 2004, Treaty establishing a Constitution for Europe, available at <http://www.conseil-constitutionnel.fr/decision/2004/2004505/eng.htm> (last visited 12 May 2010).

[114] See nn 78, 79, and 82 above.

to certain forms of religious expression as opposed to religion in general,[115] the Court has been willing to see the relationship between religion and the state in the public arena in essentially competitive terms. Furthermore, it is clear that conflict between the right to religious freedom and that of the state to control and define the nature of public spaces and institutions will generally be resolved in favour of the latter. However, unlike France, most Member States of both the Council of Europe and the EU have official links to certain religious traditions. Not only are particular faiths important sources of national identity in such states,[116] the intertwining of state and religion includes the making of references in constitutional texts to religion as something that underpins the constitutional order,[117] and permits religious bodies to undertake state functions in areas such as education and healthcare.[118] When, as in cases such as *Rommelfanger*, states have chosen to confer important public roles on certain favoured denominations, the Court has not seen the religion as a rival to the state in the public arena. Indeed, in upholding such arrangements it has, in contrast to its approach in cases such as *Sahin* and *Dahlab*, downplayed the impact of the presence of religion in the public contexts on those of different or no religion. The recognition by the Court of Human Rights of the rights of religious institutions in the public sphere can be seen, not a matter of the assertion of religious rights against the authority of the state in the public sphere, but rather as a matter of a recognition of the right of states, within limits, to define their own identity and relationship to religion, including the right to treat certain denominations, by virtue of history, as constitutional status and institutional reality, in some way part of the state's cultural identity and broader public order.

This recognition of the cultural links between certain states and certain religions has been accompanied by a clear recognition on the part of the Court that the Convention imposes limitations on the degree to which states can seek to impose a single religious identity or legislate for the religious law of a single faith. Its judgment in *Refah Partisi v Turkey* stated that a political programme aimed at introducing Islamic religious law would be 'incompatible with the fundamental principles of democracy, as set forth in the Convention',[119] noting particularly how 'the way [Islamic religious law] intervenes in all spheres of private and public life in accordance with religious precepts' meant that it 'clearly diverges from Convention values'.[120]

---

[115] See n 81 above.   [116] See Ch 2, section 4.3.   [117] Ibid, section 4.4.
[118] Ibid, section 4.5.   [119] *Refah Partisi and others v Turkey* (2003) 37 EHRR 1 para 123.
[120] Ibid.

Although these comments were, strictly speaking, *obiter*, they represent a clear indication that there is a point at which promotion of certain forms of religion through state institutions or religious influence over the state would be incompatible with the respect for pluralism and individual autonomy inherent in the Convention system. The desire to keep a degree of distance between state power and religion is also seen in *Lautsi* where, as noted above, the Court placed greater emphasis on the state's duty of 'confessional neutrality' and explicitly distinguished between recognition of the role of specific faiths in national identity, which is compatible with the Convention, and recognition by the state of the truth claims of a particular faith, which is not.

Nevertheless, the Court's upholding of the status of state churches, together with the decision in *Rommelfanger*, show recognition of the cultural role of religion in certain Member States and an unwillingness to interfere with the promotion of a religiously particular communal cultural identity by such states. Thus, the Court has not viewed the cultural identification of the state with a particular denomination, the promotion of a religiously specific communal identity, or the involvement of religious institutions in the exercise of state functions as violating Convention values despite the impact of such policies on the equal treatment of religions or on individual freedom from religion. On the other hand, apart from the rather limited internal rights recognized in cases such as *Knudsen* and *Hasan and Chaush* (above), states have not been required by the Court to provide religious institutions with the public role Dalacoura would see as necessary to the maintenance of their public role.[121] Thus, the failure of the Convention institutions in cases such as *Rommelfanger* to interfere with the granting of public sphere privileges to certain religions can be see as empowering the state to define its relationship to religion in the manner of its choosing, rather than as a requirement that such a relationship encompass certain collective privileges for religious institutions.

4.4 Religion as Part of the State

Taken together, the Strasbourg Court's characterization of the relationship between religion and the state in the public arena in competitive terms, its prioritization of the rights of the state over those of religions in the public contexts, and its upholding of the right of states to allow religious institutions

---

[121] See n 28 above.

to exercise significant public sector activities, point to a recognition of certain religions as in some way part of the state and its identity.

Despite the evolution of real and substantial limits on the influence of religion over both public and private spheres in Europe, many European states have not fully renounced the use of state power to promote religious interests or to uphold the taboos necessary for the maintenance of religious influence over society. The use of state power in this way has a potentially serious impact on individual autonomy and runs counter to the liberal rationale of the protection of religious freedom. As noted above, the Court has shown a degree of nervousness at the impact on Convention values of governmental involvement in this area by repeatedly emphasizing the state's role as a 'neutral and impartial organiser of the exercise of various religions'.[122] Nevertheless, although states have been prevented from endorsing the truth claims of religions, the Convention has not been held to mandate the institutional separation of church and state and has been interpreted so as to facilitate the use, albeit to a limited degree, of coercive power to promote the interests of certain religions and to identify the interests of certain religions with those of the state.

In *Darby v Sweden*[123] the ECtHR explicitly stated that the establishment of a single faith as a state religion did not breach Article 9 (although it did say that the terms of establishment must include safeguards for individual religious freedom). The direct collection of taxes by churches and the use of the judicial apparatus of the state to enforce payment of religious taxes have also been upheld despite the danger that such an approach may force individuals to reveal their religious beliefs to the state.[124] The Strasbourg institutions have also upheld the outright favouring of certain denominations under the taxation system provided that there are 'objective and reasonable justifications' for such discrimination[125] and have refused to find a right to recognition by the state even when such recognition brought significantly more favourable treatment from state institutions.[126]

Even more strikingly, in *Kokkinakis v Greece*,[127] the ECtHR was faced with national legislation banning proselytism. Although a process of constitutional amendment had removed the sections which explicitly favoured

---

[122] See n 119 above, para 91. See also the discussion of *Lautsi* (n 2 above).

[123] *Darby v Sweden* (1991) 13 EHRR 774.

[124] *E & GR v Austria* (Application No 9781/82) (1984) 37 DR 42.

[125] *Iglesia Bautista 'el Salvador' and Ortega Moratilla v Spain* (Application No 17522/90) (1992) 72 DR 256.   [126] *X v Austria* (Application No 8652/79) (1981) 26 DR 89.

[127] *Kokkinakis v Greece* (1994) 17 EHRR 397.

Greek Orthodoxy, the law had originally been introduced and continued to function so as to maintain the dominant position of the Greek Orthodox Church. The Court found in favour of the applicant (a Jehovah's Witness convicted of seeking to convert a Greek Orthodox woman) but did so on the basis that the Greek courts had failed to indicate with sufficient precision what element of the applicant's actions had constituted the relevant offence. It explicitly refused to condemn anti-proselytism laws in general and specifically upheld the compatibility of laws banning 'improper proselytism'. In doing so, the Court upheld what was, in effect, the use of coercive legal measures to restrict the ability of minority religions to undermine the dominance of what, as the Court noted, was in the Greek context the 'religion of the state'.[128] It was left to the dissenting judgment of Judge Martens to make the case for viewing religious freedom as essentially an individual matter and to argue that '[w]hether or not someone intends to change religion is no concern of the State's and, consequently, neither in principle should it be the State's concern if someone attempts to induce the another to change his religion'.[129]

Indeed, despite its statement that Article 9 is 'also a precious asset for atheists, sceptics and the unconcerned',[130] the ECtHR has gone as far as using it, and the notion of religious freedom in general, as justification for laws under which the state can restrict expression deemed hostile or insulting towards religion. In *Otto Preminger Institut v Austria*[131] the Court upheld a ban on the (private) showing in the, predominantly Catholic, Tyrolean region of a film the Austrian authorities felt would be insulting to Catholics, stating that 'in extreme cases the effect of particular methods of opposing or denying religious beliefs can be such as to inhibit those who hold such beliefs from exercising their freedom to hold and express them'.[132] It went on to use Article 9 as a justification for restricting freedom of expression under Article 10 on the basis that '[t]he respect for the religious feelings of believers as guaranteed in Article 9 can legitimately be thought to have been violated by provocative portrayals of objects of religious veneration; and such portrayals can be regarded as malicious violation of the spirit of tolerance, which must also be a feature of democratic society'.[133]

The Court repeated this line of argument in *Wingrove v United Kingdom*[134] where it based its decision to uphold restrictions on the distribution of an

---

[128] Ibid para 14.   [129] Ibid.   [130] *Kokkinakis v Greece* (1994) 17 EHRR 397 para 31.
[131] *Otto Preminger Institut v Austria* (1994) 19 EHRR 34   [132] Ibid para 47.
[133] Ibid.   [134] *Wingrove v United Kingdom* (1996) 24 EHRR 1.

allegedly blasphemous film on the 'right of citizens not to be insulted in their religious feelings'.[135] There is, however, no such right apparent in the text of Article 9. Moreover, there was no suggestion in either case that the films in question incited violence or hatred against any religious group. As the British High Court pointed out in its judgment upholding the refusal of the authorities to prosecute the producers of *Jerry Springer the Opera*: 'it does not seem to us that insulting a man's religious beliefs, deeply held though they are likely to be, will normally amount to an infringement of his Article 9 rights since his right to hold to and to practise his religion is generally unaffected by such insults'.[136]

In 2005 the Strasbourg Court again upheld the compatibility of blasphemy laws with the Convention in *IA v Turkey*.[137] Three of the seven judges argued strongly that 'the time has perhaps come to "revisit" [the approach in *Otto Preminger Institut* and *Wingrove*], which in our view seems to place too much emphasis on conformism or uniformity of thought and to reflect an overcautious and timid conception of freedom of the press'.[138] However, the majority relied on the precedents set in *Otto Preminger Institut* and *Wingrove* to hold that the conviction of a publisher for publishing a book which was harshly critical of the Koran met the legitimate aim of intending 'to provide protection against offensive attacks on matters regarded as sacred by Muslims'[139] and, as the book had not been seized, the measure was proportionate.[140] Such a view of Article 9 grants to the state significant latitude to use its coercive powers to maintain the taboos that Dalacoura has argued are necessary for the maintenance of the social position and influence of individual denominations and would appear to be at odds with the liberal notion of religious freedom as predominantly a means to ensure respect for individual choice within the framework of a religiously neutral state.[141]

As noted above, European society is notably a-religious in international terms and both EU and ECHR institutions have evidenced a strong concern that unfettered religious influence over the public sphere may be incompatible with Europe's shared commitment to liberal democracy. The expansive and communalist view of religious freedom seen in *Wingrove, Otto Preminger*, and *IA* has the potential to impact on liberal democratic values and freedom from religion to a significant degree, and the Court has not held to it in

---

[135] Ibid para 47.
[136] *R (Green) v City of Westminster Magistrates' Court* [2007] EWHC 2785 (Admin) para 17.
[137] *IA v Turkey* (Application No 42571/98) 13 September 2005.
[138] Ibid para 8, dissenting judgment of Judges Costa, Cabral-Barreto, and Jungwiert.
[139] Ibid para 30.   [140] Ibid para 32.   [141] See n 28 above.

all circumstances. The Court has been willing to countenance relatively clear disparities in treatment in relation to the rights of different denominations in the public sphere. In *Wingrove*, when dealing with insults towards the UK's established Christian religion, the Court had invoked the 'right of citizens not to be insulted in their religious feelings'.[142] In contrast, in *The Church of Scientology and 128 of its Members v Sweden*,[143] the Commission dismissed a complaint against the failure of the Swedish state to punish a man who had been critical of the religion on the basis that 'a right to be free from criticism' was not part of freedom of religion.[144] Similarly, in *Choudhury v United Kingdom*,[145] when faced with a UK law that criminalized blasphemy of the Christian religion but not Islam, the Commission refused to find a violation of the Convention and held that the failure to make out a claim under Article 9 also defeated arguments under Article 14, which prohibits discrimination in respect of rights protected by the Convention.[146] Thus, states have been permitted to provide protection for selected religions and to use coercive legal powers to protect those religions that form part of their communal identity.

Clearly, the liberal and egalitarian values of the Convention, and in particular the duty to respect individual autonomy in relation to religious identity, provide significant limitations on the degree to which states can use their coercive powers to favour certain chosen religions. In addition to its rulings in *Lautsi* and *Buscarini*, the Court has ruled that a failure to provide exemptions from compulsory religion classes to pupils whose parents objected to the content of the lessons was a violation of the Convention.[147] Furthermore, as noted above, the Court's judgment in *Refah Partisi v Turkey*[148] gave strong indications that attempts to introduce a theocratic system, or to legislate for religious law in such a way as to interfere significantly with rights to privacy and self-determination, would breach the ECHR.[149] Nevertheless, these values have not been interpreted so as to require separation of the interests of the state and individual religions. Despite its attachment to liberal values, the Court's approach to the relationship between religion and the state in Europe owes something to visions of religion as a collective and cultural

---

[142] See n 134 above.

[143] *The Church of Scientology and 128 of Its Members v Sweden* (Application No 8282/78) (1980) 21 DR 109, 100.　　　　　　　　　　　　　　[144] See Evans (n 3 above) 69–70.

[145] *Choudhury v United Kingdom* (Application No 17439/90) (1991) 12 *Human Rights Law Journal* 172.　　　　　　　　　　　　　　[146] Ibid.

[147] *Zengin v Turkey* (Application No 1448/04) 9 October 2007.

[148] *Refah Partisi v Turkey* (2003) 37 EHRR 1.　　　　[149] Ibid para 123.

matter in addition to liberal notions of religious freedom as an element of individual autonomy. The Court has permitted Member States to use state institutions to offer privileged treatment to certain denominations, to use coercive powers to uphold the dominant position of certain religions, and to insulate chosen faiths from the full rigours of democratic debate, thus enabling such states to maintain and promote certain religions as elements of their collective identity.

5. Conclusion

The fundamental rights obligations of the EU in respect of religious freedom have not, to date, required it to call into question the continued intertwining of religion and the state in many of its Member States. The Union is committed to the protection of religious freedom and this obligation applies across all areas of EU law. The jurisprudence of the ECtHR, which largely determines the content of the Union's fundamental rights obligations, does reflect humanist ideas to a significant degree. The Court's view of individual religious freedom as largely a private matter of identity is consistent with notions of the religiously neutral state. Decisions such as *Refah Partisi* and those relating to the wearing of Islamic dress in public institutions, reflect a fear of the consequences for individual autonomy of significant religious presence in the public arena. However, overall, the Court has shown a pragmatic acceptance of the continued importance of religion to Member State identity and has been unwilling to interpret guarantees of religious freedom in such a way as to interfere with the ability of Member States to define a relationship to religion which reflects their cultural norms. While not requiring them to do so, the ECtHR's judgments have permitted states to grant significant institutional privileges to religious bodies and have enabled them to play key roles in relation to important state functions such as the provision of healthcare and education, despite the impact that such an approach may have on individual freedom from religion and equal treatment of religions. Furthermore, it has not only upheld the recognition of official state religions, thus recognizing the pragmatic virtue of the old *cuius regio eius religio* principle, but has also endorsed the use of coercive state powers to maintain the taboos necessary for the continuance of religion's social role by upholding laws designed to maintain the dominance of certain denominations[150] or

---

[150] See, eg *Kokkinakis v Greece* (1994) 17 EHRR 397.

providing selective protection to certain faiths from ridicule or blasphemy. On the other hand, decisions such as *Lautsi* (provided that it is upheld by the Grand Chamber on appeal) have shown an increasing concern on the part of the Court to police the boundary between state recognition of a particular faith as an element of national culture, and state recognition of the truth claims of a particular religion. This greater strictness, which builds on the Court's frank recognition of the dangers of theocracy in *Refah Partisi* and which may be linked to more general concerns relating to the role of Islam in Europe,[151] may mean that, in the future, the Convention will regulate Member State relationships to religion to a greater degree, with knock-on consequences in terms of the EU's approach to these issues.

⌠Nevertheless, as matters stand, the fundamental rights framework provided by the ECHR provides significant latitude for states to maintain close relationships to certain denominations. Given religion's dual nature as an individual and collective phenomenon, it is not surprising that conflicts between protection of individual and collective religious identities have arisen. The approach of the ECtHR has been to protect individual religious identity in private. Such an approach means that Member States have not been required to abandon or revisit shared cultural norms and practices that are less challenging to adherents to culturally entrenched religions than to those seeking to follow the practices of religions whose large-scale presence in Europe is more recent and whose practices are more likely to conflict with established structures. Furthermore, in non-private contexts, the ECHR jurisprudence has, by granting to individual states the right to define and protect a denomination-specific communal cultural identity, required individual religious identity to give way to particular communal religious, political, or cultural norms in certain circumstances. Thus, religious identity is protected in a framework within which, provided that it respects the pluralism and respect for individual autonomy inherent in the liberal democratic values underpinning the Convention, the right of the state to maintain a religiously specific element to its identity and to promote such an identity through public institutions is largely upheld. ⌡Nevertheless, although the ECHR largely determines the content of EU fundamental rights norms, the admittedly limited EU jurisprudence in this area indicates a slightly broader view of the protection to be given to individual religious identities

---

[151] See Ch 6. See also R McCrea, 'De Facto Secularism in a Diversifying Religious Environment: The Changing Relationship between State and Religion in Europe' in A Sajo (ed.), *Religion in the Public Square* (Utrecht: Eleven International Publishing, forthcoming 2011).

in non-private contexts and appears to grant greater scope to individuals to require equal treatment of their particular religious identity in contexts such as employment where doing so may impinge on the ability of states to promote particular communal cultural and religious practices. Such an approach has also been seen in EU legislation in this area, which is the subject of Chapter 5.

5

The Regulation of Religion in the Single Market

1. Introduction

In line with the approach outlined in Chapter 4, this chapter shows how EU law has largely viewed religion as a matter of identity. In regulating this form of identity in the context of the Single Market, the European Union (EU) has adopted a dualist approach that sees religion both as an economic choice within the market and a phenomenon requiring protection from the economic and commercial processes of the market. As religious identity is both individual and collective in nature, the Union is therefore required to mediate conflicts between individual and collective religious identities. EU law has actively facilitated individual religious identity within the Single Market on a basis that promotes the equal treatment of all religions and potentially destabilizes denomination-specific communal market practices and structures, most notably through its prohibition of direct and indirect discrimination in employment on grounds of religion. On the other hand, the actual impact of this facilitation is limited by the need to respect the overall structures of the competitive market and by the Union's recognition of collective religious identity. EU law has recognized religion, including religiously influenced market structures and institutional arrangements, as elements of national culture that Member States are entitled to uphold. It has also granted religious institutions exemptions from anti-discrimination legislation, thus according priority to their collective identity over that of the individual identity of their employees.

However, in line with the principle of balance between religious and humanist influences, the facilitation of both individual and collective religious identities is also limited. Exemptions from anti-discrimination legislation have been narrowly drawn and are regarded as exceptional. Furthermore, the limitations on religion's political influence, which the Union sees as intrinsic to the notion of balance that underpins its public order, have also been recognized through the explicit subjugation of religious rights to those of the state in order to defend fundamental state interests and the liberal democratic order.

The chapter shows that this approach to religion, and, in particular, the characterization of religion's public role as part of national culture, has allowed 'insider' religions that have strong cultural roots in Member States to access significantly greater privileges within the marketplace. Furthermore, such privileges are limited by the needs of the market and state to a significantly lesser degree than the individual religious rights recognized in other areas of Single Market law. Finally, this chapter demonstrates how the cultural prism through which 'insider' faiths are seen causes their ideological demands to be viewed as cultural, and therefore less liable to restriction on the basis of the need to respect restrictions on religion's political influence than the demands of 'outsider' religions. Accordingly, the Union allows religious elements of national culture, and therefore denominationally specific practices and ideas of the good life, to exercise significant influence within the marketplace. The regulation of religion within the Single Market reflects the wider, culturally conditioned dialectic in EU law between the accommodation of religion's role in individual and collective identity and the need to limit the political and legal influence of religion in order to respect the principle of balance between the religious, cultural, and humanist elements that characterizes the Union's public order.

2. Dual Approach to Religion in the Market

2.1 Religion as a Market Choice

The law of the Single Market views religion in the marketplace in two distinct ways, recognizing it as both an economic choice that can be facilitated by the economic liberties of the Single Market, and an intimate, non-economic phenomenon that requires protection from those same liberties. In relation to the former, the Court of Justice has, on occasion, been willing to stretch the notion of economic activities in order to protect religiously motivated choices by individuals even when the actions in question lacked features such as exchange and commercial value, which normally characterize market transactions. For instance, in *Steymann v Staatssecretaris van Justitie*,[1] the Court assessed the right of a German national to live in a religious commune in the Netherlands solely in terms of his rights to freedom of movement and the economic aspects of his activities. In this case the applicant challenged the refusal of the Dutch authorities to grant him the residence permit to which EEC nationals employed in the Netherlands were entitled. Mr Steymann was a member of a religious commune, known as the Bhagwan Community, for whom he performed household chores and helped with the community's commercial activities. In return, the community provided for Mr Steymann's material needs.[2] However, the community provided for the needs of all of its members whether or not they performed such duties. The Dutch authorities ruled that Mr Steymann was not pursuing an activity as an employed person and refused him a residence permit on that basis. The Dutch Raad van Staat referred the following question to the Court of Justice:

Can activities which consist in, and are entirely centred around, participating in a community based on religion or on another form of philosophy and in following the rules of life of that community, whose members provide each other with benefits, be regarded as an economic activity or as a service for the purposes of the Treaty establishing the European Economic Community?[3]

The Court appeared to take a very minimalist view of the competence then held by the EC in relation to religious matters, stating that 'in view of the objectives of the European Economic Community, participation in a community based on religion or another form of philosophy falls within the field of application of Community law only in so far as it can be regarded as an economic activity within the meaning of Article 2 of the Treaty'.[4]

The Court went on to hold that the work carried out by members of the Bhagwan Community constituted an 'essential part of participation in that community'[5] and that the support given to members could be regarded as 'an indirect quid pro quo for their work'.[6]

Accordingly the Court found in favour of the applicant, holding that:

Article 2 of the EEC Treaty must be interpreted as meaning that activities performed by members of a community based on religion or another form of philosophy as part of the commercial activities of that community constitute economic

---

[1] Case 196/87 *Steymann v Staatssecretaris van Justitie* [1988] ECR 6159.   [2] Ibid para 4.
[3] Ibid para 6.   [4] Ibid para 9.   [5] Ibid para 12.   [6] Ibid.

activities in so far as the services which the community provides to its members may be regarded as the indirect quid pro quo for genuine and effective work.[7]

Thus, the Court regarded religion as relevant to EU law rights only in so far as it could be subsumed into the broad economic framework of the issue of free movement of workers. Therefore, while the judgment certainly approached the issue from an individual rights perspective, the right in question was seen as that of freedom of movement rather than freedom of religion. Indeed, the most notable aspect of the decision is the Court's concern to bring activities that were not economically motivated within the framework of commercial norms such as 'quid pro quo for genuine and effective work' and its refusal to allow the religious nature of the activity to impinge on the Court's purely economic and individualistic analysis of the issues involved. Religious choices were therefore seen as economic choices and as falling within the ambit of EU law for that reason.

In *van Rosmaalen v Bestuir van de Betrijfsvereinigingen*,[8] the Court of Justice showed a similar willingness to emphasize the commercial aspects of religious conduct, even in contexts where they did not provide the primary motivation for the relevant activities. In this case the Court was required to interpret the definition of 'self-employed' in relation to the pension entitlements of a priest who had worked for several decades as a missionary in what was then called Zaire. The Court ruled that:

The term 'self-employed person'… applies to persons who are pursuing or have pursued, otherwise than under a contract of employment or by way of self-employment in a trade or profession, an occupation in respect of which they receive an income permitting them to meet all or some of their needs, even if the income is supplied by third parties benefiting from the services of a missionary priest.[9]

In other words, the fact that during the course of the applicant's ministry, he had been maintained by the local community rather than the order of priests to which he belonged was sufficient to bring him within the definition of 'self-employed' for the purposes of EU law.

The Court offered no definition of religion in either case. Indeed, the repeated references in the *Steymann* judgment to 'religion or other form of philosophy'[10] could be seen as consistent with a view of religion as simply a

---

[7] Ibid para 14.
[8] Case 300/84 *van Rosmaalen v Bestuir van de Betrijfsvereinigingen* [1986] ECR 3097.
[9] Case 196/87 *Steymann v Staatssecretaris van Justitie* [1988] ECR 6159 para 23.
[10] Ibid para 9.

form of philosophy which is not entitled to any greater consideration or role in public life than other beliefs. Although by supporting the right of an individual to use his or her European right to freedom of movement to take part in the life of a religious community in another Member State the *Steymann* decision could be seen as showing a willingness to facilitate individual freedom of religion and the ability of individuals to construct their own identity, the failure of the Court to attribute any special significance to the religious aspects of the case, and its implicit acquiescence in the Dutch Court's characterization of religion as a form of philosophy, might be less welcome from a religious perspective in other circumstances. Therefore, although the strong emphasis placed by markets on respect for individual autonomy and choice[11] does draw on some of the same principles that form the basis for liberal theories of freedom of religion, a purely economic approach can lead to mischaracterization of individual religious behaviour to a significant degree and ignores vital elements of religion such as its collective, institutional, and cultural elements.

2.2 Protection of Religion from the Market

However, as shown in Chapter 4, the Union is required to protect religious freedom as part of its commitment to fundamental rights. EU law has therefore also recognized religion as a fundamental right requiring protection within the Single Market. The upholding of religious freedom not only involves the balancing of religious rights against the interests of broader structures such as the market and the rights of the non-religious, it also requires the reconciliation of potentially conflicting institutional, collective, and individual religious rights. The protection of religious freedom within the Single Market has led EU law to recognize various individual rights such as an individual right not to be discriminated against on the basis of one's religious identity when engaging in market activities and a right to have one's religious identity facilitated in the workplace. At the same time EU law has also acknowledged collective interests and has sought to balance the right to protect religious ethos of institutions and the religious elements of national culture against such individual entitlements.

The notion that respect for religion required a degree of active protection within the market was recognized relatively early in the history of the

---

[11] See, eg E Petersmann, 'Constitutional Economics, Human Rights and the WTO' (2003) 58 *Aussenwirtschaft* 49, 56–58.

Community. The Preamble to the European Social Charter of 1961, for example, states that 'the enjoyment of social rights should be secured without discrimination on grounds of race, colour, sex, religion, political opinion, national extraction or social origin'.[12]

In its dealings with its own employees the Community has forbidden religious discrimination for some time. For instance, the 1962 Regulations governing the recruitment and employment of Council staff,[13] and the 1976 Council Regulations regulating the conditions of employment of the staff of the European Foundation for the Improvement of Living and Working Conditions[14] and the European Centre for the Development of Vocational Training,[15] all prohibited discrimination on grounds of religion. On the other hand, none specified whether applying generally applicable rules that did not make special allowances for religious beliefs or practice would constitute such discrimination. The ruling of the Court of Justice in the mid-1970s in *Prais v Council*[16] indicated that a duty to take such active steps and to protect individual choice and identity in relation to religion may be part of the general principles of EU law. In this case the applicant had been unable to complete an examination for the recruitment of officials as it had been scheduled on a Jewish holy day on which she was unable to write or travel for religious reasons. The Council refused her request to change the date of the exam. The applicant argued that in the light of Article 9 of the European Convention on Human Rights (ECHR), the regulations governing the recruitment of Community officials should be interpreted so as to enable every candidate to complete the examination irrespective of his or her religious background. The defendant did not dispute that freedom of religion, as guaranteed by Article 9 of the ECHR, was part of the general principles of Community law or that the staff regulations required the Council to recruit without reference to the religion of applicants, but argued that to oblige it to take account of the religious requirements of all candidates would involve an excessive administrative burden. The Court ruled that if the Council

---

[12] European Social Charter 1961; *cf*, eg Art 136(1) EC.

[13] Council Regulation (EEC) 31/62 of 14 June 1962 laying down the Staff Regulations of officials and the conditions of employment of other servants of the European Economic Community and the European Atomic Energy Community [1962] OJ B045/1385, Art 27(2).

[14] Council Regulation (EEC) 1860/76 of 29 June 1976 laying down the conditions of employment of staff of the European Foundation for the Improvement of Living and Working Conditions [1976] OJ L214/24, Ch 3, Art 23.

[15] Council Regulation (EEC) 1859/76 of 29 June 1976 laying down the conditions of employment for staff of the European Centre for the Development of Vocational Training [1976] OJ L214/1, Ch 3, Art 23.   [16] Case 130/75 *Prais v Council* (unreported) 27 October 1976.

were to be informed within good time by a candidate that a particular date presented religious difficulties, then it 'should take this into account... and endeavour to avoid such dates'[17] but that 'neither the Staff Regulations nor the fundamental rights already referred to can be considered as imposing on the appointing authority a duty to avoid a conflict with a religious requirement of which the Authority has not been informed'. The judgment concludes rather cryptically, stating:

In so far as the Defendant, if informed of the difficulty in good time would have been obliged to take reasonable steps to avoid fixing for a test a date which would make it impossible for a person of a particular religious faith to undergo the test, it can be said that the Defendant in the present case was not informed of the unsuitability of certain days until the date for the test had been fixed, and the Defendant was in its discretion entitled to refuse to fix a different date.[18]

This statement left open the issue of whether the Council would have been obliged to set a new date had it been informed in good time or whether such an approach was merely desirable. The decision does, however, indicate both support for the idea of religious freedom as part of the general principles of EU law and a degree of openness on the part of the Court to the idea that individual religious freedom includes a right to adhere to one's religious identity in market contexts such as the workplace, with a corresponding duty on the part of Community institutions actively to facilitate such religious identities. Such a view of individual religious freedom would seem to go beyond the requirements of Article 9 as it has been interpreted by the European Court of Human Rights (ECtHR).[19]

This dual approach of recognizing religion both as a choice that can be facilitated as part of the commercial processes of the Single Market and as a reason to circumscribe such processes, is also seen in more recent Community legislation in relation to employment. Directive (EC) 2003/88, which regulates aspects of working time, shows a willingness to defend religious choices even when they potentially impinge on the pursuit of market imperatives such as maximum efficiency, permitting Member States to allow derogations from working time legislation for 'workers officiating at ceremonies in churches and religious communities'.[20] In doing so, the Union permits

---

[17] Ibid para 16.   [18] Ibid para 19.   [19] See Ch 4.

[20] Council Directive (EC) 2003/88 concerning certain aspects of the organisation of working time [2003] OJ L299/9 (this amended Council Directive (EC) 93/104 concerning certain aspects of the organisation of working time [1993] OJ L307/18, which had a similar provision). See Case C-14/04 *Dellas v Premier Ministre* [2005] ECR I-10253.

Member States to go beyond their minimum ECHR duties and to facilitate individual religious identities in market contexts by disapplying rules that could interfere with religious practices that are otherwise applicable to workers, despite the impact that such facilitation may have on the organization of the working day.

More significantly, the Union's anti-discrimination legislation has conferred more general protection on the religiously motivated choices of individuals in the area of employment. Despite the commitments in relation to discrimination in documents such as the European Social Charter of 1961, a treaty basis for EU legislation in relation to religious discrimination was lacking until the entry into force of the Treaty of Amsterdam in 1999. The situation changed significantly with Article 6a of the Treaty granting the Community the authority to make laws prohibiting discrimination on various grounds, including religion.[21] In late 2000, the Council used these new powers to enact Directive (EC) 2000/78 establishing a general framework for equal treatment in employment and occupation ('the Framework Directive').[22] This Directive was intended to combat discrimination on the grounds listed in Article 6a. In line with EU anti-discrimination law as it had applied in relation to gender discrimination, the Directive prohibited both direct and indirect discrimination on religious grounds. Article 2(2) of the Directive defined these concepts in the following terms:

(a) Direct discrimination shall be taken to occur where one person is treated less favourably than another is, has been or would be treated in a comparable situation, on any of the grounds referred to in Article 1 [these grounds are religion or belief, age, disability, or sexual orientation].

(b) Indirect discrimination shall be taken to occur where an apparently neutral provision, criterion or practice would put persons having a particular religion or belief, a particular disability, a particular age, or a particular sexual orientation at a particular disadvantage compared to other persons unless:

   (i) that provision, criterion or practice is objectively justified by a legitimate aim and the means of achieving that aim are appropriate and necessary.

The duality of the Union's approach to religion in the marketplace is seen here in relation to the differing approaches to direct and indirect discrimination. The prohibition in Article 2(2)(a) on direct discrimination prevents individuals' religious identity from being used to prevent them from engaging in market activities. Religious individuals are not to be prevented

---

[21] Treaty of Amsterdam [1997] OJ C340/133, Art 6a.   [22] [2000] OJ L303/16.

from engaging in the activity of employment, or to be paid less than the market worth of their labour, on the basis of their religion. Thus, the freedom of religious individuals to participate in a free market is protected. This can be seen as in some ways as comparable to the judgment in *Steymann* (above) where the religious nature of the applicant's motivation was not seen as a reason to deny him the market freedoms granted by EU law. Indeed, Article 2(2)(a) goes further and enshrines the formal religious neutrality of the Single Market. Market actors are required by the Directive to be 'religion blind' and not to hold the fact of individuals' religious identity against them. Such an approach reflects the formal equality of all religious individual identities in EU law and establishes the market as an arena within which individuals of all religious backgrounds have an equal opportunity to take part. Thus, notwithstanding the predominance of a single religious tradition in a Member State, outright favouring of adherents to particular religions in the area of employment is prohibited by the Union, which thereby enforces and upholds the notion of the formal equality of individuals as market actors.

The prohibition of indirect discrimination in Article 2(2)(b), on the other hand, takes a different approach. By providing that 'apparently neutral' provisions or practices that place individuals of a particular religion at a disadvantage are to be considered discriminatory unless objectively justified, the Directive goes beyond formal equality and requires that the religious choices of individuals be actively facilitated, thus providing the possibility of protecting such choices from standard market practices. Thus, workplace dress codes that preclude the wearing of headscarves for female Muslim employees, or arrangements in respect of working time that interfere with the ability of workers to respect religious feast days, are potentially covered by the notion of indirect discrimination. This goes significantly beyond the requirements of Article 9, which, as interpreted by the ECtHR, does 'not give individuals the right to behave in the public sphere in compliance with all the demands of their religion or belief'[23] and which involves the active facilitation of religious behaviour even when such behaviour impinges on pre-established workplace practices.

It is noteworthy that the privileges granted by the Directive are applicable to religion in general and make no distinction between culturally

---

[23] See *Arrowsmith v United Kingdom* (Application No 7050/75) (1978) 19 DR 5. Here the term 'public sphere' seems to be used in a broader sense meaning non-private contexts as opposed what Asen calls the 'realm of social life in which public opinion can be formed': R Asen, 'Toward a Normative Conception of Difference in Public Deliberation' (1999) 25 *Argumentation and Advocacy* (Winter) 115.

entrenched and newer or minority faiths. Indeed, the Directive provides significant scope for undermining denomination-specific privilege in the workplace in that it enables adherents of minority religions to characterize workplace structures built around the traditions and practices of the dominant religion as measures placing adherents of minority faiths 'at a particular disadvantage compared to other persons'. Thus, by bringing workplace practices that reflect a particular religious tradition within the notion of discrimination, EU Single Market law not only requires that such practices be objectively justified, but also seems to categorize as discrimination, and therefore implicitly to deprecate, the maintenance of communal structures that accord preferential treatment to certain religions. This approach has the potential to undermine, in the name of the rights of religious individuals, not merely the rights of employers, but also the ability of individual Member States to structure the workplace, and thereby the communal life of the state, in such a way as to reflect their predominant religious tradition.

2.3 Reconciliation of Religious Rights with Established Norms and Structures

The prohibition of indirectly discriminatory measures, as Fredman notes, can be seen as an attempt to reduce the costs to individuals of adhering to certain identities.[24] Taken together, Articles 1[25] and 2(2) of the Framework Directive place religion together with characteristics such as age, disability, or sexual orientation, which are seen as either immutable or as so fundamental to personal identity that individuals should not be asked to change or disavow them. They therefore appear to grant priority to the protection of individual religious identity and the notion of equal treatment of adherents to different religions over the right of states or employers to reflect a particular religious heritage in their workplace practices. Being centred on ideas of respect for and facilitation of individual autonomy, such an approach can be seen as being broadly in line with liberal rationales for the protection of religious freedom.[26] However, such facilitation must be reconciled with

---

[24] See S Fredman, 'Combating Racism with Human Rights: The Right to Equality' in S Fredman (ed.), *Discrimination and Human Rights: The Case of Racism* (Oxford: Oxford University Press, 2001).

[25] Article 1 reads: 'The purpose of this directive is to lay down a general framework for combating discrimination on the grounds of religion or belief, disability, age or sexual orientation as regards employment and occupation, with a view to putting into effect in the Member States the principle of equal treatment'.

[26] Such a view of the purpose of Directive 2000/78 was endorsed in the opinion of Advocate-General Poiares Maduro in Case C-303/06 *Coleman v Attridge Law* [2008] ECR I-5603.

other factors. Rights, of course, do not exist in a vacuum, and their exercise must take account of countervailing rights and interests. Unsurprisingly, the Directive provides that rights may be restricted in order to protect 'the rights and freedoms of others'.[27] Thus, religiously motivated harassment of colleagues or refusals to work with people of a particular gender or religion will not be protected. This was confirmed in the *Ladele* case in the United Kingdom, where the Court of Appeal held that an employer was entitled to require a civil registrar who had a religious objection to homosexuality to register same-sex partnerships.[28]

Nevertheless, religious rights are in certain circumstances accorded clear priority over other countervailing norms. In relation to animal cruelty, for example, EU law has provided exemptions from laws requiring humane slaughtering methods in order to facilitate religious practices in relation to meat preparation. Directive (EC) 93/119 on the protection of animals at the time of slaughter or killing[29] confers in Article 2(8) authority on religious institutions in relation to animal slaughter by providing that 'religious authority on whose behalf the slaughter is carried out shall be competent for the application and monitoring of the special provisions which apply to the slaughter according to religious rites'.[30]

The Directive's Preamble notes that it is 'necessary...to take account of the particular requirements of certain religious rites'. It goes on to provide in Article 5(2) that the requirement that animals be stunned before slaughter does not apply 'in the case of animals subject to particular methods of slaughter required by certain religious rites', thus subjugating the prevention of cruelty to animals to the religious rights of those who only wish to consume ritually killed meat.

Perhaps more significantly for the purposes of this chapter, the rights to active facilitation of religion in the marketplace conferred by EU law and the Framework Directive in particular, also have to be reconciled with the interests of the two pillars of the European public order—the market and the humanist elements of the liberal democratic state.

---

[27] Article 2(5).

[28] *Ladele v London Borough of Islington* [2009] EWCA Civ 1357.

[29] Council Directive (EC) 93/119 on the protection of animals at the time of slaughter or killing [1993] OJ L340/21.

[30] Ibid, Art 2(8). Paragraph 1 of the Preamble to Directive 2001/88, which amends Council Directive (EC) 91/630 laying down minimum standards for the protection of pigs [2001] OJ L340/33, has a similar provision.

2.3.1 Reconciliation with the Structures of the Market

Although in legislation such as the Framework Directive, EU law has provided significant protection to the right of individuals to adhere to and retain a religious identity, this facilitation must adapt itself to the overall structures of the market. A competitive market economy, such as that envisaged by the treaties, is characterized by certain features like the commercial exchange and the pursuit of profit, efficiency, and self-interest. The protection provided by EU law to the rights of religious individuals in areas such as employment can impact on the pursuit of these objectives and a balance must therefore be struck found between them.

Although in *Steymann* (above) the Court of Justice, in characterizing the relationship between the applicant and the religious community to which he belonged as one of employment, was willing to overlook the absence of genuine economic exchange or profit-seeking between them, EU law in this area has been clear that the facilitation of religion must adapt to the profit motive and the need for efficiency in the market. Article 2(2)(b)(i) of the Framework Directive makes this point explicitly, stating that an apparently neutral provision that disadvantages an individual will not be discriminatory if 'that provision, criterion or practice is objectively justified by a legitimate aim and the means of achieving that aim are appropriate and necessary'.

Therefore, workplace practices that place individuals of a particular religion at a disadvantage compared to other individuals will not be considered discriminatory if they are 'objectively justified by a legitimate aim' and the means chosen to achieve the aim are 'appropriate and necessary'. The Directive's provisions make it clear that the pursuit of market goals such as efficiency and competitiveness are to be considered to be legitimate aims in this regard. Paragraph 17 of the Directive's Preamble states that '[t]his Directive does not require the recruitment, promotion, maintenance in employment or training of an individual who is not competent, capable and available to perform the essential functions of the post concerned or to undergo relevant training'. Thus, where the beliefs or practices of a particular religious identity are incompatible with fundamental commercial demands such as the need to perform the 'essential functions' of a post, the duty to facilitate religion will give way to the need to maintain business efficiency and the duty of the employee to provide effective work in return for employment. Indeed, the concern to temper the protection of the rights of religious individuals in order to avoid unduly burdening business and administration was seen in the Court of Justice's judgment in *Prais* (above), which stressed that the duty

to schedule recruitment exams so as to avoid clashing with religiously man-
dated days of rest would only apply when the defendant had been 'informed
of the difficulty in good time' and only extended to a duty 'to take reasonable
steps to avoid fixing for a test a date which would make it impossible for a
person of a particular religious faith to undergo the test',[31] thus allowing the
duty to facilitate an individual's religious choices to be circumscribed by the
need to avoid unduly burdening the process of recruitment.

Judgments in other areas of discrimination law have shown similar concerns. Thus, the need to avoid placing 'an intolerable burden on employers'
was relied on to limit the duty of employers to justify differences in pay
between employees,[32] while 'justifiable operational reasons' were invoked
to limit the duty to facilitate employees on parental leave.[33] The needs of
the broader economy have also been seen as justifying a difference in treatment in respect of employees of small firms[34] and differences in treatment in
respect of older workers.[35] The common thread in these cases is the willingness of the Court to circumscribe rights to equal treatment and the facilitation of individual identities in order to protect the ability of enterprises to
operate efficiently within a competitive economy or to protect the ability of
the state to regulate the economy. While the Court has on occasion found
interferences with the principle of equal treatment to have been disproportionate, in general, it has shown considerable deference to the needs of
employers and the regulatory state. In relation to discrimination on grounds
of religion, therefore, the rights provided by EU law to employees are likely
to be required to accommodate the needs of the competitive market to a significant degree. In relation to indirect discrimination on religious grounds
in particular it must therefore be thought likely that certain religiously
motivated behaviour, such as a refusal on the part of Muslim supermarket
workers to handle pork or alcohol, may well be held to relate to an availability
to perform essential functions of the job and to fall outside of the protection of the Framework Directive on this basis. Writing in relation to the
EU Race Directive[36] (which contains similar provisions relating to indirect

---

[31] Case 130/75 *Prais v Council* (unreported) 27 October 1976, para 19.
[32] Case C-17/05 *BF Cadman v Health and Safety Executive* [2006] ECR I-9583 (AGO).
[33] Case C-116/06 *Sari Kiiski v Tampereen kaupunki* (unreported) 15 March 2007 (AGO)
para 47.
[34] Case C-189/91 *Kirsammer-Hack v Sidal* [1993] ECR I-6185.
[35] See Case C-411/05 *Palacios de la Villa v Cortefiel Servicios SA* [2007] All ER (D) 207 (Oct);
and Case C-144/04 *Werner Mangold v Rüdiger Helm* [2005] ECR I-9981.
[36] Council Directive (EC) 2000/43 implementing the principle of equal treatment between
persons irrespective of racial or ethnic origin [2000] OJ L180/22.

discrimination), Chalmers has suggested that minority identities are recognized 'only on the basis that they transform themselves so that they be judged according to the "rules of the game" of the existing model of political economy, whatever hidden structures or biases it contain'.[37]

Given that matters such as the range of products sold in shops are likely to have been influenced by wider cultural norms that are themselves partly the product of particular (and in Europe, mainly Christian) religious traditions, it is inevitable that the subordination of the right to maintain a religious identity in the workplace to the need to ensure that employees carry out the essential functions of their jobs will impinge to a greater degree on followers of minority religions, whose practices are more likely to clash with established business patterns. Accommodation of the beliefs of any worker, no matter how such beliefs impacted on the operation of business, would indeed have the potential severely to affect the ability of businesses to function and it is clear both from the case law of the Court and the provisions of the Framework Directive that EU anti-discrimination law is not intended to displace the influence of the commercial elements of the market economy. Indirectly discriminatory measures that seek to safeguard the ability of an enterprise to compete in the marketplace will therefore be regarded as having the legitimate aim necessary to withstand challenge on grounds of religious discrimination.

The accommodation of economic interests is not absolute, and directly discriminatory measures that prevent individuals from entering the marketplace on the basis of the mere fact of their religious identity will not be upheld on this basis, even if the employer's commercial interests are at stake, for example where a large number of customers dislike being served by a Jewish staff member. Neither will measures that are disproportionate, as for instance an unwillingness, on grounds of efficiency, to allow an employee to respect his or her religious day of rest in a context where the relevant tasks could be performed on other days, be upheld. However, while economic interests will not be accorded priority in every occasion, the protection of religion within the Single Market, at least in so far as it involves active facilitation of religious behaviour as opposed to protecting the mere fact of religious identity, will have to accommodate itself, to a significant degree, to the centrality of commercial norms such as the pursuit of profit and efficiency in EU law.

---

[37]   D Chalmers, 'The Mistakes of the Good European?' in Fredman (n 24 above) 220.

2.3.2 Reconciliation with the Structures and Norms of the Liberal Democratic Polity

(a) Religion as part of the public order of the EU   The interests that EU law recognizes as being capable of justifying restrictions on religious rights are not solely economic. The accommodation of religion within the Single Market also has to take account of the desire of EU law to maintain certain restrictions on the public role of religion (particularly in the political arena) in order to maintain the balance between religious, humanist, and cultural influences which underpins its public order and which is seen as having given rise to the Union's liberal democratic ethos.

While certain limitations are imposed on this basis, the EU is not a strictly secular policy and does recognize both the promotion of a particular public status for religion, including a degree of protection from liberal principles such as freedom of expression, as part of its public order. Indeed, the EU's own public order has notably un-secular elements, with Single Market legislation both accommodating religious perspectives and seeing the promotion of an elevated cultural and social status for religion as an element of the public good. For example, the law of the Single Market has characterized the enforcement of respect for religious taboos, the prevention of the denigration of religion, and the promotion of an elevated public status for religion as part of the public good, as well as providing recognition of religious perspectives within its regulatory law.

Union law on trade marks, for instance, has contemplated restrictions motivated by a desire to protect religious taboos around certain symbols by providing that Member States may 'provide that a trade mark shall not be registered or, if registered, shall be liable to be declared invalid where and to the extent that: ... (b) the trade mark covers a sign of high symbolic value, in particular a religious symbol'.[38] Similarly, the 2007 Broadcasting Directive requires that 'Member States shall ensure by appropriate means that audiovisual media services provided by media service providers under their jurisdiction do not contain any incitement to hatred based on race, sex, religion or nationality',[39] thus protecting those who hold religious but not other

---

[38] Council Directive (EC) 89/104 to approximate the laws of the Member States in relation to trade marks [1989] OJ L40/1, Art 3(2)(b).

[39] Council Directive (EC) 2007/65 amending Council Directive (EC) 89/552 on the coordination of certain provisions laid down by law, regulation or administrative action in Member States concerning the pursuit of television broadcasting activities [2007] OJ L332/27, Ch A, Art 3b.

kinds of beliefs. More significantly, the Broadcasting Directive also provides that '[n]o television advertising or teleshopping shall be inserted during religious services',[40] thereby attempting to ensure by legislative means a degree of reverence for religious services. Furthermore, in addition to promoting a particular status for religion, the Union has, in certain circumstances, recognized the validity of the promotion of religious morality by means of 'public morality' clauses in legislation as a valid element of EU law. Restrictions on cloning and bio-technology[41] and on gambling[42] have been recognized on this basis. Therefore, in contrast to strictly secular polities,[43] EU law does recognize religious perspectives as a valid element of law-making and appears to regard the promotion of an elevated public status for religion in general as part of the public good.

(b) Limitations on religion as part of the public order of the EU   The accommodation of religion is, however, part of a broader context in which significant limitations on the degree of public influence that can be exercised by religion are seen as a key element of the balance between religious, cultural, and humanist influences inherent in the liberal democratic nature of the Union's public order. The Union's approach to migration and enlargement shows that it regards the limitation of religious influence over law and politics as perquisites for the respect of fundamental rights such as privacy and equal treatment.[44] Furthermore, the duty to accept these limitations has been seen both as a duty of states wishing to join the Union[45] and as an individual duty of individuals seeking to reside there.[46] The ECtHR has also been explicit that preponderant religious influence over law and politics is repugnant to the democratic values underlying the rights that the EU has undertaken to respect.[47]

---

[40] Ibid, Ch IIC, section 14.

[41] Council Directive (EC) 98/44 on the legal protection of biotechnological inventions [1998] OJ L213/13.

[42] Case C-275/92 *Her Majesty's Customs and Excise v Gerhart Schindler and Jörg Schindler* [1994] ECR I-1039. See also Joined Cases C-338/04, C-359/04, and C-360/04 *Placanica* [2007] ECR I-1891 para 47. See discussion in Ch 3.

[43] The Preamble to the Turkish Constitution, for example, requires that 'there shall be no interference whatsoever by sacred religious feelings in state affairs and politics' and in Article 24 prohibits 'even partially basing the fundamental, social, economic, political, and legal order of the state on religious tenets'. See the Constitution of the Republic of Turkey, English translation available from the Office of the Prime Minister at <http://www.byegm.gov.tr/sayfa.aspx?Id=78> (last visited 26 May 2010).

[44] See Ch 6.   [45] Ibid.

[46] Ibid.   [47] *Refah Partisi and others v Turkey* (2003) 37 EHRR 1.

Such limitations are also seen in EU Single Market legislation. Article 2(5) of the Framework Directive provides that:

This Directive shall be without prejudice to measures laid down by national law which in a democratic society, are necessary for the public security, for the mainten-ance of public order and the prevention of criminal offences, for the protection of health and for the protection of the rights and freedoms of others.

A similar limiting clause has not been included in any of the other anti-discrimination directives to date, so it can be assumed that it was a feature or features of the grounds protected in the Framework Directive (sexual orien-tation, religion or belief, disability, and age) that were thought to render such a clause necessary. The fact that the grounds given in Article 2(5) are strikingly similar to those given in Article 9(2) of the ECHR ('such limita-tions as are prescribed by law and are necessary in a democratic society in the interests of public safety, for the protection of public order, health or morals, or the protection of the rights and freedoms of others') would seem to indicate that it was the inclusion of religion in the Directive that gave rise to this limitation clause.

The idea that religious rights, like all other rights, are to be limited by the need to respect the rights of others is not remarkable. However, Article 2(5) of the Directive goes further and limits the protection of religion in the market in order to safeguard the principle of balance between religious and humanist influences and the fundamental interests of the liberal demo-cratic state. The Union's overall approach to religion is characterized by both a respect for religion's role in individual and communal identity and an awareness that a high level of religious influence over public institutions (particular in the legal and political arenas) can pose a threat to the state, to democracy, and to the humanist elements of the balance between religious and humanist influences required by the EU's public order.[48] Just as the prohibition in Article 2(2) on discrimination on religious grounds repre-sents this respect for religious identity, Article 2(5) can be seen as reflecting the Union's desire to maintain certain limitations on religion's public role in the interests of the state, liberal democracy, and the principle of balance which underpins its approach to religion. The provisions of Article 2(5) subordinate the prohibition on discrimination in the Directive specifically to 'the interests of public safety' and 'the protection of public order' in so far as such subordination is 'necessary in a democratic society'. The invocation

---

[48] See Chs 3 and 6.

of ideas such as 'public order' and 'public security' would seem to reflect a view that there are core elements related to the authority and security of the modern state which cannot be expected to accommodate individual or collective identities in general, and religion in particular, without undermining the stability of the public order as a whole. Such an approach has much in common with the restrictions on the assertion of religious claims to truth in the political arena outlined in Chapter 3. Thus, the need of a democratic society to maintain public order, or indeed, to promote 'morals' or to protect the personal freedom that is part of a shared European public morality[49] ('the rights and freedoms of others') trumps the need to respect religious freedom in the marketplace. Notably, unlike the 'objective justification' exemption in Article 2(2)(b)(i), the exemption provided by Article 2(5) covers both direct and indirect discrimination. Accordingly, adherents to religions that are seen as contrary to the public order, or that are hostile to the notion of balance, and the accommodation of humanist and cultural influences that it entails, may be excluded from employment in, for example, the security services or the army, on the basis of their religious identity alone rather than an inability on the part of the employer to accommodate their religious behaviour.

2.3.3 *Accommodation of Existing Religious Privilege in the Market*

However, in addition to its personal aspects, religion is also a communal phenomenon, and most mainstream European faiths regard an approach to religious freedom based solely on protection of individual autonomy as gravely deficient.[50] The right of individuals not to be discriminated against on grounds of their religion can be inconsistent with the rights of religious institutions to organize themselves in accordance with their religious beliefs. Indeed, the relevant ECHR case law,[51] and therefore in all likelihood the general principles of EU law,[52] suggest that the protection of the collective religious identity of religious organizations requires that exemptions from anti-discrimination laws be provided to religious bodies, at least in relation to those employed to carry out religious tasks such as preaching. However, the role of religious bodies in the marketplace is not restricted to the employment of clergy.

Certain religions have achieved privileged status in many Member States. More importantly, in terms of Single Market law, religious institutions continue to play a key role in the provision of public services such as

---

[49] See Ch 3.   [50] See Ch 4.   [51] Ibid.   [52] Ibid.

health and education in several EU Member States.[53] The EU has specifically undertaken not to interfere with this institutional role for religion at
Member State level. In 1998 the Member States agreed to append a Declaration on the Status of Churches to the Amsterdam Treaty.[54] This Declaration has also been included in the Lisbon Treaty,[55] and provides that '[t]he
European Union respects and does not prejudice the status under national
law of churches and religious associations or communities in the Member
States'.[56]

The Union has therefore undertaken to avoid interfering with the status
that Member States choose to grant, or not to grant, under national law
to individual denominations or to religious organizations in general. Thus,
EU law recognizes that it cannot be used to force a state to reconsider, in
general terms, its decision to promote, to some degree, a religiously specific
collective identity in public contexts, nor, for example, to require a Member
State to disestablish a state church or, potentially, to restrict the public role
exercised by religious institutions in individual Member States.[57] The centrality of the role of the Member States in relation to the demarcation of the
public role of religious bodies is underlined by the fact that no definition of
'religion', 'religious', 'association', or 'church' is provided by EU law which,
under the terms of the Declaration, would appear to be bound to defer to the
definitions of national law in these matters.

This commitment to respecting the pre-existing market privileges
granted to religions by Member States is given concrete form in the Framework Directive, which significantly limits the applicability of the prohibitions on direct and indirect discrimination on grounds of religion on this

---

[53] See Ch 2.

[54] Declaration No 11 to the last act of the Treaty of Amsterdam [1997] OJ C340/133.

[55] Treaty of Lisbon amending the Treaty on European Union and the Treaty establishing the
European Community [2007] OJ C306/42, Art 16C.

[56] The Declaration also states that 'The European Union equally respects the status of philosophical and non-confessional organisations'; however, such organizations do not have the institutional and legal status held by various denominations under Member States' laws, meaning
that the inclusion of this rider could be seen as something of a meaningless gesture designed to
lessen the degree to which the EU appeared to be granted special treatment to religious bodies.

[57] However, as noted in Ch 4, the ECtHR has held that recognition of a particular religious
identity cannot spills over into state recognition of the truth claims of a particular religion (see
the discussion of *Buscarini v San Marino* and *Lautsi v Italy* in Ch 3). Distinguishing between
recognition of religion as a matter of culture and recognition of the truth claims of a religion
is entirely in keeping with the EU's conception of what constitutes a fair or proper balance
between religious and humanist influences (see Chs 3 and 6).

basis. Paragraph 24 of the Preamble to the Directive specifically invoked the Declaration, stating:

The European Union in its Declaration No. 11 on the status of churches and of non-confessional organisations, annexed to the Final Act of the Amsterdam Treaty, has explicitly recognised that it respects and does not prejudice the status under national law of churches and religious associations or communities in the Member States and that it equally respects the status of philosophical and non-confessional organisations. With this in view, Member States may maintain or lay down specific provisions on genuine legitimate and justified occupational requirements which might be required for carrying out an occupational activity

The substantive provisions of the Directive reflect this accommodation of collective institutional religious privilege. In Article 4(1), which deals with 'occupational requirements', the Directive states that Member States may provide that acts that would otherwise be considered discriminatory:

shall not constitute discrimination where, by reason of the nature of the particular occupational activities concerned or of the context within which they are carried out, such a characteristic constitutes a genuine and determining occupational requirement, provided that the objective is legitimate and the requirement is proportionate.

Article 4 provides protection for the internal autonomy of religious organizations by exempting them from the duty not to discriminate in relation to employment related to religious practices. Accordingly, the restriction of membership of the clergy to believers or, for those religions for which it is necessary, to members of one gender, are not prevented by the Directive. Importantly, these privileges are granted not directly to the relevant institutions but instead provide Member States with the right to grant such privileges if they so desire.

However, the exemption granted to Member States by the Directive may go beyond the accommodation of genuine occupational requirements. Article 4(2) substantially curtails the application of the key EU law of principle non-discrimination to religious institutions, while leaving it to apply with full rigour to other kinds of institutions. It states:

Member States may maintain national legislation in force at the date of adoption of this Directive or provide for future legislation incorporating national practices existing at the date of adoption of this Directive pursuant to which, *in the case of occupational activities within churches and other public or private organisations the ethos of which is based on religion or belief,* a difference of treatment based on a person's religion or belief shall not constitute discrimination where, by reason of the nature of these activities or of the context in which they are carried out, *a person's religion or belief constitute a genuine, legitimate and justified occupational requirement, having regard to the organisation's ethos.* This difference of treatment shall be implemented taking account of Member States' constitutional provisions and principles, as well as the general principles of Community law, and should not justify discrimination on another ground.

Provided that its provisions are otherwise complied with, this Directive shall thus not prejudice the right of *churches and other public or private organisations, the ethos of which is based on religion or belief,* acting in conformity with national constitutions and laws, *to require individuals working for them to act in good faith and with loyalty to the organisation's ethos.* (emphasis added)

There are a number of noteworthy features of this article. First, it covers religious bodies alone. However, its scope goes beyond that of mere internal autonomy for churches and extends to 'other public or private organisations the ethos of which is based on religion or belief'. Thus, the notion of 'occupational requirement' is deliberately extended to ensure that religious bodies exercising public functions can protect the religiously specific nature of the public services they provide by granting scope within EU law to exempt them from otherwise applicable non-discrimination norms. Indeed, the Directive goes even further in the second paragraph of Article 4(2), which contemplates the extension of the rights of religious institutions as employers to require individual employees to act 'in good faith and loyalty to the organisation's ethos'. This approach involves significant curtailment of principles such as the prohibition on discrimination against individuals on grounds of religion and individual freedom from religion in favour of the collective rights of religious bodies. Moreover, the wording of Article 4(2) does not make it clear whether the duty to act 'in good faith and with loyalty to the organisation's ethos' applies only in the context of posts for which 'religion or belief constitute a genuine and legitimate occupational requirement'. The Directive gives scope for religious employers to argue that they are permitted to prioritize their collective religious freedom over the individual right not to be discriminated against in relation to functions that are not specifically religious. Such an approach would enable discriminatory actions that result from a particular ethos to be exempt from the normal standard of 'genuine and determining occupational requirement' applied by Article 4(1) to other kinds of employers. Instead, it would permit religious employers to bring their beliefs into the calculation of what constitutes a 'genuine legitimate and justified occupational requirement'. Thus, a religious organization that operates a publicly funded hospital or school may be permitted to import its religious rules relating, for example, to appropriate sexual behaviour, into the law by gaining exemptions from prohibitions on discrimination on this ground in order to defend its 'ethos'. Such an approach supports the protection of a broad, collective, institutional, religious identity in public contexts such as the provision of healthcare or educational services, even when such protection impacts on the rights of individual employees in the private arena (insofar as the conduct of an employee of an organization with a religious ethos in his or her private life could be seen as failing to act 'in loyalty to organisation's ethos'). The fact that a decision to discriminate is religiously motivated is, on this view, regarded as a reason to curtail the applicability of the otherwise generally applicable principle of non-discrimination.

Moreover, the term 'ethos' is not defined, meaning that it could be extended to cover almost any form of otherwise-prohibited discrimination, provided that the discriminatory intent is religious in nature. In addition, while under Article 2(2)(b)(i) of the Directive indirect discrimination against an individual on the grounds of his or her religion (or on any of the other prohibited grounds) is permitted only when it can be 'justified by a legitimate aim, and the means of achieving that aim are appropriate and necessary', no such limitation is placed on discrimination necessitated by 'an ethos which is based on religion or belief'. Thus, religiously motivated discrimination alone is not required to justify itself in terms of legitimacy of it aims, necessity, or appropriateness. This appears to place religion outside of the norms governing the public behaviour of institutions in modern liberal societies and to characterize religion as a kind of non-rational, non-modern phenomenon whose actions cannot be regulated or assessed according to generally applicable modern norms without impinging on its essence. In other words, by exempting acts that result from the religious ethos of an organization from generally applicable principles of non-discrimination, while refusing to define what such an ethos may or may not encompass, EU law seems to suggest that religion cannot be expected to account for itself in the rationally structured norms that apply to other organizations in modern liberal democratic societies.

This approach suggests that EU law recognizes religion as an exceptional phenomenon whose communal rights and public role are entitled to broad recognition not accorded to other kinds of bodies. However, although many of the rights provided by the Directive are wide-ranging and specifically religion-related, they do not indicate a broad prioritization of the rights of religious institutions at the expense of principles such as equal treatment or the protection of individual identity. Instead, the provisions of Article 4(2) can be seen as an attempt on the part of the Union to ensure that its embrace of norms like equal treatment on grounds of religion does not interfere with the established institutional privileges and public role of certain religions in the market in several Member States.

This deference towards *pre-existing* religious structures in the market is shown by the fact that the exemptions provided by EU law in respect of religious employers take the form of a right, not a duty, of Member States to impose a standstill clause maintaining such privileges. Furthermore, although EU law, as noted above, does recognize the promotion of a particular public status for religion as part of the public good and accommodates religious perspectives in its regulatory framework, it also implicitly characterizes such exemptions from the principle of equal treatment as anachronistic and anomalous.

This view of such privileges as anachronistic is illustrated by the fact that only those national practices that predated the Directive are protected by the exceptions provided by Article 4(2) ('Member States may maintain national legislation in force at the date of adoption of this Directive or provide for future legislation incorporating national practices existing at the date of adoption of this Directive'). Thus, while EU law is willing to provide recognition to established Member State practices, it is not willing to require the rolling modification principle of equal treatment into the future in order to facilitate religious privilege. The status of these privileges as anomalies is seen in several ways. First, the structure of the Directive establishes non-discrimination as a general principle from which religious bodies are then granted an exception. The norm, to which the religious privileges are exceptions, is therefore that of the liberal principle of equal treatment. Secondly, although non-religious bodies do not have the public role that would enable them to benefit from the exemptions in Article 4(2) (one does not find, for example, publicly funded socialist, environmentalist, or fascist hospitals and schools at Member State level), nevertheless those who agreed the terms of the Directive felt constrained to indicate, at least rhetorically, a commitment to the equality of religious and non-religious beliefs by including in Article 4(2) 'churches and *other public or private organisations* the ethos of which is based on religion *or belief*' (emphasis added). Although the practical impact of this inclusion is limited, it does represent an implicit denial that religion is by its nature entitled to privileged status to which other belief systems are not.

Furthermore, even the accommodation of pre-existing religious structures is constrained by the religion-limiting elements of the broader dialectic within EU law between recognition of religion and a desire to limit the public role of religion in the interests of the balance between religious, cultural, and humanist influences which is seen as underlying liberal democratic values. Thus, the public role accorded to religion by Article 4(2) is one that is exceptional and must be reconciled with the wider hegemony of liberal values. As a result, although discriminatory actions motivated by an institution's religious ethos are exempt from the otherwise applicable standards of legitimacy, necessity, and appropriateness, the limited and non-hegemonic public role assigned to religion by the Directive is nevertheless underlined by the fact that it specifically requires that the communal rights provided under Article 4(2) be implemented 'taking account of Member States' constitutional provisions and principles, as well as general principles of Community law' and that they 'should not justify discrimination on another ground'. This reference to the principles of Member State constitutional law and the general principles of EU law, coupled with the provisions of Article 2(5)[58] (which subjugates the rights conferred by the Directive to public security and the rights and freedoms of others, and which apply equally to the provisions dealing with religious institutions), make it clear that the privileges granted to religion are viewed as exceptions that fall to be justified against the overall constitutional principles (and therefore, to an extent, collective identity) of both the Member States and the Union and can therefore be seen as an element of an overall public order that embodies contrary elements and is, in the final instance, defined by the secular institutions of the polity. Indeed, in the UK litigation relating to the implementation of the exemptions provided in Article 4(2), the courts have stressed that, as departures from the principle of equal treatment, they need to be narrowly interpreted.[59]

Of course, these principles of national constitutional law are themselves not entirely secular and are likely, particularly in countries where religious

---

[58] Article 2(5) provides: 'This Directive shall be without prejudice to measures laid down by national law which, in a democratic society, are necessary for the public security, for the maintenance of public order and the prevention of criminal offences, for the protection of health and for the protection of the rights and freedoms of others'.

[59] *R (Amicus and others) v Secretary of State for Trade and Industry* [2004] EWHC 860 (Admin). See also the narrow interpretation given to the exemption in a case where the Bishop of Hereford was found to have breached the rights of a gay applicant for a diocesan social work job when he questioned him about his sexual life in a way in which a heterosexual employee would not have been questioned. See 'Bishop urged to resign after iocese loses gay bias case', *Guardian*, 19 July 2007, available at <http://www.guardian.co.uk/gayrights/story/0,,2129741,00.html> (last visited 13 May 2010).

institutions are granted a major public role, to reflect the religious identity of the very institutions whose public role they may be invoked to limit. For example, Irish legislation implementing Article 4(2) takes a broad approach, providing exemptions from the duty not to discriminate to:

A religious, educational or medical institution which is under the direction or control of a body established for religious purposes or whose objectives include the provision of services in an environment which promotes certain religious values shall not be taken to discriminate against a person [in contravention of the Act] if—

(a) it gives more favourable treatment, on the religion ground, to an employee or a prospective employee over that person where it is reasonable to do so in order to maintain the religious ethos of the institution, or

(b) it takes action which is reasonably necessary to prevent an employee or a prospective employee from undermining the religious ethos of the institution.[60]

Furthermore, in the Irish case, the country's heavily Catholic Constitution may well prove unlikely to provide significant grounds for restriction of the exemptions in the Directive given that Irish courts have in the past upheld the dismissal of a teacher in a Catholic school on the grounds that she was unmarried and pregnant.[61]

Thus, the institutional privileges granted by Article 4(2) are subject to certain limitations in the name of respect for balance, liberal democracy, and the restrictions on the public role of religion they entail. However, these limitations are provided by such humanist and secular elements as there may be in the public orders of both the Member States and the EU, which may themselves bear the influence of particular religious traditions or regard the promotion of an elevated (albeit limited) public status for religion in general as part of the public good. On the other hand, the European Commission has taken a narrow view of the exemptions granted, and in late 2009 commenced a process that may lead to Article 226 proceedings against the United Kingdom for breach of the Directive. British legislation allowed employers 'to apply a requirement related to sexual orientation in respect of employment for an organised religion in order to comply with the doctrines of the religion or so as to avoid conflicting with the strongly held religious convictions of a significant number of the religion's followers'.[62] The Commission

---

[60] Employment Equality Act 1998, s 37(1).   [61] *Flynn v Power* [1985] IR 648.

[62] Commission of the European Communities, Reasoned Opinion addressed to the United Kingdom under Article 226 of the Treaty establishing the European Community, on account of failure to transpose correctly Articles 2(4), 4 and 9 of Council Directive 2000/78/EC of 27 November 2000 establishing a general framework for equal treatment in employment and

argued that this exemption was too broad and that exemptions granted to religious employers had to be restricted to situations where a decision to discriminate was the result of a genuine and determining occupational requirement, a legitimate objective, and where the requirement was proportionate.[63] Attempts to narrow the exemption were rejected by the Upper House of the British Parliament so the case may well end up before the Court of Justice.

Accordingly, EU law in this area engages in a complex balancing of individual and collective identity rights in relation to religion that is informed and limited by its commitment to an overall balance between religious, cultural, and humanist influences over law. While the Union recognizes both a right to engage in religion as a market activity and a right to protection for religious identity and activities within the market, these rights must adapt to established structures, norms, and institutional arrangements. While the right not to be penalized for being a believer in a particular faith (and therefore individual religious identity) is protected to a very significant degree, the right to act in accordance with religious beliefs in the marketplace can be limited when such actions clash with fundamental market norms such as the pursuit of profit or efficiency. Both the right to hold a religious identity and to act in accordance with such an identity in the market are also limited, not only by the requirement that it be balanced with other rights but also by the fundamental interests of the state and the liberal democratic public order. Furthermore, the facilitation of individual religiosity and the attempt by EU law to restrict discrimination on religious grounds is also required to accommodate the pre-existing religious structures in the marketplace, thus enabling significant departure from key principles such as equal treatment in order to facilitate the maintenance of the public role of certain religions in individual Member States.

3. Cultural Autonomy, Single Market Law, and Religion

There is a further means through which religion is recognized within the Single Market that also reflects the desire of EU law not to interfere with the established structures underpinning the role of certain religions in the public life of Member States. The role played by religion in national culture

occupation, 20 November 2009, quoting the Employment Equality (Religion or Belief) Regulations 2003 (SI 2003/1660) and the Employment Equality (Sexual Orientation) Regulations 2003 (SI 2003/1661) para 15.   [63] Ibid para 18.

enables it to achieve a degree of recognition in the marketplace, but in addition it is not subject to the same degree to the limitations imposed by the market, the state, and liberal values that constrain the rights accorded to religion in other areas of Single Market law.

The EU is a pluralist public order committed to respecting the cultural autonomy of its Member States (including the right of each state to define its own notions of public morality).[64] Indeed, as an institution of limited democratic legitimacy, attempts on the part of the EU to interfere with cultural autonomy could have very serious consequences for its stability. On the other hand, as Taylor points out, sustainable political communities are not made up of 'a scratch team of history with nothing more in common that the passenger list of some international flight',[65] but require some kind of common identity.[66] While Weiler has noted the 'constitutional tolerance' of the Union for the particularities and national identities of its Member States, he also notes that it is necessary that the Union be based on shared values in order that the people of the Member States will be willing to be bound by the decisions of common European institutions in certain areas.[67] Seen in this light, it is hardly surprising therefore that the Union has repeatedly referred to itself as a 'community of values' and has attempted to promote the 'common cultural heritage'[68] of Europe.

This dual approach, which respects Member State cultural autonomy while promoting a common cultural identity derived from these various national cultures, is reflected in Article 151 of the EC Treaty, which provides that:

(1) The Community shall contribute to the flowering of the cultures of the Member States, while respecting their national and regional diversity and at the same time bringing the common cultural heritage to the fore.

...

(4) The Community shall take cultural aspects into account in its action under other provisions of this Treaty, in particular in order to respect and to promote the diversity of its cultures.

[64] See Ch 3.

[65] C Taylor, 'Liberal Politics and the Public Sphere', Discussion Paper 15 (The Centre for the Study of Global Governance, London School of Economics, 1995) 19.   [66] Ibid.

[67] JHH Weiler, *The Constitution of Europe* (Cambridge: Cambridge University Press, 1999).

[68] Treaty Establishing the European Community, Art 151.

3.1 Definition of Culture in EU Law

According to predominant contemporary perceptions, culture is seen as an ethnographic or anthropological state of affairs covering matters of values and beliefs and the generation of meaning, as well as practices relating to matters such as food, leisure rituals, or clothing.[69] Such a view of culture is not readily understandable in terms of rational argument or teleology.[70] Indeed, the existence of a national culture in particular is seen as requiring no justification in rational terms or in terms of the attainment of greater goals.[71]

Neither does culture, as a phenomenon that is not goal oriented, fit readily into the competitive structures of the free market, and has in general been protected from the impact of the market in significant ways. As Sassoon noted in relation to post-war Europe, '[e]ven after the boost in the ideological strength of the free market following the post-war boom, hardly any political party...was willing to support the strict application of the market mechanism in the field of culture'.[72]

The distinctiveness of individual cultures has also been seen as a good in itself.[73] The placing of a high value on distinctiveness for its own sake underlines culture's specific and particularist nature. As a culture is constituted by certain habits, ideas, and practices shared by a certain group, it defines itself in relation to existing practices and structures that are linked in some way to past practices and structures of the same group. Furthermore, as it is constituted by certain shared distinctive features, culture is inherently particularist as, by definition, it excludes those who do not share such commonalities. The law of the Single Market has repeatedly adapted to and facilitated these features.

The valuing of cultural distinctiveness is also seen in EU law, most notably in the commitment in Article 151 EC to respect 'national and regional diversity' in cultural matters.

---

[69] See F Inglis, *Culture* (Cambridge: USA Polity Press, 2004) 28–29. See also C Barker, 'Culture' in *The SAGE Dictionary of Cultural Studies* (London: Sage, 2004) 45.

[70] Ibid 12.

[71] D Sassoon, *The Culture of the Europeans: From 1800 to the Present* (London: Harper Collins, 2006) 861. This exemption from standards of rationality is also seen, as noted above, in relation to Art 4(2) of the Framework Directive, which notably fails to require that discriminatory decisions justified on the grounds of religious ethos be justified in terms of rationality or reasonableness.

[72] Ibid 867.

[73] See arguments of Von Herder, quoted in Inglis (n 69 above) 14.

Single Market legislation has repeatedly recognized culture's non-economic nature and the need to protect a shared cultural heritage from the impact of the free market. The Preamble to the 2007 Broadcasting Directive provides that the status of audio visual services as 'cultural services' and their 'growing importance . . . for education and culture justifies the applications of special rules to these services'.[74] It also noted that Article 151(4) EC 'requires the Community to take cultural aspects into account in its action under other provisions of the Treaty, in particular in order to respect and to promote the diversity of its cultures'[75] and that the European Parliament had resolved that 'cultural activities, goods and services have both an economic and a cultural nature, because they convey identities, values and meanings, and must therefore not be treated as solely having commercial value',[76] thus acknowledging both culture's role in generating meaning and identities, as well as recognizing that this important role could be threatened by the regulation of cultural matters in accordance with purely commercial and economic principles.

Religion is, of course, a key element of many national cultures and has accordingly been explicitly recognized by EU law as forming part of cultural identity not only in the case law of the Court of Justice which, in the *Eman* case, defined culture as 'the totality of individuals linked by the fact of sharing traditions, culture, ethnicity, religion, and so on',[77] but also in legislation. For instance, Council Regulation (EC) 3911/92 on the export of cultural goods, includes 'elements forming an integral part of artistic, historical or religious monuments' and the 'inventories of ecclesiastical institutions' in its definition of 'cultural objects'.[78] Council Directive (EC) 93/7 on the return of cultural objects unlawfully removed from the territory of a Member State adopts the same definition.[79] These Directives therefore recognize the role of religion in national culture by including church records and religious objects as parts of national heritage, the preservation of which the Union acknowledges as a legitimate ground for departure from normal rules of the free market. Thus,

---

[74]   Council Directive (EC) 2007/65 amending Council Directive (EC) 89/552 on the coordination of certain provisions laid down by law, regulation or administrative action in Member States [2007] OJ L332/27, Preamble, para 3.   [75]   Ibid para 4.

[76]   Ibid para 5.

[77]   Case C-300/04 *Eman v College van Burgenmeester en Wethaiders van den Haaq* [2006] ECR I-8055.

[78]   Council Regulation (EC) 3911/92 of 9 December 1992 on the export of cultural goods [1992] OJ L395/1, Annex, Art A2.

[79]   See Preamble to Council Directive (EC) 93/7 on the return of cultural objects unlawfully removed from the territory of a Member State [1993] OJ L74.

the Union attempts to shelter certain elements of national culture, including religion, from the impact of the exercise of its powers to regulate the Single Market. In doing so it recognizes a specific religious heritage as part of the collective identity of the state, which the institutions of the state are entitled to promote and protect on grounds of cultural autonomy.

EU legislation does not merely see religion as a historical and symbolic element of identity. It has also recognized religion as an element of a broader cultural communal way of life, which Member States are entitled to seek to maintain. As noted in Chapter 3, this includes the promotion of particular views of 'public morality' that may be religiously influenced. It also includes the protection of certain market structures that may also be linked to particular religious traditions. Thus, Directives 94/33 on the protection of young people at work[80] and 93/104 concerning certain aspects of the organisation of working time[81] enable Member States to designate Sunday as part of the weekly rest period if they so choose (although in doing so they are required to take account of 'the diversity of cultural, ethnic, religious and other factors').[82] These Directives establish exceptions that enable Member States to promote communal practices resulting from particular religious practices and to shield such practices from the impact of the a-religious free market orientation of EU law. The Court of Justice, in line with its anthropological definition of culture in *Eman*, has taken a similar approach, categorizing a decision to ban Sunday trading by a local authority as an instance of 'certain political and economic choices in so far as their purpose is to ensure that working and non-working hours are so arranged as to accord with national or regional socio-cultural characteristics'.[83]

Such an approach sees the regulation of workplace practices in a manner that is influenced by a particular religious tradition as a legitimate exercise of cultural autonomy by Member States whose regulatory approach is permitted to promote a particular communal identity for the state. The Christian Sabbath can therefore be legally protected, not on the basis of its religious significance per se, nor on the basis of a duty to respect individual choice (though this right may be protected by other EU laws), but due to its status as a collective 'regional socio-cultural characteristic'. Such an approach is consistent with the Union's approach to the accommodation of the choices

---

[80] Council Directive (EC) 94/33 on the protection of young people at work [1994] OJ L216/12.

[81] See Preamble to Council Directive (EC) 93/104 concerning certain aspects of the organisation of working time [1993] OJ L307/18.   [82] Ibid.

[83] Case C-145/88 *Torfaen Borough Council v B & Q plc* [1989] ECR 3851.

of Member States in relation to matters of public morality on the basis of its respect for the cultural autonomy of Member States[84] and with the approach of the ECtHR, which has distinguished between state recognition of a particular religion as an element of national culture, which is acceptable, and state recognition of the truth claims of an individual faith, which is not.[85] The provisions of the Framework Directive relating to indirect discrimination in the workplace do place some limits on the degree to which Member States are free to define general rules that disadvantage adherents of minority religions;[86] nevertheless, Directives 94/33 and 93/104 make it clear that EU law does enable Member States to take account of, and grant legal privilege to, practices linked to certain religious traditions in defining general rules, such as those relating to weekly rest periods, and to shield such facilitation of religious practices in the marketplace from the operation of commercial market norms.

While such an approach enables certain denominations to use the power of the state to regulate the market to promote their specific religious practices, it does not grant rights to religions as religions but instead empowers the state to define its identity and public culture in such a way as to reflect the cultural importance of (and thereby benefit) specific religions should it choose to do so. It therefore enables the promotion of a religiously specific identity in public matters and the embrace of a religious element to the identity of the state at the same time as enabling the refusal to grant a public role to religions that are seen as either culturally or ideologically incompatible with the predominant ideological or cultural norms of this culturally specific state. Certain religions may therefore access significant legal privilege in communal life. However, they do so not as religion per se but merely as elements of the broader communal identity of a particular state that is equally free to exclude religious elements from the public order should it choose to do so.

3.1.1 Institutional Arrangements as Culture

The recognition by EU law of the religious element of national cultural identity has extended to cover not merely religious practices but also particular institutional arrangements between certain religions and Member

---

[84] See Ch 3.

[85] See the discussion of *Lautsi v Italy* and *Buscarini v San Marino* in Ch 4. See also R McCrea, 'De Facto Secularism in a Diversifying Religious Environment: The Changing Relationship between State and Religion in Europe' in R McCrea, *Religion in the Public Square* (Utrecht: Eleven International Publishing, forthcoming 2011).   [86] See section 2.2 above.

States. In Decision 1982/2006,[87] which related to the Union's actions in relation to research and technological development, the Council of Ministers called for activities that would promote 'the citizen in the European Union', including promotion of 'respect for Europe's diversities and commonalities in terms of culture, religions, cultural heritage, institutions and legal systems, history, languages and values as building elements of our European multi-cultural identity and heritage'.[88]

This recognition of religion as an element of culture and the Council's placing of religion in the context of notions of 'diversities', 'multi-cultural identity', and 'institutional and legal systems' is also consistent with the Declaration on the Status of Churches appended to the Amsterdam Treaty[89] and included in the Lisbon Treaty[90] which, as noted above,[91] provides that '[t]he European Union respects and does not prejudice the status under national law of churches and religious associations or communities in the Member States',[92] thus linking existing institutional arrangements, such as those surrounding the role of certain religions in individual Member States, to broader issues around the Union's obligation to respect Member State identity in the exercise of its powers. Indeed, the fact that the right to grant or to withhold the exemptions from the principle of non-discrimination contained in Article 4(2) of the Framework Directive is given to Member States, underlines the fact that these institutional religious privileges can equally be seen as recognition within EU law of Member State cultural autonomy rather than the institutional autonomy religions.

3.2 Culture as Discrimination between Religions

3.2.1 Culture, Insider Religions, and Compatibility with the Public Order

Culture, therefore, is seen in EU law as a matter of contemporary habits, ideas, customs, and institutional structures which distinguish particular groups, as well as containing important elements from the past that give

---

[87] Council Decision (EC) 1982/2006 concerning the Seventh Framework Programme of the European Community for research, technological development and demonstration activities (2007–2013) [2006] OJ L412/1.   [88] Ibid section 8.

[89] Declaration No 11 to the last act of the Treaty of Amsterdam [1997] OJ C340/133.

[90] Article 16C.   [91] See n 56 above.

[92] The Declaration also states: 'The European Union equally respects the status of philosophical and non-confessional organisations'; however, such organizations do not generally have the institutional and legal status held by various denominations under Member States' laws, meaning that the inclusion of this rider could be seen as something of a meaningless gesture designed to lessen the degree to which the EU appeared to have granted special treatment to religious bodies.

meaning to such habits, ideas, customs, and structures. Thus, it is a dynamic phenomenon in which present interpretations of a shared past are constantly reinvented and renewed. Recognition of a practice or structure as part of national or European culture is also a privileged category in legal terms, with the Union permitting the exemption of such cultural phenomena from the standards its law applies to other matters.[93] There is no legal definition of the contents of such culture; indeed, given its dynamic and non-rational nature, it is difficult to imagine how such a definition could be arrived at. Accordingly, political understandings of what is and is not part of such culture play an important role in determining what will be recognized as coming within this legally privileged category. Nevertheless, despite its influence over law, culture is viewed as in some way separate from the rationalism and ideological nature of political sphere.[94] The strong historical and cultural role of the mainstream Christian denominations means that the public role of Christian institutions is likely to be recognized as part of the national cultural identities, which EU Single Market law is bound to respect. However, despite the recognition of the promotion of an elevated cultural and social status for religion as an element of the public good, and the accommodation of religious perspectives in the Single Market law noted above,[95] such culturally characterized religious privilege is, like other religious privileges in this area, subject to real limitations in the name of the protection of the principle of balance and the liberal democratic values to which such balance is viewed as giving rise. There are strongly humanist and secular elements of the public order of the EU which are themselves seen as part of European culture and identity. The humanist and secular elements of European culture highlighted in Chapter 2 are reflected in the Union's enlargement policy, migration legislation, and the rulings of the ECtHR, all of which make it clear that religious domination of politics and law and state recognition of the truth claims of a particular faith, particularly in the political and legal arenas, are incompatible with EU membership. Furthermore, as noted above, the provisions of Article 2(5) of the Framework Directive provide limitations

[93] See, eg the manner in which the Framework Directive exempts discriminatory actions motivated by religious ethos from the generally applicable standards of having a legitimate aim and being reasonably necessary (section 2.3.3 above), the exemption of religious slaughtering practices from animal cruelty legislation (section 2.3.1 above), or the deference to religious choices in relation to rest days (section 3.1 above).

[94] See A Gramsci, *Selections from the Prison Notebooks* (New York: International Publishers, 1971) 238; and S Žižek, *In Defense of Lost Causes* (London: Verso, 2008) 21, both of whom acknowledge that despite this perception, culture is a site of political power and is not ideologically neutral.   [95] See section 2.3.3 above.

on religious privilege in the name of the 'rights and freedoms of others' and the needs of a 'democratic society'. These elements of the Union's approach to religion restrict the influence of all religions. However, due to their more limited cultural influence in Europe, and as the expectations of their adherents in relation to the appropriate role of religion in law, politics, and society may not have been moulded to the same degree by the secularizing influences of European history, 'outsider' religions whose large-scale presence in Europe is a more recent phenomenon, may find the Union's approach to be more restrictive than the historically entrenched 'insider' religions whose relationship to the law and the state has been shaped by their role in European history and whose cultural role can enable them to indirectly influence EU law. Furthermore, EU law's culturally saturated view of religion and the view of the influence of cultural norms over law as in some way non-political lead to a situation where 'insider' religions are seen in cultural and less ideological and political terms than 'outsider' faiths. 'Outsider' religions are viewed, both within the legal and political arenas, much more in terms of their ideological elements and, consequently, are seen as greater threats to the humanist secular elements of the public order that require limitations on religious influence, particularly the curtailment of recognition of religious truth claims in the political arena. Of course, accommodating religion as an element of a broader culture is very different from accommodating religious truth claims in the political arena. As the process of cultural evolution is open to all in a way in which the evolution of the norms of a particular faith is not, the basing of legislation on explicitly religious grounds is more damaging to the equality of individual citizens in the political arena than basing legislation on cultural norms.[96] Furthermore, in the European context such cultural norms include a strong tradition of individual liberty. Nevertheless, the boundary between the cultural and the political is not clear-cut and, in terms of fundamental rights, one's liberty is no less restricted by being forced to adhere to a collective cultural norm than being forced to do the same in the name of respecting a collective religious norm.

The difficulties arising from the EU's approach can be seen in matters such as the regulation of employment, advertising, and gambling. In these areas the Union has been willing to carve out exemptions from liberal or market principles to enable Member States to allow religion to continue to play an active public role. In dealings with religions whose large-scale presence in Europe is a more recent phenomenon and which have not been

---

[96] See R Rorty, 'Religion as a Conversation Stopper' (1994) 3(1) *Common Knowledge* 1.

subject to the same historical and cultural forces, European officials and institutions have demonstrated concern that granting similar exemptions to such religions may pose a greater threat to the overall principle of balance and therefore to the liberal democratic nature of the public order.[97] In other words, mainstream Christianity, as a formative influence on European culture, is seen as consistent with the European public order, including its humanist and secular elements, to a degree to which other religions are not. For instance, the Union's approach to the issue of religious offence in advertising contrasts somewhat to the attitude taken by some of its institutions to the controversy surrounding the publication of cartoons of the Prophet Mohammed by the Danish newspaper *Jyllands Posten*. In a statement on the issue to the European Parliament Commission, President Jose Manuel Barroso stated:

Our European society is based on respect for the individual person's life and freedom, equality of rights between men and women, freedom of speech, and a clear distinction between politics and religion. Our point of departure is that as human beings we are free, independent, equal and responsible. We must safeguard these principles. Freedom of speech is part of Europe's values and traditions. Let me be clear. Freedom of speech is not negotiable.[98]

These views were repeated almost verbatim by Franco Frattini, Vice President of the Commission, in an interview with the EU's official anti-racism body, the European Monitoring Centre on Racism and Xenophobia ('the EUMC'). Although the Commissioner criticized the publication of the cartoons of the Prophet Mohammed in the Danish newspaper *Jyllands Posten* as 'thoughtless and inappropriate', he went on to say:

During the debate, we have recognised that the publication of the cartoons aggrieved many Muslims all over the world, and that it is important to respect sensitivities.... Equally, we have reaffirmed that our European society is based on the respect for the individual person's life and freedom, equality of rights between men and women, freedom of speech and a clear distinction between politics and religion.

---

[97] This argument also appears in relation to France, specifically in O Roy, *Secularism Confronts Islam* (New York: Columbia University Press, 2007).

[98] Jose Manuel Barroso, President of the European Commission, statement on the issue of the cartoons of the prophet Muhammad, European Parliament, Strasbourg, 15 February 2006, available at <http://europa.eu/rapid/pressReleasesAction.do?reference=SPEECH/06/86&format=HTML&aged=1&language=EN&guiLanguage=en (last visited 26 May 2010)>

We have said clearly and loudly that freedom of expression and freedom of religion are part of Europe's values and traditions, and that they are not negotiable.[99]

Later in the same interview he reiterated the same point saying: 'Let me be clear, even if European societies become multicultural, freedom of speech as an essential part of Europe's values and traditions, is simply not negotiable'.[100]

In relation to Islam, therefore, the right to freedom of expression was characterized as a non-negotiable element of Europe's values and traditions. Both the Commission President and Commissioner Frattini furthermore seemed to imply that such an approach to freedom of expression was part of Europe's tradition of freedom of religion. The fact that the two statements are so strikingly similar suggests that this view is one that has been agreed collectively to some degree by the Commission. Freedom of expression is an important element of the Union's public order. However, given that, at the time, the laws of several Member States and the relevant EU broadcasting legislation (the 1989 Broadcasting Directive)[101] explicitly restricted statements that are offensive to religious beliefs (the changes effected by the 2007 Broadcasting Directive are assessed below), it is difficult to see the Commission's statement as a fair depiction of the true situation. Rather, it would seem to be the case that under EU law some legal suppression of religious offensive material is permitted and that freedom of expression can be restricted on this basis. However, such protection is viewed in the context of a strong collective commitment to free expression and is contingent on a perceived acceptance on the part of such religions of the principle of balance between religious, cultural, and humanist influences and the non-hegemonic nature of religion's role in such a public order.[102] Furthermore, the granting of such privileges to religion is seen as promoting respect for culture and identity[103] rather than an attempt to assert claims of religious truth in the political

---

[99] See *Equal Voices* Issue 18, June 2006, published by the European Monitoring Centre on Racism and Xenophobia, 5.   [100] Ibid.

[101] Council Directive (EC) 89/552 on the coordination of certain provisions laid down by law, regulation or administrative action in Member States concerning the pursuit of television broadcasting activities [1989] OJ L298/23.

[102] The ECtHR, for example, has upheld denomination-specific blasphemy laws in *Choudry v United Kingdom* (Application No 17439/90) (1991) 12 *Human Rights Law Journal* 172, while Directive 89/552 is likely to benefit well-established majority religions whose services are far more likely to be the subject of television broadcasts than the services of minority or non-mainstream faiths.

[103] Directive 89/552 focuses on the need to avoid the broadcast of material that is offensive to political beliefs as well as religious ones (Art 12(c)) and defends personal identity more generally

arena or to subjugate liberal principles, such as freedom of expression, to religious norms as part of a wider ideological aversion to the humanist elements of Europe's public order. Thus, the privileges granted to culturally entrenched religions are seen as being less threatening than the expectations of the leadership and members of such religions in relation to the uses to which such privileges can be put are expected to have been moderated by their contextualization within a broader culture that contains significant secular and humanist elements. As a number of sociologists of religion have pointed out, many religious traditions whose large-scale presence in Europe is a more recent phenomenon have not been exposed to such secularizing influences to the same degree and have a more muscular and political view of the role of religion in society.[104] Of course, the statement of individual Commissioners does not necessarily represent the view of the Union as a whole; however, the Commissioners' statements can be seen as evidencing a justifiable concern that, in a more multicultural and multi-faith environment, restrictions on free speech in relation to religious matters may take a much greater toll on the principle of free expression than has previously been the case. The Commission's approach is underpinned by the assumption that the exercise of legal privileges granted to culturally entrenched mainstream Christian denominations will be tempered by a shared approach to liberal enlightenment values, such as freedom of expression, along with a concern that religions such as Islam, which have been less influenced by the European social, historical, and political norms, might, if accorded similar status, make excessive use of such privileges in a way that would be incompatible with democratic society. Such views have not been restricted to the European Commission. As will be seen below, other European institutions also appear to consider that the expectations of Christian religions with long histories in Europe in relation to their public role will have been conditioned by long exposure to the historical and cultural forces that brought about the modern European nation state.

---

by prohibiting advertising that encourages discrimination on grounds of race, sex, or nationality (Art 12(b)).

[104] Davie has noted that rejection of 'live and let live' privatized religion is not restricted to Muslim immigrants by any means but is in fact prevalent among immigrants of many religions. See G Davie, 'Religion in Britain: Changing sociological assumptions' (2000) 34 *Sociology* 113–28. She further argues that the difference in attitude to religion of native Europeans and immigrant communities 'has led to persistent and damaging misunderstandings' (ibid). See also P Norris and R Inglehart, *Sacred and Secular: Religion and Politics Worldwide* (Cambridge: Cambridge University Press, 2004).

Ferrari has argued that the 'constituent religions' (Catholic, Protestant, and Jewish) that were then present on the European public scene were party to 'a new Westfalia', which was 'genetically inscribed in the crucial hairpin bend of the period after the Second World War' and under which they accepted the political supremacy of the liberal democratic state in return for a 'constitutional secularism that is less and less interpreted as separation and more and more as integration', enabling them to take a full part in civil society.[105] Religions such as Islam, which were largely absent from the European scene at the time, are not seen as having curtailed their political ambitions in this way and are consequently considered a greater threat to democratic societies. Similarly, in relation to the role of Islam in France, Roy argues that suspicion is generated 'by the appearance of new communities of believers who do not feel bound by the compromises laboriously developed over the past century between cathos and laïques'.[106]

While Martin has argued that Christianity was particularly well-suited to adapt to secularism,[107] as Roy points out, the embrace by mainstream Christian religions of the principles of liberal democracy has as often been for reasons of *realpolitik* as for theological reasons. Nevertheless, mainstream Christian denominations appear to be viewed in Europe as more likely to have reconciled themselves to the limitations on their political and social influence that have emerged in Europe since the Enlightenment and therefore as being more trustworthy recipients of access to legal or political privilege. Roy notes how even political stands on the part of Christian denominations are not seen as threatening to the state. The opposition of the Catholic Church to the policies of many Member States in relation to abortion, for instance, is not seen as evidence of its threatening nature 'because the two parties accept precisely that the debate will not turn into opposition to the political system'.[108]

In this vein, the resolution of the Parliamentary Assembly of the Council of Europe in relation to blasphemy laws[109] suggested that 'blasphemy, as an

[105] A Ferrari, 'Religions, secularity and democracy in Europe: for a new Kelsenian pact', Jean Monnet Working Papers Program (NYU School of Law, 2005).

[106] O Roy, *Secularism Confronts Islam* (translated by George Holoch) (New York: Columbia University Press, 2007) 6.

[107] See D Martin, *On Secularisation: Towards a Revised General Theory* (Aldershot: Ashgate, 2005).

[108] See n 106 above, 21–2.

[109] Recommendation 1805 (2007), 'Blasphemy, religious insults and hate speech against persons on grounds of their religion', Assembly debate on 29 June 2007 (27th Sitting) (see Doc 11296, report of the Committee on Culture, Science and Education, rapporteur: Mrs Hurskainen, Doc 11319, opinion of the Committee on Legal Affairs and Human Rights, rapporteur:

insult to religion, should not be considered a criminal offence'.[110] It noted that several Member States of the Council of Europe do criminalize blasphemy but also significantly that '[e]ven though today prosecutions in this respect are rare in member states, they are legion in other countries of the world'.[111] In other words, such laws are dead letters in the mainstream European cultural context but, as the Mohammed Cartoons controversy (which partly prompted the resolution in question) showed, these cultural values are not universally shared. As Chapter 6 discusses, such ideas seem to have been influential in the Union's enlargement policy[112] and are, it is submitted, also to be seen in its attitude to freedom of speech. Whether such assumptions in relation to the attitudes of adherents of traditional European religions are justified is a matter for theologians and sociologists rather than a work such as this book. It must be noted, however, that satire and ridicule of elements of the Christian religion are far more common in Europe than is similar treatment of Islam in Muslim majority countries. The furore surrounding the *Jyllands Posten* cartoons and the *Satanic Verses* affair[113] highlighted that even mainstream adherents to religions that have not been moulded to the same degree by the secularizing influences of European history as mainstream European Christianity, have more extensive views of the kind of criticism or ridicule of religion that a commitment to free speech requires us to accept. However, although the Catholic Church has been exposed to and participated in the conflicts surrounding the emergence of the modern European state, its attitude to the *Jyllands Posten* controversy demonstrated that it may still be striving for more extensive use of the law to suppress criticism or mockery of religion; Vatican representatives at the United Nations used the controversy generated by the cartoons and subsequent protests to call for legislation to suppress expression considered offensive to religion.[114] In Ireland and the United Kingdom,

Mr Bartumeu Cassany, and Doc 11322, opinion of the Committee on Equal Opportunities for Women and Men, rapporteur: Mr Dupraz). Text adopted by the Assembly on 29 June 2007 (27th Sitting), available at: <http://assembly.coe.int/Mainf.asp?link=/Documents/AdoptedText/ta07/EREC1805.htm> (last visited 13 May 2010). [110] Ibid para 4.

[111] Ibid.   [112] See Ch 6.

[113] Many Muslims felt that the book *The Satanic Verses* by Salman Rushdie was blasphemous. There were widespread protests (including in European countries) by Muslims calling for the banning of the book and the punishment of its author. Iranian government placed the author under death sentence and there were attacks on those who published and translated it.

[114] See 'Intervention of the Holy See at the ordinary session of the United Nations Human Rights Council on Religious Freedom, Address of H.E. Msgr. Silvano M. Tomasi, Geneva, 22 March 2007', available at <http://www.vatican.va/roman_curia/secretariat_state/2007/documents/rc_seg-st_20070322_religion_en.html> (last visited 13 May 2010). In 2010 the Vatican distanced itself from the concept of 'defamation of religion', arguing that it was dan-

fringe Christian elements have also attempted to take prosecutions in respect of cartoons and theatre productions that they felt were disrespectful towards Christianity but were blocked by decisions of national courts.[115] Yet, as Roy notes, European states appear to believe that 'Christian dogma is compatible with *laïcité* or that the Church's political acceptance of *laïcité* exonerates it from any suspicion about theological content'.[116]

While the comments of Commission President Barroso and Commissioner Frattini do not necessarily represent the view of the Union as a whole, they, along with the approach of the Council of Europe's Assembly, provide neat examples of concerns that 'outsider' religions may present a greater threat to individual rights and European liberal democracy than culturally entrenched Christian denominations. Furthermore, their views are very much in line with the approach of EU institutions in other areas, such as the emphasis placed by the Council of Ministers on the need for liberal and secular values to trump religious beliefs in relation to the integration of migrants from outside the EU[117] and the Commission's declaration that 'democratic secularism' was a condition of Turkey's accession to the Union, despite the lack of consensus around issues of secularism and church-state relations among existing Member States.[118] All of these approaches seem to posit a degree of symbiosis between versions of Christianity traditionally dominant in Europe and liberal democracy that enables exemptions from generally applicable liberal norms to be granted to such religions without imperilling the overall liberal democratic nature of the public order. The implication appears to be that a condition of the privileged status granted by EU law religion in public life is an acceptance by such religions of the legitimacy of humanist perspectives and the non-hegemonic role of religion in the overall public order. European institutions appear to consider that through a combination of *realpolitik*, historical experience, or even

---

gerously vague. It did, however, continue to argue that freedom of expression does not authorize a 'lack of respect for the values commonly shared by a particular society'. See 'Religious freedom does not require complete secularization, Archbishop Tells UN', *Catholic News Agency*, 24 March 2010, available at <http://www.catholicnewsagency.com/news/religious_freedom_does_not _require_complete_secularization_archbishop_tells_un/> (last visited 13 May 2010).

[115] See *Corway v Independent Newspapers* [1999] 4 IR 485; and *R (Green) v City of Westminster Magistrates' Court* [2007] EWHC 2785 (Admin) para 11.   [116] Roy (n 106 above) 22.

[117] See Ch 6.

[118] Speech by Olli Rehn, Commission for Enlargement in the Open Debate on Enlargement, European Parliament, Foreign Affairs Committee, Brussels, 7 May 2007, available at <http:// europa.eu/rapid/pressReleasesAction.do?reference=SPEECH/07/287&format=HTML&aged=0 &language=EN&guiLanguage=en> (last visited 13 May 2010).

theological conviction, mainstream Christian denominations accept this peripheral status and can therefore be trusted to moderate the use they may make of such public privilege. On the other hand, religions such as Islam, which have not been subject to similar pressures and experiences, would appear to be seen as less 'trustworthy' in this regard, the suggestion being that its adherents may use such privileges in ways that might impact on the overall principle of balance between religious and humanist influences to a greater degree.

The characterization of the public role of certain denominations at Member State level as a matter of national culture exacerbates this tendency by characterizing the ideological preferences of culturally entrenched religions in respect of gender or sexuality as instances of culture, and accommodating them in the marketplace on this basis while categorizing similar ideological preferences of non-culturally entrenched faiths as ideological aims and claims to recognition of religious truth claims that are incompatible with the principle of balance and with liberal norms of equality. There are indications that the existing model of European secularity, under which the cultural roots of historically European faiths obscure the ideological elements of such faiths, is coming under pressure in a more multicultural context. Klausen's study of European Muslims involved in public life noted arguments that concerns about the role of Islam in Europe were pushing many European states towards a more comprehensive secularism, with a resultant reduction in the public role of culturally entrenched faiths. She quotes a Muslim member of the Bundestag, who suggested that 'when the history of how Muslims changed Europe will be written [sic], the conclusion will be that they promoted secularism and the separation of church and state'.[119] There is indeed some evidence that such a process may be underway and may lead to a strengthening of the humanist and secular elements of the European public order. In the aftermath of the Mohammed cartoons controversy not only, as noted above, did the Parliamentary Assembly of the Council of Europe call for the abolition of blasphemy laws, EU law broadcasting legislation was amended so as to reduce significantly the restrictions it imposed on free speech in order to prevent criticism of, or insults to, religion. In the 1989 Broadcasting Directive the Union used its powers to regulate television advertising to restrict expression that would be 'offensive' to religious beliefs. Article 12(c) of the Directive provided that '[t]elevision advertising shall not

---

[119] J Klausen, *The Islamic Challenge: Politics and Religion in Western Europe* (Oxford: Oxford University Press, 2005) 179.

be offensive to religious...beliefs'. When a revised version of the Directive was under consideration in 2007 this prohibition was initially retained.[120] Several secularist groups objected to the retention of Article 12(c) on the basis that there was no valid distinction to be drawn between religious and political beliefs and the article in question offered 'far too strong a power of suppression of legitimate communication to people who are liable to be ultra-sensitive'[121] and noting that 'the idea of protecting political beliefs is dangerous. Politics is a realm of robust debate and those putting forward political views must be open not just to criticism but to mockery etc.'[122]

The final version of the 2007 Directive, while retaining the prohibition on transmitting advertisements during the broadcast of religious ceremonies, deleted the prohibition of expression offensive to religious beliefs in Article 12(c).[123] While too much should not be read into a single piece of legislation, it is notable that in deleting Article 12(c), European institutions implicitly changed the balance between the principle of free speech and legal enforcement of respect for religion in a secular direction. Furthermore, in doing so the Union also drew the line at the facilitation of religious identity rights at the point at which such rights could impact on political debate and therefore the autonomy of, and equality of participants in, the public sphere. Such an approach further underlines the Union's distinction between the cultural and the political in relation to its facilitation of religion.

There is therefore some validity in accusations that the EU engages in discrimination between religions. This discrimination does not arise because of the Union's refusal to accommodate religious truth claims in the political arena or because of its recognition of the fact that particular faiths are important parts of the cultural identity of Europe and its nation states. Rather, it arises from the failure of the Union to recognize the complex nature of the relationship between the cultural and the political and, most significantly, the continuing ambiguities in the approaches of culturally entrenched European faiths to the question of the proper relationship between law, religion,

---

[120] Coordination of certain of the Member States' provisions on television broadcasting (amending directive 89/552/EEC, règl. 2006/2004/EC) ('Television without Frontiers') (COD 2005/260).

[121] See response of the British Humanist Association to the Department of Culture consultation on the proposed directive, available at <http://www.culture.gov.uk/NR/rdonlyres/262BF0AA-244E-4E2B-A5C4-50D47151F51C/0/BritishHumanistAssociation.docx> (last visited 26 May 2010).   [122] Ibid.

[123] Council Directive (EC) 2007/65 amending Council Directive (EC) 89/552 on the coordination of certain provisions laid down by law, regulation or administrative action in Member States concerning the pursuit of television broadcasting activities [2007] OJ L332/27.

and the state and the limitations on religious influence in the legal and political arenas. However, the combination of the strong religious element to national cultures, the Union's commitment to pluralism, and its weak democratic legitimacy, means that any attempts to address this discrimination by taking a stricter line in relation to the privileging of culturally entrenched faiths would be immensely difficult. On the other hand, the recent decision of the ECtHR in *Lautsi v Italy*[124] may indicate some movement in this regard. As noted in Chapter 4, in this case the Court held unanimously that the presence of crucifixes in Italian state schools amounted to an unacceptable endorsement of the truth of the Catholic faith by the Italian state. This may indicate that European institutions may police the boundary between recognition of religion as an element of national culture and state recognition of the truth claims of particular religions more strictly, with knock-on consequences for the degree of privilege and recognition that states may legitimately confer on 'insider' religions. This decision has, however, been very controversial, and is under appeal to the Grand Chamber.

As will be discussed more fully in Chapter 6, attempts to assert and protect secular elements of European approaches to religion, including those by the EU, have been criticized as discriminatory and even racist. It is true that, insofar as it assumes a congruence between the ambitions of culturally entrenched faiths and liberal democracy, which it does not assume in the case of religions such as Islam, the Union's approach can validly be criticized and give encouragement to those whose support of such limitations is merely an opportunistic ruse to support of racist or discriminatory agendas. On the other hand, given that Europe's changing religious make-up is bringing the grey areas and contradictions in European approaches to the relationship between religion, the law, and the state (in particular the disconnect between the exalted symbolic status of insider faiths and their limited *de facto* influence over law) into sharper relief, the Union is operating in a particularly complex and challenging environment. As Chapter 6 shows, the secular elements of European approaches to religion are being made more explicit in many states as the cultural consensus limiting the impact of concessions granted to religions begins to break down. The limitations on religious influence over law and politics imposed by the Union serve extremely valuable purposes, but the entanglement between national cultures and particular religions makes the process of asserting and maintaining such limitations very complex.

---

[124] *Lautsi v Italy* (Application No 30814/06) 3 November 2009.

The Union does need to be vigilant in order to ensure that its approach is not abused by those seeking simply to exclude on racial or other grounds those who wish to take part in European society and who respect its liberal democratic values. It must also, however, respect the limitations on its ability to impose change on Member States in this area. It is perhaps inevitable that greater religious diversity will require reconsideration of the privileges granted to particular faiths by Member States, but, as the undertaking in Article 16 of the Lisbon Treaty to respect the status of churches under national law recognizes, this process will largely be one for the Member States themselves to undertake. The Union can only set down broad parameters and ensure that its own public order upholds the limitations on religion in a fair way. This task is complicated by the overlapping nature of competences in the Union and the importance attached by the EU to cultural autonomy, which make the process of change slow and fraught with difficulty. Nevertheless, changes such as those made to the Broadcasting Directive in 2007 and the clear distinction drawn between recognition of religion as an element of culture and recognition of religious truth claims seen in the decision in *Lautsi* (which will have a knock-on impact on the Union's fundamental rights norms) indicate that the limitations imposed on religion within the EU public order are increasingly being applied even when this calls into question a privilege previously enjoyed by insider faiths and are not merely nativist prejudice masked as constitutional principle.

3.2.2 Culture and Religions Viewed as Contrary to the Public Order

Indeed, any unevenness in the application of limitations to religious influence in the legal and political arenas may not be the most serious issue of discrimination arising out of the Union's approach to religion. Although religions such as Islam may have less access to public privileges than culturally entrenched religious denominations, they are, nevertheless, recognized by EU law as religions and are capable of accessing the significant privileges outlined above, which are granted to religion in general by EU law in areas such as employment, broadcasting, and ritual slaughter. While EU law does seem to attribute theocratic ambitions to such outsider religions to a greater degree than insider religions such as the Catholic Church, Islam itself is not in general seen as something intrinsically threatening to Europe's public order. On the other hand, despite the Union's commitment to the protection of religious freedom and the recognition of respect for religion in general as a part of the public order, newer religions that do not have institutional links to the state or a long history in Europe have been characterized as actively hostile to the public order and have received scant protection of either the public or private elements of their religious freedom in many EU Member States. Such religions have been excluded not merely from the marketplace benefits accorded to dominant, culturally entrenched religions, but also from recognition as religions.[125] The Church of Scientology in particular has been the target of significant restriction of religious freedom. The German Government denies that Scientology is even a religion[126] and has been accused by the US State Department of 'harassing and intimidating members of the Church of Scientology merely because of their belonging to an organisation... not because of any actions [Scientologists] have taken'.[127] Allegations that Scientologists who are civil servants have been disciplined by the Bavarian Government were also noted by the UN Special Rapporteur on Religious Intolerance in 1994.[128] The authorities in other Member States have also manifested a strong degree of hostility towards newer religions.[129] Such religions are, as Ferrari notes, generally opposed on the basis that they tend to isolate their adherents from society, or, as he himself states, because they represent 'centrifugal forces which estrange individuals from the circuits of democratic citizenship'.[130] In other words, the

[125] 'The New Europe: Sects, Orthodoxy and Discrimination by the State', paper presented by the Rutherford Institute to the OSCE Human Dimension Seminar on Constitutional and Administrative aspects on the Freedom of Religion, Warsaw, 16–19 April 1996, 4; quoted in Peter Cumper, 'The Rights of Religious Minorities: The Legal Regulation of New Religious Movements' in P Cumper and S Wheatley (eds), *Minority Rights in the New Europe* (The Hague: Martinus Nijhoff Publishers, 1999) 171.

[126] See 'The Scientology Organisation', paper submitted by the German delegation at the OSCE Human Dimension Seminar on Constitutional and Administrative aspects on the Freedom of Religion, Warsaw, 16–19 April 1996, 6, where the German Government states that 'goals are clearly oriented to economic activity and its claim to be such a denomination or community is simply a pretext... it is straightforward profit [rather than religion or faith] that lies at the heart of scientology'.

[127] Cumper (n 125 above).

[128] See the report of Abdelfattah Amor, Special Rapporteur on Religious Intolerance to the UN Commission on Human Rights, 22 December 1994, E/CN.4/1995/91.

[129] See *Les sectes en France. Rapport fait au nom de la commission d'enquête sur les sectes* (Paris: Les Documents d'information de l'Assemblée Nationale, 1996). For criticism by scholars and the mainstream churches, see Massimo Introvigne and J Gordon Melton (eds), *Pour en finir avec les sectes. Le débat sur le rapport de la commission parlementaire* (Paris: Dervy, 3rd edn, 1996) ; and Chambre des Réprésentants de Belgique, *Enquête parlementaire visant à élaborer une politique en vue de lutter contre les pratiques illégales des sectes et le danger qu'elles représentent pour la société et pour les personnes, particulièrement les mineurs d'âge* (Brussels: Chambre des Représentants de Belgique, 1997) (two volumes).

[130] Ferrari (n 105 above).

failure of adherents of such religions to accept the peripherality of religion in terms of the public life of the state and their individual public duties as citizens, renders the religion a threat to the principle of balance between religion and humanism and therefore a threat to the public order. Indeed, criticisms of Scientology by the German authorities explicitly make this point, arguing that it 'engenders a marked friend-foe mindset in its members', which can cause a weakening of links to family and society.[131] These concerns that the individual's role and responsibilities as citizen may be overwhelmed by their religious beliefs have, it must be conceded, also been seen in the approach of several Member States to Muslim migrants who have been required, through residence and citizenship exams, to indicate their acceptance of secular, liberal values as a precondition of citizenship or residence rights.[132] Nevertheless, no Member State has considered subjecting Islam (which, despite its status as a minority religion, has a long cultural history in Europe) to the kind of restrictions faced by newer religions such as Scientology. Despite the Union's commitment to upholding religious freedom, EU institutions have failed to intervene or to criticize Member State actions in this area.[133] This contrasts with the strongly worded warnings to respect European human rights norms in other areas. The Polish Government, for instance, following the election victory of conservative parties in 2005, was warned by the Commission that it would have to uphold gay rights or risk losing voting rights in the Council of Ministers.[134]

The case law of the Court of Justice also indicates that Member States appear to have a relatively free hand to restrict the religious liberty of newer, non-mainstream religions in the context of the Single Market. In contrast to courts in other jurisdictions,[135] the Court has never attempted to define

---

[131] 'The Scientology Organisation', paper submitted by the German delegation at the OSCE Human Dimension Seminar on Constitutional and Administrative aspects on the Freedom of Religion, Warsaw, 16-19 April 1996; quoted in Cumper (n 125 above).   [132] See Ch 6.

[133] See JT Richardson and M Introvigne, 'Brainwashing Theories in European Parliamentary and Administrative Reports on "Cults" and "Sects"' (2001) 40(2) *Journal for the Scientific Study of Religion* 143.

[134] 'Polish President Warned over Ultra-Right Shift', *The Independent*, 25 October 2005, available at <http://www.independent.co.uk/news/world/europe/polish-president-warned-over-ultraright-shift-512413.html> (last visited 26 May 2010).

[135] See, eg the decisions of the US Supreme Court in *US v Seegar* 380 US 163, 180–1 (1965); *Wisconsin v Yoder* 406 US 203, 215–216 (1972); and *Thomas v Review Board of the Indiana Employment Security Division* 450 US 707, 714 (1981). See also the decision of the Australian High Court in *Church of the New Faith v Commissioner for Pay-Roll Tax (Vic)* 154 CLR 120, 173 (1983).

religion and has appeared to be willing to ignore the issues of religious freedom raised by the treatment of new religions such as Scientology. In early
1996, the Association Église de scientologie de Paris and the Scientology
International Reserves Trust asked the French authorities to repeal a French
law that enabled the authorities to require that prior authorization be given
to all international financial transactions deemed by the French Government to represent a 'threat to public policy [and] security'.[136] The Government refused to do so and proceedings taken by the two Scientologist
organizations were referred to the Court of Justice for preliminary ruling.[137]
The applicants alleged that the law in question represented an impermis-
sible interference with the free movement of capital. The relevant treaty
provisions permitted Member States to maintain such restrictions as were
justified on grounds of 'public policy or public security'.[138] The Court noted
that:

while Member States are still, in principle, free to determine the requirements of
public policy and public security in the light of their national needs, those grounds
must, in the Community context and, in particular, as derogations from the fundamental principle of free movement of capital, be interpreted strictly, so that their
scope cannot be determined unilaterally by each Member State without any control
by the Community institutions.[139]

It further held that 'Public security may be relied on only if there is a genuine and sufficiently serious threat to a fundamental interest of society'.[140]

Such measures were, furthermore, subject to a proportionality test, with
the Member State being required to show that its restrictions were 'necessary for the protection of the interests which they are intended to guarantee
and only in so far as those objectives cannot be attained by less restrictive
measures'.[141]

Given that the impugned measures were intended to restrict the ability
of the Church of Scientology to function in France, it may have been antici-
pated that the issue of religious freedom would have played a prominent role
in this case as, for instance, potential restrictions on freedom of expression

---

[136] Article 5-1(I)(1) of Law No 66-1008, introduced by Law No 96-109 of 14 February 1996 on
financial relations with foreign countries in regard to foreign investments in France.

[137] Case C-54/99 *Association Église de scientologie de Paris and Scientology International Reserves
Trust v The Prime Minister* [2000] ECR I-1335.

[138] Ibid para 16 (the relevant EC Treaty article is Art 65(1)(b)).   [139] Ibid para 17.

[140] Ibid.   [141] Ibid para 18.

were considered in the Court's judgment in the *ERT* case.[142] At the very least it would have been expected that, given the fundamental nature of the right to religious freedom, the proportionality argument would have played an important role in the decision and that the French authorities would be asked to justify their failure to take less draconian measures in their attempts to prevent the transfer of funds to the French Scientology organization. The Court did strike down the relevant French legislation. However, it did so on the basis that:

the essence of the system in question is that prior authorisation is required for every direct foreign investment which is such as to represent a threat to public policy and public security, without any more detailed information.... Such lack of precision does not enable individuals to be apprised of the extent of their rights and obligations deriving from Article 73b of the Treaty. That being so, the system established is contrary to the principle of legal certainty.[143]

No mention of the religious aspect of the case appears anywhere in the judgment. Given that, as noted above, the aim of the actions of the Member State authorities were intended to restrict the capacity of a religious organization to operate in the state in question, the absence of any mention of the issue of religious freedom is remarkable. This lack of concern for the institutional rights of minority religions contrasts strongly with the protection afforded to the institutional interests of the more established, Member-State-favoured churches by Single Market law, most notably under the Framework Directive. Indeed, in the *Église de Scientologie* case it appears that the Court of Justice simply did not consider that issues of religious freedom were raised by attempts to impede the functioning of the Church of Scientology. This is despite the fact that, under its ruling in the *ERT* case, measures such as those in this case, which are adopted by Member States in derogation of their duty to respect the four freedoms under EU law, are subject to compliance with EU fundamental rights norms. The relevant fundamental rights clearly include the right to freedom of religion,[144] yet the Court failed even to mention religious freedom as a pertinent issue.[145]

---

[142] Case C-260/89 *ERT* [1991] ECR I-2925. See Ch 4, section 3.

[143] Case C-54/99 *Association Église de Scientologie de Paris and Scientology International Reserves Trust v The Prime Minister* [2000] ECR I-1335 paras 21 and 22.

[144] Freedom of religion is recognized in specific articles by both the EU Charter of Fundamental Rights (Art 10) and the ECHR (Art 9).

[145] The Court of Justice recognized as much in Case 130/75 *Prais v Council* (unreported) 27 October 1976 in 1975 (see Ch 4). Furthermore, freedom of religion is protected by Art 9 of the

It is true that the Court of Justice has, on occasion, preferred to side-step sensitive topics in its judgments and has, perhaps deliberately, in cases such as *Grogan*,[146] which dealt with Irish anti-abortion legislation, tended to base its decisions on less controversial areas of the law. Nevertheless, even in *Grogan*, the Court acknowledged the wider controversy, albeit only to state that arguments about the moral nature of abortion were irrelevant.[147] In *Église Scientologie*, the Court failed to make any such acknowledgement despite the clear status of freedom of religion as a part of EU law. If one considers a scenario under which the Court was required to assess Member State legislation that imposed similar financial penalties on the Catholic Church on the basis that the Member State in question felt that it represented a threat to public policy, it is difficult to imagine the case being decided without some mention of the principle of religious freedom or some attempt to seek justification from the Member State in question for its characterization of the Church in those terms.[148]

The Union's linking of issues of culture and religion would appear therefore not only to have influenced not only its view of the appropriateness of the role of certain denominations in the public sphere, but has also conditioned its view of what can be considered to be religion, with knock-on consequences for the protection provided by EU law to both the public and private elements of religious freedom in the Single Market. It is true that, in the context of employment discrimination, individual adherents to newer religions may be able to access some protection from direct discrimination under the provisions of the Framework Directive.[149] Nevertheless, while religion may be seen as part of the public order, and even allowed a certain degree of societal, legal, and political influence on this basis, religions such as Scientology, which are identified as contrary to this public order, receive scant protection of their communal or institutional rights. The Union's categorization of religion as a cultural matter, and its failure to recognize newer religions as religions at all, avoids the necessity of addressing awkward questions posed by its approach to religion and the limitations required on

ECHR whose role in the determination of the content of the EU's fundamental rights norms was recognized in Case 36/75 *Rutili v Ministre de l'Intérieur* [1975] ECR 1219.

[146] Case C-159/90 *Society for the Protection of Unborn Children Ireland Ltd v Stephen Grogan and others* [1991] ECR I-4685. [147] Ibid para 20.

[148] In Case 196/87 *Steymann v Staatssecretaris van Justitie* [1988] ECR 6159 the Court similarly ignored the element of religious freedom in coming to its decision that the applicant's work in a religious commune for which he received food and accommodation was 'employment' for the purposes of Community law.

[149] See section 2.2 above.

religious influence in a liberal democratic public order. By recognizing religion as a matter of culture and identity the Union allows certain religions to play a privileged role within the public order and facilitates the maintenance of a culturally and religiously specific element to the identity of the state. However, religion cannot be seen in purely cultural terms. Religion is also ideological and, as the Union has emphasized in other areas, it can also pose a threat to liberal democracy and fundamental rights on this basis. While it may be happy to recognize a religious tradition discouraging work on Sundays as a 'regional socio-cultural characteristic', the EU would surely hesitate to defer on a similar basis to a legislative recognition of religious traditions discouraging women from working in the labour market or from venturing outside unaccompanied by a male relative.

The European Union has declared equal treatment to be one of its fundamental principles. On the face of it, the granting of influence (albeit influence that operates indirectly through culture) to certain faiths would appear to contravene this principle. On the other hand, the rights sought by some religions may place greater pressure on humanist elements of the European public order (most notably values such as individual autonomy and non-discrimination on grounds of gender or sexuality) than those sought by other religions. Categorization of religion as a cultural matter and failure to recognize in all circumstances newer religions as religions for the purposes of European guarantees of freedom of religion, allow the Union to avoid the politically unpalatable options of stating explicitly its view that certain religions are more compatible with the European public order than others or of recognizing that its view of the appropriate public role of religion is historically, culturally, and politically specific.

4. Conclusion

The regulation of religion in the Single Market is influenced by the wider dialectic within EU law between the recognition and facilitation of individual and collective religious identity and the desire to maintain certain limits on religion's public role required by the principle of balance between religious, cultural, and humanist influences, which the Union sees as key to its liberal democratic public order. Single Market law approaches the regulation of religion in two different ways, treating it both as an economic choice that can be facilitated by the market and as a phenomenon whose importance to individual and collective identity entitles it to protection from the market. Legislation prohibiting discrimination against individuals on religious grounds in employment, or protecting ritual slaughter methods in food production, protects individual religious identity in areas beyond the purely private contexts in which the ECHR requires that it be protected. The Union has also recognized collective religious identity and has, in some contexts, accorded it a degree of priority over individual identities by curtailing the applicability of the principle of non-discrimination to religious bodies. However, although the Union does recognize the promotion of a particular public status for religion as an element of its own public order and is willing to accommodate religious perspectives in its regulation of the market, the public role allowed to religion under Single Market law is, in accordance with the elements of the balance to which the Union is committed in relation to religion, limited by the need to respect the overarching structures of the market and the humanist and cultural influences which are also part of the EU's public order.

Religion also achieves recognition within the Single Market through the confluence of the recognition accorded to its role in national culture and the Union's commitment to deferring to national cultural autonomy. This deference towards national cultural autonomy extends to the facilitation of significant aspects of the public role of individual religions within the public life and public orders of the Member States. In line with the leeway given to states by the ECtHR,[150] EU law has recognized the right of the state to define national collective identity and to promote this identity, which can include the promotion of particular forms of religion (short of state endorsement of the truth of a particular faith), through law. This involves the recognition by EU law, and the accommodation within the regulation of the Single Market, of religion as sets of practices and as a way of life and the facilitation of particular institutional arrangements between certain denominations and Member States, which enable religions to play important public roles in areas such as health and education. Such recognition can significantly undermine the potential of the prohibitions on discrimination on grounds of religion, recognized elsewhere in EU law, to destabilize established religious privileges.

Nevertheless, in accordance with the overall approach of EU law to the accommodation of religion in public life, this cultural role is also subject to limitations. Restrictions based on the need to respect the structures of the

---

[150] See Ch 4.

market are somewhat limited because EU law specifically recognizes that cultural matters should not be subordinate to market forces. Nevertheless, the broader approach of EU law of seeking to impose limits on the public role of religion in order to safeguard the principle of balance does limit the privileges that religion can assert in this way. Limitation on this ground is, however, less stringent than that which applies to rights provided to religions that are not linked to respect for national cultural autonomy. First, there is a degree of circularity in that institutional privileges granted by Member States to certain denominations are reflective of the important role played by such denominations in the very public orders that could act to limit these privileges. Secondly, the religion-limiting elements of the EU's dialectical approach to the issue of religious privilege are based on a distinction between recognizing religion as an element of culture and recognition of the truth claims of a particular faith. Underpinning this is a recognition that religion can be an ideological threat to the humanist elements of the Union's public order, including key liberal values such as equal treatment, personal autonomy, and the autonomy of the public sphere from religious domination. As culture is seen as in some way non-political and non-ideological, the recognition of the public role of 'insider' faiths as a cultural matter obscures the ideological element of the exercise of public influence by such denominations, thus limiting the scope for restricting the role of culturally entrenched religions on the basis of the need to restrict religious influence within the political arena. Indeed, EU institutions have, in general, appeared to assume compatibility between culturally entrenched religions such as Roman Catholicism and the humanist elements of the Union's public order, even when the privileges that these faiths seek to assert are inconsistent with humanist and egalitarian values (as in the case of the desire to discriminate against employees whose behaviour is inconsistent with the ethos of the organizations in which they work, or in relation to the criminalization of blasphemy). On the other hand, EU institutions have been quicker to recognize the ideological elements of outsider religions such as Islam and the threat that these elements can pose to humanist values. Even more notably, new religions such as Scientology, which have few cultural roots and are seen as actively contrary to the liberal democratic public order, have not, in some circumstances, even been recognized as religions and have received scant protection of their rights in the marketplace. The Union's assumption of a congruence between the ambitions of culturally entrenched faiths and the limitations it requires on religious influence over law and politics raise issues of equal treatment, which the complex relationship between culture and religion and the Union's weak legitimacy and commitment to respecting Member State cultural autonomy make difficult to resolve. On the other hand, recent developments, such as the 2007 Broadcasting Directive, show a greater willingness to uphold such limitations even when doing so impinges on privileges previously held by religious bodies.

Therefore, the overall picture is one in which the right to individual religious identity and the sometimes competing right to collective religious identity are both protected by EU law. The balance between these two sets of rights takes place within the context of the Union's commitment to the notion of balance between religious, cultural, and humanist influences, and of the recognition of the right of states to promote particular forms of religion as an element of their national cultures. Therefore, although individual religious identity is protected on a denomination-neutral basis by Single Market law, this protection must adapt itself to predominant market structures and humanist-influenced political and constitutional norms. The protection of collective religious identity in the form of religious notions of morality, communal religious practices, and institutional religious structures are also accorded protection in the Single Market, but largely on the basis of respect for the established religious structures in the marketplace and national cultural autonomy. Thus, it is largely those values, institutions, and practices that are compatible with pre-existing practices, values, and institutional structures recognized by the Member States—many of which retain close identifications with, and promote important public roles for, certain Christian denominations—that will be recognized. To describe the Single Market as a 'Christian Market' on this basis would go too far. It is certainly true that Christian denominations have a greater level of influence and privilege within Single Market law and that other religions are accorded lower levels of privilege. However, many of these collective rights (such as exemptions from anti-discrimination legislation) are characterized by EU law (in so far as they clash with the right to individual identity) as anachronistic and anomalous exceptions to established humanist elements of the Union's public order, such as individual autonomy and equal treatment. Furthermore, although there is reluctance on the part of EU institutions to recognize the ideological nature of the influence over law wielded by culturally entrenched Christian denominations, this may be changing, and the continued exercise of privilege by such denominations within the Single Market can be seen as contingent. Acceptance of the notion of balance, and the limitation of religious influence and truth claims in the political arena that such balance involves, has been attributed to insider denominations by

EU law and they must therefore avoid seeking a degree of privilege inconsistent with these principles. Indeed, these privileges (as the *Lautsi* decision
and the above-mentioned changes in the 2007 Broadcasting Directive made
in relation to religiously offensive speech indicate) may be vulnerable to rising fears in relation to the role of religion in public life and perceived threats
to humanist elements of Europe's public order, which may result in more
vigilant policing of the limitations on religious influence over the political
sphere and a consequent restriction of the cultural influence of insider religions over law.

6

Competing Identities Limiting Religious Influence within the EU Legal Order

1. Introduction

Previous chapters have shown the significant facilitation of both religious identities and religious influence over law provided by the public order of the European Union (EU). However, they have also indicated that such facilitation is limited by the humanist elements of that public order. In particular, the accommodation of the promotion of collective religious morality, by virtue of the status of such morality as a part of national cultural identity, has been limited by the Union's own public morality, which draws on its fundamental rights commitments, most notably to individual liberty. Although the Union has welcomed the participation of religious bodies in its policy-making process, acceptance of limitations on religious influence in the legal and political arenas has been identified as a fundamental element of the Union's public order. Analysis of elements of the EU's enlargement and immigration policies demonstrates that acceptance of limitations on religious influence over law and politics has been seen both as a prerequisite of membership of the Union and as something that may legitimately be required of outsiders seeking to live there.

Specifically, the Union has regarded attempts to legislate for religious morality, to an extent that is overly intrusive in relation to personal private autonomy, as incompatible with a desire to join the EU. It has also identified a desire to subordinate the political sphere to religious influence, or to legislate on explicitly religious grounds, as similarly inconsistent with EU membership and the proper balance between religious and humanist influences that the EU requires, thus mirroring the restrictions on the assertion of religious truth claims in the political arena seen in other areas such as the

Union's outreach to religious bodies. Religious influence over law and the promotion through law of religious morality are permitted under the EU's public order, provided that this influence is based on religion's cultural role and the principle of individual autonomy is respected. On the other hand, religion's ability to achieve the same ends in its capacity as a political or ideological movement is considerably more restricted. Such a restriction on religion's political role impacts more heavily on outsider religions whose demands cannot as readily be characterized as elements of national culture.

These features of the Union's approach are seen in relation to its dealings with Turkey, and Islam's controversial role in Turkish politics. Although it is part of Turkish national culture, Muslim influence in Turkey has been seen in more political than cultural terms, and Islamic attempts to exert influence in the political and legal arenas have not been regarded as compatible with the EU's public order to the same degree as the public role played by mainstream Christian denominations such as Roman Catholicism or Orthodox Christianity in EU Member States. The Union's commitment to distinguishing between accommodating religion as a matter of culture and accommodating religious truth claims in relation to law and politics is seen, in its hostility to religious attempts, to influence law in ways that cannot be characterized as the promotion of national culture. This arises most notably in relation to the issue of the integration of immigrants. EU law has facilitated measures requiring migrants to indicate their acceptance of either the right of the state to embrace principles such as gender equality and individual autonomy in sexual matters or acceptance of such principles themselves, even when such principles, which are rejected by many mainstream European faiths, contradict their religious beliefs. The EU has therefore sanctioned state interference in the private sphere of beliefs and opinions in order to protect the general principles of the supremacy of secular law and the autonomy of the individual in the private sphere.

These measures indicate that the Union regards limitations on the influence of religion over law and politics as fundamental elements of its public order. Limitations in relation to the protection of individual autonomy are applied to all religions. Within the political arena, the EU's hostility to theocracy similarly restricts recourse to religious arguments on the part of all faiths. However, there are significant grey areas in relation to the role of religion in the legal and political arenas in Europe. Many faiths, including culturally entrenched 'insider' faiths, retain ambitions to mould law and policy in line with their teachings, particularly in relation to 'lifeworld'

issues.[1] This chapter shows that the EU, while demonstrating some awareness of the dangers to liberal democracy posed by the political ambitions of
some outsider religions, has not fully recognized the ambiguities that exist
in the approach of insider religions to the relationship between religion, the
law, and the state. Furthermore, insider religions can get around limits on
religion's political role by exercising influence through their cultural role.
Therefore, the approach of the Union raises questions of equal treatment
between insider and outsider religions. However, it is the application of the
limitations imposed by the EU's public order that are problematic, rather
than their substance. There is doubtless a danger that limitations will be
abused by those motivated by racist or other exclusionary motives. On the
other hand, there is also the danger that legitimate concerns in relation to
racism will undermine necessary limitations on religious influence over law
and politics and important principles such as gender equality, individual
autonomy, equal democratic participation, and free expression that such
limitations protect. As Baykal argues, the quest for shared values for the
EU remains vital to the future of the Union as a sustainable polity.[2] Limits
on religious influence over law and politics are a major element of European
culture and, although some with racist motives may seek to use them, they
are not in themselves racially discriminatory. Provided such limitations are
applied across the board they are entirely defensible. However, as this chapter shows, the achievement of across-the-board application faces significant
challenges.

2. Enlargement and Religion in the Public Sphere

As was shown in Chapter 2, since the Reformation and Enlightenment, relations
between religious institutions and those of the state have been characterized in
Europe by a gradual decline in religious power and the establishment of a legal
order in which humanist notions such as individual autonomy and the authority
of secular political institutions achieved major influence.[3] On the other hand,

---

[1] See Ch 2.
[2] S Baykal, 'Unity in Diversity? The Challenge of Diversity for European Political Identity,
Legitimacy and Democratic Governance: Turkey's EU Membership as the Ultimate Test Case',
Jean Monnet Working Papers Series 09/2005, NYU School of Law.
[3] See Ch 2.

'grey areas' persist in the relationship between religion, the law, and the state in Europe with a significant difference between the *de jure* and *de facto* influence of culturally entrenched faiths.[4] Nevertheless, although the balance between religious, humanist, and cultural influences, which the EU sees as having emerged from European history, enables religious institutions to continue to play a role in law-making, including at EU level, religious bodies have much less political impact than in other areas of the world. The limited nature of religious influence over legal norms in Europe is shown by the fact that, even in relation to the law governing what Casanova terms 'lifeworld' issues (namely those relating to the beginning and end of life, family, and sexuality), which are the highest political priority for mainstream European religious[5] and which embodied the largely conservative approach of the Abrahamic religions to a significant degree as recently as 60 years ago, liberal norms of personal autonomy, privacy, and equality have become increasingly dominant. This approach embodies the arguably Western notion of religion as a largely private matter with limited influence over law and political life and contrasts markedly with the situation in much of the rest of the world,[6] most notably Islam,[7] where religious principles continue to exercise a much greater influence over certain areas of law.[8]

2.1 Enlargement, Conditionality, and Human Rights

Even prior to 1989, it was clear that the criteria for inclusion in the European Community amounted to more than adoption of a market economy. As far back as the 1960s, the Community was stressing the importance of respect for democratic principles and human rights in assessing Greece's application for

---

[4] See ibid. See also R McCrea, 'De Facto Secularism in a Diversifying Religious Environment: The Changing Relationship between State and Religion in Europe' in A Sajo (ed.), *Religion in the Public Square* (Utrecht: Eleven International Publishing, 2011, forthcoming).

[5] See Ch 2.

[6] P Berger and G Weigel (eds), *The Desecularization of the Modern World: Resurgent Religion and Modern Politics* (Grand Rapids Michigan: Erdemans Publishing Company and Public Policy Center, 1999). See also P Norris and R Inglehart, *Sacred and Secular: Religion and Politics Worldwide* (Cambridge: Cambridge University Press, 2004).

[7] Norris and Inglehart (ibid). See also B Lewis, *The Crisis of Islam: Holy War and Unholy Terror* (London: Phoenix, 2003) 14–17.

[8] Private consensual sexual behaviour continues to be regulated by the criminal law to a significant extent in many largely Muslim societies. For instance, homosexuality remains a crime in the largely Muslim countries of Afghanistan, Algeria, Bahrain, Bangladesh, Iran, Iraq, Lebanon, Libya, Malaysia, Mauritania, Morocco, Oman, Pakistan, Somalia, the United Arab Emirates, and Yemen; see <http://www.gaylawnet.com/> (last visited 17 May 2010). In relation to the greater level of religiosity found in societies outside Europe, see Norris and Inglehart (n 6 above).

membership.[9] From the 1970s onwards, human rights achieved an increasing prominence in the Community.[10] Following the collapse of Communism, the speed with which newly liberated countries sought membership of the Union meant that European institutions were required to make explicit the criteria that would be used to determine who could and could not become a member of the Community. The resulting 'Copenhagen Criteria' were outlined in Copenhagen at the European Council of June 1993. The criteria specified that '[m]embership requires that candidate country has achieved stability of institutions guaranteeing democracy, the rule of law, human rights and respect for, and protection of, minorities, the existence of a functioning market economy as well as the capacity to cope with competitive pressure and market forces within the Union'.[11]

The act of setting out such explicitly political criteria was a recognition by Member States that a state eminently suitable for membership in economic terms would not be permitted to join the Community unless it showed a commitment to certain ideals (democracy, protection of human rights, etc), adherence to which was deemed necessary for the proper functioning of the European polity. These criteria have played a prominent role, not only in the enlargement process but also in the EU's view of itself. The Maastricht Treaty gave this process constitutional status stating, in Article 6, that the EU was 'founded on the principles of liberty, democracy, respect for human rights and fundamental freedoms, and the rule of law' and pledging in the same article to respect the principles of the European Convention on Human Rights (ECHR). Article 49 TEU now provides that states applying to join the Union must respect 'the values of respect for human dignity, freedom, democracy, equality, the rule of law and respect

---

[9] For an account of how democracy and human rights moved from implicit to explicit conditions of EU membership, see H Sjursen, 'Enlargement in Perspective: The EU's Quest for Identity', paper given as part of the European Institute Research Seminar series at the London School of Economics, 24 May 2006.

[10] See the 1977 Tripartite Declaration on Human Rights of the Parliament, Council and Commission [1977] OJ C103/1). This process continued into the 1990s with direct reference being made to the European Convention on Human Rights in the Amsterdam Treaty and the adoption of a Bill of Rights for the EU in the Nice Treaty. See also the series of rulings of the European Court of Justice in cases such as Case 29/69 *Stauder v City of Ulm-Sozialamt* [1969] ECR 419, through to Case C- 260/89 *ERT* [1991] ECR I-2925, and see Ch 4.

[11] See European Council in Copenhagen, 21–22 June 1993, 'Conclusions of the Presidency', SN 180/1/93 REV 1, available at <http://ue.eu.int/ueDocs/cms_Data/docs/pressdata/en/ec/72921.pdf> (last visited 17 May 2010).

for human rights, including the rights of persons belonging to minorities'.[12] The European Commission is charged with assessing whether candidate countries meet these conditions. It makes a recommendation to the Member States, which must unanimously decide to open negotiations.[13] Formal accession negotiations have never been opened by the EU with a state that has not been judged by the Commission to be in compliance with the Copenhagen Criteria.

The criteria themselves do not, on their face, appear to mandate any particular approach to management of the relationship between religion, law, and politics. However, given that many mainstream religions advocate, or have advocated, the use of the law to enforce compliance with religious teachings to a degree that may be inconsistent with individual autonomy and equality in sensitive areas such as gender and sexuality, states that allow religions to determine the content of their laws are likely to face difficulties in satisfying the Union's accession criteria and, at certain times in the accession process, the EU has indicated that adherence to the criteria and the liberal democratic values underlying them does require limitations on the role played by religion and religious norms in law-making.

2.2 Romania and Homosexuality

In 1996 the Romanian legislature amended Article 200 of the Penal Code to criminalize private homosexual acts and outlaw membership of gay and lesbian organizations. This law was strongly supported by the Romanian Orthodox Church, with a former foreign minister identifying ecclesiastical

---

[12] Consolidated Versions of the Treaty on European Union and the Treaty Establishing the European Community OJ C321 E/35, Art 49. See also the Commission Regular Report of 2002 COM(2002)700, which states that 'since the entry into force of the Treaty of Amsterdam in May 1999, these [political] requirements have been enshrined as constitutional principles in the Treaty on European EU'. See also C Hillion, 'The Copenhagen Criteria and Their Progeny' in C Hillion (ed.), *European Enlargement: A Legal Approach* (Oxford: Hart Publishing, 2004), where it is argued that '[t]he novelty of the Copenhagen criteria also lies in the way the obligations they embody have been enforced: their gradual "constitutionalisation" has resulted in them being applied more strictly' (3) and that '[o]ne may suggest that the political conditionality has been implicit in the Community legal order from the very outset, and made progressively more explicit' (4).

[13] Consolidated Versions of the Treaty on European EU and the Treaty Establishing the European Community, Art 49. See 'How Does a Country Join the EU', European Commission, DG Enlargement, available at <http://ec.europa.eu/enlargement/questions_and_answers/background_en.htm> (last visited 17 May 2010).

opposition as a key factor behind the retention of the law.[14] The Romanian Government attempted to repeal Article 200 in 1998 but this was rejected by its parliament after a vociferous campaign by the Orthodox Church. Church officials referred to gays and lesbians as 'the ultimate enemy' and 'Satan's army' and accused legislators of being 'scared by the huge European pressures'.[15] In September 2000 the Orthodox Church appealed to legislators not to amend Article 200. Acknowledging the European dimension to the controversy, Archbishop Nifon stated that he did not 'believe that European Union integration hinges on the [homosexuality] issue'.[16]

At the time of the announcement of the Copenhagen Criteria in June 1993, the EU had no competence in relation to sexual orientation discrimination,[17] nor had criminalization of homosexuality been raised as an issue in any previous enlargement.[18] However, notwithstanding this lack of internal competence or consensus among Member States,[19] the Union embraced the repeal of laws criminalizing homosexual activity as part of the accession process. Importantly, however, it did so on the grounds that such laws constituted an interference with the human rights of gays and lesbians. In its 1998 report on Romania's progress towards accession, the Commission noted that a proposal to reform the Penal Code, which included a proposal to decriminalize homosexuality had been rejected by the Romanian Parliament[20] and that there were 'reports of inhuman and degrading treatment by the police, especially of Roma, children, homosexuals and prisoners' by the police. These references were made in the section of the report dedicated to 'Human Rights and the Protection of Minorities' and not in the section

[14] See 'It's Still No Breeze for Gays, Even Diplomatic Ones', *New York Times*, 17 October 2001. Note in particular the comments of former Foreign Minister Mircea Geoana attributing key importance to the Orthodox Church in the debate over decriminalization.

[15] See Florian Buhuceanu, 'ACCEPT Country Report on the Status of LGBT', available at <http://www.globalgayz.com/romania-news.html> (last visited 17 May 2010).

[16] See 'Romanian Orthodox Church Denounces Homosexuality', *Reuters News Agency*, 13 September 2000, available at <http://www.ilga.org> (last visited 17 May 2010).

[17] The Amsterdam Treaty of 1997 widened the scope of the EU's ability to legislate against discrimination to include discrimination on grounds of sexual orientation but such legislation required unanimity in the Council and was not enacted until late in the year 2000 (Council Directive (EC) 2000/78 establishing a general framework for equal treatment in employment and occupation [2000] OJ L303/16).

[18] Homosexual acts were illegal in Scotland and Northern Ireland at the time of the accession of the United Kingdom in 1973. A similar prohibition was part of the law of the Republic of Ireland until July 1993.   [19] Ibid.

[20] See section 1.2 of *Regular Report from the Commission on Romania's Progress towards Accession*, available at <http://ec.europa.eu/enlargement/archives/pdf/key_documents/1998/romania _en.pdf> (last visited 17 May 2010).

covering 'Democracy and the Rule of Law', indicating that the Commission saw the matter as a question of interference with the fundamental rights of a minority rather than a structural question relating to the role of religious norms in legislation.

The European Parliament was also particularly active on this issue. In September 1998 it adopted a resolution calling on Romania and Cyprus to abolish their anti-homosexual legislation. The Resolution 'deplored the refusal of the Romanian Chamber of Deputies to adopt a reform bill presented by the Government to repeal all anti-homosexual legislation provided by Article 200 of the penal code'.[21] It also specifically linked the issue of decriminalization to the question of accession, expressing the European Parliament's refusal to 'give its consent to the accession of any country that, through it legislation of policies, violates the human rights of lesbians and gay men'.[22] The European Parliament repeated these sentiments in subsequent resolutions in March 2000 and July 2001.[23] In the summer of 2001 the European Parliament's Intergroup for Lesbian and Gay Rights held a hearing on the situation of lesbians and gays in the accession states. These activities contributed to an increase in pressure on the Commission to take a more proactive stand in relation to the issue of homosexuality and enlargement. Like the Commission, the European Parliament's resolutions were phrased solely in terms of the implications of criminalization for the human rights of gays and lesbians and did not address the controversy's religious aspects.

In remarks to the European Parliament in September 2001, the Commissioner responsible for enlargement, Gunter Verheugen, stated that he wished to make it clear that the Commission would continue to press for human rights and non-discrimination in enlargement negotiations, including on grounds of sexual orientation.[24] The Commissioner's representative to the Intergroup on Gay and Lesbian Rights further stressed that there would be 'no flexibility' on this issue on the part of the Commission. Commissioner Verheugen was even more explicit in a letter sent to the International Lesbian and Gay Association in which he stated that applicant states would be expected to accept the elimination of discrimination based

---

[21] Resolution B4-0852/98, adopted 17 September 1998. See in particular para F.

[22] Ibid, para J.

[23] Resolution A5-0223/2001, adopted 5 July 2001, paras 80, 83 and Resolution A5-0050/2000, adopted 16 March 2000, paras 59, 60.

[24] D Cronin, 'Enlargement Chief Rapped for "Understating" Bias against Gays', *European Voice*, quoted in ILGA Europe, Euroletter No 97, April 2002, available at <http://www.france .qrd.org/assocs/ilga/euroletter/97.html> (last visited 26 May 2010)

upon sexual orientation and that 'equal treatment of gays and lesbians is a basic principle of the European Union'.[25] In December 2001, faced with the determined opposition of the Orthodox Church and conscious of its failure to push decriminalization through the Parliament on the previous occasion, the Romanian Government resorted to an emergency ordinance to amend Article 200 and finally decriminalized homosexuality.[26]

European institutions had therefore succeeded in forcing the Romanian authorities to remove from their statute book a legal measure which enshrined in the criminal law religiously influenced norms against homosexuality and had done so in the face of a vociferous and popular campaign by religious leaders of Romania's state church in favour of retaining the law. However, despite this, the Union saw the issue not as a primarily religious one but as a question of human and minority rights. It was to take a different approach in its dealings with Turkey.

2.3 Turkey and Adultery

2.3.1 Background: Turkey and EU Membership

The issue of Turkish accession is perhaps the most controversial aspect of the entire enlargement process. Although its first attempt to join what was then the EEC predated the collapse of Communism in Europe by almost 30 years,[27] Turkey has seen the traditionally Christian countries of Central and Eastern Europe overtake it in the race to join the EU. The prospect of Turkish accession has proved far more unpopular with European electorates than any previous enlargement and has triggered the opposition of many prominent figures in European politics such as Valéry Giscard d'Estaing,

---

[25] See R Wockner, 'Anti-Gay Nations May Not Join European EU', *International News Report*, 31 July 2001, available at <http://gaytoday.badpuppy.com/garchive/world/073101wo.htm> (last visited 17 May 2010).

[26] Lavinia Stan and Lucian Turcescu, 'The Romanian Orthodox Church and Post-Communist Democratisation' (2000) 52(8) *Europe-Asia Studies* 1480. See also the account given by the Romanian gay rights group ACCEPT (which has received EU funding for it work) at <http://accept-romania.ro/en/despre-noi/istoric/> (last visited 26 May 2010).

[27] Turkey made its first application to join the EEC in 1959 and concluded an association agreement with the Community in 1963. It applied for membership again in 1987. It was not recognized as a candidate for membership until 1999. Membership negotiations are still ongoing. Although the membership applications of the formerly communist states of Eastern and Central Europe all post-dated Turkey's 1987 application, 10 such states had become Member States by January 2007.

Jacques Delors, and Angela Merkel.[28] Much of this opposition has centred on the idea of cultural incompatibility, based on the fact of Turkey's status as a state whose large Muslim majority contrasts with the predominantly Christian heritage of existing Member States.

Nevertheless, as is shown below, much of the concern shown by the Union in relation to Turkish accession has focused on worries that Turkey is insufficiently secular rather than insufficiently Christian. While Turkey is officially a secular republic, religion plays a far larger role in its political life than in most EU Member States.[29] Furthermore, the state is heavily involved in managing religious affairs and, while this state of affairs is not unusual in Europe, the Turkish state does impose certain restrictions on the practice of religions other than Sunni Islam, which have been highlighted by groups opposed to its admission to the EU.[30] Others have rejected the notion of Turkish membership outright on the grounds that Europe's identity and foundations are Christian and that a mainly Muslim country is therefore, by its nature, an inappropriate candidate for membership of the EU.[31] Nevertheless, since the rejection of its membership bid of April 1987 on human rights and economic grounds, Turkey has made significant efforts to bring its human rights standards up to the levels required by the EU. Restrictions on the use of the Kurdish language have been removed and the death penalty has been abolished as part of wide-ranging legal and administrative reforms. This has allowed Turkey to make significant progress along the road to

---

[28] See, eg the opposition of Valéry Giscard d'Estaing stated in an interview with *Le Monde* newspaper, 'Pour ou contre l'adhésion de la Turquie à l'union européenne', *Le Monde*, 9 November 2002, available at <http://www.medea.be/index.html?page=&lang=&doc=1298> (last visited 17 May 2010). Sjursen has noted how Member States described the accession of the historically Christian states of Eastern and Central Europe as a process of 'rejoining' a Europe from which they had been artificially separated while Turkish accession is seen as 'joining' a Europe of which it had not previously been part.

[29] See A Çarkoğlu and B Rubin (eds), *Religion and Politics in Turkey* (London: Routledge, 2006).

[30] The Conference of European Churches (CEC-KEK), which represents Protestant churches in Europe, issued a report that was highly critical of restrictions on religious freedom in Turkey and questioned whether Turkey could acceded to the EU in the absence of fundamental change in the situation in this regard. See *The Relation of the European and Turkey from the Viewpoint of the Christian Churches*, Discussion Paper, February 2004, available at <http://www.cec-kek.org/pdf/EUandTurkey.pdf> (last visited 17 May 2010).

[31] Then Cardinal Ratzinger (now Pope Bendedict XVI) argued that 'Turkey always represented another continent throughout history' and that accession by Turkey would be 'a mistake'. See 'Ratzinger Asserts Vatican Stand against Turkey EU Membership', *Catholic News*, 16 August 2004, available at <http://www.orthodoxytoday.org/articles5/CatholicNewsRatzinger.php> (last visited 26 May 2010).

membership. A customs union with the EU was agreed in 1995, and in 1999 the Tampere European Council declared that Turkey was a candidate for membership. The Copenhagen European Council, in late 2002, declared that negotiations with Turkey could begin if the December 2004 European Council decided (on the basis of a report from the European Commission) that Turkey fulfilled the Copenhagen Criteria.[32]

2.3.2 *The Criminalization of Adultery and the EU Response*

In the autumn of 2004, the Turkish Government presented its overhaul of the criminal code to Parliament as part of its attempt to win the backing of the European Council (scheduled for later that year) for the opening of accession negotiations with the EU. Despite the limited nature of EU competence in this area, it was the criminal law as it related to the 'lifeworld' issues of gender and sexuality that received the greatest attention.[33] Indeed, as the *Deutsche Welle* newspaper noted, 'with pressure from the EU, women's rights groups were able to outlaw rape in marriages and get old fashioned terms like "chastity", "honor", and "moral" out of criminal law books'[34] However, despite the fact that the Turkish Constitutional Court had abolished the crime of adultery in 1996 (on the grounds that it unfairly penalized women),[35] the 2004 reforms proposed that it be recriminalized. Prime Minister Erdoğan defended the measure on the grounds that the law represented a 'vital step' towards preserving the family and 'human honour'. He further argued that although Turkey wanted to join the European Union it did not have to adopt its 'imperfect Western morals'.[36] Although several EU Member States retained laws criminalizing adultery until relatively recently[37] the European Commission reacted strongly to this proposal, with the Commission's official

---

[32] See Copenhagen European Council, 12 and 13 December 2002, Presidency Conclusions 15917/02, 5, para 19, available at <http://ue.eu.int/ueDocs/cms_Data/docs/pressData/en/ec/73842.pdf> (last visited 17 May 2010).

[33] See 'Turkey Changes Laws to Meet EU Standards', *Deutsche Welle*, 1 September 2004, available at <http://www.dw-world.de/dw/article/0,2144,1314044,00.html> (last visited 17 May 2010). [34] Ibid.

[35] See 'Verheugen Warns Turkey on Adultery Law', *Deutsche Welle*, 10 September 2004, available at <http://dw-world.de/dw/article/0,1564,1324102,00.html> (last visited 17 May 2010).

[36] Quoted in 'Turkey's adultery ban splits the nation', *The Age*, 7 September 2004, available at <http://www.theage.com.au/articles/2004/09/06/1094322712399.html?from=storylhs> (last visited 17 May 2010).

[37] Irish law criminalized adultery until 1981, French law until 1975, and Austrian law until 1997. In the United States, 23 states have similar laws. See K Gajendra Singh, 'EU-Turkish

spokesman stating that the proposal 'certainly cast doubts on the direction of Turkey's reform efforts and would risk complicating Turkey's European prospects'.[38] Certain Member States also expressed reservations, with UK Foreign Secretary Jack Straw asserting that the proposal 'would create difficulties for Turkey'.[39] However, although Turkish women's groups had been among those most strongly opposed to the law,[40] the EU response did not stress the impact of the law on women or ideas of gender equality. Instead, the response of Günther Verheugen, the Commissioner with responsibility for the enlargement process, consisted of an uncompromising attack on the proposal, which focused on the need to separate religious from legal norms. The Commissioner described the proposal to criminalize adultery as 'a joke' and that he '[could] not understand how a measure like this could be considered at such a time'. While stating that he was not 'defending adultery', Verheugen went on to note that it was important that 'Turkey should not give the impression . . . that it is introducing Islamic elements into its legal system while engaged in a great project such as the EU'.[41] The Commissioner further characterized such a move a completely out of step with Europe and as unacceptable to the EU.[42]

According to Commissioner Verheugen, therefore, the feature of the proposed change that was most unacceptable to the EU was not the repression of adultery. After all, the EU has very limited competence in this area and the Commissioner made it clear that he was 'not defending adultery'. What was out of step with European values and inconsistent with membership of the EU was to attempt to introduce 'Islamic elements' into the legal system. Faced with this reaction from the Commission and certain Member States, the proposal was withdrawn within a matter of days.[43]

Engagement: A Must for Stability of the Region', South Asia Analysis Group Papers, available at <http://www.southasiaanalysis.org/papers12/paper1127.html> (last visited 25 May 2010).

[38] See 'Adultery Fault Line with EU', *Turkish Daily News*, 18 September 2004, available at <http://www.turkishdailynews.com.tr/archives.php?id=37707> (last visited 18 October 2006).

[39] See 'Turkey Backs off Plan to Outlaw Adultery', Associated Press, 14 September 2004, available at <http://wwrn.org/articles/7164/?&place=turkey&section=legislation> (last visited 26 May 2010).

[40] See 'Verheugen Warns Turkey on Adultery Law' (n 35 above).   [41] Ibid.

[42] See 'EU warns Turkey not to recriminalize adultery', D Wes Rist, 8 March 2005, available at <http://jurist.law.pitt.edu/paperchase/2005/03/eu-warns-turkey-not-to-recriminalize.php> (last visited 17 May 2010).   [43] See n 33 above.

2.4 A Difference in Approach?

The manner in which the Copenhagen Criteria have been interpreted by the institutions of the EU means that a measure of respect for a private zone of autonomy within which citizens are free to define their own sexual existence without being forced to adhere to religious norms is seen as a fundamental requirement of accession to the Union. As the EU's own practice of consulting extensively with religious organizations shows, this does not require a complete removal of religious influence from the law-making process. However, such influence has, in line with the principle of balance between religious, cultural, and humanist influences, to be constrained by the principles of personal autonomy, political pluralism, and the respect for privacy rights. Accordingly, while religious bodies are welcome to contribute to the law-making process, religious claims to a monopoly on truth cannot be accommodated, nor can religious dogma be the sole determinant of the content of such laws, particularly when the demands of such dogma are inconsistent with the autonomy of individuals to determine their identity and private conduct. As the case studies show, these principles were applied to both Romania and Turkey as part of the enlargement process.[44]

However, there was a notable difference in the approaches adopted by the Commission in dealing with the two countries. In both cases religious elements in societies with a single dominant religion (Sunni Islam and Orthodox Christianity respectively) had succeeded in pressuring the government into attempting to enact (or to retain) legislation giving religiously influenced norms, which condemned certain private sexual behaviour, the force of law. In the Romanian case, the EU viewed this solely as a question of the human right of gays and lesbians to be left alone by the state. In the Turkish case, however, the proposal was seen not as a human rights issue or even as an issue of privacy, but was instead framed as an issue of the general relationship between religion and the law. While the problem with the Romanian law was that it violated gay and lesbian human rights, the problem with the Turkish legislation was, according to the Commission, that it appeared to be 'introducing Islamic elements into its legal system'. Despite the leading

---

[44] This analysis is further supported by the limited case law in this area. In EFTA Surveillance Authority Decision 336/94 it was held that restrictions imposed by Member States on slot-machines could not be justified solely on religious grounds, while the rulings of the Court of Justice in Case C-260/04 *Commission v Italy* [2007] ECR I-7083 para 35 and Case C-65/05 *Commission v Greece* [2006] ECR I-10341 make it clear that 'religious factors' can be taken into account by Member States exercising their margin of appreciation in regulating gambling. See the discussion in Ch 5.

role played by the Orthodox Church in the campaign to retain Article 200, Romania was never warned against introducing 'Orthodox elements' into its legal system and the close institutional relationship between the Orthodox Church and the Romanian State was assumed by the EU to be in accordance with acceptable norms. The attempt to criminalize adultery, on the other hand, was viewed as emblematic of a wider, potentially systemic problem in the relationship between the law and religion in the Turkish state, the inclusion of Islamic elements in the legal system being seen as incompatible with the balance between religion, humanism, and culture that characterizes the public order of the EU. A right to be free from religiously inspired rules was upheld for 'sinners' in both Romania and Turkey, but the manner in which the EU framed its demands that this right be respected differed markedly.

2.4.1 Sexual Orientation Discrimination: A European Norm?

The difference in approach may, of course, be explained by the fact that homosexuality had already been the subject of debate within the Union for some years, during which time a distinctive EU norm in relation to gay and lesbian rights had emerged. Although the Union's acquisition of substantive powers in relation to sexual orientation discrimination post-dated the controversy in relation to Romania, its institutions had, since the early 1980s, been debating and formulating an approach to the issue of gay and lesbian rights which, by 1998, had, in certain respects, become relatively liberal. By 1998, outright criminalization had been condemned by the European Court of Human Rights (ECtHR), the European Parliament had voiced its support for gay and lesbian equality on several occasions, and the treaties had been amended so as to enable the Union to legislate in this area.[45] There had been no similar process in relation to the laws regulating adultery that had not been the subject of any debate at EU level, nor had adulterers either organized themselves or been recognized as a minority group to the same degree as gays and lesbians. It is therefore arguable that the EU's characterization of the Romanian issue solely in terms of its human rights implications arose from the fact that the EU had already established a common approach on

---

[45] In relation to the acquisition of powers in relation to sexual orientation discrimination, see n 17 above. In relation to the activity of the European Parliament on this issue, see Resolution on Human Rights in the Soviet EU, 17 May 1983, [1983] OJ C161/67, Document 1-1358/83, Rapporteur: Vera Squarcialupi, at the request of the Committee on Social Affairs and Employment 13 February 1984, available at: <http://www.xs4all.nl/~heinv/hearingintergroup/documents/squarcialupi.pdf> (last visited 17 May 2010), and Resolution A3-0028/94, adopted 8 February 1994.

this issue under which discrimination against gays and lesbians was seen as a violation of human rights. This certainly chimes with Commissioner Verheugen's statement in the summer of 2001 that 'equal treatment of gays and lesbians is a basic principle of the European Union'.[46] As Romania was seeking to join a polity that increasingly defined itself as a 'Community of Values', a failure to decriminalize homosexuality could be seen as a failure to adhere to the common value the EU had established in relation to sexual orientation. An attempt to criminalize adultery did not involve such an established value and was therefore approached in a different manner from that of the criminalization of homosexuality.

However, despite the Commissioner's assertion that equal treatment of homosexuals was 'a basic value of the European Union', in the period in which the Commission was dealing with the issue of Article 200 of the Romanian Penal Code, acceptance of the principle of equal treatment of gays and lesbians in the EU was in fact limited. In its 1997 decision in *Grant v South West Trains*,[47] the European Court of Justice specifically ruled that discrimination on grounds of sexual orientation was not prohibited by the Treaties and that gay and lesbian equality was not a fundamental principle of EU law. Indeed, at paragraph 31 of the judgment the Court specifically stated that '[w]hile the European Parliament, as Ms Grant observes, has indeed declared that it deplores all forms of discrimination based on an individual's sexual orientation, it is nevertheless the case that the Community has not as yet adopted rules providing for such equivalence'.

While the Treaty of Amsterdam did provide the Union with competence to legislate in this area, it could only do so on the basis of unanimity and did not do so until late 2000. Even when it did finally act in this area, the EU deferred significantly to religious sensibilities giving religious bodies (including institutions such as healthcare and educational establishments whose purposes were not exclusively religious) scope to continue to discriminate on the basis of sexual orientation in the Employment Directive[48] and allowing Member States not to recognize civil partnerships between same-sex couples in the 2004 Citizenship Directive.[49] Therefore, although it may now apply, a norm relating to the equality of sexual orientations had not

---

[46] See n 25 above.   [47] Case C-249/96 *Grant v South West Trains* [1998] ECR I-621.

[48] Council Directive (EC) 2000/78 establishing a general framework for equal treatment in employment and occupation [2000] L303/16, Art 4(2).

[49] Council Directive (EC) 2004/58 on the right of citizens of the EU and their family members to move and reside freely within the territory of the Member States [2004] OJ L229/35, Arts 2(2)(b),3(2)(b).

been definitively embraced by the Union at the time it pressured Romania to decriminalize homosexuality and was, at most, emergent and subject to continuing dispute.

2.4.2 Religion in General or Islam?

A second explanation for the difference of approach outlined above is that the EU saw, in the attempt by the Turkish authorities to criminalize adultery, something very different from the efforts of Romanian leaders to retain the ban on homosexuality. More specifically, the criminalization of adultery may have been seen as representative of a wider desire to increase the influence of religion over the Turkish state to a degree that might threaten the balance between religious, humanist, and cultural influences that underpins the liberal democratic nature of the EU's public order. Romanian legislation on homosexuality, on the other hand, merely represented a specific failure to respect privacy rights which, although religiously motivated, did not concern the overall role of religion in the Romanian legal and political system.

Turkey is a secular republic. However, Turkish secularism is different from the secularism found in most EU Member States. In Turkey, secularism has come to represent the control of religion by the state rather than the separation of religion and the state. As noted above, the Turkish state is, for example, heavily involved in the training of Sunni Muslim clergy and the administration of religious institutions.[50] Furthermore, many in Turkey perceive the state's secularity to be under threat.[51] The army in particular has intervened on several occasions to protect the country's secular system from what it sees as the threat of Islamic movements. The Turkish Government that sought to criminalize adultery was made up of the Justice and Development Party (AKP). The AKP is the successor to the Welfare Party (Refah Partisi), which had been forced out of office in 1997 by the Turkish military and was later banned for threatening the secular nature of the Turkish republic. The AKP's Islamist past has meant that although it now portrays itself as a moderate conservative party that supports democratic principles, it has been viewed with extreme suspicion both by the secular elements of Turkey's establishment and by some EU governments. This

---

[50] See, eg 'Basic Principles, Aims and Objectives', statement of the Presidency of Religious Affairs of the Republic of Turkey (the Diyanet), a state body responsible for regulating religious matters, available at <http://www.diyanet.gov.tr/english/tanitim.asp?id=13> (last visited 17 May 2010).

[51] See, eg E Özbudun, *Contemporary Turkish Politics: Challenges to Democratic Consolidation* (London: Lynne Rienner Publishers, 2000).

history may have caused the EU (along with many in Turkey) to view the attempt to criminalize adultery as part of a wider strategy aimed at increasing the role of Islam in public life in Turkey and undermining the secular nature of the state.

As shown in Chapter 3, many current EU Member States are not, in institutional terms, officially secular, with official state churches and close institutional and financial links between certain denominations being a prominent feature of the European constitutional landscape. Moreover, explicitly Christian parties are part of governments in several EU states such as Germany, Sweden, and the Netherlands, and have often resisted policy proposals, such as the legalisation of same-sex marriage, that are opposed by most Christian churches. On the other hand, religious influence over law, politics, and society is notably weaker in EU Member States than in most countries with Muslim majorities.[52] EU law has tended to see in Islam a greater threat to the notion of balance, and therefore to the liberal democratic order, than other religions. Roy has noted a similar dynamic in France where, in relation to Roman Catholic opposition to the legalisation of abortion, 'both parties accept precisely that opposition will not turn into opposition to the political system' and 'the church's political acceptance of *laïcité* exonerates it from any suspicion about theological content' but where there has been significant concern that Muslim resistance to principles such as gender equality may represent a broader opposition to the liberal democratic and secular nature of the political system and efforts to aid the development of an Islamic theology that is compatible with secularism.[53] Similarly, the EU's approach can be seen as reflecting a suspicion that the desire of Turkey's Islamist-leaning government to criminalize adultery represented a broader opposition to secularism, and the limitation of religious influence over law and politics in general. Seen in this way, Commissioner Verheugen's statement that Turkey could not afford to give the impression that it was 'introducing Islamic elements into its legal system' can be seen as reflecting a view on the part of the EU that the criminalization of adultery was representative of a broader project aimed at the eventual domination of the

---

[52] See Norris and Inglehart (n 6 above). See also Ch 2.

[53] O Roy, *Secularism Confronts Islam* (translated by George Holoch) (New York: Columbia University Press, 2007) 21–4. The French Government refused citizenship to a man who forced his wife to wear a full fail on the basis that this indicated his failure to accept the principle of secularism and equality of the sexes. See: 'France refuses a citizenship over full Islamic veil', *BBC News*, 3 February 2010, available at <http://news.bbc.co.uk/1/hi/8494860.stm> (last visited 17 May 2010).

political and legal arenas by religion along with the allied concern that a religiously influenced legal system might fail to respect the degree of private autonomy required by respect for the humanist elements of the EU's liberal democratic public order. In other words, the Union fear was not that Turkey was the wrong religion (ie Muslim rather than Christian) but that it was too religious (ie that its government intended to allow religion an excessive degree of influence over law and politics).

This concern cannot be separated from the fact that the majority religion in Turkey is Islam. The compatibility of Islam with Western liberal democracy has been the subject of much debate in recent years. The role played in Islam by the *Sharia*, with its interventionist and conservative approach to issues of gender and sexuality, has been a prominent aspect of discussion in this area. Those who assert that a degree of incompatibility exists have focused on two main aspects. The first relates to the low level of secularization experienced by largely Muslim societies. In a protracted process beginning with the Enlightenment and Reformation, the major Christian denominations in Europe, either voluntarily or after protracted conflict, accepted significant limitations on the scope of religious authority in relation to matters of public policy.[54] Lewis argues that this process has not occurred to the same extent in the Muslim majority countries (which also provide many of Europe's immigrants). Such societies are, he believes, 'still profoundly Muslim, in a way and in a sense that most Christian countries are no longer Christian'.[55] The second (and possibly related) argument asserts that mainstream Islamic theology is incompatible with the secular state and the notions of personal autonomy and distinction between public and private morality underlying the liberal democratic project. Joffé argues that 'representative democracy is seen as alien to Islam'[56] and that 'the holistic nature of normative Islamic society does not accept the premise of the socio-political atomism that is implicit in the democratic and capitalist projects'.[57] Gabriel notes that 'in modern western societies many matters are considered as more liable to moral scrutiny and judgment rather than legal investigation' but that such matters 'are still within the ambit of law in Islamic societies'.[58]

---

[54] See Ch 2.

[55] B Lewis, *The Crisis of Islam: Holy War and Unholy Terror* (London: Phoenix, 2003) 14.

[56] G Joffé, 'Democracy, Islam and the Cult of Modernism' (1997) 4(3) *Democratization* 134; quoted in P van Ham, *European Integration and the Postmodern Condition* (London: Routledge, 2001) 211.   [57] Ibid.

[58] T Gabriel, 'Is Islam against the West?' in R Geaves *et al.* (eds), *Islam and the West Post 9/11* (Aldershot: Ashgate, 2004) 15.

In a similar vein, Lewis and Roy argue that 'few...practising Muslims are interested in a privatized faith as it is experienced by most Western Europeans and sometimes advanced as a model for Muslims'.[59] All of these views point to a potential incompatibility between mainstream versions of Islam, as a faith based on an all-encompassing system of holy law (the *Sharia*) and the liberal democratic system, acceptance of which is a prerequisite for EU membership. Indeed, the influential Muslim commentator Tariq Ramadan has argued that to require European Muslims to adopt the Western 'privatized' approach to religion effectively requires Muslims to 'be Muslim without Islam' and that such an approach is based on 'a widespread suspicion that to be too much a Muslim means not to be really and completely integrated into the Western way of life and its values'.[60] However, the idea that Islam is in some way incompatible with the modern state or liberal democracy is, notwithstanding its high levels of popular support,[61] highly controversial, with many commentators arguing that such views are tainted with orientalism and even racism.[62]

The true nature of Islam and the beliefs of Muslims are matters to be addressed by theologians and sociologists of religion rather than this book. What is important for our purposes is to note that the European Union has appeared to attribute a higher level of acceptance of secularism and liberal democracy to Christian denominations than to Islam. Thus, the campaign by the Romanian Orthodox Church to retain legislation criminalizing homosexuality was viewed as an individual instance of interference by the state (albeit largely at the behest of religious authorities) with the privacy

[59] JS Fetzer and JC Soper, *Muslims and the State in Britain, France and Germany* (Cambridge: Cambridge University Press, 2005) 150, summarizing the arguments made by B Lewis, *Islam and the West* (Oxford: Oxford University Press, 1993) 173–86 and O Roy, *Vers un islam européen* (Paris: Editions Esprit, 1999) 89–103.

[60] T Ramadan, *To Be a European Muslim* (Leicester: Islamic Foundation, 1999) 184–185.

[61] A Pew Research poll in 2006 interviewed some 14,000 people in 13 countries across the world. European respondents showed very high levels of hostility towards, and fear of, Islam among Europeans. Relations between Muslims and Westerners were seen as 'generally bad' by 70 per cent of Germans, 66 per cent of French people, 61 per cent of Spaniards, and 61 per cent of British people. Clear majorities in Germany, Britain, and Spain also agreed that there was 'a conflict between being a devout Muslim and living in a modern society' (although a large majority of French respondents rejected this view). High percentages of respondent in all countries stated that they considered Muslims to be fanatical (Spain 83 per cent, Germany 78 per cent, France 50 per cent, and Britain 48 per cent). See Pew Research Foundation, 'The Great Divide: How Westerners and Muslims View Each Other', 22 June 2006, available at <http://pewglobal.org/reports/display.php?ReportID=253> (last visited 17 May 2010).

[62] See R Geaves, 'Who Defines Moderate Islam "post" September 11?' in Geaves *et al.* (n 58 above) 66.

rights of a minority group, while the attempt by the formerly Islamist governing party of Turkey to enact legislation criminalizing adultery was seen as representative of a far wider and more serious issue—the maintenance of the more general limitations on Islamic influence over the legal system which were seen as necessary for Turkey to remain eligible for EU membership (the introduction of 'Islamic elements' into the Turkish legal system being seen by the Commission as *ipso facto* inconsistent with its desire to join the Union). This approach was underlined in May 2007 when Enlargement Commissioner Olli Rehn, while discussing Turkish membership in the European Parliament, stated that 'if a country wants to become a member of the EU, it needs to respect the principle of democratic secularism, part of our Copenhagen Criteria', thus identifying secularism as a part of the Criteria for the first time.[63] The Commissioner's statement was supported by Dr Hannes Swoboda MEP, a vice-president of the Party of European Socialists, despite his acknowledgement that there was no common approach to secularism among existing Member States and that the Union had not stressed secularism in previous enlargements.[64]

The resistance to the insertion of 'Islamic elements' into the Turkish legal system contrasts with the symbolic and institutional privileges granted to culturally entrenched Christian religions in many current Member States. However, this does not mean that the Union would accept Christian theocracy but reject a Muslim theocracy. The public order of the EU requires limitations on the political ambitions of all religions. However, the EU appears not to perceive that the same danger of religious domination of the political arena arises from Christian denominations as from Muslim denominations. In effect, it assumes that the actual impact of the privileges granted to culturally entrenched Christian denominations will be moderated by shared cultural assumptions (shared also by the Christian faithful) relating to the limited nature of the permissible influence of religion over law and politics.[65] It does not make the same assumption in relation to Islam. Whether or not this assumption is factually correct, there is significant scope for criticizing the approach of the Union in this regard. The imposition of limitations on religious influence over law and politics are not in themselves problematic.

---

[63] Olli Rehn, European Commissioner for Enlargement, Open Debate on Enlargement, European Parliament Foreign Affairs Committee, Brussels, 7 May 2007, available at <http://europa.eu/rapid/pressReleasesAction.do?reference=SPEECH/07/287&format=HTML&aged=0&language=EN&guiLanguage=en> (last visited 17 May 2010).   [64] Ibid.

[65] For analysis of the operation of these assumptions and cultural norms in the European context, see McCrea (n 4 above).

The Union is also correct to recognize the danger posed by ambitions of political Islam to liberal democracy and individual rights. It is the failure to apply these limitations across the board that poses difficulties. Although the mainstream Christian denominations that predominate in Europe have, to a large degree, accepted and adapted to the secularization of the legal and political arenas, certain ambiguities remain.[66] A notable recent example is the support of many Christian denominations for legislation criminalizing homosexuality in Uganda.[67] While the different cultural context within which the European versions of these denominations operate may mean that European churches would not support such a law, the disagreement within denominations (and the ambivalent attitude of the Vatican)[68] show that the assumption that Christian denominations will necessarily accept limitations on their influence over and on the assertion of religious truth claims in the political arena may not always be justified. Indeed, there are signs, most notably in the *Lautsi* decision of the ECtHR, that European institutions are coming to recognize that stricter control of the symbolic and institutional privileges of entrenched denominations may be increasingly necessary in order to uphold the boundary between state recognition of religion as an element of culture and state recognition of the truth claims of a particular religion.[69]

2.4.3 *The European Convention on Human Rights, Islam, and Militant Democracy*

The perception that political Islam and the role of *Sharia* therein are inconsistent with the notions of personal autonomy, privacy, and pluralism and are therefore particularly threatening to the European public order is also to be seen in the jurisprudence of the ECtHR, whose decisions, while not part of EU law, are very influential in determining the scope the EU's human rights obligations.[70] Most notably, in the case of *Refah Partisi and others v*

---

[66] Ibid. See also Ch 2.

[67] See, eg the Vatican's opposition to a United Nations motion calling for an end to the criminalization and punishment of individuals on the grounds of their sexual orientation: 'The Pope's Christmas Gift: A Hard Line on Church Doctrine', *Time Magazine*, 3 December 2008. The Vatican later clarified that it was not necessarily in favour of criminalization of homosexuality. However, it did not object to the principle of criminalization of homosexuality in Uganda in 2009–2010 and actively objected to moves to decriminalize homosexual conduct in Ireland as late as 1993. See Kieran Rose, *Diverse Communities: The Evolution of Lesbian and Gay Politics in Ireland* (Cork: Cork University Press, 1994) 27 and 44.   [68] Ibid.

[69] *Lautsi v Italy* (Application No 30814/06) 3 November 2009. See Ch 4.

[70] See Case C-540/03 *Parliament v Council* [2006] ECR I -5769.

Turkey[71] the Grand Chamber of the Strasbourg Court upheld the dissolution of the predecessor of Erdoğan's AKP by the Turkish Constitutional Court on the grounds that it was a 'centre of activities contrary to the principle of secularism'.[72] The Court's judgment reflected a profound fear of the political nature of Islam and, in debates in which euphemism normally plays such a dominant role, made strikingly clear pronouncements in relation to the role of *Sharia* in European political life.

In 1995 the Refah Partisi won the largest number of votes (22 per cent) in the Turkish general election. It subsequently entered into a coalition government with another party and its leader became prime minister. In May 1997 the Principal State Counsel at the Court of Cassation brought proceedings in the Turkish Constitutional Court to dissolve Refah, on the grounds that it was 'a centre of activities against the principle of secularism'. The application cited acts and speeches by leaders and members of the party which were alleged to show that the party aimed to introduce *Sharia* law and a theocratic regime, both of which were said to be incompatible with a democratic society.[73]

Refah applied to the European Commission on Human Rights in May 1998. In July 2001 the Chamber of the Court held by four votes to three that there had been no violation of Article 11 of the ECHR (which protects the right of freedom of association) and (unanimously) that no separate claim arose under Articles 9, 10, 14, 17, or 18).[74] Refah's lawyers appealed this decision to the Grand Chamber of the Court, which unanimously held that the actions and speeches that formed the basis of the decision of the Turkish court showed the party to have a long-term aim of setting up a regime based on *Sharia*. It further found that such a system would be incompatible with the democratic values of the Convention and that the opportunities Refah had to put such policies into practice meant that its dissolution could be considered to have met a 'pressing social need' and to have been within the restricted margin of appreciation afforded to contracting states in this area.

The degree to which the Court viewed an Islamist political orientation as threatening to the European political order is shown by the fact that on the three previous occasions on which the Strasbourg institutions had been called upon to rule on the compatibility of the decision by the Turkish

---

[71] *Refah Partisi and others v Turkey* (2003) 37 EHRR 1.   [72] Ibid para 12.
[73] See the summary of the facts of the case, available at the Court's website at <http://www.echr.coe.int/Eng/Press/2003/feb/RefahPartisiGCjudgmenteng.htm> (last visited 17 May 2010).   [74] Ibid.

authorities to dissolve a political party (all non-religious parties) it found a violation of the Convention in each case.[75] Furthermore, it noted that the dissolution of a political party was 'a drastic measure' and that such severe measures could be used 'only in the most serious cases'.[76] The Court noted that democracy was the 'only political model contemplated by the Convention and, accordingly, the only one compatible with it'.[77] It also appeared to endorse a secular model of church–state relations in stating that it had 'frequently emphasized the State's role as the neutral and impartial organizer of the exercise of various religions' and characterizing the adoption of such a role as a 'duty'.[78] Recalling previous decisions in which it had upheld limitations on the right to wear an Islamic headscarf in certain contexts[79] the Court declared that in the Turkish context:

> the Convention institutions have expressed the view that the principle of secularism is certainly one of the fundamental principles of the State which are in harmony with the rule of law and respect for human rights and democracy. An attitude which fails to respect that principle will not necessarily be accepted as being covered by the freedom to manifest one's religion.[80]

Accordingly, the political order upheld by the Convention may require religions to adapt and submit to secular government in order to be covered by the protection provided to religion under the Convention system. The Convention instruments may therefore refuse even to recognize as religious (for the purposes of the protection of Article 9) a movement which, like some interpretations of Islam, does not recognize the legitimacy (and supremacy within its sphere) of the secular state. This approach by the Court is in line with predominant 'Western' views of religion. As Esposito points out, the notion of religion as a system of personal beliefs as opposed to a comprehensive phenomenon 'integral to politics and society' is both 'modern and Western in origins'.[81]

---

[75] The cases in question are: *United Communist Party of Turkey and Others v Turkey* (133/1996/752/951) 30 January 1998; *Socialist Party and Others v Turkey* (20/1997/804/1007) 25 May 1998; *Freedom and Democracy Party (ÖZDEP) v Turkey* (Application No 23885/94) 8 December 1999.

[76] *Refah Partisi and others v Turkey* (2003) 37 EHRR 1 para 133.

[77] Ibid para 86.   [78] Ibid para 91.

[79] *Dahlab v Switzerland* (Application No 42393/98) 15 February 2001 and *Yanasik v Turkey* (Application No 14254/89) (1993) DR 74.

[80] *Refah Partisi and others v Turkey* (2003) 37 EHRR 1 para 93.

[81] J Esposito, *The Islamic Threat: Myth or Reality* (Oxford: Oxford University Press, 2002) 199.

The Court went on to declare its belief in the incompatibility of *Sharia* with democracy and human rights, noting in particular the issues of the pluralism of the public sphere and protection of private autonomy, which have also been a key element of the EU's approach to religion's participation in the public sphere.[82] It stated that:

Sharia, which faithfully reflects the dogmas and divine rules laid down by religion, is stable and invariable. *Principles such as pluralism in the political sphere or the constant evolution of public freedoms have no place in it.*...It is difficult to declare one's respect for democracy and human rights while at the same time supporting a regime based on Sharia, which clearly diverges from Convention values, particularly with regard to its criminal law and criminal procedure, its rules on the legal status of women and *the way it intervenes in all spheres of private and public life in accordance with religious precepts.* In the Court's view, a political party whose actions seem to be aimed at introducing Sharia in a State party to the Convention can hardly be regarded as an association complying with the democratic ideal that underlies the whole of the Convention.[83] (emphasis added)

The Court underlined the limitations on expressly political religion inherent in predominant European approaches to the relationship between the law and religious truth claims, stating that 'freedom of religion, including the freedom to manifest one's religion by worship and observance, is primarily a matter of individual conscience,' and that 'the sphere of individual conscience is quite different from the field of private law'.[84]

The Court left no doubt that Islamist political projects, or indeed the ambitions of any religious movement that seeks to establish a religiously based political order and to base the legal system on the teachings of a particular religion, are incompatible with the ECHR.

The judgment specifically notes elements of Islamic law that its sees as incompatible with the ideals of the Convention.[85] In particular the judgment highlights the manner in which it believes *Sharia* violates the key Convention norms of privacy and personal autonomy. The degree of danger to liberal democracy that the Court saw as being posed by such a project is shown by the fact that, as Boyle points out, the Court was willing to uphold the dissolution of the party not for actual attempts to introduce Islamic law,

---

[82] See Ch 3, section 3.   [83] See n 80 above, para 123   [84] Ibid para 128.
[85] While explicitly Christian political parties in existing Member States may, due to the influence of their religious texts, have a similarly conservative approach to sexual morality, a desire to introduce biblical sexual morality into the secular law has not been attributed to them by European institutions.

'but rather because of what it might do, should it, at some point in the future, become the outright party in power'.[86] The threat posed by a party that was thought to harbour concealed desires to introduce Islamic elements was therefore considered by the Court to be such that the 'drastic' measure of dissolving a political party that had won a plurality of votes in the most recent election was justified. In upholding the dissolution of a political party that had recently won a fair and free election on the grounds that its Islamist ideology represented a threat to the democratic order, the Court not only embraced the 'militant democracy'[87] but also endorsed the proposition that there is a degree of incompatibility between political religion in general, political Islam in particular, and the liberal democratic norms on which the Council of Europe is based. The views of the Court of Human Rights on these questions have the potential to influence the approach of EU institutions to such matters to a significant degree.[88] Furthermore, the Court's approach in this area is strikingly similar to the approach adopted by the EU to the adultery issue, where the legislation in question was viewed as being representative of broader but concealed desires to introduce 'Islamic elements' into the Turkish legal system.

The notion that EU law regards views held by some Muslims of the appropriate relationship between religion, the law, and the state as potentially threatening towards public and private autonomy and therefore to the balance between religion and humanism that characterizes the EU's public order, is also seen in developments in the law of migration both of the Union itself and of individual EU Member States, which are the subject of the second set of case studies in this chapter.

3. Migration, Integration, and the EU

EU law and policy governing migration and the rights of long-term residents from non-EU countries increasingly demand explicit reassurances

---

[86] K Boyle, 'Human Rights, Religion and Democracy: The Refah Party Case' (2004) 1(1) *Essex Human Rights Review* 1, 10.

[87] See, eg P Macklem, 'Militant democracy, legal pluralism and the paradox of self-determination' (2006) 4(3) *International Journal of Constitutional Law* 488; P Harvey, 'Militant Democracy and the European Convention on Human Rights' (2004) 29(3) ELR 407; M Kocak and E Orucu, 'Dissolution of Political Parties in the Name of Democracy: Cases from Turkey and the European Court of Human Rights' (2003) 9(3) *European Public Law* 399.

[88] See n 70 above.

from migrants that they are either willing to respect or are personally committed to the limitations on religious influence inherent in the EU's commitment to the notion of balance between religious, cultural, and humanist influences, which it regards as underpinning its liberal democratic values. Developments at EU level have both influenced and complemented similar developments in the law governing citizenship and the integration of migrants at Member State level.

In recent years, the question of the integration of immigrant communities has been particularly prominent in European politics. Much of this concern has centred on a perceived incompatibility between what are seen as the liberal democratic values of European societies and the more intensely religious and conservative values adhered to by some immigrants, particularly those of Muslim backgrounds. Kofman has noted that the increased diversity of migration to Europe has led European states to create more complex systems that differentiate between migrants on the basis of their mode of entry and legal status and grant differential access to civil, economic, and social rights on this basis.[89] In addition to distinguishing between migrants on the basis of mode of entry and legal status, the migration law of both the EU and several Member States has begun to differentiate between migrants on the basis of their adherence to certain values, with those who fail to hold certain 'European' values being disfavoured in relation to the granting of citizenship and residence rights. Furthermore, just as the Union has assumed the secular bona fides of entrenched Christian denominations to a greater degree than Islam, the ideological elements of the migration laws of Member States and the EU have, in some instances, been applied to a greater degree to Muslim than non-Muslim immigrants.

One of the key 'European' values promoted by EU migration and integration law is the acceptance of limitations on the public role of religion and the legitimacy of a zone of individual freedom from religion and its prescriptive norms. Just as the EU saw an inconsistency with important elements of the EU's public order in the attempt by the Turkish Government to criminalize adultery, EU migration and integration law, having been influenced by emerging trends at Member State level, sees the failure of *individual* immigrants to accept norms such as gender and sexuality (where the views of devout Muslims diverge most notably from those of indigenous Europeans), or at least a failure to accept the right of the state to protect such norms,

---

[89] E Kofman, 'Contemporary European migrations: civic stratification and citizenship' (2002) 21 *Political Geography* 1035.

as a threat to public and private autonomy and therefore to the humanist elements of the EU's public order. Viewed in this way, the holding of private views becomes a matter of concern for the state justifying the penalization of the holding of such beliefs through withholding benefits such as citizenship or residence rights. Thus, in order to protect the privacy rights of personal autonomy of individual citizens guaranteed by its public order, the Union either interferes with, or facilitates efforts by individual Member States to interfere with, the private views and conduct of individual (generally Muslim) immigrants. Like the ECtHR's embrace of the notion of 'militant democracy', such an approach restricts the exercise of a particular right (in this case that of private autonomy) by those opposed to core elements of that right in order to protect the right from being destroyed.

3.1 The EU's 'Basic Principles on Integration'

In recent times both migration policy statements and substantive Community legislation have increasingly emphasized the need for migrants to adopt 'European values', and have viewed a failure to do so as a threat to European societies. Although less explicit than the measures adopted in the Netherlands, France, and parts of Germany (which will be discussed below), the output of Community institutions has nevertheless, in common with the emerging law in these Member States, seen a failure to restrict the public role of religious principles (particularly in relation to gender and sexuality) as a potentially threatening phenomenon that can be the subject of regulation in the interests of disempowered groups and the development of European society as a whole.

In 2003 the European Commission began to monitor the integration policies of Member States through its 'Synthesis Report on National Integration Policies'.[90] The European Council of June 2003 continued this development by stressing the need for the 'issue of the smooth integration of legal migrants into EU societies [to be] further examined and enhanced'.[91] The conclusions also stated that integration policies should be understood as 'a continuous, two-way process based on mutual rights and corresponding obligations of legally residing third-country nationals and the host societies'.[92]

---

[90] *Communication on Immigration, Integration and Employment*, COM(2003) 336 Final, 44 *et seq.* (section 2.6), Annex 1, '2003 Synthesis Report on National Integration Policies'.

[91] Council of the European Union, Thessaloniki European Council, 19 and 20 June 2003, Presidency Conclusions 11638/03 POLGEN 55 para 9.

[92] Ibid.

However, the later development of this principle of mutuality indicates that dilution of the principle of freedom from religion is not what the Union had in mind in endorsing such mutuality. The conclusions of the European Council held at Brussels on 4 and 5 November 2004 called for the establishment of 'the common basic principles underlying a coherent European framework on integration', which were to 'form the foundation for future initiatives in the EU'.[93] It then set out a list of basic minimum elements of such principles, which restated the conclusion of the Thessaloniki Council that integration was 'a continuous, two-way process' and stressed 'frequent interaction and intercultural dialogue'.[94] However, it supplemented these rather multicultural principles with an assertion that integration also 'implies respect for the basic values of the European Union and fundamental human rights'.[95] The delineation of the precise relationship between these potentially conflicting principles was left for the Justice and Home Affairs Council.

The Justice and Home Affairs Council met later the same month and, in a meeting chaired by Dutch Immigration Minister Rita Verdonk, agreed on the content of the 'Common Basic Principles for Immigrant Integration in the European Union'.[96] The principles noted that 'the precise integration measures a society chooses to implement should be determined by individual Member States' but also stated the EU's interest in the issue, noting that '[t]he failure of an individual Member State to develop and implement a successful integration policy can have in different ways adverse implications for other Member Stats and the European Union'.[97] In a theme that would become more explicit in the principles themselves, it stated that such failure 'can have impact [sic] on the economy and the participation at [sic] the labour market, it can undermine respect for human rights...and it can breed alienation and tensions within society'.[98] The invocation of the state interest in the promotion of respect for human rights as a relevant factor in relation to immigrant integration is particularly pertinent as this provides the basis for the interference with the religious beliefs and cultural practices of individual immigrants authorized by the principles on integration.

The principles clearly endorse a model of immigrant integration under which the religious beliefs of immigrants, in so far as they appear inconsistent with the notion of balance in relation to religion and may thereby affect the

---

[93] Ibid.   [94] Ibid.   [95] Ibid.
[96] See Press Release, 2618th Council Meeting, Justice and Home Affairs, Brussels, 19 November 2004, 14615/04 (Presse 321).   [97] Ibid 16.   [98] Ibid.

freedom from religion of others or cause the evolution of society in undesirable directions, are seen as a legitimate subject of state regulation. The first principle restates the conclusion of the Thessaloniki and Brussels Councils that '[i]ntegration is a dynamic, two-way process of mutual accommodation by all immigrants and residents of Member states'.[99] However, the explanation provided by the Council for this principle makes it clear that what is envisaged is not a process of mutual transformation of political, legal, and cultural values. The explanation states that 'the integration process involves adaptation by immigrants, both men and women, who all have rights and responsibilities in relation to their new country of residence. It also involves the receiving society, which should create the opportunities for the immigrants' full economic, social, cultural and political participation'.[100]

Therefore, integration is seen as a process of adaptation on the part of immigrants coupled with facilitation on the part of the native population. Native populations are required to facilitate the participation of immigrants in their societies but are not required to adapt their own values or culture. Immigrants, on the other hand, are under an obligation to engage in a process of 'adaptation . . . in relation to their new country of residence'.[101]

The second principle makes this point equally clearly. It states that '[i]ntegration implies a respect for the basic values of the European Union'.[102] The explanation states that:

[e]verybody resident in the EU must adapt and adhere closely to the basic values of the European Union as well as to Member State laws. The provisions and values enshrined in European Treaties serve as both baseline and compass, as they are common to the Member States.[103]

Adherence to the values of the EU is therefore categorized as an individual duty to which residents must adapt if necessary. The explanation goes on to assert that:

Member States are responsible for actively assuring that all residents, including immigrants, understand, respect, benefit from and are protected on an equal basis by the full scope of values, rights, responsibilities, and privileges established by the EU and Member State laws. Views and opinions that are not compatible with such basic values might hinder the successful integration of immigrants into their new host society and might adversely influence society as a whole.[104]

There are a number of important features of this principle. First, while the Member States are required to ensure that all residents (and not just immigrants)

---

[99] Ibid 19.   [100] Ibid.   [101] Ibid.   [102] Ibid.   [103] Ibid.   [104] Ibid.

understand and respect the EU's basic values, a failure to adhere to these values on the part of immigrants is seen as more serious on the basis that such a failure will 'hinder their integration into their new host society' and 'might adversely influence society as a whole'. Adherence to the EU's basic values is seen as an important part of the society the Union and its Member States are trying to build. More importantly, the principles make it clear that it is the holding of 'views and opinions that are not compatible with such basic values' that constitutes the threat to immigrant integration and the construction of the kind of society desired by the Union and its Member States. The holding of such views therefore generates a sufficient state interest to justify regulation by the law of the Member State or the Union. This approach clearly chimes with the approach of the governments of France, the Netherlands, and certain German states outlined below, which sees, in the ongoing adherence to religiously influenced conservative attitudes to sexuality and gender by certain immigrant communities, a threat to the continued acceptance of key values within their societies. The idea that the promotion of certain values is an important goal of the state is also seen in other principles. Principle 5 notes the importance of education to immigrant integration and states that '[t]ransferring knowledge about the role and working of societal institutions and regulations and transmitting the norms and values that form the binding element in the functioning of society are also a crucial goal of the educational system'.[105]

Having defined individual adherence to certain views, opinions, and values as an important goal for the state and as a potential site of legal regulation, the crucial question becomes how far the duty to accept such values should prevail over the rights of migrants to cultural and religious freedom. Principle 8 has a definite answer. It states that '[t]he practice of diverse cultures and religions is guaranteed under the Charter of Fundamental Rights and must be safeguarded, unless practices conflict with other inviolable European rights or with national law'.[106]

The requirement of respect for diverse religions and culture is therefore specifically subordinated to the need to protect 'other inviolable European rights' or 'national law'. This notable rejection of multiculturalism's aversion to the imposition of host society standards on migrant communities is made even more explicit in the accompanying explanation, which states:

Member States…have a responsibility to ensure that cultural and religious practices do not prevent individual migrants from exercising other fundamental rights

---

[105] Ibid 21.   [106] Ibid 23.

or from participating in the host society. This is particularly important as it pertains to the rights and equality of women, the rights and interests of children, and the freedom to practice or not to practice a particular religion.[107]

The explanation also expresses a preference for the use of non-coercive measures as a means of 'addressing issues relating to unacceptable cultural and religious practices that clash with fundamental rights' but goes on to state that 'if necessary according to the law, legal coercive measures can also be needed'.[108] The EU's policy framework for the integration of immigrants, therefore, specifically subordinates the religious autonomy of individual migrants to the need to protect European basic values and the fundamental rights of others. While not naming any religion in particular, the framework deliberately emphasizes issues such as the equality of men and women, which have been prominent in debates around the practice of Islam in Europe.[109]

3.2 The Refugee, Long-term Residents, and Family Reunification Directives

Although the basic principles are not binding, the ideas underpinning them are clearly visible in the 'hard law' enacted by the EU in this area. Indeed, the principles themselves are specifically referred to in the Preamble to the Directive establishing minimum standards for the granting of refugee status, which anticipates the establishment of such principles in Article 36 and which states that '[t]he implementation of the Directive should be

---

[107] Ibid.   [108] Ibid.

[109] This decisively non-multicultural approach and the importance of the idea of limitations on the public role of religion in this area have been further underlined by the statements of Commissioner Fratini concerning the controversy that erupted over the publication of cartoons by the Danish newspaper *Jyllands Posten*, which were perceived by many Muslims as being insulting towards the prophet Mohammed. While recognizing that 'it is important to respect sensitivities', the Commissioner went on to state: 'Equally, we have reaffirmed that our European society is based on the respect for the individual person's life and freedom, equality of rights between men and women, freedom of speech and a clear distinction between politics and religion. We have said clearly and loudly that freedom of expression and freedom of religion are part of Europe's values and traditions, and that they are not negotiable.' See interview with Commissioner Fini, 'The Right to Offend and Not To Be Offended: An Interview with EU Commission Vice President Frattini', *Equal Voices*, Issue 18, June 2006, published by the European Monitoring Centre on Racism and Xenophobia (EUMC), available at <http://fra.europa.eu/fraWebsite/attachments/ev18en.pdf> (last visited 26 May 2010).

evaluated at regular intervals, taking into consideration in particular...the development of common basic principles for integration'.[110]

In a number of directives relating to the legal status of immigrants, EU law has defined a failure on the part of individual immigrants to indicate acceptance of humanist-influenced liberal and egalitarian values as a threat to key public policy goals, particularly protection of the right of individuals to live their lives in ways that conflict with religious doctrine. In particular, the directives legitimize actions on the part of individual Member States that seek to penalize those immigrants (or would-be immigrants) who fail to indicate their acceptance of limitations on the influence of religious principles on law and public policy and liberal democratic values such as pluralism and individual autonomy. Under this approach, the religious and political views of immigrants become a legitimate site of state regulation notwithstanding the EU's commitments to freedom of conscience.

Two directives in particular have been distinctly marked by the decidedly non-multicultural ideas on which the basic principles are based. In September 2003 the Council adopted a directive on the right to family reunification of third country nationals residing in the EU.[111] The Preamble to the Directive states that 'Member States should give effect to the provisions of this Directive without discrimination on the basis of sex, race, colour,...religion or beliefs, political or other opinions'.[112]

This would seem to indicate that the religious or political views of those seeking family reunification are not a basis on which such a benefit could be refused. However, the provisions of the Directive to which this non-discrimination principle applies indicate that such views can be taken into account by Member States in considering applications under the Directive. Paragraph 11 of the Preamble states that:

the right to family reunification should be exercised in proper compliance with the values and principles recognised by the Member States, in particular with respect to the rights of women and children; such compliance justifies the possible taking of restrictive measures against applications for family reunification of polygamous households.

---

[110] Council Directive (EC) 2004/83 on minimum standards for the qualification and status of third country nationals or stateless persons as persons who otherwise need international protection and the content of the protection granted [2004] OJ L304/12.

[111] Council Directive (EC) 2003/86 on the right of family reunification [2003] OJ L251/12.

[112] Ibid, Preamble, para 5.

While the issue of polygamy is singled out, it is nevertheless made clear that the need to comply with 'the values and principles recognised by the Member States' applies across the board.

The general grounds for refusal of family reunification are set out in paragraph 14 of the Preamble, which states that:

the person who wishes to be granted family reunification should not constitute a threat to public policy or public security. In this context it has to be noted that the notion of public policy and public security covers also cases in which a third country national belongs to an association which supports terrorism, supports such an association or has extremist aspirations.

Thus, it is made clear that supporting an organization which supports terrorism or holds certain political views ('extremist aspirations') can be sufficient grounds for the refusal of family reunification. Article 6 of the Directive dealing with refusal of applications for family reunification does not specifically mention the holding of extremist opinions as a ground for refusal, stating instead that 'Member States may reject an application...on grounds of public policy, public security or public health'[113] and that, 'when taking the relevant decision, the Member State shall consider...the severity or type of offence against public policy or public security committed by the family member, or the dangers that are emanating from such a person'.

Taken together, paragraph 14 of the Preamble and the provisions of Article 6 endorse the view that the holding of certain opinions by migrants is seen as a threat to either public security or public policy, both of which are seen as dependent on the continued attachment of residents to the liberal democratic system. This approach lies at the heart of recent changes in immigration law and policy at Member State level, which are outlined below. References to the rights of women in paragraph 11 of the Preamble further support the view that such policies are necessary for the protection of certain groups who may be victimized should the 'extremist' worldview of certain migrants increase its influence in the host society.

As well as endorsing the notion that beliefs and opinions of migrants are a valid factor to be taken into account in immigration law, the Directive also contains measures designed to facilitate Member State efforts to encourage integration on the part of their migrant populations. Article 4(1) provides that Member States may require children over the age of 12 to satisfy 'a condition for integration provided for by existing legislation on the date of

---

[113] Ibid, Art 6(1).

implementation of this Directive'. This is supplemented by a more general provision in Article 7(2), which provides that 'Member States may require third country nationals to comply with integration measures, in accordance with national law', thereby protecting the religion-related measures taken at Member State level outlined below. The compatibility of certain cultural/religious practices with the aim of greater integration is directly addressed in Article 4(5), which states that '[i]n order to ensure better integration and to prevent forced marriages Member States may require the sponsor and his/her spouse to be of a minimum age, and at a maximum 21 years, before the spouse is able to join him/her'.

Articles 4(1), (5), and 7(2) were all absent from the Commission's initial draft of the Directive but were included at the behest of certain Member States. Germany and Austria pushed strongly for Articles 4(1) and (along with the Netherlands) 7(2), which were inserted in September 2001[114] and November 2002[115] respectively. Article 4(5) was inserted during the final stage of negotiations in February 2003 by the Dutch and German Governments.[116] These three Member States have, as will be shown below, taken a leading role in changing domestic immigration law in such a way that Muslim migrants in particular are required to give assurances that they are willing to place limits on the public and political role of their religion as a prerequisite for the granting of residence or citizenship rights.

These provisions have proved highly controversial. As noted above, many of the provisions that permitted the imposition of integration requirements were introduced by the Council at a very late stage in the legislative process. Indeed, the insertion of the relevant provisions came so late that parliamentary debates on the subject focused almost exclusively on the question of the acquisition of competence in the native languages of Member States by immigrant populations. Furthermore, Article 4(6), which enabled Member States to place an age limit of 15 years on applications for reunification as minor children, was inserted after the consultation of the European Parliament, which had advocated a less restrictive approach.[117] In December 2003,

[114] See Council document 12022/01 of 24 September 2001; see also K Groenendijk, 'Legal Concepts of Integration in EU Migration Law' (2004) 6(2) *European Journal of Migration and Law* 119.

[115] See Council document 14272/02 of 26 November 2002. For an account of the disputes among Member States in relation to this measure, see Groenendijk (n 114 above) 119–20.

[116] See Council document 6912/03 of 28 February 2003. See also Groenendijk (n 114 above).

[117] The Rapporteur backed the idea of language integration but balked at the proposal that failure to meet it could result in a refusal of a permit. See the report of Baroness Ludford MEP, A5-0436/2001, COM(2001)127-C5-0250/2001-2001/0074(CNS)).

the Parliament applied to the Court of Justice to annul certain aspects of the Directive which, it alleged, violated the right to respect for family life and the non-discrimination principle, both of which were asserted to form part of the general principles of law protected by the Court.

The Parliament did not seek the annulment of the Directive as a whole, but sought instead to have the provisions allowing for the imposition of integration conditions (along with a further provision allowing Member States up to three years to process applications) struck down and severed from the rest of the Directive, which was to remain in force. The specific provisions challenged by the Parliament were:

- the final subparagraph of Article 4(1) enabling Member States to require that a child aged over 12, who arrives independently from the rest of his/her family, meet an integration condition before he or she is granted entry and residence;
- Article 4(6) allowing Member States to request that applications under the Directive for reunification of minor children be submitted before the child reaches the age of 15;
- Article 8 enabling Member States to provide a waiting period of no more than three years between the making of an application and the issuing of a permit.[118]

The Advocate-General advised the Court to dismiss the application on the grounds that it was not possible to sever the impugned provisions without altering the substance of the Directive and thereby trespassing on the territory of the Community legislature. In relation to the merits, she found that the failure to consult the Parliament in relation to Article 4(6) rendered its adoption by the Council void[119] (though this point had not been argued by the Parliament's lawyers and was not taken up by the full court). She also found that Article 8 potentially permitted a situation where Member States could violate the fundamental rights of applicants under the Directive by applying a waiting period of up to three years, and that it was therefore contrary to Community law.[120] Most importantly for the purposes of this discussion, the Advocate-General upheld paragraph 4(1) of the Preamble as a proportionate means through which Member States can pursue their legitimate desire to 'to integrate immigrants as fully as possible'.[121]

---

[118] Case C-540/03 *Parliament v Council* [2006] ECR I-5769. [119] Ibid para 59.
[120] Ibid para 105.   [121] Ibid paras 112–113.

The Grand Chamber of the Court issued its judgment at the end of June 2006.[122] The Court resolved the admissibility question by holding that:

the fact that the contested provisions of the Directive afford the Member States a certain margin of appreciation and allow them in certain circumstances to apply national legislation derogating from the basic rules imposed by the Directive cannot have the effect of excluding those provisions from review by the Court of their legality as envisaged by Article 230 EC.[123]

It was also held that the issue of severability could only be resolved by consideration of the substance of the case.[124]

As noted above, the ECtHR has adopted a very clear approach to the issue of Islamism, the relationship between religion and law, and liberal democracy. In its ruling in relation to the Directive on family reunification, the Court of Justice went out of its way to stress the importance of the role played by the ECHR in determining the substance of the general principles that form part of EU law and which are upheld by the Court of Justice.[125]

Thus, the ECHR was recognized by the Court of Justice as being of special significance in the determination of the substance of the human rights norms protected in EU law. Furthermore, in its analysis of the provisions of the Directive impugned by the Parliament, the Court showed a striking degree of deference to the decisions of the ECtHR. The judgment noted that the Preamble to the Directive states that it 'respects the fundamental rights and observes the principles recognised in particular in Article 8 of the European Convention for the Protection of Human Rights and Fundamental Freedoms and in the Charter of Fundamental Rights of the European Union'.[126]

Although it failed to ask the Court to annul Article 7(2) of the Directive, which allows Member States to impose integration conditions on third country nationals, the Parliament argued that, in relation to the right to family life of applicants under the Directive:

a condition for integration does not fall within one of the legitimate objectives capable of justifying interference, as referred to in Article 8(2) of the ECHR, namely, national security, public safety, the economic well-being of the country, the prevention of health of morals and the protection of the rights and freedoms of others.[127]

This seemed to indicate a somewhat wider objection to such measures. The Court explicitly relied on several rulings of the ECtHR in coming to

---

[122] Ibid.   [123] Ibid para 22.   [124] Ibid para 29.   [125] Ibid para 35.
[126] Ibid para 38.   [127] Ibid para 42.

its decision not to annul the relevant parts of the Directive. In particular, it noted the decisions in *Sen v The Netherlands, Gül v Switzerland,* and *Ahmut v The Netherlands,* from which it concluded that Article 8 'may create positive obligations inherent in effective "respect" for family life' and that 'regard must be had to the fair balance that has to be struck between the competing interests of the individual and of the community as a whole [in relation to which] the State enjoys a margin of appreciation'.[128]

It found that Article 4(1) of the Directive merely partially preserved this margin of appreciation in circumstances where a child over 12 arrives independently of the rest of his or her family. Accordingly:

the final subparagraph of Article 4(1) of the Directive cannot be regarded as running counter to the right to respect for family life. In the context of a directive imposing precise positive obligations on the Member States, it preserves a limited margin of appreciation for those states which is no different from that accorded to them by the European Court of Human Rights.[129]

The Court specifically endorsed the compatibility of integration conditions with the ECHR in paragraph 66, where it stated that: 'It does not appear that such a condition is, in itself, contrary to the right to respect for family life set out in Article 8 of the ECHR.... In any event, the necessity for integration may fall within a number of legitimate objectives referred to in Article 8(2) of the ECHR.' This does not, however, indicate that Member State discretion in this area is unfettered, as the Court points out:

The fact that the concept of integration is not defined cannot be interpreted as authorising the Member States to employ that concept in a manner contrary to general principles of Community law, in particular to fundamental rights. The Member States which wish to make use of the derogation cannot employ an unspecified concept of integration, but must apply the condition for integration provided for by their legislation existing on the date of implementation of the Directive in order to examine the specific situation of a child over 12 years of age arriving independently from the rest of his or her family.[130]

The Directive may therefore act as a kind of 'stand still' measure, with Member States being unable to introduce further restrictions. However, the stand still provision, as the Court made clear, applies only in relation to

---

[128] Ibid para 54. *Sen v The Netherlands* (2001) 36 EHHR 81; *Gül v Switzerland* (1996) 22 EHRR 93; *Ahmut v The Netherlands* (1996) 24 EHRR 62.

[129] Case C-540/03 *Parliament v Council* [2006] ECR I-5769 para 62.

[130] Ibid para 70.

this relatively narrow area of the Directive and does not affect the right of individual states to introduce other restrictive measures in the immigration arena in general. Moreover, the idea of compulsory integration, including a duty to adhere to 'European' or national values (which was already a feature of national legislation in certain Member States), was not, of itself, contrary to Community law.

The Grand Chamber also rejected the Parliament's arguments in relation to Article 4(6), on the basis that an age limit on applications interfered with family life and was discriminatory. The Council argued that encouraging immigrant families to bring their children at a young age in order to facilitate their integration was a legitimate objective under Article 8(2) of the ECHR.[131] The Court held that '[i]t does not appear that the contested provision infringes the right to respect for family life set out in Article 8 of the ECHR as interpreted by the European Court of Human Rights' and that the fact that Article 5(5) of the Directive requires Member States to take the best interests of the child into account meant that 'Article 4(6) cannot be regarded as running counter to the fundamental right to respect for family life'.[132]

Article 8 of the Directive was upheld on similar grounds. The Court held that the provision:

preserves a limited margin of appreciation for the Member States by permitting them to make sure that family reunification will take place in favourable conditions, after the sponsor has been residing in the host State for a period sufficiently long for it to be assumed that the family members will settle down well and display a certain level of integration. Accordingly, the fact that a Member State takes those factors into account and the power to defer family reunification for two or, as the case may be, three years do not run counter to the right to respect for family rights set out in particular in Article 8 of the ECHR as interpreted by the European Court of Human Rights.[133]

The judgment is notable in several respects. First, the Court of Justice endorses integration of immigrants as a legitimate objective that can be pursued by states under Article 8(2) of the ECHR. It seems willing to uphold relatively substantial interferences with the Article 8 rights of immigrants in order to enable Member States to pursue the integration policies that they see fit. Moreover, the Court's heavy reliance on the judgments of the

---

[131] Ibid para 79.   [132] Ibid para 90.   [133] Ibid para 98.

ECtHR in order to determine the content of the EU's fundamental rights guarantees may prove important for the future development of EU law as it relates to the interaction of questions of religion, integration, and the right of states to require adherence to certain religion-related norms from individual immigrants. The primary reason given by the Court for upholding the three impugned provisions of the Directive was that each complied with Article 8 of the ECHR as interpreted by the ECtHR. The judgment of the Court of Justice therefore appears to indicate that legislation appearing to comply with the standards set down by the ECtHR will, almost inevitably, not be found to be in violation of the fundamental rights norms forming part of EU law. The judgment in the *Refah Partisi* case (discussed above) indicates that the ECtHR is willing to uphold extensive interferences with Convention rights in order to defend the liberal democratic order, including the principles of public and private autonomy, from what it sees as the threat of political Islam. Should EU law follow this approach, interference by Member States with rights to religious liberty and privacy in the defence of 'European' values are unlikely to fall foul of EU human rights norms.

The approach adopted by the Council in relation to the Directive on family reunification has been repeated in a second directive establishing the rights of third country nationals who are long-term residents of the EU.[134] Like the Directive on family reunification, the Preamble to the Directive on long-term residents, which was adopted in late 2003, states that Member States should not discriminate, *inter alia*, on grounds of religious or political beliefs in giving effect to the Directive.[135] However, it also subordinates this duty to a requirement that third country nationals seeking to use the Directive 'should not constitute a threat to public policy or public security'.[136] Article 5(2) of the Directive specifically states that 'Member States may require third country nationals to comply with integration conditions, in accordance with national law'.

Article 6 states that 'Member States may refuse to grant long-term resident status on grounds of public policy or public security'.[137] Member States, therefore, can refuse long-term resident status on the grounds that the applicant is a threat to public policy or public security. At the same time, Article 5 makes it clear that applications may be refused if integration conditions are

---

[134] Council Directive (EC) 2003/109 concerning the status of third country nationals who are long-term residents [2004] OJ L16/44.   [135] Ibid, Preamble para 5.
[136] Ibid, Preamble, para 9. Paragraph 21 of the Preamble also mentions public policy and public security as relevant factors along with public health.   [137] Ibid, Art 6(1).

not met. A failure on the part of migrants to integrate is, therefore, a permissible ground for refusal of status under Article 6 as a threat to either public policy or public security. Furthermore, Article 9(3) makes it clear that long-term resident status can be withdrawn from those who constitute a threat to public policy, while Article 12 permits the expulsion of such people provided they are shown to constitute 'an actual and sufficiently serious threat to public policy or public security'.[138]

As with family reunification, the requirement contained in Article 5(2) was not present in the Commission's initial draft of the legislation but was inserted by Member States. Indeed, at the insistence of the Austrian and German Governments the phrase 'integration measures' was strengthened to 'integration conditions' in order to emphasize that failure to adhere to such conditions could potentially result in refusal of the relevant permit.[139] The Court of Justice's ruling in relation to the Directive on family reunification makes it unlikely that such provisions will be held to fall foul of the EU's human rights commitments.

Therefore, in the light of both the statement of basic principles and the ruling of the Court of Justice in *Parliament v Council*, the directives passed in this area clearly provide space within EU law for Member States to take active steps to regulate the religious views of individual migrants and to refuse concrete legal benefits to migrants whose views do not adhere to the fundamental values of the Union or individual Member State. By categorizing a failure on the part of such migrants to adhere to the fundamental values of the Union as a threat to public policy and/or public security, EU legislation provides justification for laws aimed at limiting the degree to which those who adhere to conservative, religiously influenced norms in relation to gender and sexuality can seek to enshrine such norms in law and public policy (or even to advocate such enshrinement). Groenendijk argues that previous migration-related legislation in the Union had focused on integration primarily as something that can be encouraged by enhancing the residence status of immigrants and providing for equal treatment. He notes that Regulation 1612/68 (which enshrines free movement of EU citizens) does not allow for any integration tests and restricts language examinations to situations where knowledge of the language of the relevant Member State is necessary to carry out the relevant employment.[140] However,

---

[138] Ibid, Art 12(1).   [139] See Groenendijk (n 114 above) 122–3.

[140] Ibid 116. Regulation (EC) 1612/68 on freedom of movement for workers within the Community [1968] OJ L257/2.

Regulation 1612/68 deals with free movement within the Union so the conditions it imposes were always likely to be significantly less onerous than those imposed in legislation dealing with the immigration of non-EU citizens. Groenendijk is, however, correct to note that since 2003, EU law has increasingly adopted an approach under which 'the lack of integration or the assumed unfitness to integrate are grounds for refusal of admission to the country'.[141] This change is perhaps a reaction to the general move away from multicultural approaches to integration in Europe in recent years.[142] The heavy reliance by the Court of Justice on the jurisprudence of the ECtHR in order to determine the limitations that the fundamental rights norms of the EU will place on such a policy substantially lessens the likelihood of large-scale interference with this policy on the part of the Court of Justice.

4. Developments at Member State Level

4.1 The Netherlands

The increasing emphasis placed by EU law on integration and adoption of 'European values' by immigrants has occurred against a background of similar developments at Member State level. In recent years several Member States have radically overhauled their approach to migrant integration and have placed the question of religion at the centre of such changes. The approach of the Netherlands to these issues of religion, migration, and citizenship has been extremely influential. The Netherlands is a country with a libertarian and egalitarian approach to questions of sexuality. Prostitution and pornography are tolerated, while same-sex marriage has been legal since 2001. It also has a Muslim population of over one million (out of a total population of approximately 16 million). A series of events in the late 1990s and early 2000s, such as increases in attacks on gays and lesbians in Dutch cities[143] and the murders of and death threats against figures such as Pim Fortuyn, Theo van Gogh, and Ayaan Hirsi Ali (who were severely critical of Muslim attitudes towards gender, sexuality, and freedom of expression),

---

[141] Groenendijk (n 114 above) 113.

[142] F Fukuyama, 'Europe vs. Radical Islam', *Policy Review*, 27 February 2006.

[143] See 'It may be Europe's most liberal city, but if you are gay you had best beware', *The Times*, 14 May 2005, available at <http://www.timesonline.co.uk/tol/news/world/article522264.ece> (last visited 18 <May 2010).

raised the issue of the problems of multiculturalism up the political agenda in the Netherlands.

These trends and events led to a situation where 'old-style multicultural-ism' was, as Fukuyama says, 'widely seen as a failure in Holland'.[144] Dutch Government policy changed radically to deal with these concerns. In 2000, 2002, and 2003 legislative changes were introduced that required applicants for naturalization to indicate their 'integration' into Dutch society by means of a series of exams testing knowledge of Dutch society and the Dutch lan-guage.[145] Worries that the 'importation' of spouses by Muslim immigrants from their countries of origin was hampering integration efforts led to an increase in the minimum age above which spouses could benefit from fam-ily reunification. Tighter rules were introduced providing that religious preachers from abroad had to attend integration courses in which Dutch values would be explained to them. Most strikingly, a new test for immi-grants with accompanying explanatory video was introduced in 2006.

The immigration test requires immigrants to answer a series of questions about the Netherlands, such as its provincial structure and the role of the monarchy. It also requires immigrants to show an awareness of Dutch norms in relation to sexual liberalism and gender equality. Questions in the exam ask how people would react if they see two men kissing or whether hitting women or female circumcision are acceptable practices.[146] Those who wish to sit the exam are required to take extensive language classes and are sent an instructional video that shows footage of topless bathing and a same-sex couple kissing. Those who pass the test are required to swear allegiance to Holland and its constitution within five years.

The claim that the test is aimed at Muslims is strengthened by the fact that immigrants from non-European 'Western' countries, such as the United

---

[144]   Fukuyama (n 142 above).

[145]   Royal Decree of 14 April 2002, *Staatsblad* 2002, No 197, Royal Decree of 15 March 2003, *Staatsblad* 2003, Royal Decree No 118 on the entry into force of the Act of 21 December 2000, *Staatsblad* 2000, No 618.

[146]   See 'The Civic Integration Exam Abroad', published by Immigratie-en Naturalisatie-dienst (the Dutch Immigration and Naturalization Service), available at <http://www.ind.nl/en/Images/bro_inburgering_tcm6-105967.pdf> (last visited 18 May 2010). In particular, p 23 specifies that in addition to EU citizens, American, Canadian, Australian, New Zealand, Japa-nese, Norwegian, and Swiss nationals are exempt from the test. See also 'Holland launches the immigrant quiz', *Sunday Times*, 12 March 2006, available at <http://www.timesonline.co.uk/article/0,,2081496,00.html> (last visited 18 May 2010).

States, Canada, and Australia are exempt.[147] Muslim groups severely criticized the proposal. The Islamic Human Rights Commission, a British-based organization, described the test as 'Islamophobic' and said that it sent out a message that 'Muslims are not only unwelcome...but those that are already [in the Netherlands] do not conform to a uniform idea of what should be a citizen' [sic].[148] Dutch theologian Karen Steenbrink of Utrecht University also criticized the video on the grounds that it was 'offensive to Muslims' and noted that topless bathing is in fact rarely seen in the Netherlands.[149] Emecmo, a group representing Moroccans in the Netherlands, described the video as provocation rather than education and said it was clearly intended to stop Muslim immigration.[150] This was denied by the Government. Rita Verdonk, the then immigration minister, asserted that '[i]t is important to make clear demands of people. They need to subscribe to our European values, respect our laws and learn the language'.[151] The film was also backed by Mohammed Sini, chairperson of 'Islam and Citizenship' (a national Muslim organization), who described homosexuality as 'a reality' and who called on immigrants 'to embrace modernity'.[152]

Religion in general and Islam in particular have therefore been prominent elements in the debate over the new Dutch policy in relation to immigration. While part of the overall objective of these measures has been to decrease immigrant numbers (visa fees were also significantly increased), the central role accorded to gender and sexuality in the measures adopted demonstrates that an equally important objective of the policies in question has been to make acceptance of sexual liberalism, gender equality, and the restriction of religious influence on public policy into prerequisites for the acquisition of

---

[147] 'Dutch immigration kit offers a revealing view', *New York Times*, 17 March 2006, available at <http://www.iht.com/articles/2006/03/16/news/dutch-5852942.php> (last visited 18 May 2010).

[148] See 'A Testing Time for Immigrants', *Al Jazeera*, 6 April 2006, available at <http://english.aljazeera.net/archive/2006/04/2008410133654309799.html> (last visited 27 May 2010). The film, however, received the backing of Mohammed Sini, chairperson of Islam and Citizenship (a national Muslim organization), who described homosexuality as 'a reality' and who called on immigrants 'to embrace modernity': see 'Immigrants Exposed to Liberal Dutch Ways', MSNBC, 16 March 2006, available at <http://www.msnbc.msn.com/id/11842116/> (last visited 27 May 2010)   [149] Ibid.

[150] Ibid.

[151] See 'Europe raises the bar for immigrants', *Boston Globe*, 22 May 2006, available at <http://www.boston.com/news/world/europe/articles/2006/05/22/europe_raises_bar_for_immigrants/> (last visited 18 May 2010).

[152] 'Immigrants Exposed to Liberal Dutch Ways', MSNBC, 16 March 2006, available at <http://www.msnbc.msn.com/id/11842116/> (last visited 27 May 2010).

Dutch citizenship. While it is clearly unable to determine the political and religious views of established citizens, the Dutch Government has made it clear that those who choose to apply to become Dutch can be required to accept these values or, at the very least, to be willing to place limitations on their desires to see religious norms hostile to such values reflected in public policy. The tests clearly make the holding of certain views by individual migrants the subject of a degree of state regulation. The focus on requiring acceptance of gay relationships or the freedom of women to wear revealing clothing indicates that what is being sought is acceptance on the part of individuals of the right of others to engage in conduct thought sinful by many religions (most notably mainstream Islam). A failure to adhere to such libertarian values can result in a denial of the right to live in the Netherlands.

As both the exemption of 'Western' immigrants from the tests and the reactions of Muslim leaders show, these requirements are aimed at, and prove most challenging for, Muslim immigrants. Research by the European Commission[153] and Klausen[154] has shown that even among otherwise moderate Muslims, many do not accept the concept of gay rights or the right of the state to promote them. The Dutch Government has therefore taken the view that immigration may be placing in danger the personal autonomy and freedom from religion of elements of Dutch society, particularly gays and lesbians and others whose private lives violate traditional religious norms. It has therefore been willing to require those who choose to come to the Netherlands to confine their disapproval of homosexuality, pre-marital sex, or the free mixing of genders, to the private sphere.

---

[153] See J Césari, A Caeiro, and D Hussain, *Islam and Fundamental Rights in Europe*, Final Report, October 2004, European Commission, DG Justice and Home Affairs Centre National de la Recherche Scientifique, École Pratique des Hautes Études, Groupe de Sociologie des Religions et de la Laïcité, Executive Summary para 3.

[154] Klausen's survey of European Muslims who were actively engaged in civic life (a group she acknowledges to be made up of a disproportionate number of moderate and more Western-oriented Muslims) also showed little evidence of an acceptance of sexual liberalism. Even interviewees who expressed views that were otherwise liberal were unequivocal in their opposition to greater toleration of homosexuality, with some going as far as to suggest that no secular state had the right to impose toleration of gays and lesbians on Muslims: see J Klausen, *The Islamic Challenge: Politics and Religion in Western Europe* (Oxford: Oxford University Press, 2005). See interview with young Danish Imam at pp 15 and 16, the opposition of the Muslim Council of Britain to gay rights at p 34, and the description of the opposition of 'the voluntarists' to all gay rights at p 92. Hussein attributes some of the decline in support for the Labour Party among British Muslims to the Blair Government's support for gay rights legislation: D Hussein, 'The Impact of 9/11 on British Muslim Identity' in Geaves *et al.* (n 58 above) 120.

4.2 Germany

The Dutch approach to these issues has been very influential both on the policies of other Member States and on the approach of EU policy and legislation in this area. In Germany, changes in the nationality laws that came into force on 1 January 2000 loosened the link between blood line and nationality but made 'proof of commitment to the values of the Basic Law'[155] a prerequisite of citizenship. There is at least some evidence that elements of Islamic belief and practice are seen as potentially inconsistent with these values. Klausen has noted how the requirement has been 'a sticking point' for many German Muslims. Moreover, the federal agency for the protection of the Constitution (BundesamtFürVerfassungsschutz) has blacklisted Milli Görüs, one of the largest Muslim organizations in Germany, describing its as an 'Islamist' organization whose social work amongst the young is 'disintegrative...antidemocratic and antiwestern'.[156]

The CDU Federal Minister for the Interior, Wolfgang Schäuble, praised the new Dutch immigration regulations, saying that Germany 'can learn from the Netherlands'.[157] Under German law individual states have power to assess whether potential citizens truly accept the principles of the Basic Law to which federal law requires them to sign an oath of allegiance. The state of Baden-Württemberg was the first to use these powers to propose a citizenship that examined the compatibility of the values of aspirant citizens with the values of the German constitutional order. It was quickly followed by the state of Hesse, which proposed a similar examination. Tests in both states were again clearly aimed at assessing the degree to which Muslims were willing to separate religious attitudes towards gender and sexuality to the private sphere and to accept liberal notions of individual self-determination. Indeed, in Baden-Württemberg the state government explicitly mentioned Muslims as the targets of the new policy.[158] Questions in the Hesse examination, for example, asked immigrants: 'A woman should not be allowed to move freely in public or travel unless escorted by a close male relative. What is your standpoint on this?' and 'What possibilities do parents have to influence their sons' or

---

[155] Klausen (n 154 above) 21.   [156] Ibid 43.

[157] See 'Testing the Limits of Tolerance', *Deutsche Welle*, 16 March 2006, available at <http://www.dw-world.de/dw/article/0,2144,1935900,00.html> (last visited 18 May 2010).

[158] See 'New Rules for Muslims in German State Blasted', *Deutsche Welle*, 5 January 2006, available at <http://www.dwworld.de/dw/article/0,2144,1840793,00.html> (last visited 18 May 2010).

daughters' choice of partner? Which practices are forbidden?'[159] Similarly, the Baden-Württemberg test asked questions relating to forced marriage ('What do you think of the fact that parents forcibly marry off their children?'), homosexuality ('Does the holding of office by open homosexuals disturb you?'), and women's rights ('Do you think that a woman should obey her husband and that he can beat her if she is disobedient?').[160] Both tests also focused on other issues seen as particularly relevant to Muslims. The Hesse test examined attitudes towards Israel ('Explain the term "Israel's right to exist"') and Holocaust denial ('if someone described the Holocaust as a myth or a fairytale, how would you respond?');[161] while the Baden-Württemberg exam asked whether the 9/11 hijackers were 'terrorists or freedom fighters'.[162]

As in the Netherlands, the proposals were severely criticized for interfering with private attitudes and stereotyping Muslims.[163] Volker Beck, a leading member of the Green Party, noted that the anti-gay attitudes of Baden-Württemberg's (Christian) interior minister meant that 'he himself would probably fail the test'.[164] The Federal Parliament took up the issue in February 2006, with the CDU minister for integration policy, Maria Böhmer, noting how 'the United States gives courses in the constitution, history, culture and values of the country'.[165] In May 2006 the federal and state governments worked out a series of guidelines that fell short of introducing a federal immigration test but included an 'integration course', which was intended to focus on 'the German constitution and German values such as gender equality'.[166] In June 2008 the federal government introduced a citizenship test requiring applicants to demonstrate knowledge of German legal and political structures. Although the test did not itself address issues of conscience and religion, it left in

[159] See 'Becoming German: Proposed Hesse Citizenship Test', *Der Spiegel*, 5 September 2005, available at <http://service.spiegel.de/cache/international/0,1518,415207,00.html> (last visited 2 June 2006). The guidelines for the test provided by the Baden-Württemberg government can be accessed at <http://www.baden-wuerttemberg.de/de/Meldungen/171636.html> (last accessed 18 May 2010).   [160] Ibid.   [161] Ibid.
[162] See 'Europe raises bar for immigrants', *Boston Globe*, 22 May 2006, available at <http://www.boston.com/news/world/europe/articles/2006/05/22/europe_raises_bar_for_immigrants/> (last visited 18 May 2010)
[163] See 'How To Be a German', *Inter Press Service News Agency*, 31 May 2006, available at <http://www.ipsnews.net/news.asp?idnews=33203> (last visited 18 May 2010)
[164] See n 159 above.
[165] See n 159 above.
[166] See n 163 above.

place the requirement that potential citizens demonstrate a commitment to upholding the values of the German Constitution.[167]

4.3 France

The French Government has adopted a similar approach to Germany. As far back as 2000, the Government began to seek assurances from Muslim groups in relation to their commitment to values of the French Republic. In January of that year the minister for the interior, Jean Pierre Chevènement, concluded an agreement with Muslim organizations that sought to establish principles on which a structured relationship with state institutions could be based. The French Government proposed that all Muslim groups participating in the exercise would be obliged to sign up to a statement of 'Fundamental Principles',[168] which:

Solemnly confirmed their attachment to the fundamental principles of the French Republic and especially... to freedom of thought and religion, to Article 1 of the Constitution which affirms the secular character of the Republic and the respect this principle accords to all beliefs and finally to the provisions of the law of 9 December 1905 concerning the separation of the churches and the State.[169]

Other religious groups were not required to make similar declarations. Chevènement justified this targeting of Islam on the grounds that the country was faced with an 'exceptional' situation and that, unlike Christianity, Islam:

has experienced neither the Renaissance nor the Reformation. Certainly, Islam does distinguish between the religious and temporal domains. However, there is

---

[167] See 'Germany to Introduce Controversial New Citizenship Test', *Der Spiegel*, 11 June 2008, available at <http://www.spiegel.de/international/germany/0,1518,559021,00.html> (last visited 18 May 2010).

[168] See S Ferrari, 'The Secularity of the State and the Shaping of Muslim Representative Organizations in Western Europe' in J Césari and S McLoughlin (eds), *European Muslims and the State* (Aldershot, Ashgate, 2005) 16–17. The statement was called '*Principes et fondements juridiques régissant les rapports entre les pouvoirs publics et le culte musulman en France*' and is available at: <http://oumma.com/Status-type-des-conseils-regionaux> (last visited 27 May 2010). Césari also notes that '[m]any Muslim representatives considered the request to sign this declaration a demonstration of suspicion': see J Césari, 'Islam in France: The Shaping of a Religious Minority' in Y Yazbeck Haddad, *Muslims in the West from Sojourners to Citizens* (Oxford: Oxford University Press, 2002) 40.

[169] Ferrari (ibid) (translation mine). The original French version reads: '*confirment solennellement leur attachement aux principes fondamentaux de la République française et notamment... à la liberté de pensée et à la liberté de religion, à l'art. 1 de la constitution affirmant le caractère laïque de la République et respect par celle-ci de toutes les croyances et enfin aux dispositions de la loi du 9 décembre 1905 concernant la séparation des Églises et de l'État*'.

no shortage of Muslims to show that this distinction calls for a level of coordination [between the two domains] and consequently permanent involvement of religion in the temporal sphere.[170]

Cesari notes that several Muslim organizations considered that this request showed that they were viewed with suspicion by the French authorities.[171]

In 2003 media attention in relation to the question of the role of Islam in French society focused on a law to ban the wearing of 'ostentatious' religious symbols in public schools, which was widely seen as being motivated by concerns relating to the wearing of the Muslim headscarf by pupils in state schools. However, in the course of proposing this ban to Parliament, the then Prime Minister, Jean-Pierre Raffarin, placed the issue of the headscarf into the wider context of immigration, citizenship, and common values, saying that '[i]ntegration is a process that presupposes a mutual wish to [integrate], a shift towards certain values, a choice of a way of life, a commitment to a certain view of the world proper for France'.[172] At the same time he announced that the Government would be introducing a 'contract' for immigrants under which learning the French language and 'attachment' to France and French values would be preconditions for the granting of residence permits.[173] The announcement of measures to encourage immigrants to adopt French values at the same time as legislation targeting the headscarf on the basis of its incompatibility with secular values was being introduced, gives an indication of the thinking of the French authorities. Along with their colleagues in other EU Member States, they viewed (rightly or wrongly) elements of Islam (and in particular those relating to gender and sexuality and the relationship between religion and the law), as incompatible with native values. Furthermore, the solution to such incompatibility lay in the adoption by immigrants of the secular values whose acceptance was to become a prerequisite of citizenship. Thus, in a move which certain commentators

---

[170] Translation mine. The original French version reads '*à la différence du christianisme, l'Islam n'a connu ni la renaissance ni la Réforme. Certes, l'Islam distingue le domaine religieux et le domaine mondain. Mais il ne manque pas de musulmans pour faire observer que cette distinction appelle une coordination et, par conséquent, une implication permanente du religieux dans le mondain*'. See *Déclaration de M. Jean-Pierre Chevènement, ministre de l'intérieur, sur l'organisation du culte musulman en France dans le cadre de la laïcité et de la loi de 1905 sur la séparation de l'Église et de l'État*, Paris le 28 janvier 2000, available at <http://discours.vie-publique.fr/notices/003000469.html> (last visited 27 May 2010). See Ferrari (n 168 above).

[171] Many Muslim representatives considered the request to sign this declaration a demonstration of suspicion and lack of trust—a quote from Césari (n 166 above) 40.

[172] Klausen (n 154 above) 176.

[173] Ibid 123–4. These measures were introduced in April 2006.

have seen as at least partly prompted by the importance accorded to integration in the EU directives on long-term residents and family reunification,[174] France amended its 1945 law to require immigrants to satisfy a condition of 'Republican Integration'.[175] Under these laws a failure to indicate acceptance of the fundamental values of the French constitutional order has become a valid ground to refuse French citizenship. In July 2008, the Conseil d'État upheld a refusal to grant French nationality to a (Muslim) woman on the grounds that her 'radical practice of her religion', which included the wearing of a niqab, was incompatible with the basic values of French society, including gender equality.[176] In February 2010 the French justice minister refused to accord citizenship to a man who required his wife to be fully veiled and who was found to have failed to accept the principles of gender equality and secularism.[177]

4.4 Other Member States

The trend towards incorporating an acceptance of the idea of the right of freedom from religion as part of citizenship can also be seen in other Member States. In 2002, for example, Austria introduced a compulsory 'Integration Agreement' as part of reforms of its Aliens Act,[178] while in 2005 Britain introduced a 'Life in the UK Test', which examines the knowledge of applicants for British citizenship of British values, culture, and history. Included in the tests are questions probing acceptance of principles such as gender equality and the importance of tolerance.[179] In late 2006, the then Prime Minister, Tony Blair, stressed the importance of these principles in a speech in which he criticized a 'new and virulent form of ideology associated

---

[174] See S Barbou des Places and H Oger, 'Making the European Migration Regime: Decoding Member States' Legal Strategies' (2004) 6(4) *European Journal of Migration and Law* 361.

[175] See article 6(3) of Loi no 2003-1119 du 26 novembre 2003 relative à la maîtrise de l'immigration, au séjour des étrangers en France et à la nationalité, *Journal Officiel* no 274, 27 novembre 2003).

[176] Section du contentieux, 2ème et 7ème sous-sections réunies. Séance du 26 mai 2008. Lecture du 27 juin 2008, Mme M, available at <http://www.conseil-etat.fr/ce/jurispd/index_ac _ld0820.shtml> (last visited 18 May 2010).

[177] See 'France refuses a citizenship [sic] over full Islamic veil', *BBC News*, 3 February 2010, available at <http://news.bbc.co.uk/1/hi/world/europe/8494860.stm> (last visited 18 May 2010).   [178] See Barbou (n 173 above) 360.

[179] See 'Core British Values', *BBC News*, 17 May 2006, available at <http://news.bbc.co.uk/2/hi/programmes/politics_show/4988946.stm> (last visited 18 May 2010) and also 'New UK citizenship testing starts', *BBC News*, 1 November 2005, available at <http://news.bbc.co.uk/2/hi/uk_news/politics/4391710.stm> (last visited 18 May 2010).

with a minority of our Muslim community' and warned migrants that 'our tolerance is part of what makes Britain, Britain. Conform to it; or don't come here.'[180]

These laws have focused on actual or perceived resistance among Muslim populations to gender equality and sexual liberalism which have become emblematic of wider fears surrounding the willingness of some Muslims to respect individual rights to a zone of freedom from religious norms. The response of some European governments has been to stipulate acceptance of liberal values in these areas as a prerequisite of citizenship in order to test the willingness of immigrants to accept limitations on the use of religious precepts as a basis for public policy (on the basis that it is in relation to areas such as gender and sexuality that religiously inspired views are strongest) and thus to accept the kind of limitations on public religion that have evolved in Europe over recent centuries. These countries see in the religious views of certain migrants, a threat to the humanist and liberal characteristics of their societies and the rights to privacy and individual self-determination that such societies uphold. Their desire to protect these humanist and liberal elements (which are seen as important both culturally and as a means to protect certain groups such as women and homosexuals), renders the beliefs and opinions of potential citizens and residents legitimate subjects of legal regulation. Therefore, the linking of acceptance of the principle of freedom from religion to the granting of citizenship or residence rights potentially interferes, in the name of protecting privacy and autonomy, with the privacy and autonomy of those who hold views that condemn or seek the use of the law to regulate the private conduct of others.

These developments have influenced EU law in this area in two ways. First, EU legislation has been careful not to impinge upon the ability of Member States to regulate the religious beliefs of migrants.[181] Secondly, in both substantive legislation[182] and in its broader statements of policy[183] the Union has endorsed the view of a failure to adopt certain 'European values' and to confine one's religious convictions to the private sphere, as a threat to public policy justifying legal intervention. Furthermore, EU law has in turn influenced national laws, with certain Member States using what has been

---

[180] See 'Conform to our society says PM', *BBC News*, 8 December 2006, available at <http://news.bbc.co.uk/2/hi/uk_news/politics/6219626.stm> (last visited 18 May 2010).

[181] See the provisions of the Directives on family reunification and long-term residents allowing for the imposition of integration conditions by individual Member States (above).

[182] See discussion of the grounds for refusing status in the Directives (above).

[183] See JHA Press Release (n 95 above).

termed the 'alibi' of restrictive European legislation in relation to integration matters to introduce such an approach into national law.

5. Conclusion

The EU's approach to the issues of enlargement and immigration demonstrates that it regards the principle of balance between religious and humanist influences as requiring limitations on religious influence over law and politics. These limits are therefore seen as necessary elements of membership of the Union. Any state that enforces religious morality through law to an extent that unduly interferes with individuals' right to private autonomy in sexual matters or allows religion to dominate its political system (for example, by allowing religious truth claims to form the basis for legislation) will not be regarded as maintaining the proper balance between religious and humanist influences required by the EU's public order. The EU has evinced a concern that certain kinds of religious identities may not accept these limitations and may therefore pose a threat to core elements of EU's public order such as pluralism in the public sphere as well as to the key liberal democratic values of personal autonomy, equality, and respect for privacy. The history of the Crusades and Inquisition, as well as more contemporary examples such as law and government in modern day Saudi Arabia and Iran, show that religion can act as the basis for many serious violations of human rights and exercise a degree of control over the political and personal spheres that is incompatible with liberal democratic values. As the judgment of the ECtHR in *Refah* correctly highlighted, and as the restrictions on the role of religion in the political arena outlined in Chapter 3 underline, the enactment of 'divine' law as the basis of the legal system is inconsistent with the openness to change, pluralism, and equal participation in public debate necessary to liberal democratic systems.

As a polity committed to balance in religious matters and to the protection of fundamental rights, the EU is not merely entitled but obliged to ensure that states that seek to join it impose limitations on religious influence over law and politics necessary for liberal democratic values to thrive. Its dealings with Romania and Turkey demonstrate that the Union has used the Copenhagen Criteria on enlargement to ensure that applicant states balance their desire to promote religious morality through law with respect for notions of individual equality and autonomy. The introduction of a mechanism to deprive states that fail to respect fundamental rights norms in Article 7 of the EU Treaty[184] of some of the rights under the Treaty means that such requirements may be more actively imposed on existing Member States, as is indicated by the Commission's 2005 warning to the Polish Government that it risked losing voting rights in the Council should it fail to respect gay rights.[185]

In the area of immigration, the Union encouraged Member States to require migrants to the Union to indicate, as a prerequisite to the granting of residence rights or citizenship, that they accept the principles of the autonomy of the public sphere and individual private autonomy, as well as accepting limitations on the reflection in law of the conservative, interventionist, and patriarchal approaches of many religions to issues of gender and sexuality. This approach involves a significant degree of interference with religious liberty and with the private views and identity rights of migrants. However, in an approach analogous to the 'militant democracy' espoused by the ECtHR in *Refah*, the Union has permitted Member States to interfere with private views and individual autonomy in order to secure respect for these principles in relation to issues such as gender and sexuality. Roy has pointed out that issues of demography must be recognized as part of the discussion of how Europe deals with religion and immigration.[186] Experiences such as those of gays and lesbians in urban areas in the Netherlands,[187] or the Mohammed cartoons affair in Denmark, show that the growth of significant immigrant populations, elements of which have more restrictive attitudes to matters such as sexual liberalism or freedom of expression, may impact significantly on freedoms previously widely accepted in particular societies. States are entitled to ensure that immigration does not become a means through which cherished values and hard won freedoms are eroded, and can justifiably ask those who choose to come to a country to accept that country's basic values. Indeed, in the context of migration, states regularly select migrants on the basis that they have certain desirable traits (the youthful, highly skilled, and those with cultural or ethnic ties to certain states are often granted favourable treatment under immigration laws). It is not, therefore, inherently objectionable for EU Member States to select migrants on

[184] Consolidated versions of the Treaty on European EU and the Treaty on the functioning of the European EU, 15 April 2008, 6655/08, Art 7.

[185] See 'Polish President Warned over Ultra-Right Shift', *The Independent*, 25 October 2005, available at <http://www.independent.co.uk/news/world/europe/polish-president-warned-over-ultraright-shift-512413.html> (last visited 26 May 2010).   [186] See n 54 above, 32.

[187] See n 143 above.

the basis of commitment to certain basic values or for the Union to encourage the selection of migrants committed to the values of its own public order, such as respect for the notion of balance between religious and humanist influences.

However, there is a significant danger that such limitations will be used by those with racist or other reprehensible agendas as a means to promote nativist prejudice. As Baykal has pointed out, given Islam's status as Europe's primary historical 'other', the accession of Turkey provides the acid test of the EU's commitment to diversity. Baykal argues that none of the values to which the Union has committed itself place the EU in the kind of 'thick cultural space' that would require exclusion of Turkey from membership on cultural grounds.[188] The key question, he argues, is 'what would happen if our significant other embraces "our" values and wants to become one of us?'[189]

The requirement that states wishing to join the EU, or individuals seeking to live there, accept limitations on religious influence over law and politics does not itself fail such a test. States and individuals of any racial background are capable of accepting and embracing limitations on religious influence over law and politics. Indeed, as Habermas has pointed out, liberal democracy requires a degree of self-restraint and cognitive dissonance on the part of all missionary faiths, not just Islam.[190] On the other hand, Baykal rightly notes that 'the public reaction to Turkish membership does hint at the existence of some kind of thick identity between current Member States which Turkey is seen as lacking'.[191] Some Member States and a significant element of European public opinion appears to be unwilling to countenance Turkish accession, even if Turkey fully embraces an approach to religion that is compatible with European norms. Similarly, the approach adopted in Baden-Württemberg, where a state government that has been distinctly uncommitted to gay rights[192] devised an integration test requiring immigrants to show acceptance of those rights, shows the significant danger that limitations on religion may function so as to give cover to racist agendas.

---

[188] Baykal (n 2 above) 68.   [189] Ibid 54

[190] J Habermas, 'Intolerance and Discrimination' (2003) 1(1) I.CON 2, 7 (discussed in Ch 3, section 3).   [191] Baykal (n 2 above) 76.

[192] The leader of the Baden-Württemberg government has expressed opposition to gay pride events, calling them 'repellent'. See 'Homo-Gegner neuer Ministerpräsident in Baden-Württemberg: CSD für Stefan Mappus "abstossend"', available at <http://www.ggg.at/index.php?id=62&tx_ttnews[tt_news]=2834&cHash=e953e7410781096e15c714ca5ca43b03> (last visited 18 May 2010).

It is therefore vital that limitations on religion are applied equally. The EU's approach is not entirely satisfactory in this regard. It rightly imposes limits on religious influence over law and politics in relation to applicant states and immigrants. However, its application of these limits to insider religions is marred by an uncritical assumption of compatibility between such limits and the ambitions of culturally entrenched, mainstream Christian denominations.[193] The attribution of an uncomplicated acceptance of limitations on religious influence over law and politics to such denominations was seen in the failure to view the criminalization of homosexuality at the behest of the Romanian Orthodox Church as even possibly indicative of any kind of systemic failure to keep religious influence over law within proper limits. It is also seen at Member State level in the exemptions granted to nationals from Western countries to the integration tests operated by the Dutch authorities and those of some German states.

This does not mean that attempts to require immigrants to accept gay rights or other limitations on religious influence over law and politics are illegitimate or that they should be abandoned. On the contrary, the right principles should still be supported even when some support them for the wrong reasons. They must, however, be applied to all. Thus, the failure to apply the Dutch test and those of some German states to migrants from Western countries can rightly be condemned as discriminatory (one can imagine that many Americans who belong to conservative Christian political movements would fail the Baden-Württemberg test). While the Court of Justice has upheld the principle of requiring immigrants to satisfy integration tests, it has not been asked to rule on the selective application of such tests. In so far as such tests are applied in this selective manner within the field of application of EU law (for example in relation to the Directives on long-term residence and family reunification), they may well fall foul of fundamental rights commitments to equal treatment. On the other hand, the French approach cannot be criticized on this ground as it requires all prospective citizens to embrace the fundamental values of the Republic. It is true that elements of the changes adopted by the French authorities may have been motivated by

---

[193] See the February 2009 Human Rights Watch report, 'Discrimination in the Name of Neutrality', available at <http://www.hrw.org/ja/node/80829/section/2> (last visited 18 May 2010). It is noteworthy that Baden-Württemberg's legislation restricting the wearing of headscarves in schools exempted Christian symbols such as nuns' habits. This was justified on the basis that human rights were Christian in origin. For discussion of the complex and, at times, antagonistic, relationship between Christianity and many of the key fundamental rights recognized in Europe, see Chs 2 and 3.

a desire to address manifestations of the Muslim religion to a greater degree than other faiths. However, the religious make-up of European states is in the process of change and the large-scale presence of religions that were previously only marginal presences may raise new issues and challenges. In a changing religious environment, maintenance of existing approaches to religion may require new principles and laws to address issues relating to religion that did not arise in the religious environment of the past. As the large-scale presence of Muslims in metropolitan France is a relatively recent phenomenon, issues surrounding the interaction of manifestations of the Muslim faith with the principle of secularism would not have been prominent considerations during the period in the late nineteenth and early twentieth centuries, during which French legal arrangements on religion were decided upon. Therefore, new laws may well now be required in order to uphold the principles established by the French state at that time. Accordingly, the fact that the changes made to French law may have been motivated by concerns relating to Islam to a greater degree than other faiths does not mean that such changes cannot claim to be genuinely seeking to defend the principles and rights upon which the French state wishes to base its public order.[194]

It may be the case that European believers in religions that are culturally entrenched within EU Member States have come to accept limitations on their influence over law as a result of historic exposure to the secularizing forces that have marked European history.[195] Acceptance of the EU's limitations may therefore be more challenging for those from religious traditions such as Islam that have not had similar historical experiences. However, valuable constitutional principles should not be abandoned merely because they are not palatable to some. Any indirect discrimination that may exist can be justified by the important ends served by limitations on religious influence over law and politics. Such limitations are essential to preserve pluralism, equal democratic participation, and, given the beliefs of many religions, free expression, gender equality, and private autonomy. If Muslims were indeed

---

[194] Much of the support for these measures also came from those motivated by racist or other improper motives. This does not mean that the law itself is racist. Opportunistic embrace of worthy principles by those with unworthy motives is, sadly, a recurrent fact of political life.

[195] Indeed, several commentators have noted that rejection of 'live and let live' privatized religion is not restricted to Muslim immigrants, but is in fact prevalent amongst immigrants of many religions. See G Davie, 'Religion in Britain: Changing sociological assumptions' (2000) 34 *Sociology* 113–28. Davie further argues that the difference in attitude to religion of native Europeans and immigrant communities 'has led to persistent and damaging misunderstandings' (ibid). See also Norris and Inglehart (n 6 above).

incapable of accepting liberal democratic norms or respecting personal autonomy then significant Muslim immigration to European states would raise very serious issues for the future of liberal democracy and the protection of fundamental rights in Europe. However, Muslims are as capable as all other human beings of developing diverse approaches to their religion and of realizing that not everyone may wish to adhere to the teachings of their faith. Those who claim that the very idea of requiring immigrants to sign up to liberal democratic norms or tolerance of homosexuality and gender equality is 'Islamophobic' are correct only if Islam is regarded as inherently incapable of tolerating such norms, and are therefore themselves as guilty of essentializing Islam as those who seek to apply such requirements to Muslims alone.

However, the need to apply limitations on religious influence over law and politics equally means that the EU and its Member States cannot continue to assume absolute compatibility between these limitations and the ambitions of culturally entrenched faiths. As secularization occurred gradually and unevenly over centuries in Europe, many grey areas, where the precise terms of the implicit compact between culturally entrenched religions and the state may have been understood differently by each side, have remained.[196] Even if there is such absolute compatibility (and the long history of Christian attempts to mould 'lifeworld' legislation in line with their teaching and the reaction of the Catholic Church to the Mohammed cartoons affair indicates that this may not be a safe assumption),[197] Member States must still explicitly hold these faiths and their adherents to the same standards to which they seek to hold others. Otherwise the protection of the necessary limitations on religious influence risks turning into a smokescreen for nativist prejudice.

In the long run, it may be that greater religious diversity may lead to a more complete secularization of Europe as fears linked to the more muscular religiosity of many immigrants lead to the replacement of symbolic privileges, whose impact has been limited by cultural convention, with more black-and-white arrangements specifying the actual limitations on religious influence and power.[198] In the interim, the Union and its Member States must be vigilant to ensure that the entirely legitimate commitment to balancing religious and humanist influences, and the limitations on religious influence over law and politics that such balance entails, are not misused. Due to the

---

[196] See Ch 2.   [197] See Ch 2, Ch 3, section 2, and Ch 5, section 3.

[198] This view is expressed by a Muslim German politician in Klausen (n 153 above) 179. For an account of some developments in this regard, see McCrea (n 4 above). See also the discussion of the *Lautsi v Italy* case in Ch 4.

strong role played by religion in national cultures and the EU's commitment to respecting Member State cultural autonomy, this process will have to take place largely at Member State level. The fact that the Union permits the indirect reflection of religious notions of morality in law through its recognition of the right of Member States to derogate from EU law duties to reflect national cultural values, means that culturally entrenched religions can exercise, albeit indirectly, a degree of influence over law without falling foul of restrictions on religious influence over politics. Comparable influence is denied to faiths whose cultural role in Member States is more marginal. That said, it is simply a matter of historical reality that certain faiths have played a greater role than others in the formation of national cultures in Europe. Laws are not made in a vacuum and it is therefore inevitable that the laws of European states will be influenced by dominant faiths to a greater degree than other religions. This disparity does not render any less important the need to maintain limits on the accommodation of religious truth claims in the political arena. Religious influence exercised by means of religion's status as one element of a broader culture is much less damaging to the principle of equal democratic participation and does not involve the same degree of subjugation of the political process as direct attempts to base laws on religious truth claims, by definition,[199] exclude those who do not belong to a particular faith from political deliberations. However, although its ability to ensure absolute equality between religions at Member State level is limited, the Union can and should take action within its own sphere to ensure that limitations on religious influence over law and politics are equitably applied. It should therefore ensure that the integration conditions mentioned in directives relating to immigration and the conditions applied to applicant states as part of the enlargement process are applied to all religions with equal rigour and should not assume, as it appeared to do in its dealings with Romania, that the political ambitions of culturally entrenched Christian denominations are necessarily compatible with the EU public order.

---

[199] This is particularly dangerous when, as in most EU Member States, adherents to a particular faith make up a large majority of the population.

7

Conclusion

1. Religion and Humanism: The Two Pillars of the EU's Public Order

This book has endeavoured to provide a broad account of the relationship between religion and the public order of the European Union (EU). It has addressed issues of religious freedom but has also considered the complex relationships between religion, individual rights, democracy, and collective (particularly national) identities seen in the context of the EU's *sui generis* and highly pluralist legal order.

In the context of increasing religious and cultural diversity in Europe, the EU has constructed a public order that aims to balance the two major influences on contemporary European approaches to the relationship between religion, law, and state—a mainly, but not exclusively, Christian religious tradition and a humanist tradition that sprang from, but nevertheless has often come into conflict with, Christianity.[1] These two traditions are present in the legal systems of all Member States.[2] However, the relative importance accorded to each, along with the degree of cultural identification with particular faiths, varies greatly from country to country.[3] The EU lacks the authority to reconstruct the relationship between the state, the law, and religion in a fundamental fashion. It therefore has to devise an approach that synthesizes the national traditions of its Member States.

The EU's public order seeks to uphold its commitment to balancing religious and humanist traditions and to give scope to Member States to continue to pursue their own particular relationships to religion, by treating

---

[1] These two influences are discussed in the work of Le Goff, discussed in Ch 2, section 2.
[2] See Ch 2, section 4, which details the contemporary role of religion in EU Member States.
[3] Ibid.

it as a form of identity. Approaching religion in this way contributes to balance between these traditions by restricting religious influence in the political arena while facilitating religion's cultural role, in particular its role in national cultures. In line with predominant anthropologically focused approaches, culture in general, and therefore religion's cultural role, is seen under EU law as separate, to a degree, from the rationalism of the political sphere and the economic imperatives of the market.[4] This cultural role allows religion to be recognized as part of the EU's public order in its own right. Although protection of religion's cultural role allows it to achieve a degree of facilitation within both the market and the political arena, including recognition of religion's historical role in defining communal moral standards,[5] such facilitation must also respect and adapt to the commercial needs of the market and to the strong humanist and secular elements, including respect for individual autonomy, which are part of the same public order and which restrict religious influence over law and politics.[6] This balancing of religious and humanist influences is seen as part of Europe's ethical identity and inheritance and as normatively desirable in its own right.[7]

2. The Effects of an Identity-based Approach to Religion

Treating religion as a form of identity impacts on the nature of the role played by religion within the EU legal order. Identity covers both individual self-definition ('who am I?') and broader shared identities that provide a framework for, and give meaning to, individual identities and choices ('what am I?'). While respecting individual self-definition can be seen as a humanist goal (albeit one with which individual religions may agree), protecting collective identities can, in addition to respecting human choices, involve

---

[4] EU legislation has repeatedly recognized that cultural goods and activities must not be treated solely on the basis of their commercial value and that culture is entitled to protection from the free market (see Ch 5, section 3.1). See also the discussion in Ch 5, section 4.

[5] EU law has recognized that religious bodies make a 'particular contribution' to policy-making and has facilitated religious participation in this field (see Ch 3, section 3).

[6] Facilitation of the religious identity of employees under EU law is limited by the need to respect the commercial nature of the market (see Ch 5, section 2.3.1). The EU has made it clear that religious domination of the public sphere and excessive interference with private autonomy in order to promote religious norms are incompatible with EU membership (see Ch 4).

[7] The Preamble to the Lisbon Treaty recognizes both religious and humanist influences as elements of its constitutional values (see Ch 3, section 2). For a discussion of the importance of the principle of balance in EU law, see Ch 3, section 5.2.

valorizing factors such as national or religious identities which are seen as having significance beyond subjective human experience and is not necessarily therefore entirely humanist in its orientation. The fact that viewing religion as a form of identity covers both of these individual and collective aspects can pose problems for religions in terms of the coherence of the demands they may make of the law, as the individual identity rights underpinning individual claims to facilitation of religious identity may clash with the collective identity rights through which a particular religion may seek to play a broader role by, for example, operating public institutions such as schools and hospitals or promoting the use of the law to enforce its theological norms.

The form of recognition accorded to religion by EU law as a consequence of its status as a form of identity is marked by these tensions. As a form of identity, religion can claim a degree of protection from the law. Such protection can involve the defence of individual religious identity rights, as in relation to the prohibition on discrimination on religious grounds in employment.[8] However, it can also involve claims for the protection of collective rights that restrict individual identity rights, as in the case of the rights to promote particular notions of public morality[9] or to operate religious institutions in accordance with the ethos of a particular faith.[10] Religion's status as a form of identity also enables it to claim a degree of special treatment under the law. In individual terms this is seen in the prohibition of indirect discrimination on religious grounds, which enables individuals to be treated in accordance with their religious characteristics rather than in the same way as all other individuals.[11] Claims to different treatment are also seen at a collective level where Member States are permitted to invoke religious elements of their cultural identity in order to derogate from EU law duties on grounds of public morality,[12] and to excuse religious institutions from the duty to respect the identities of employees in order to promote the identity of such institutions.[13] The EU's recognition of religion as a form of identity also entitles religion to a place in civil society, where it has been recognized as making a 'particular contribution' and has been facilitated on this basis.[14]

---

[8] See Ch 5, section 2.2.   [9] See Ch 3, section 4.   [10] See Ch 5, section 2.3.
[11] See Ch 5, section 2.2.   [12] See Ch 3, section 4.   [13] See Ch 3, section 2.3.
[14] See Ch 3, section 3.

3. Competing Identities Limiting Religious Influence within the EU Legal Order

EU law therefore enables religion to influence law both through its status as an element of individual identity, which entitles it to protection on grounds of respect for individual autonomy, and on the basis of its role in collective identity, particularly national cultural identity, which permits facilitation of religion's institutional role and its contribution to notions of public morality. However, these roles are limited by other elements of the EU's public order, including the importance of the market economy and those that reflect Europe's strong humanist and secular traditions of protecting individual autonomy and questioning and limiting religious influence over law and politics. Indeed, the strong, though not exclusively, humanist orientation of an identity-based approach to religion means that restrictions on the facilitation of religion are likely to be greater when the facilitation in question involves greater intrusion with key elements of human identity or individuals' public status as equal citizens.

Therefore, in relation to the interests of the competitive market, which is a relatively impersonal, technical phenomenon and is somewhat removed from core issues of identity, the facilitation of religious identity is permitted to demand relatively significant accommodation. Although in certain instances EU law has recognized religion as an economic choice,[15] it has repeatedly stated that culture is not a purely commercial matter and, by recognizing religion as an element of national culture, has suggested that there are limits on the extent to which religious and cultural actions can be quantified and transacted.[16] Direct discrimination on religious grounds in matters of employment is not permitted even when such discrimination may be necessary to protect the commercial interest of the employer.[17] Even in relation to indirect discrimination, an employer must show an 'intolerable burden' or an inability to perform 'the essential functions'[18] of a post in order to restrict the religious identity rights of an employee.

---

[15] See the discussion of the ruling in Case 196/87 *Steymann v Staatssecretaris van Justitie* [1988] ECR 6159 in Ch 5, section 2.1 where religious choices were characterized as economic choices by the Court of Justice.

[16] See the discussion of EU legislation in this area in Ch 5, section 3.1.

[17] See Ch 5, section 2.   [18] See Ch 5, section 2.3.1.

In contrast, in relation to the public sphere, which is of vital importance to notions of equality of citizenship, equal respect, and dignity,[19] religious claims to special treatment have been restricted to a far greater degree. Indeed, as the EU's commitment to respecting religion as an element of identity is merely the predominant mechanism through which it puts its wider commitment to balancing Europe's religious and humanist traditions into operation, EU law has made it clear, both internally and externally, that the facilitation of religious identity must give way to the protection of the autonomy of the public sphere and the equality of all participants therein. Internally, this approach is seen in the framework provided by the Union to enable religious bodies to contribute to law- and policy-making. While the EU recognizes the 'particular contribution' of religious bodies, it has refused to grant such bodies similar exemptions from the principle of mutual respect for all identities as those it provides in relation to the rights of religious institutions in the context of the labour market. It has therefore required religions to make their contributions to law-making through structures that require them to acknowledge the legitimacy of different religious choices and forms of identity and which therefore preclude the assertion, within the political arena, of claims to a monopoly of truth on the part of particular faiths.[20] Externally, this principle has been seen in relation to the EU's approach to enlargement and particularly in relation to the requirements it has sought from Turkey concerning the limitation of religious influence over the Turkish legal and political systems.[21]

In a similar vein, the Union has also required that religious influence over law be limited by the need to respect the principle of private autonomy, which has a strong tradition in European humanism. The leading religious traditions in Europe continue to seek to mould the law in accordance with their theological convictions, particularly in areas such as sexuality and the beginning and end of life, which are closely linked to individual identity

---

[19] See, eg J Rawls, *Political Liberalism* (New York: Columbia University Press, 1993) and R Dworkin, *Taking Rights Seriously* (Cambridge, MA: Harvard University Press, 1977).

[20] The structures provided by the EU in this regard are open to all religious and philosophical groups, including secularist and humanist groups. Such structures cannot therefore readily accommodate contributions based on the claims on the part of a particular faith to a monopoly on truth (see Ch 3, section 3).

[21] The EU has required Turkey to maintain its secular system as a condition of membership and has warned it against introducing 'Islamic elements' into its legal system, while the European Court of Human Rights has made it clear that theocracy is repugnant to the European Convention on Human Rights (see Ch 5, section 3.2 and Ch 6, section 2.3).

and autonomy.[22] The EU's identification of respect for personal autonomy as a key element of the EU's public order and of EU membership has placed restrictions on the degree to which religious bodies can realize such goals. The commitment of EU law to personal autonomy is manifested in the protection of the right of individuals to choose between national moral frameworks through free movement rights[23] and through the EU's fundamental rights commitments, which have been interpreted to require Member States to refrain from legislating to force compliance with religious or, indeed, cultural, norms to a degree that impinges on individual autonomy to too great an extent. Thus, the criminalization of private adult sexual conduct such as adultery or homosexuality by candidates for EU membership has been identified as inconsistent with accession to the Union.[24]

These restrictions underline the limitations on the political role of religion inherent in the notion of balance between Europe's religious and humanist traditions. They are based on the recognition of the particular characteristics of religion as a form of identity. In particular, the facts that religion is such a powerful form of identity and that religious arguments are neither amenable to debate on rational grounds nor accessible to non-believers, mean that unrestricted religious influence over the political arena, especially the accommodation of religious truth claims in law-making, could preclude the meaningful participation of all groups in the political process and violate the anti-totalitarian principles of personal autonomy and privacy which have been central to Europe's post-war legal order. Europe's humanist tradition requires that the facilitation of religion cannot go so far as to override the notion of the individual as autonomous in private matters and as an equal in the legal and political arenas.

The fundamental importance of humanist ideas (some of which may be shared by particular faiths) to Europe's legal order means that religions that are seen as failing to respect the principles of public and private autonomy are not merely excluded from the public role and influence accorded to religion by EU law. Such religions are, in fact, seen as potential threats to the EU's public order and have been restricted as a result.[25] Indeed, despite (or perhaps, because of) the importance placed on the notion of individual

---

[22] See Ch 2, section 4.2.   [23] See Ch 3, section 4.   [24] See Ch 4, section 2.

[25] See the failure of the EU to intervene in relation to the suppression of religions such as Scientology even in areas governed by EU law (Ch 5, section 3.2.2), the identification of religions that seek restrictions on freedom of speech or the introduction of *Sharia* as contrary to the EU's public order (Ch 5, section 3.2.1 and Ch 6, section 2.4), and the EU's principles on immigrant integration requiring Member States to ensure that individual migrants subjugate religious

autonomy by the Union, EU law has been willing, in the context of immigration policy, to require migrants to indicate their willingness to respect gender equality and gay rights, thus interfering with the personal autonomy of individuals whose religious beliefs are seen as inconsistent with respect for public and private autonomy and therefore as threatening to the limits on religion inherent in the EU's public order.[26] This potentially paradoxical approach highlights the ambivalent nature of the relationship between many forms of religion and private autonomy within the EU legal order. On the one hand, religious identities can be protected on the basis of their status as elements of identity, which our respect for individual autonomy requires us to protect. Religious identities can, however, be restricted on the basis of collective interests. These collective interests can relate to the preservation of the autonomy of the public sphere or promotion of principles such as gender equality. However, such collective values can also include religious ideas that are recognized as part of public morality. Religion can therefore be both a beneficiary of the protection of private autonomy and a reason for the curtailment of such autonomy.

4. The Problems, Power, and Limits of Religion's Cultural Role

It is at this point that the EU's cultural identity framework for dealing with religion's public role gives rise to complications. As national cultures have been recognized by EU law as being entitled to protection from market forces, recognizing religion as an element of national culture entitles the practices of those faiths that are culturally entrenched to a greater degree of protection than those of 'outsider' faiths and provides scope for the promotion of religious morality through law on grounds of cultural autonomy. In relation to the protection of public and private autonomy, the approach adopted by the EU faces significant difficulty in distinguishing between the reflection in law of religious ideas on the basis of religion's role in cultural identity and political attempts to use law and the political process to enforce compliance with religious teachings. The EU's recognition of the reflection in law of religious teachings that are predominant in a particular Member

---

objections to a duty to respect private autonomy in relation to issues of gender and sexuality (Ch 6, section 3).   [26] See Ch 6, sections 3 and 4.

State as a legitimate exercise of cultural autonomy enables the promotion of religious norms through law on the part of culturally entrenched faiths.[27] Accordingly, such 'cultural' attempts to influence the law to religious ends are not seen as representative of a desire on the part of religion to dominate the public sphere or to pursue theocratic agendas. On the other hand, equivalent attempts on the part of outsider religions that are not similarly culturally entrenched are seen as political, not cultural, and are therefore restricted by the limitations[28] on religion's political role imposed by the EU's public order. Furthermore, the fact that such outsider religions are seen as having political aims means that they are susceptible to being regarded as potential threats to the non-theocratic nature of the EU's public order and to restriction on this basis. Thus, culturally entrenched religions may be able to exercise a degree of indirect influence over law that is denied to outsider faiths. The issues of equal treatment this raises are made more serious by the adoption of a sometimes uncritical assumption on the part of EU institutions and Member States that culturally entrenched religions unconditionally accept limitations on their political and legal influence and a consequent failure, as in the case of both enlargement and immigration policy,[29] to require such insider faiths to demonstrate their secular bona fides to the same degree as is required of outsider faiths.

Fear of the consequences of enabling outsider religions to play the same public role as culturally entrenched faiths is part of a broader context in which the relationship between religion, law, and state in Europe is in a state of flux due the pressure increasing religious diversity has placed on established patterns of dealing with religion. In particular, the common European pattern of church–state relations based on an exalted symbolic status for particular faiths moderated by shared cultural conceptions of religion's role in society that limit the political influence granted by such status, has come under some pressure as European populations come to be made up of larger numbers of people whose religious experience has not been marked to the same degree by the religion-limiting influences of European history.[30]

[27] See Ch 3, section 4. Note, however, the limitations of such national public morality on the basis of respect for individual autonomy and free movement rights described in Ch 3, section 5.
[28] Ibid.   [29] See Ch 6.
[30] Davie has argued that the difference in attitude to religion of native Europeans and immigrant communities 'has led to persistent and damaging misunderstandings, not least amongst groups whose religious commitments form the very core of their existence and for whom a pick-and-mix, live-and-let-live attitude simply will not do': G Davie, 'Religion in Britain: Changing Sociological Assumptions' (2000) 34 *Sociology* 113.

In such a context, the symbolic status granted to religion by the state, or previously largely symbolic laws relating to matters such as blasphemy, have come to be seen in a new light as the cultural consensus that limited their impact breaks down. Therefore, just as the unused and symbolic powers of the British monarchy would be threatened by the arrival in the United Kingdom of significant numbers of people who genuinely believed in monarchical government, the symbolic status of European religions has been called into question by the increase in the number of adherents to religious traditions whose relationship to politics and law has not been moulded by the same conflicts and compromises that have influenced the relationship between culturally entrenched forms of Christianity and the state in Europe.

The European Union has therefore had to develop its balance and identity-focused approach to religion and to distinguish between cultural and political religious influence over law in this context where increasing cultural diversity is contributing to highlighting the ambiguities and contradictions of the established system. Addressing the claims of unequal treatment arising under the current approach could involve a 'levelling up' of religious influence where restrictions on religion's political influence are relaxed in order to enable outsider religions to achieve a comparably broad role to that of insider faiths. It could also involve a degree of 'levelling down' under which the influence of insider religions over law is more strictly controlled, with consequent restriction of Member State derogations from EU law obligations on cultural grounds.

To date, no consensus has emerged in this regard and in some ways both 'levelling up' and 'levelling down' bring as many problems as solutions. Some have argued that the more muscular religiosity of many immigrants may lead to a process in which the secular elements of the European public order are made more explicit. Indeed, an un-named German politician, quoted by Klausen in her study of politically active European Muslims, predicted that the result of the increased presence of Muslims in Europe will be the institution of greater separation between church and state.[31] However, such an outcome is far from inevitable. Powerful voices have spoken out against the notion of a more secular Europe and have called for a reassertion of Europe's Christian identity,[32] while the Catholic Church has used controversies such

---

[31] J Klausen, *The Islamic Challenge: Politics and Religion in Western Europe* (Oxford: Oxford University Press, 2005) 179.

[32] See Ch 3, sections 2 and 3, in particular the arguments of JHH Weiler in *Un'Europa Cristiana* (Milano: Biblioteca Universale, 2003).

as that surrounding the publication of cartoons of the Prophet Mohammed in the Danish press to push for measures to restrict freedoms such as the right to satirize religion, which emerged from past conflicts between Christianity and secular forces in Europe.[33]

The option of 'levelling up' and significantly reducing restraints on religious influence over law and politics brings with it major drawbacks. Such an approach is inconsistent with the overall notion of balance between religious and humanist influences, which underpins the overall approach of the EU in this area. As non-believers cannot contribute meaningfully to the formation of laws justified on religious grounds, it also risks compromising the ability of all groups to participate in public debate. Furthermore, given that major European religions such as Roman Catholicism and mainstream versions of Islam retain ambitions to use the law to enforce compliance with their teachings in relation to 'lifeworld' matters, 'levelling up' risks imperilling the valuable European tradition of protection of privacy and individual autonomy.[34] It may also, as the reaction of the Vatican to the Mohammed cartoons affairs showed, encourage insider religions to seek to unpick existing implicit compacts to win back powers, such as the ability to stifle criticism, which religions in Europe had lost over preceding centuries.

On the other hand, to attempt to cure the political inequalities that result from the ill-defined nature of the boundary between the cultural and political realms by insisting on absolute equality of religions in the cultural arena represents the kind of radically multiculturalist approach which has not found favour with European electorates in recent times[35] and which would deny the right of nation states to develop their own cultural identity and to retain cultural links to a shared past (imagined or otherwise)—a key element of any national identity. As Taylor rightly points out, sustainable political communities are not made up of 'a scratch team of history with nothing more

---

[33] See 'Intervention of the Holy See at the ordinary session of the United Nations Human Rights Council on Religious Freedom', Address of HE Msgr Silano M Tomasi, Geneva, 22 March 2007, available at <http://www.vatican.va/roman_curia/secretariat_state/2007/documents/rc_seg-st_20070322_religion_en.html> (last visited 18 May 2010).

[34] See Ch 2, section 4.2. See also the Vatican's opposition to a United Nations motion calling for an end to the criminalization and punishment of individuals on the grounds of their sexual orientation: 'The Pope's Christmas Gift: A Hard Line on Church Doctrine', *Time Magazine*, 3 December 2008.

[35] Parties running on anti-multiculturalist platforms have had significant success in the Netherlands and Denmark. Policies in relation to immigration have increasing stressed integration over multiculturalism in recent years (see Ch 6, section 4).

in common than the passenger list of some international flight'.[36] Although 'levelling down' may bring fewer problems in terms of political and individual autonomy, it would, in its most intense form, involve significant restriction on the ability of European states to maintain a vibrant and distinctive shared culture. European history, art, and music have all, for better or worse, been heavily influenced by Christianity. An education system in a Member State that is historically predominantly Catholic or Protestant, for example, which devoted as much time to studying Islam and Hinduism as to Christianity, would give students an inaccurate and defective understanding of their national cultural heritage and would leave them with a much weaker sense of connection to a shared cultural past. Similarly, the state recognition of festivals such as Christmas and Easter or the feasts of Saint Joan in Catalonia or Saint Patrick in Ireland as national holidays is clearly not strictly neutral in religious terms but also helps to maintain the sense of community promoted by shared holidays and celebrations. An approach that insisted on the removal of all religious elements of state identity, even in the cultural arena, would risk undermining the very idea of shared cultural norms and common cultural identity, with a consequent impoverishment of the public and cultural life of European states. Furthermore, such an approach would be politically impossible for the EU and would violate its long-standing and valuable commitments to pluralism and respect for the cultural autonomy of its Member States.

It is therefore unavoidable that within the Union and its Member States, certain religious traditions will exercise a greater degree of indirect influence over law than faiths whose cultural influence has been more marginal. Moreover, the Union is an organization of limited competence that is intimately linked to the nation state and has limited authority to reshape European approaches to religion. Whether or not it is desirable, and notwithstanding the fact that it grants insider religions a degree of indirect influence denied to others, the continuing role of particular faiths in the national cultures of various Member States is a reality with which the Union must live and is something it has specifically undertaken to respect.[37] By defining religion's role as cultural, EU law recognizes religion as part of a specific and particular identity shared by a particular society (or, for the purposes of EU, a

---

[36]   C Taylor, 'Liberal Politics and the Public Sphere', Discussion Paper 15 (The Centre for the Study of Global Governance, London School of Economics, 1995) 19.

[37]   Consolidated Version of the Treaty on the Functioning of the European EU [2008] OJ C115/47, Art 17(1), available at <http://eur-lex.europa.eu/LexUriServ/LexUriServ.do?uri=OJ :C:2008:115:0047:0199:EN:PDF>. See discussion in Ch 3, sections 2 and 3.

particular Member State), which need not necessarily be shared by others.[38] As respecting the cultural identity of Member States is acknowledged by the Union to be one of its duties, its definition of the institutional role and the influence over public morality matters granted by a Member State to a particular religion as a cultural matter, means that such particularities do not have to be characterized as appropriate for all Member States, or as justifiable in rational terms, but are protected purely as a result of their status as a part of the identity of that Member State. However, the Union does not merely passively reflect Member State religious identities. The characterization of religion's influence over law as a cultural matter also involves the characterization of this role as non-political and non-ideological in nature. Gramsci[39] and Zizek[40] have noted the degree to which cultural norms and practices are thought of as non-political and non-ideological. Of course, as both authors acknowledge, such ostensibly non-ideological and non-political matters are in fact far from ideologically and politically neutral. Nevertheless, the distinction between religion as culture and religion as a truth claim is central to the EU's idea of proper balance between religious and humanist influences. Therefore, within the explicitly political context of the public sphere, the Union has been notably less accommodating of the particularism and exemption from the requirements of rational justification and general applicability that it is content accommodate in relation to cultural claims on law, including such claims with religious aspects, and has thereby reinforced the notion of cultural claims as being non-political in nature or, at the very least, less of a threat to the autonomy of the public sphere than purely religious claims.[41]

By adopting this approach, the Union establishes limits on religion's role within the overtly political public sphere and provides protection to the

---

[38] Inglis and Barker both note how such specificity and particularlism are intrinsic to cultural identity. See F Inglis, *Culture* (Cambridge: Polity Press, 2004) 28–29; C Barker, 'Culture' in *The SAGE Dictionary of Cultural Studies* (London: Sage, 2004) 45. The EU's close relationship to nation states means that the cultural autonomy it respects is necessarily national in nature. As the EU cannot define national cultures for the Member States, multicultural national identities are therefore likely to be recognized at EU level only to the extent to which a particular Member State itself decides to embrace such a vision of its national identity.

[39] Gramsci speaks of culture as 'a network of cultural values and institutions not normally thought of as political': A Gramsci, *Selections from the Prison Notebooks* (New York: International Publishers, 1971) 238.

[40] Žižek argues in relation to cultural norms that 'in a given society certain features, attitudes and norms of life are no longer perceived as ideologically marked, they appear as neutral': S Žižek, *In Defense of Lost Causes* (London: Verso, 2008) 21.

[41] See Chs 3, 5, 6.

principle of formal political equality between religions and between individuals. Although it cannot ensure the equal influence of all religious traditions, the distinction drawn by the EU's public order between the cultural and political elements of religion's influence over law enables it to oblige religious participants in its own public sphere to provide rational and generally applicable justifications for their claims and to recognize the validity of the contributions and claims of other forms of identity.[42] Although it does not impose the same constraints on religious claims made under the guise of Member State cultural autonomy, this approach also permits the EU to require Member States to maintain the autonomy of their public spheres from the explicit domination of any particular faith without removing religious elements of Member State identity.[43] Thus, by distinguishing between explicitly religious claims and cultural claims, which may include religious elements, the Union attempts to reconcile the notion of balance between religious and humanist influences and the limitations on religious influence over the public sphere that this principle entails, with respect for the role of religion in Member State identity.

Although this approach inevitably involves a degree of privilege for insider faiths, it is not immutable, and routing religious claims through the notion of culture is less damaging to the principle of equal citizenship than 'levelling up' and can help to ensure a greater degree of inclusion of minority groups than would otherwise be the case. Facilitation of direct religious influence by accommodating religious truth claims in the political arena excludes those who do not share a particular faith from political debate and undermines the idea of the law-making process as one in which common ground is sought rather than as a process for the articulation of the particular demands of individual groups. Furthermore, in societies where one denomination is a clear majority, acceptance of religious truth claims as a basis for law risks the domination and capture of the political process by that particular faith.[44]

---

[42] See Ch 3, section 3. This separation of the political from the religious has been cited by Habermas and Derrida as one of the foundation elements of a common European identity: J Habermas and J Derrida, 'February 15, or What Binds Europeans Together: A Plea for a Common Foreign Policy, Beginning in the Core of Europe', (2003) 10(3) *Constellations* 291.

[43] See Ch 5, section 3.2 and Ch 6, section 2.3.

[44] Consider, for example, the likely fate of a proposal to introduce same-sex marriage in countries such as Saudi Arabia, Iraq, or Iran, whose constitutions make it clear that all legislation must be compatible with the *Sharia* (see Saudi Arabian Constitution, Chapters 1, 2, 6, Constitution of the Islamic Republic of Iran, Arts 2–5, Constitution of Iraq, Art 2(1st)(a)). It is also notable how legislators who oppose granting more rights to women in Pakistan and Afghanistan have argued against such laws on explicitly religious grounds: see 'Strong feelings over Pakistan

Facilitation of religion as an element of a broader set of cultural values does not bring the same risks. While national cultural identities do have strong links to the past, culture is an evolving phenomenon which has many elements in addition to religion and which is constantly subject to change and development, as occurred, for example, in relation to gender equality when long-standing patriarchal European traditions were replaced by more egalitarian approaches. Although individual religions can also evolve and encompass widely divergent worldviews, participation in this evolutionary process is only open to those who accept the divinely inspired nature of a religion's founding text or basic beliefs. Participation in the process of cultural evolution and change is not necessarily similarly restricted and can be open to the contributions of all. Even in a society in which a particular faith has been dominant, the cultural role of this dominant faith may evolve and take on board the viewpoints and traditions of minority groups. Such developments must, however, take place at Member State level and cannot be imposed by the EU, whose public order will therefore continue to be influenced by the religious particularities of its Member States.

Furthermore, in a European Union of 27 states, no single cultural approach may claim automatic acceptance at EU level, meaning that the possibility of exclusion of those who dissent from particular national cultural norms from public debate at EU level is significantly reduced. Moreover, cultural claims in respect of EU law relate largely to claims for exemptions and derogations from Community law obligations on the part of individual states. Such derogations are limited in effect to those states and do not therefore involve the same degree of risk of the imposition of a particular cultural approach on all as would be posed by the acceptance in the law-making arena of religious truth claims whose effects would not be similarly restricted. The EU's embrace of the principles of the autonomy of the public sphere and the protection of fundamental rights, particularly individual private autonomy, as both basic principles of its public order and as prerequisites of EU membership, also provide a bulwark against large-scale expansion of the influence of a particular faith over law and political life and the subjugation of individual autonomy to the promotion of collective religious and cultural goals at Member State level, thereby promoting

---

rape law', *BBC News*, 15 November 2006, available at <http://news.bbc.co.uk/1/hi/world/south _asia/6152520.stm> (last visited 18 May 2010) and 'Afghan Women Protest New Law on Home Life', *New York Times*, 15 April 2009, available at <http://www.nytimes.com/2009/04/16/world/ asia/16afghan.html?_r=1> (last visited 18 May 2010).

the degree of pluralism necessary for cultural evolution to remain an open and reflexive process. These requirements show that certain constraints on Member State choices regarding the relationship between religion, the individual, and the law, including those that are culturally based, are part of the EU's public order. While these features do not entirely cure the inequality caused by the EU's facilitation of religion's cultural influence over law, in the light of the EU's limited authority and commitment to respecting Member State autonomy, they may represent the maximum degree of regulation of such relationships of which the Union is capable.

5. Conclusion

The relationship between religion and the EU's public order is unmistakably linked to a Christian humanist tradition that seeks to balance Europe's dual tradition of largely Christian religiosity, on the one hand, with a strong humanist tradition that stresses notions of individual autonomy and the separation of religion and law, on the other. The identity-focused framework through which the Union pursues this balance recognizes religion as an element of communal identity and thus as a contributor to the definition of shared norms. Such an approach enables the pursuit of religious goals and the promotion of religious morality through law. However, this approach also limits religious influence over law by restricting the degree to which claims to religious monopolies on truth can be asserted in the political sphere and by its emphasis on respect for choice and identity rights that strengthens claims to individual autonomy and freedom from religious norms. This gives the Union a public order which both facilitates the predominantly Christian cultural role of religion in influencing law but which is also avowedly non-theocratic. Such a public order is therefore able to accommodate the requirements of cultural and legal pluralism that are particularly important in the light of the diversity of approaches to the relationship between religion and law shown by the Member States. Although this approach comes at the cost of a degree of inequality between religions, such a situation is the inevitable outcome of Christianity's immense cultural and historical influence in Europe and the EU's limited authority and need to defer to the cultural autonomy of its Member States. This relationship to religion is in line with the EU's approach more generally which, as Weiler notes, is based on a 'constitutional tolerance' under which the Union requires commitment to a limited range of shared values but does not seek to supplant the national identities of Member States.[45]

There is, of course, the danger that requirements that states or individuals accept limitations on religious influence over law and politics may be used as a smokescreen by those with racist motives to exclude those who come from different racial or cultural backgrounds. Indeed, the Union has at times appeared to attribute uncomplicated acceptance of these limitations to insider faiths and their adherents while examining more rigorously the secular bona fides of states and individuals whose background is influenced by outsider faiths, most notably Islam.[46] This is something that the Union and its Member States need to address. Requiring those who seek to join or to come to live in the Union to accept the limitations on religious influence necessary for liberal democracy to thrive is entirely justifiable. People of all religions are capable of realizing that others do not share their faith and of practising the self-restraint required in liberal societies under which individuals do not seek to use the law to force everyone to live in accordance with the teachings of their particular religion. Some states or individuals may not be capable of accepting these principles. The Union is entitled to take the view that states joining the Union must accept it values and, similarly, Member States may equally decide that those who cannot accept the fundamental values of their state should not be permitted to immigrate. Neither membership of the Union nor the choice to immigrate into Europe are, after all, obligations, and the growth of significant populations committed to totalitarianism or theocracy may undermine the protection of key values within the EU and its Member States. On the other hand, in the light of the danger of the misuse of limitations for racist purposes, the Union should be vigilant to ensure that the limitations it imposes on religion in the context of enlargement policy and immigration are not selectively applied. The Commission should verify that states with predominantly Christian histories have embraced the 'democratic secularism' and the limitations on religious influence over law that this entails, in the same way that it has done in the case of Turkey. The Court of Justice has upheld the principle of integration requirements but has not yet ruled on their selective

---

[45] JHH Weiler, *The Constitution of Europe* (Cambridge: Cambridge University Press, 1999).
[46] See Ch 6.

application. In the light of the commitment to non-discrimination in the Charter of Fundamental Rights, it should seriously consider stepping in to block the selective application of integration conditions, within the field of application of EU law in an appropriate case.[47]

Such an approach may involve requiring culturally entrenched religions and their adherents to address some of the 'grey areas' and ambiguities in their attitudes towards the relationship between law, religion, and the state. It may be that increasing religious diversity will bring about a situation where European countries are required to address the grey areas in their own relationships to religion and to replace systems characterized by *de jure* privilege, which is moderated by shared cultural norms, with more black-and-white norms that more accurately reflect the *de facto* situation of limited religious influence. This process cannot, however, be imposed by a Union committed to respecting the cultural autonomy of the Member States and which has explicitly committed itself in the Lisbon Treaty to respecting the status of national churches.[48]

The pluralism of the EU's constitutional order and the significant facilitation of religion's cultural and political role provided by EU law mean that the approach of the EU's public order to the regulation of religion does not represent the kind of secularist break with the past that some have alleged.[49] However, the Union requires commitment to certain shared values if it is to be a sustainable polity, and there are definite limits to this pluralism. The commitment to balance between religious and humanist influences is therefore perhaps better seen as a commitment to a *proper* balance between these influences, which is informed by the humanist tradition of challenging and limiting religious influence over law and politics as much as by Europe's Christian heritage. Respect for proper balance between these traditions is a key element of the EU's public order, which precludes the reversal of principles such as respect for the autonomy of the public sphere and for individual autonomy in the private sphere, as well as requiring limitation of the accommodation of religious claims to a monopoly of truth in the political arena.

---

[47] Examples of immigration-related EU law are the Directives on family reunification and long-term residents, which permit the application of integration conditions by Member States (see Ch 6).

[48] Consolidated Version of the Treaty on the Functioning of the European EU [2008] OJ C115/47, Art 17(1).

[49] See n 32 above. See also The Catholic Communications Office, 'Cardinal Seán Brady's Bishop Stock Address at the Humbert Summer School', 24 August 2008, available at <http://www.catholiccommunications.ie/Pressrel/24-august-2008.html> (last visited 18 May 2010).

In recent years, religion has come to occupy a level of importance in global politics that would have shocked the legions of sociologists who confidently predicted its demise.[50] Some have proclaimed the return of religion to the political sphere.[51] Others have argued that immigration and demographic factors make it inevitable that European democracies will have to accommodate and accord greater political and legal power to religious movements in the future.[52]

Although the EU's public order is not strictly secular, the Union may well prove to be a limiting factor should such a broad return of religious influence come to pass. In particular, the EU's recognition of the legitimacy and worth of Europe's humanist tradition and its commitment to individual autonomy are inconsistent with wholesale enforcement of religious morality by legal means on the basis of either explicitly religious or cultural claims. As importantly, its adherence to strict formal neutrality in its own public sphere, its identification of the autonomy of the public sphere from religious influence as a necessary condition of accession, and its valorization of religion on the basis of its significance to human identities and consequent unwillingness to facilitate the assertion of religious claims to truth in public debate, all establish the notion of a degree of separation between religion and the law as an indispensable element of Europe's public order. Indeed, the weakness of the EU's own cultural identity and the diversity of the identities of its Member States mean that EU law is created within a political system in which no one religious or cultural tradition can assume automatic acceptance. In this sense it can be seen as encouraging participants in its political sphere to repackage particularist religious or cultural arguments into forms which are, in theory, generally accessible, including those who do not share such a cultural or religious background. Therefore, despite the significant accommodation of the religious and cultural particularities of Member States, this public order is a promising environment for the promotion of ideas such as public reason, which require religious justifications for law to be 'translated'[53] so that they are in principle accessible to those

---

[50] P Berger and G Weigel (eds), *The Decsecularization of the Modern World: Resurgent Religion and Modern Politics* (Grand Rapids Michigan: Erdemans Publishing Company and Public Policy Center, 1999). [51] Ibid.

[52] See, eg Davie (n 30 above); B Bawer, *While Europe Slept: How Radical Islam Is Destroying the West from Within* (New York: Doubleday, 2006); and *Sunday Times*, 'Down with Godless Government', 22 April 2007.

[53] For discussion of this notion of translation, see J Habermas, 'Religion in the Public Sphere' (2006) 14(1) *European Journal of Philosophy* 1.

with differing religious views. The Union may therefore help to maintain the reflexivity of European culture while acting as a bulwark against any theocratic tendencies that may emerge in the future, and is likely to be an important site in future conflicts in relation to religion's role in European liberal democracies.

BIBLIOGRAPHY

Books and Articles

Abbott, WM (ed.), *The Documents of Vatican II* (Piscataway: American Press, 1966)

Alfeyev, H, 'Christian Witness to Uniting Europe: A View from a Representative of the Russian Orthodox Church', *The Ecumenical Review*, January 2003

Asen, R, 'Toward a Normative Conception of Difference in Public Deliberation' (1999) 25 *Argumentation and Advocacy* (Winter) 115

Barbou des Places, S and Oger, H, 'Making the European Migration Regime: Decoding Member States' Legal Strategies' (2004) 6(4) *European Journal of Migration and Law* 361

Barker, C, 'Culture' in *The SAGE Dictionary of Cultural Studies* (London: Sage, 2004) 45

Barrett, D (ed.), *World Christian Encyclopedia: A Comparative Study of Churches and Religions in the Modern World AD 1900–2000* (New York: Oxford University Press, 1982)

Bawer, B, *While Europe Slept: How Radical Islam Is Destroying the West from Within* (New York: Doubleday, 2006)

Baykal, S, 'Unity in Diversity? The Challenge of Diversity for European Political Identity, Legitimacy and Democratic Governance: Turkey's EU Membership as the Ultimate Test Case', Jean Monnet Working Papers Series 09/2005, NYU School of Law

Bellamy, R and Castiglione, D, 'Lacroix's Constitutional Patriotism: Response' (2004) 52 *Political Studies* 187

Bengoetxea, J, MacCormick, N, and Moral Soriano, L, 'Integration and Integrity in the Legal Reasoning of the European Court of Justice' in G de Burca and JHH Weiler (eds), *The European Court of Justice* (Oxford: Oxford University Press, 2001) 64

Berger, P, *A Far Glory: The Quest for Faith in an Age of Credulity* (New York: Free Press, 1992)

—and Weigel, G (eds), *The Decsecularization of the Modern World: Resurgent Religion and Modern Politics* (Grand Rapids Michigan: Erdemans Publishing Company and Public Policy Center, 1999)

Boyle, K, 'Human Rights, Religion and Democracy: The Refah Party Case' (2004) 1(1) *Essex Human Rights Review* 1

Bruce, S, *From Cathedrals to Cults: Religion in the Modern World* (Oxford: Oxford University Press, 1996)

Cantwell Smith, W, *The Meaning and the End of Religion* (New York: The Macmillan Company, 1963)

Çarkoğlu, A and Rubin, B (eds), *Religion and Politics in Turkey* (London: Routledge, 2006)

Carcassonne, G, 'France: Conseil Constitutionnel on the European constitutional Treaty' (2005) 1 *European Constitutional Law Review* 293.

Casanova, J, *Public Religions in the Modern World* (Chicago: University of Chicago Press, 1994)

Césari, J, 'Islam in France: The Shaping of a Religious Minority' in Y Yazbeck Haddad, *Muslims in the West from Sojourners to Citizens* (Oxford: Oxford University Press, 2002) 40

—and S McLoughlin (eds), *European Muslims and the State* (Aldershot: Ashgate, 2005)

—Caeiro, A, and Hussain, D, *Islam and Fundamental Rights in Europe*, Final Report, October 2004, European Commission, DG Justice and Home Affairs Centre National de la Recherche Scientifique, École Pratique des Hautes Études, Groupe de Sociologie des Religions et de la Laïcité

Chalmers, D, 'The Mistakes of the Good European?' in S Fredman (ed.), *Discrimination and Human Rights: The Case of Racism* (Oxford: Oxford University Press, 2001) 220

Cox, J, 'Master Narratives of Long-Term Religious Change' in H McLeod and W Ustof (eds), *The Decline of Christendom in Western Europe, 175–2000* (Cambridge: Cambridge University Press, 2003) 203

Crouch, C, 'The Quiet Continent: Religion and Politics in Europe' in D Marquand and RL Nettler (eds), *Religion and Democracy* (Oxford: Blackwell Publishers, 2000) 90

Cumper, P, 'The Rights of Religious Minorities: The Legal Regulation of New Religious Movements' in P Cumper and S Wheatley (eds), *Minority Rights in the 'New' Europe* (The Hague: Martinus Nijhoff Publishers, 1999) 171

Cvijic, S and Zucca, L, 'Does the European Constitution need Christian Values?' (2004) 24(4) OJLS 744

Dalacoura, K, *Islam, Liberalism and Human Rights: Implications for International Relations* (London: IB Tauris, 1998)

Davie, G, 'Religion in Britain: Changing sociological assumptions', (2000) 34 *Sociology* 113–28.

—*Religion in Europe: A Memory Mutates* (Oxford: Oxford University Press, 2000)

—*Europe: The Exceptional Case: Parameters of Faith in the Modern World* (London: Longman Todd, 2002)

—'Morality Clauses and Decision Making in Situations of Scientific Uncertainty: the Case of GMOs' (2007) 6(2) *World Trade Review* 249

Dershowitz, A, *Rights from Wrongs: A Secular Theory of the Origins of Rights* (New York: Basic Books, 2004)

Durkheim, É, *The Elementary Forms of the Religious Life* (Oxford: Oxford University Press, 2001)

Dworkin, R, *Taking Rights Seriously* (Cambridge, MA: Harvard University Press, 1977)

Enyedi, Z, 'The Contested Politics of Positive Neutrality in Hungary' in JTS Madeley and Z Enyedi (eds), *Church and State in Contemporary Europe The Chimera of Neutrality* (London: Frank Cass, 2003) 1

Esposito, J, *The Islamic Threat: Myth or Reality* (Oxford: Oxford University Press, 2002)

Evans, C, *Freedom of Religion under the European Convention on Human Rights* (Oxford: Oxford University Press, 2001)

Evans, M, *Religious Liberty and International Law in Europe*, (Cambridge: Cambridge University Press, 1997)

Ferrari, A, 'Religions, secularity and democracy in Europe: for a new Kelsenian pact', Jean Monnet Papers Series NYU School of Law, 2005

Ferrari, S, 'The Secularity of the State and the Shaping of Muslim Representative Organizations in Western Europe' in J Cesari and S McLoughlin (eds), *European Muslims and the State* (Aldershot: Ashgate, 2005) 6

Fetzer, JS and Soper, JC, *Muslims and the State in Britain, France and Germany* (Cambridge: Cambridge University Press, 2005)

Foley, EP, *Liberty for All: Reclaiming Individual Privacy in a New Era of Public Morality* (New Haven, CT: Yale University Press, 2006)

Foley, M, *The Silence of Constitutions* (London: Routledge, 1989)

Fredman, S, 'Combating Racism with Human Rights: The Right to Equality' in S Fredman (ed.), *Discrimination and Human Rights: The Case of Racism* (Oxford: Oxford University Press, 2001) 9

Fukuyama, F, 'Europe vs Radical Islam', *Policy Review*, 27 February 2006

Fuller, L, *The Morality of Law* (New Haven, CT: Yale University Press, 1969)

Gabriel, T, 'Is Islam against the West?' in R Geaves, T Gabriel, Y Haddad, and J Idleman Smith (eds), *Islam and the West Post 9/11* (Aldershot: Ashgate, 2004) 15

Gajendra Singh, K, 'EU-Turkish Engagement: A Must for Stability of the Region', South Asia Analysis Group Papers, available at <http://www.southasiaanalysis.org/papers12/paper1127.html> (last visited 25 May 2010)

Geaves, R, 'Who Defines Moderate Islam "post" September 11?' in R Geaves, T Gabriel, Y Haddad, and J Idleman Smith (eds), *Islam and the West Post 9/11* (Aldershot: Ashgate, 2004) 66

Gramsci, A, *Selections from the Prison Notebooks* (New York: International Publishers, 1971)

Groenendijk, K, 'Legal Concepts of Integration in EU Migration Law' (2004) 6(2) *European Journal of Migration and Law* 119

Gunn, TJ, *Adjudicating Rights of Conscience under the European Convention on Human Rights* in JD Van Der Vyver and J Witte (eds), *Religious Human Rights in Global Perspective: Legal Perspectives* (The Hague: Martinus Nijhoff Publishers, 1996) 305

Habermas, J, Intolerance and Discrimination' (2003) 1(1) *International Journal of Constitution Law* 2

—'Religion in the Public Sphere' (2006) 14(1) *European Journal of Philosophy* 1

—and Derrida, J, 'February 15, or What Binds Europeans Together: A Plea for a Common Foreign Policy, Beginning in the Core of Europe' (2003) 10(3) *Constellations* 291

Halman, L and Pettersson, T, 'Differential Patterns of Secularization in Europe: Exploring the Impact of Religion on Social Values' in L Halman and O Riis (eds), *Religion in Secularizing Society: The Europeans' Religion at the End of the 20th Century* (Leiden: Brill, 2003) 54

—and Riis, O (eds), *Religion in Secularizing Society: The Europeans' Religion at the End of the 20th Century* (Leiden: Brill, 2003)

Harvey, P, 'Militant Democracy and the European Convention on Human Rights' (2004) 29(3) ELR 407

Hervieu-Léger, D, *La Religion pour mémoire* (Paris: Le Cerf, 1993)

—*Vers un nouveau christianisme* (Paris: Le Cerf, 1993)

Hillion, C, 'The Copenhagen Criteria and Their Progeny' in C Hillion (ed.), *European Enlargement: A Legal Approach* (Oxford: Hart Publishing, 2004) 3

Hirschman, AO, *Exit, Voice, and Loyalty: Responses to Decline in Firms, Organizations, and States* (Cambridge, MA: Harvard University Press, 1970)

Hitchens, C, *God is Not Great: How Religion Poisons Everything* (New York: Twelve Books, 2007)

Hussein, D, 'The Impact of 9/11 on British Muslim Identity' in R Geaves, T Gabriel, Y Haddad, and J Idleman Smith (eds), *Islam and the West Post 9/11* (Aldershot: Ashgate, 2004)

Inglis, F, *Culture* (Cambridge: Polity Press, 2004)

Introvigne, M and Gordon Melton, J (eds), *Pour en finir avec les sectes. Le débat sur le rapport de la commission parlementaire* (Paris: Dervy, 3rd edn, 1996)

Jansen, T, 'Europe and Religions: the Dialogue between the European Commission and Churches or Religious Communities' (2000) 47(1) *Social Compass* 103

Joffé, G, 'Democracy, Islam and the Cult of Modernism' (1997) 4(3) *Democratization* 134

Jones, P, 'The Ideal of the Neutral State' in R Goodin and A Reeve (eds), *Liberal Neutrality* (London: Routledge, 1989) 5

Klausen, J, *The Islamic Challenge: Politics and Religion in Western Europe* (Oxford: Oxford University Press, 2005)

Kocak, M and Orucu, E, 'Dissolution of Political Parties in the Name of Democracy: Cases from Turkey and the European Court of Human Rights' (2003) 9(3) *European Public Law* 399

Kofman, E, 'Contemporary European migrations: civic stratification and citizenship' (2002) 21 *Political Geography* 1035

Kumm, M, 'The Idea of Thick Constitutional Patriotism and Its Implications for the Role and Structure of European Legal History (2005) 6(2) *German Law Journal, Special Issue—Confronting Memories* 319

Le Goff, J, *The Birth of Europe* (Malden, MA: Blackwell, 2005)

Lewis, B, *Islam and the West* (Oxford: Oxford University Press, 1993)

——— *The Crisis of Islam: Holy War and Unholy Terror* (London: Phoenix, 2003)

Locke, J, 'Letters on Toleration' in *The Works of John Locke* Vol. VI (London: Thomas Davison, 1823)

MacCormick, N, 'The Maastricht Urteil: Sovereignty Now' (1995) 1 *European Law Journal* 259

Macklem, P, 'Militant democracy, legal pluralism and the paradox of self-determination' (2006) 4(3) *International Journal of Constitutional Law* 488

Madeley, JTS, 'European Liberal Democracy and the Principle of State Religious Neutrality' in JTS Madeley and Z Enyedi (eds), *Church and State in Contemporary Europe: The Chimera of Neutrality* (London: Frank Cass Publishing, 2003) 1

Maréchal, B, (ed.), *Muslims in the Enlarged Europe: Religion and Society* (Leiden: Koninlijke Brill NV, 2003)

Martin, D, *A General Theory of Secularisation* (Oxford: Blackwell, 1978)

—*On Secularisation: Towards a Revised General Theory* (Aldershot: Ashgate, 2005)

Massignon, B, 'Les relations des organismes Européens religieux et humanistes avec les institutions de l'Union Européene: Logiques nationales et confessionnelles et dynamiques d'européanisation' in Commissariat Général du Plan, *Croyances religieuses, morales et ethiques dans le processus de construction européenne* (Institut Universitaire de Florence, Chaire Jean Monnet d'études Européennes, 2002) 23

Mavrogordatos, G Th, 'Orthodoxy and Nationalism in the Greek Case' in JTS Madeley and Z Enyedi (eds), *Church and State in Contemporary Europe: The Chimera of Neutrality* (London: Frank Cass Publishing, 2003) 120

McCrea, R, 'De Facto Secularism in a Diversifying Religious Environment' in A Sajo (ed.), *Religion in the Public Square* (Utrecht: Eleven International Publishing, 2011 forthcoming)

Menendez, AJ, 'Review of A Christian Europe' (2005) 30(1) ELR 133

Meny, Y and Knapp, A, *Government and Politics in Western Europe* (Oxford: Oxford University Press, 1998)

Mill, JS, *On Liberty* (London: Wordsworth Classic Edition, 1996)

Minkenberg, M, 'The Policy Impact of Church-State Relations: Family Policy and Abortion in Britain, France and Germany' in JTS Madeley and Z Enyedi (eds), *Church and State in Contemporary Europe: The Chimera of Neutrality* (London: Frank Cass Publishing, 2003) 202

Modood, T, 'Anti-Essentialism, Multiculturalism and the "Recognition" of Religious Groups' (1998) 6 *Journal of Political Philosophy* 378

Monsma, S and Soper, C, *The Challenges of Pluralism; Church and State in Five Democracies* (Oxford: Rowman and Littlefield, 1997)

Norris, P and Inglehart, R, *Sacred and Secular: Religion and Politics Worldwide* (Cambridge: Cambridge University Press, 2004)

O'Reilly, E, *Masterminds of the Right* (Dublin: Attic Press, 1992)

Özbudun, E, *Contemporary Turkish Politics: Challenges to Democratic Consolidation* (London: Lynne Rienner Publishers, 2000)

Petersmann, E, 'Constitutional Economics, Human Rights and the WTO' (2003) 58 *Aussenwirtschaft* 49

Phelan, DR, 'The Right to Life of the Unborn v the Promotion of Trade in Services' (1992) 55 MLR 670

Procter, M and Hornsby-Smith, M, 'Individual Context Religiosity, Religious [sic] and Values in Europe and North America' in L Halman and O Riis (eds), *Religion in Secularizing Society: The Europeans' Religion at the End of the 20th Century* (Leiden: Brill, 2003) 110

Ramadan, T, *To Be a European Muslim* (Leicester: Islamic Foundation, 1999)

Rawls, J, *A Theory of Justice* (Cambridge, MA: Harvard University Press, 1971)

—*Political Liberalism* (New York: Columbia University Press, 1993)

Raz, J, *The Morality of Freedom* (Oxford: Clarendon Press, 1988)

Richardson, JT and Introvigne, M, 'Brainwashing Theories in European Parliamentary and Administrative Reports on "Cults" and "Sects"' (2001) 40(2) *Journal for the Scientific Study of Religion* 143

Robbers, G, 'State and Church in the European Union' in G Robbers (ed.), *State and Church in the European Union* (1st edn; Baden-Baden: Nomos Verlagsgesellschaft, 1996) 323

—*State and Church in the European Union* (2nd edn; Baden-Baden: Nomos Verlagsgesellschaft, 2005)

Rorty, R, 'Religion as a Conversation Stopper' (1994) 31 *Common Knowledge* 1

Rose, K, *Diverse Communities: The Evolution of Gay and Lesbian Politics in Ireland* (Cork: Cork University Press, 1993)

Roy, O, *Vers un islam européen* (Paris: Editions Esprit, 1999)

—*Secularism Confronts Islam* (translated by George Holoch) (New York: Columbia University Press, 2007)

Rynkowski, M, 'Remarks on Art I-52 of the Constitutional Treaty: new Aspects of the European Ecclesiastical Law? (2005) 6(11) *German Law Journal* 1

Sassoon, D, *The Culture of the Europeans: From 1800 to the Present* (London: Harper Collins, 2006)

Sjursen, H, 'Enlargement in Perspective: The EU's Quest for Identity', paper given as part of the European Institute Research Seminar series, at the London School of Economics, 24 May 2006

Stan, L and Turcescu, L, 'The Romanian Orthodox Church and Post-Communist Democratisation' (2000) 52(8) *Europe-Asia Studies* 1480

Stark, R and Iannaccone, LR, 'A supply-side reinterpretation of the "secularization" of Europe' (1994) 33(3) *Journal for the Scientific Study of Religion* 230

Taylor, C, 'Liberal Politics and the Public Sphere', Discussion Paper 15 (The Centre for the Study of Global Governance, London School of Economics, 1995) 19

—*A Secular Age* (Cambridge, MA: Harvard University Press, 2007)

van Ham, P, *European Integration and the Postmodern Condition* (London: Routledge, 2001)

Weber, M, *The Protestant Ethic and the Spirit of Capitalism* (New York: Scribner's, 1930 [1904])

Weigel, G, *The Cube and the Cathedral: Europe, America and Politics without God* (New York: Basic Books, 2005)

Weiler, JHH, *The Constitution of Europe* (Cambridge: Cambridge University Press, 1999)

—*Un'Europa Cristiana: Un saggio esplorativo* (Milan: BUR Saggi, 2003)

Williams, A, *EU Human Rights Policies: A Study in Irony* (Oxford, Oxford University Press, 2004)

Yamane, D, *The Catholic Church in State Politics: Negotiating Prophetic Demands and Political Realities* (Lanham: Rowman and Littlefield Publishers, 2005)

Žižek, S, *In Defense of Lost Causes* (London: Verso, 2008)

News Reports (alphabetically by publication name)

365gaycom, 'EU Warns Poland on Gays' 26 October 2005, available at <http://www365gaycom/newscon05/10/102605poland.htm>

The Age, 'Turkey's Adultery Ban Splits the Nation' 7 September 2004

Associated Press, 'Turkey Backs off Plan to Outlaw Adultery' 14 September 2004

BBC News, 'God Missing from EU Constitution' 6 February 2003

BBC News, 'Muslim Schools Citizenship Warning' 17 January 2005

BBC News, 'New UK Citizenship Testing Starts' 1 November 2005

BBC News, 'Core British Values' 17 May 2006

BBC News, 'Strong Feelings over Pakistan Rape Law' 15 November 2006

BBC News, 'Conform to Our Society Says PM' 8 December 2006

BBC News, 'France refuses a citizenship over full Islamic veil' 3 February 2010

Boston Globe, 'Europe Raises the Bar for Immigrants' 22 May 2006

Catholic News, 'Ratzinger Asserts Vatican Stand against Turkey EU Membership' 16 August 2004

Catholic News Agency, 'Religious freedom does not require complete secularization, Archbishop tells UN' 24 March 2010

Conscience, 'Slovak Government Falls over Concordat with Vatican' June 2006

Deutsche Welle, 'Turkey Changes Laws to Meet EU Standards' 1 September 2004

Deutsche Welle, 'Verheugen Warns Turkey on Adultery Law' 10 September 2004

Deutsche Welle, 'New Rules for Muslims in German State Blasted' 5 January 2006

Deutsche Welle, 'Testing the Limits of Tolerance' 16 March 2006

Equal Voices, Issue 18, June 2006, 'The Right to Offend and Not To Be Offended: An Interview with EU Commission Vice President Frattini', published by the European Monitoring Centre on Racism and Xenophobia

European Consortium for Church and State Research Newsletter, 'The EU and the Cartoons of the Prophet Mohammed' Year 7 Issue 7 July 2007

Guardian, 'Bishop Urged to Resign after Diocese Loses Gay Bias Case' 19 July 2007

The Independent, 'Polish President Warned over Ultra-Right Shift' 25 October 2005

Inter Press Service News Agency, 'How to Be a German' 31 May 2006

International News Report, 'Anti-Gay Nations May Not Join European Union' 31 July 2001

London Times, 'It May Be Europe's Most Liberal City, but If You Are Gay You Had Best Beware' 14 May 2005,

Le Monde, 'Pour ou contre l'adhésion de la Turquie à l'union européenne' 9 November 2002

Newsweek, 'The New Crusade; Fighting for God in a Secular Europe, Conservative Christians, the Vatican and Islamic Militants' 1 November 2004

New York Times, 'It's Still No Breeze for Gays, Even Diplomatic Ones' 17 October 2001

New York Times, 'Dutch Immigration Kit Offers a Revealing View' 17 March 2006

New York Times, 'Afghan Women Protest New Law on Home Life' 15 April 2009

Reuters News Agency, 'Romanian Orthodox Church Denounces Homosexuality' 13 September 2000

Der Spiegel, 'Becoming German: Proposed Hesse Citizenship Test' 5 September 2005

Der Spiegel, 'Germany to Introduce Controversial New Citizenship Test' 11 June 2008

Sunday Times, 'Holland Launches the Immigrant Quiz' 12 March 2006

Sunday Times, 'Down with Godless Government' 22 April 2007

Time Magazine, 'The Pope's Christmas Gift: A Hard Line on Church Doctrine' 3 December 2008

Turkish Daily News, 'Adultery Fault Line with EU' 18 September 2004

Turkish Daily News, 'Democratic Secularism is a Copenhagen Criterion for Turkey' 10 May 2007

US Newswire, 'Catholics Join European NGOs in Coalition in Appeal to Convention Not to Give Religion Unfair Influence in Constitutional Treaty' 22 May 2003

Washington Times, 'Netherlands Issues Immigration Test' 16 March 2006

Official Publications

Belgium

Enquête parlementaire visant à élaborer une politique en vue de lutter contre les pratiques illégales des sectes et le danger qu'elles représentent pour la société et pour les personnes, particulièrement les mineurs d'âge, 2 vols (Brussels: Chambre des Représentants de Belgique, 1997)

France

Les sectes en France Rapport fait au nom de la commission d'enquête sur les sectes (Paris: Les Documents d'information de l'Assemblée Nationale, 1996)

Germany

The Scientology Organisation, paper submitted by the German delegation at the OSCE Seminar on Religious Freedom, Warsaw, 16–19 April, 1996

Religionsfreiheit heute - zum Verhältnis von Staat und Religion in Deutschland, Rede von Bundespräsident Johannes Rau beim Festakt zum 275 Geburtstag von Gotthold Ephraim Lessing in der Herzog-August-Bibliothek zu Wolfenbüttel wolfenbüttel, 2212004

The Netherlands

The Civic Integration Exam Abroad, Immigratie-en Naturalisatiedienst (Dutch Immigration and Naturalisation Service) 2007

The Vatican

The Syllabus of Errors, Propositions 15 and 78, The Holy See, 8 December 1864

Doctrinal Note on Some Questions Regarding the Participation of Catholics in Political Life, The Congregation for the Doctrine of the Faith, 16 January 2003

Post-Synodal Apostolic Exhortation Ecclesia in Europa of His Holiness Pope John Paul II to the Bishops, Men and Women in the Consecrated Life and All the Lay Faithful on Jesus Christ Alive in His Church the Source of Hope for Europe, 28 June 2003

Publications of Non-governmental Organizations

Abortion Law, History and Religion, Childbirth by Choice Trust
ACCEPT Country Report on the Status of LGBT, Accept Romania, 2008
Equality for Lesbians and Gay Men, A Report of ILGA Europe, The International Lesbian and Gay Association, June 1998
Secretariat to the Debate on the Future of the European Union in the European Convention, COMECE, Brussels, 21 May 2002
The Great Divide: How Westerners and Muslims View Each Other, Pew Research Foundation
The Future of Europe, Political Commitment, Values and Religion: Contribution of the COMECE, 22 June 2006
The Relation of the European Union and Turkey from the Viewpoint of the Christian Churches, Discussion Paper, Conference of European Churches, February 2004
The Treaty Establishing a Constitution for Europe: Elements for an Evaluation, COMECE, Brussels, 11 March 2005
World Legal Survey, The International Lesbian and Gay Association, November 2006

INDEX